Logics of Failed Revolt

FRENCH THEORY AFTER MAY '68

PETER STARR

Logics of Failed Revolt

FRENCH THEORY AFTER MAY '68

STANFORD UNIVERSITY PRESS
STANFORD, CALIFORNIA

Stanford University Press
Stanford, California

Printed in the United States of America

CIP data appear at the end of the book

Stanford University Press publications are distributed exclusively by Stanford University Press within the United States, Canada, Mexico, and Central America; they are distributed exclusively by Cambridge University Press throughout the rest of the world.

For Alice

Acknowledgments

Since its beginnings as a conference paper in early 1987, this book has benefited from a great deal of support, both personal and institutional. A Summer Stipend from the National Endowment for the Humanities and a grant from the University of Southern California's Faculty Research and Innovation Fund allowed me to spend the summer of 1988 in the libraries of Paris. Much of the book's conceptual work was accomplished in 1988–89 while I was an Andrew W. Mellon Faculty Fellow at Harvard University. Special thanks to Richard Hunt and Per Nykrog for helping to make that year an especially productive one. A leave from USC in the spring of 1991 allowed me to write a significant portion of this study. For that leave, and for their unwavering support throughout the project, I thank Marshall Cohen and Albert Sonnenfeld.

Many of my colleagues and friends have spent long hours with my manuscript in various stages of its completion. If the notion of community is more alive in academia than elsewhere, it is because of people like David Bell, Svetlana Boym, Arden Reed, Lawrence Schehr, Hilary Schor, and Margaret Waller. They all know how much I owe them.

More intangible—but no less valuable—was the help I received from Leo Braudy, Antoine Compagnon, Jean-Jacques Courtine, Vincent Farenga, Suzanne Guerlac, Michael Hardt, Anne Higonnet, Alice Jardine, Barbara Johnson, Jann Matlock, Jeffrey Mehlman, Kevin Newmark, Marjorie Perloff, and Susan Suleiman.

At a time when there is much ado about mentoring, I take particular pleasure in thanking a number of colleagues who have mastered the art. Ross Chambers, Peggy Kamuf, Lawrence Kritzman, Juliet Flower MacCannell, and Nancy Vickers have supported this project in numerous ways—reading drafts, writing letters, and offering unfailing encouragement. Each has been a model friend and critic, for which I am very grateful. Michael Fried, Neil Hertz, and Richard Macksey had little to do with the present book, but their examples and their support over the years have been invaluable to me. I suspect Frank Paul Bowman saw this book as a regrettable detour from the more serious business of nineteenth-century French studies. Special thanks to him for not telling me so.

Helen Tartar has been in on this project for more years than she (or I) would care to count. I continue to marvel at her special blend of high professionalism and great good humor. Many thanks also to Marilyn Martin and to Ellen F. Smith of Stanford University Press for helping shepherd the manuscript through to the finished volume. Anca Mitroi gave me invaluable help with the preparation of an index.

No one, however, has been more constantly supportive of this project than Alice Hill. If anyone ever deserved to cosign a book they did not write, it is she. All my love and thanks to her, and to our daughters, Liza and Julia, who have thus far proven blissfully ignorant of the traps of specular doubling.

An earlier version of Chapter 9 appeared in *Esprit créateur* 32, 4 (1992). Thanks to the editors and publishers of that journal for permission to use this material here.

P.S.

Contents

PART IV. AFTERTHOUGHTS

Note on Translations and Citations

Throughout this volume, citations from published translations of French texts give the page reference for the translation, followed in italics by the corresponding page(s) of the French edition (for example: Lacan, *Écrits,* 20; *114*). In many cases I have modified the published translation to bring out textual features essential to my argument. Responsibility for such modifications, as well as for the rendering into English of all hitherto untranslated French texts, is of course my own.

In the case of texts only partially translated into English—such as Althusser et al.'s *Lire le Capital,* Kristeva's *Révolution du langage poétique,* or Lacan's *Écrits*—a single page number in italic type indicates my translation of a passage from the French edition that was not included in the English edition. For texts available only in French, citations in Chapters 1–10 are also given with a page citation in italic type.

All publication dates given within the text are those of the original (usually French) edition. This is the case even when the work's title is given in English.

Unless otherwise noted, all references to Lacan's seminars in these pages will be marked by an "*S*" (for *Séminaire*), followed by a roman numeral designating the seminar number. Thus a passage cited as *S* XX, *52* is to be found on page *52* of *Le Séminaire XX: Encore.*

The short form *Brèche* refers to Edgar Morin, Claude Lefort, and Cornelius Castoriadis, *Mai 1968: La Brèche, suivi de vingt ans après.*

Logics of Failed Revolt

FRENCH THEORY AFTER MAY '68

Introduction

> The insistence with which it has been repeated, on both sides, that, whatever happens, *afterwards* can no longer be like *before* doubtless translates, in the mode of denial, the fear (or the hope) that in fact *afterwards* will become *before*.
>
> — Roland Barthes, "Writing the Event"

Prior to 1789, the word "revolution" signified a great sea change in political affairs, without significant prejudice as to its "progressive" or "regressive" nature. Indeed the origins of the concept of revolution in the field of celestial movement long sustained a relative emphasis on particularly cyclical or recurrent forms of political mutation, forms that effected a return to the past fully as much as a break from that past. In seventeenth-century England, for example, the restoration of monarchy with the overthrow of the Rump Parliament in 1660 could lay as great a claim to the status of revolution as the expulsion of the Stuarts in 1688.[1]

Our modern sense of the "revolutionary" originated largely in the context of the French Revolution, with its radical project of inventing new, specifically republican forms of community in a society profoundly shaped by a monarchical past. In a masterly study of Revolutionary culture and symbolism as the cornerstone of a new republican consensus, Lynn Hunt supports her contention that a will to break with the national past distinguishes the French from previous revolutionary moments by citing passages such as the following, from a Radical document of 1793:

> There is nothing, absolutely nothing in common between the slave of a tyrant and the inhabitant of a free state; the customs of the latter, his principles, his sentiments, his action, all must be new. (29)

But the very insistence with which the French republicans propounded their cult of the new plainly reflected a profound, and not unwarranted, fear of the old:

> A revolution is never made by halves; it must either be total or it will abort. All the revolutions which history has conserved for memory as well as those that have been attempted in our time have failed because people wanted to square new laws with old customs and rule new institutions with old men. . . . REVOLUTIONARY means outside all forms and all rules. (Marat-Mauger, cited by Hunt, 26–27)

From the beginning, therefore, the modern concept of revolution as a radical departure from the customs and laws of the past (monarchical or otherwise) has been haunted by the ghost of revolution in its pre-modern sense, as an abortively cyclical return to a point of departure in already institutionalized norms and structures. Ironically, in other words, it is the very suppression of this older sense of revolution as cyclical repetition that would seem to have condemned modern theorists and practitioners of revolution to an obsessively repetitive fascination with revolution *as* repetition.

The purpose of this book is to explore the effects of this fascination on a significant portion of that body of literary, philosophical, and psychoanalytic work that we in America have come to know as French theory. More precisely, it is to examine the strategically central role played by a series of commonplace "explanations" for the failure of revolutionary action—or what I call "logics of failed revolt"—in representative texts by Jacques Lacan, Roland Barthes, Julia Kristeva, Hélène Cixous, Jacques Derrida, and others.[2] My study focuses on a twelve-year period defined by the revolutionary events of May 1968, a period beginning with a resurgence of leftist activism in 1965 and ending with the massive abandonment of Marxist models exemplified by the "New Philosophy" debates of 1976 and 1977. For the threat of repetition endemic to the project of modern revolution, the danger that (in Barthes's words) "afterwards" would simply slip back into "before," has arguably never received more explicit theoretical formulation than it did in the France of the late 1960s and early 1970s—that is to say, within that period of recent French history that oversaw (or so it appeared to contemporary writers) a definitive breakdown of the modern revolutionary model of political change (Barthes, *Rustle*, 150; *177*).

In the texts I shall be examining here, as in so many others of the period in question, the modern fascination with revolution as the agent of historical repetition habitually expresses itself through one of three broad genetic scenarios. According to the first, or what I call the "logic of specular doubling," revolutionary action is doomed to repetition because revolutionaries invariably construct themselves as mirror images of their rivals. Derived from Lacan's work on narcissistic aggressivity in the mirror stage, and with significant roots in nineteenth-century anarchist polemics, this logic is commonly conflated with a second logic, a "logic of structural repetition," that I trace to a structuralist misprision of the critiques of Stalinist bureaucracy articulated by such forerunners of the French New Left (*le gauchisme*) as Cornelius Castoriadis and Claude Lefort. Roland Barthes gives voice to this logic when he speaks, in a passage from *The Pleasure of the Text,* of a "structural agreement between the contesting and the contested forms" (55; *87*). Complementing these logics of structural repetition and specular doubling, one often finds various "logics of recuperation," whereby specified forms of revolutionary action are said to reinforce, and thus to be co-opted by, established structures of power. The heuristic imperative to distinguish among these commonplace logics of recuperation, specular doubling, and structural repetition is all the more compelling, I shall argue, because in recent theoretical usage they are eminently gregarious structures, prone to keep company with one another through (often unspoken) relations of implication.

My project is a threefold one. First, it is to trace the genealogy of the logics of failed revolt as a constellation of theoretical commonplaces with direct political implications. Second, it is to use those logics as what the French call "des révélateurs"—to look beyond remarkable consistencies in their formulation and application to the ways they might serve to disclose and to highlight (to develop, in the photographic sense) fundamental differences in their respective political, psychoanalytic, deconstructionist, feminist, or "semanalytic" contexts. Finally, it is to subject the logics of failed revolt to the Lacanian question "Where is it that *it* [*ça*] satisfies them, tricks like that?" in order ultimately to explore (or begin to explore) the cultural determinants of a theoretical moment largely shaped by the events of May 1968 (*S* XX, *52*).

No single series of events looms larger on the cultural landscape of Fifth Republic France than that historical syncope, that explosion of direct democracy, cultural politics, and street theater that was May '68. For my purposes, the theoretical moment defined by *les événements* (the events) begins in 1965, a year Pascal Ory and Jean-François Sirinelli have rightly called the "year of the first cracks" in the wall of the Gaullist order (*212*). Massive American bombing of North Vietnam in March 1965 effectively catalyzed the rebirth of a left that had lain dormant since the end of the Algerian War. Henceforth, young French revolutionaries commonly looked to the liberation struggles of the Third World for models of a revolutionism untainted by the blandishments of capitalist society—a phenomenon known as *le tiers-mondisme* (Third-Worldism). Likewise, dissolution of the French Communist Party's student organization, the Union des étudiants communistes, engendered two of the revolutionary *groupuscules* (from "groupe miniscule") that would play crucial roles in the events of May: the Trotskyist Jeunesse communiste révolutionnaire and the Maoist Union des jeunes marxistes-léninistes de France (*Idées, 217*). The year 1965 also marked the beginning of agitation around the question of parietal rights in university residences, agitation intensified by the overly timid Fouchet reforms, which allowed women to visit male dormitories but not vice versa (Joffrin, *42–44*).

Not surprisingly, 1965 also proved a watershed moment in the history of French thought. Althusser's *For Marx* appeared in September, followed two months later by the collective *Reading Capital*. December brought the first installment of Jacques Derrida's "Of Grammatology" (originally serialized in the review *Critique*). Equally remarkable were the publications of the following year, which included the first number of *Cahiers pour l'analyse* in February, Michel Foucault's *The Order of Things* in April, Jacques Lacan's *Écrits* in November, and the first major essays of Julia Kristeva, "Word, Dialogue, and Novel" (first translated for *Desire in Language*) and "Pour une sémiologie des paragrammes" (Toward a semiology of the paragram; in *Semeiotiké*).

If the theoretical moment treated in this study thus began in 1965, it came to an end in 1977, at the end of the French intelligentsia's long process of disengagement from the ideals of Marxism-Leninism. Set into motion in 1956 by Khruschev's anti-Stalinization campaign and the subsequent invasion of Hungary, this process was reversed for a time in the late 1960s and early 1970s, only to be renewed by the economic crisis of 1973–74 and the publication of Solzhenitsyn's *Gulag Archipelago* (1974). At their 22nd Congress in February of 1976, the French Communist Party (PCF) abandoned the Leninist "dictatorship of the proletariat" line and admitted the peaceful, democratic transition to socialism. Likewise, *le tiers-mondisme* never recovered from the blows dealt it by the Lin Biao affair (1971) and the crisis of Mao's succession (1976), the Khmer Rouge massacres (from 1976), and the exodus of the Vietnamese "boat people" (from 1976). The vehement (often well-nigh hysterical) anti-Marxism of "New Philosophers" such as Bernard-Henri Lévy and André Glucksmann was but the most visible sign of a shift in which "the entire Left Bank changed course like a school of dolphins" (Jean-Claude Guillebauden, cited by Ory and Sirinelli, *231*). The year 1977 is especially significant for the purposes of this study, moreover, because several of the most concise formulations of the logics of failed revolt occur in texts dating from that year: Barthes's "Inaugural Lecture" (*Leçon*), Kristeva's "A New Type of Intellectual: The Dissident," and *Tel Quel*'s special number on the United States.

This highly publicized turn from Marxism plainly exemplifies the axiom that historical shifts are played out in mind long after they have been played out in fact. In a 1967 piece explaining the decision to suspend publication of the seminal leftist review, *Socialisme ou Barbarie*, Cornelius Castoriadis spoke of the depoliticized and privatized nature of modern society, the transformation of workers into salaried employees, and a resultant blurring of class boundaries as precluding the constitution of a revolutionary political organization consonant with the radical restructuring of Marxist theory proposed by the journal ("Suspension," *422*). May '68 ultimately belied Castoriadis's assumption that the contemporary situation tended to prohibit the development of "a positive collective reaction against the alienation of modern society" (*422*). But his essay would appear remarkably prophetic in light of the disenchantments of the mid-1970s. It is curious, therefore, that the last number of *Socialisme ou Barbarie* appeared in August 1965.

To the militants who assembled in the courtyard of the Sorbonne on May 3, 1968, to protest "the fascist terror and police repression" undergone by the Nanterre-based March 22nd movement (*Mouvement du 22 mars*), the revolutionary idea was of course far from dead. By prompting police intervention, and thus uncovering a violence inherent in the ostensibly harmonious Gaullist order, these militants effectively touched off the student phase of the events—a time of demonstrations, denunciations, and wall-writings, culminating in the first night (May 10–11) on the barricades of the Quartier Latin. With the general strike of May 13 and the coming together of students and trades unionists in a triumphal procession through the quarters of the Left Bank, the events took a decisive turn. Action spread to the factories, to the ORTF (Office de Radiodiffusion Télévision Française), to the lycées. Daily life in France soon ground to a halt. On the afternoon of May 29, de Gaulle flew unannounced to a French army outpost in Baden-Baden, determined to take refuge from the Communist-provoked "paralysis" he saw gripping the country (Joffrin, *280*). And yet by the next day the unrest was largely over: a newly combative de Gaulle delivered a radio address dissolving the National Assembly, warning against the "intimidation, intoxication, and tyranny" of the agents of "totalitarian communism," and promising a popular referendum on his presidency (cited by Joffrin, *295–96*). As dusk fell, half a million supporters marched up the Champs Elysées on his behalf. On June 23 and 30, de Gaulle and the constitution of 1958 won a massive victory in a pair of referenda subsequently referred to in leftist circles as the *élections-trahisons* (betrayal elections).

Much of the interpretive pleasure to be had in studying the May events derives from a need to track the very real ambivalences and political tensions at the heart of a revolutionary "fused group" comprised of (among others) traditional Marxist-Leninists, Maoists, Trotskyists, situationists, anarchists, and Christian leftists.[3] Calls for the overthrow of the late capitalist order and the replacement of bureaucratic structures with forms of revolutionary self-management (*autogestion*) were routinely coupled with calls for sexual liberation, for a radical disalienation of a modern subject caught in an increasingly technocratic world, for guerrilla art, or for new conceptions of urban space.

Merging into such nominally revolutionary projects were a series of reformist demands, beginning with appeals to reform a university system reeling under the effects of a two-fold increase in enrollment in seven years. Liberalized systems of instruction and examination, protection of open access to the university for all holders of the Baccalauréat, a greater adaptation of university curricula to the demands of the job market: such were the specific motivations that drove substantial numbers of students and professors to militate in the events. Meanwhile, outside the university doctors, lawyers, architects, and magistrates sought to modernize and liberalize their professional organizations; workers at the ORTF struck for freedom of information; increased self-determination was the watchword everywhere (Touraine, *May Movement 218, 224*). All these various elements "crossed paths, crossed swords, and cross-fertilized" (Morin in *Brèche, 15*).

For the purposes of a study centered on the symptomatic and strategic functions of the logics of failed revolt, the central fact of May was perhaps its failure to effect what Pascal Ory and Jean-François Sirinelli have called, thinking of student leader Dany Cohn-Bendit and the March 22nd movement, "a fragile synthesis of two, ordinarily irreconcilable dogmatic logics—one of Marxist inspiration, the other libertarian" (*218*). With the passing of the revolutionary moment, the gulf between these two logics came to appear all but unbridgeable, thus giving rise to perceptions of a fundamental theoretical schism. In a 1986 essay entitled "Mai 68: complexité et ambiguïté" Edgar Morin articulated a widely accepted distinction between two primary lines of descent in May's intellectual genealogy: a "Marxist-Leninist-religious" line represented by the Maoists, the Trotskyists, and later by certain of the "New Philosophers" and a "libertarian-communitarian" line emblematized by the various movements in favor of sexual, racial, and regional difference and theorized by the ideologues of "desire," Deleuze and Guattari in their 1972 *Anti-Oedipus* and Jean-François Lyotard in his 1974 *Libidinal Economy* (*Brèche, 176*; cf. Ory and Sirinelli, *291*).

I find Morin's distinction a useful heuristic tool, but would add two caveats. First, some of the most interesting theoretical production in France after May '68 continued to take aim at the synthesis sought by Cohn-Bendit and his March 22nd cohorts, thus patently traversing Morin's genealogical divide. In her work up to and including the 1974 *Revolution in Poetic Language*, for instance, Julia Kristeva paid a singular homage to the "Marxist-Leninist-religious" line by synthesizing with it elements more characteristic of its "libertarian-communitarian" counterpart, including focus on the body and its fragmentation through *la jouissance* (orgasm, bliss) and the elaboration of a specifically cultural politic. And yet Kristeva was far too aware of the dangers of recuperation and had been far too assiduous a participant in Lacan's seminar to fall into an easy liberationist rhetoric.

My second caveat would be that Morin's genealogy should not be used to overstate the effect of continuity between the May events and that period which French historians typically call *l'après-Mai* (the after-May). The years immediately following May '68 were witness to a remarkable fracturing of the French left, a diversion of the revolutionary impetus unleashed by the May events into a series of so-called micropolitical projects. Although several of these were direct precipitates of the original revolutionary ferment—most notably the Worker's Self-Management movement, which culminated in the grand experiment with *autogestion* at the Lip watch factory in 1973—the majority (primarily those on the "libertarian-communitarian" side of Morin's ledger) represented concerns quite particular to the post-May period. The founding of the Mouvement de libération des femmes (MLF) in 1970, for example, has been widely interpreted as a reaction against an overblown machismo on the barricades, against a revolutionary moment that, as Guy Hocquenghem wrote in the tenth-anniversary issue of *Autrement*, "gave his final blaze of glory to the guy-in-battle-dress-whose-woman-puts-on-the-coffee" (cited by Reader, 70).

The order of the day included ecologism, consumerism, and regionalism; the defense of the rights of minorities and gays; anti-psychiatry and the liberation of "desire." "Difference" was the password and the right to difference the fundamental stake in political struggles. Or, more precisely, the celebration of difference stood athwart the political, eschewing politics proper while claiming real political effects, in accordance with an extension of the political, most commonly associated with Foucault, to include all life situations governed by differential relations of power.[4] Between the events of May and the theoretical work of the period that followed, there was both a commonality of concern and a significant effect of rupture, a play of continuity *and* discontinuity that is perfectly captured by the expression *l'après-Mai* and that it will be one of my tasks to delineate here.

Considered in light of earlier accounts (by Cornelius Castoriadis, Jean-Paul Sartre, and others) of the inevitable betrayal of a revolution's aims through the process of its institutionalization, the so-called logics of failed revolt appear strikingly impoverished. As with most received ideas, they are not wholly false. Yet, as I argue in Chapter 1, they attain their easy iterability and mythic power at the price of significant simplification. At the heart of such logics one typically finds absolutist conceptions of Power and Mastery, linked to an eternalist elision of all positive (if often tangential) historical effects. The significance of these logics for French theory of the immediate post-May period thus had less to do with their truth value than with their ability to catalyze two broad types of secondary gain. On the one hand, they allowed theorists to work over the trauma attendant to the perceived failure of May '68 by theorizing its eternal necessity; the work of former Maoists turned New Philosophers Christian Jambet and Guy Lardreau exemplifies this dynamic. On the other hand, these logics served as argumentative pretexts, allowing Barthes, Kristeva, Cixous, and others to construct the existing political field as an impasse in order to justify significant displacements of political energies (including a politicization of the literary text).

The paradox of the May events has been that, while they ultimately furthered the breakdown of that all-or-nothing criterion on which the commonplace logics of revolutionary failure depended, they were seen in their immediate aftermath as illustrative of an infernal conjunction of those logics. If one undertakes direct, political action, the argument went, then the logics of specular doubling and structural repetition apply. But if one refuses such action, as the student revolutionaries had tended to do, then one's revolt will at best be hopelessly marginal, at worst a reinforcement of institutionalized power.

It was in the face of this revolutionary double bind, outlined in Chapter 2, that the work of Jacques Lacan would come to appear exemplary to a significant number of post-May intellectuals. For not only had Lacan worked since the 1940s to theorize the logics of recuperation and specular doubling in specifically psychoanalytic terms, more recently he had turned to instituting a series of impasse structures within analytic theory itself. Chapter 3 traces Lacan's appeal to the "tragic ear" of certain post-May theorists to a double movement inherent in that ethic first outlined in Lacan's seminar of 1959–60. For Lacan, the ethics of psychoanalysis point first and foremost toward a suspension of desire in the tragic, purificatory experience of being-for-death.

But since it is in the very nature of human experience for such a suspension of desire to prove untenable, tragic purification triggers the reemergence of an endless, specifically comic flight of desire. Analysis of Lacan's elliptical pronouncements on the subject of revolutionary politics in general, and on May '68 in particular, shows them to be inscribed in a textuality that likewise fosters an oscillation between tragic insight into the impasse that is human desire and desire's comic reprise. Indeed, as I argue in Chapter 5 through a reading of *L'Ange* (The angel, 1976), Christian Jambet and Guy Lardreau's requiem for their Maoist past, Lacan's work actively reinforces that endless alternation of revolutionary despair with revolutionary hope that has so conspicuously shadowed the revolutionary project in modern France. It does so, moreover, despite Lacan's cogent critique of the narcissism underlying the rebel's demand for a confirmation of his revolutionary hope. Thus Lacan's own texts pursue a duplicitous, ironic strategy. The only solution to the fundamental impossibility of desire (political or otherwise), they suggest, is to "supplement" or "develop" that impossibility—either in the training of future analysts or in writing itself. The only true hope, in short, is to *textualize* the play of despair and hope.

This argument points to an ambivalence within Lacan's work that assures its centrality for the purposes of this study. On the one hand, Lacanian theory tends to reproduce characteristics of the political impasse as it would come to be formulated, in Lacanian terms, by theorists of *l'après-Mai*. The chapters of Part II, "Politics as Tragic Impasse," explore this tendency first in the texts of Lacan himself (Chapter 3); then in those of another *maître à penser* to the post-May generation, Louis Althusser

(Chapter 4); and finally in the work of Jambet and Lardreau (Chapter 5). More specifically, they trace a complex pattern of mutual implication between the notions of specularity, bipolarity, inversion, negation, psychosis, and rigor. Why, they ask, do Lacan and Althusser attempt to counter the vicious circles of ideologically driven, specular miscognition by deploying an aggressive theoretical circularity? What might this circularity have to do with psychosis, defined by Lacan as a "trial in rigor"? How does Lacan's privileging of psychotic miscognition serve to block the dialectical movement proper to Hegel's *schöne Seele* (beautiful soul) scenario, and so constitute the very "dialectical impasse" he finds characteristic of the revolutionary as *belle âme*? And why would Jambet and Lardreau choose to reconceive cultural revolution precisely on the model of the beautiful soul?

But Lacan's work must also be read as setting the stage for a rethinking of the political outside traditional bipolar or antinomic frameworks, and thus ultimately for an explicit politicizing of symbolic practice. The Lacanian logic of specular doubling allowed a wide range of theorists to depict established politics as trapped in a dualistic, paranoid world where rivalry masks indifferentiation or identification and where the partisan rejection of one's rival springs from the narcissistic illusion of one's own subjective unity. In so doing, it served to rationalize new forms of cultural politics grounded in the practice of a programmatic multiplicity (of meaning, drives, styles, or erotic sites). Like the related logic of structural repetition, it effectively displaced the political—some would say the revolutionary—away from that tragicomic play of despair and hope endemic to modern revolution (and reenacted for readers of Lacan) and toward the ironic tactic of "subtle" (Barthes) or "discrete" subversion (Kristeva on Mallarmé). What the logics of specular doubling and structural repetition sanctioned, in other words, was the elaboration of duplicitous, transgressive forms of writing that presuppose a tactical yet "fatal complicity" (Derrida) with the power relations to be displaced or deconstructed.

I have spoken of the logics of structural repetition and specular doubling as rhetorical pretexts. In the France of the late 1960s and early 1970s, many of the suppositions underlying these logics—the assumption, for example, of a bipolarized political sphere inhabited by rival totalizing systems—were becoming increasingly obsolete. To utter such a logic was thus to reenact an exorcism that had largely taken place in fact, if not always in mind—to "conjure" an impasse, in the full ambivalence of that verb. For in the context of post-May France, the image of the revolutionary (or revolutionary organization) as double to the powers-that-be was increasingly that of a ghost, made to be called forth and exorcised—or rather, called forth precisely to be exorcised—in the interest of a politics of transgression.

To the theorists discussed in Part III, "Conjuring the Impasse," it is literature or fiction that best illustrates this new, specifically transgressive cultural politic. Picking up where Chapter 2 had left off, Chapter 6 explores a gesture inherent in the tripartite structure of the logics of failed revolt, that of dismissing established political rivals "back to back" (*dos à dos*) in the interest of a "third term" or "third way." Through analysis of texts by Barthes and Kristeva, this chapter shows how the back-to-back dismissals of the post-May period effectively broke with a long history of (predominantly socialist) third-way positions—from the "nonconformists" of the 1930s through Sartre and Castoriadis—by reconceiving the third term as both plural solution and touristic destination. Chapter 7 focuses on Kristeva's complex, neo-Hegelian revision of the third term scenario in *Revolution in Poetic Language*, showing how her portrayal of fascism and Stalinism as specular doubles ultimately serves to justify transgressive forms of poetic practice on the margins of an advanced capitalist order. In Chapter 8 I examine how Cixous's positing of a comic "flight" outside the tragic impasses that plague masculine politics leads her to the rhetorics of anarchism and hysteria, two (seemingly untimely) forms of magical thinking that nonetheless hold the key to her rethinking of the modern community.[5]

> In 1980, it has been said, the French rediscovered narrative.

> The constraint came from politics, and from revolutions, which invariably baffled us; some because, just as we rolled up our sleeves and got ready to go to work, they turned their backs on us, and others because they showed signs of transforming themselves into dictatorships. . . . The narrative provided a kind of reef we could catch hold of, just enough to indicate and describe what we had thought. As Bizot put it, "The narrative remobilizes thought." (Clément, *Lives*, 54; *68*).

To narrate on the far side of the revolutionary moment was thus a reactive gesture, a desperate brake on political confusion and disillusionment. And yet this reactive gesture invigorated, reactivated thought.

This study was written by one who experienced May '68 and (to a lesser extent) the glory days of French theory at a temporal and geographic remove. It would be presumptuous, and perhaps simply wrong, to claim that the paralysis that comes from political confusion and the loss of revolutionary illusions has played no role in this project. But my reasons for turning to narrative's capacity to remobilize thought have grown primarily out of the American context in which I think and write. I have chosen to tell a story (to a point) from the desire to contextualize and to historicize a series of French theoretical commonplaces that American readers, unfamiliar with the intellectual climate of France after World War II, have all too often taken to be eternal verities.

In pursuing this project, I have learned much from the still-growing body of critical studies on specific French theorists (including Borch-Jacobsen, Žižek, Marini, Roustang, Rose, and MacCannell on Lacan; Callinicos on Althusser; Roger, Culler, Ungar, and Miller on Barthes; Lewis and Moi on Kristeva; Conley and Rabine on Cixous). But my aim has been to bridge the gap between such studies on the one hand and the work of historians and sociologists on the other (Hunt and Furet on the Revolution; Debray, Ory, and Sirinelli on the intellectual in France; Anderson and Poster on Western Marxism; Castoriadis on Stalinism; Maitron and Sonn on anarchism; Morin, Lefort, and Touraine on May '68; Goldstein and Glazer on hysteria; and Roudinesco and Turkle on psychoanalysis in France). Only by reading French theory of *l'après-Mai* contextually, I would argue, can one avoid that sterile alternative of deification or vilification to which such theory has so often been subjected.

The danger involved in narrating a series of theoretical attempts to conjure a certain paranoid impasse is of course that the narration itself may fall hostage to an obsessive quest for singular meaning that is paranoid in its demand for coherence. (It is worth recalling in this connection that the revival of narrative in the 1980s brought us not only Catherine Clément's fine book on Lacan, cited a moment ago, but also Francis Fukuyama's curiously self-congratulatory "The End of History?") My response to this danger has been to narrate duplicitously, to sketch out large evolutional shifts that will be problematized in particular readings and to use points where historical meaning tends to cohere to open up others where it can only be anticipated.

The readings that follow thus track a series of evolutions that are never total, rarely contemporaneous, and occasionally at cross purposes: from tragicomic oscillation to ironic subversion, from the cosmic fatalism of the rebellious outsider to the fatal complicity of the transgressive insider, from a will to overcome subjective contradictions in the name of revolutionary purity to apologies for the tactical duplicity of the fissured subject, from the paranoid suppression of the other to a hysterical traversing of that other, or from bipolarity to polyvalence and plurality. In significant ways, these evolutions point to a larger movement from politics to ethics—or better, toward attempts to elaborate a new political ethics. What is the function of the body in recent conceptions of an ethics of transgression? How might such an ethics imply a "permanent revolution"? What is the ethico-political stake of the split subject (Barthes's "perverse" subject, Kristeva's "subject in process / on trial," Cixous's hysteric)? And how could we reconceive collectivity on the basis of that subject? How might a new status of the modern community depend on the salutary contagion of "exemplary actions," such as one finds at work in that revolutionary spectacle that was May '68? These are among the principal questions that inform my readings in Part III, and that return in a pair of brief essays on more recent developments, presented in Part Four under the rubric "Afterthoughts."

PART I

Revolution as Repetition

CHAPTER 1

Logics of Failed Revolt

It is not unpleasant to discover that a received idea is false. But if such an idea is false *absolutely*, so that one need only appeal to the most basic human experience to grasp its falsehood, then a more curious (and perhaps more difficult) problem arises. How did it become a received idea in the first place? Of what stuff is it wrought? What uses does it serve? In short, the question is no longer whether the received idea is true or false, but rather why it *is*.

— Jean Paulhan, *Les Fleurs de Tarbes*

In a 1978 dialogue with Gayatri Spivak on the subject of the so-called New Philosophers (principally Bernard-Henri Lévy, André Glucksmann, Christian Jambet, and Guy Lardreau), Michael Ryan once remarked, "If the new philosophy has a coherent theory of revolution, it is this: revolution is impossible because the same always returns in the opposite. The Master can never be altogether eliminated because to oppose him is merely to reaffirm his power. And whatever alternative is set up in opposition to the Master will be yet another Master" (76). This passage conjoins, quite off-handedly, two of the theoretical commonplaces I call, as a group, the logics of failed revolt. According to the first of these, a "logic of recuperation," to oppose the Master (in specifiable ways) is merely to consolidate the Master's power. According to the second, a "logic of substitution," any figure that sets itself up as an alternative to the Master risks becoming a Master in its turn.

In Chapter 2, I shall argue that the tendency among New Philosophers and others to ascribe equal validity to the logics of substitution and recuperation, indeed to conjoin them (as here) into a seamless political impasse, arises from a common misreading of the lessons of May '68. The purpose of the present chapter will be to examine the effects of simplification specific to such commonplace logics of revolution as repetition. For if the apodictic tone captured in Ryan's (quite accurate) reformulation effectively militates against the New Philosophy's claim to political acumen, it also reflects (albeit in an especially naive, nonduplicitous fashion) the effects of simplification and certainty endemic to the logics of failed revolt as such.

To set us on the track of more contemporary formulations of these logics, I shall begin with a brief look backwards at a crucial episode of their nineteenth-century prehistory, the debates pitting Marxists against anarchists in the context of a struggle for control of the First International.

In its classic Marxist form, the logic of recuperation typically insisted that any revolutionary action that fails to undertake an explicitly political (even "authoritarian") campaign against the bourgeois State will inevitably serve to reinforce its power. Thus Friedrich Engels, a master of the genre, wrote in 1872, "I know nothing more authoritarian than a revolution, and when one's will is imposed on others with bombs and bullets, as in every revolution, it seems to me an act of authority is being committed. It was the lack of centralisation and authority that cost the Paris Commune its life" (Marx, Engels, and Lenin, 68).

At its most virulent, this logic commonly found its place in *ad hominem* forms of revolutionary polemic. In the campaign of innuendoes Marx and Engels waged against the Bakuninites prior to the latter's expulsion from the International in 1872, the essential charge was that Bakunin's Alliance of Socialist Democracy was a well-disciplined band of *agents provocateurs,* whose invective had "wakened approving echoes in the police press of all countries" and whose aim was "to decapitate the International" (Marx, Engels, and Lenin, 120).

The structure of the logic of recuperation as a truncated or degraded dialectic followed from this *ad hominem* reduction. By presenting the failure of revolutionary action simply *as* failure, by blocking that movement from particular to universal through which the dialectic relentlessly overcomes apparent impasses, the recuperative logic denied the subsumption of revolutionary failure within a dialectical progress toward revolution evoked by Marx in this well-known passage from the *Class Struggles in France*: "In a word: the revolution made headway not by its immediate tragicomic achievements, but on the contrary by the creation of a powerful, united counter-revolution, by the creation of an opponent in combat with whom the party of revolt first ripened into a real revolutionary party" (33).

Whereas the *Eighteenth Brumaire of Louis Bonaparte* had portrayed true proletarian revolution as a titanesque dialectical struggle against an adversary who is thrown down "only in order that he may draw new strength from the earth and rise again, more gigantic, before them," anarchist revolutionism was seen to merit theorization only as a truncated dialectic befitting those who preached what Engels called "the emasculating doctrine of absolute abstention from political action" (Marx, *Brumaire,* 107; Marx, Engels, and Lenin, 81). Marx's cry, "The revolution is dead! Long live the revolution!" thus offered the revolutionary dialectic as a heroic, fully virile counterpart to the phoenix-like spirit of anarchy expressed by Engels when he wrote, "The anarchists commit suicide every year and arise anew from the ashes every year; this will continue until anarchism is persecuted in earnest. It is the only socialist sect which can really be destroyed by persecution" (Marx, Engels, and Lenin, 170).

To the Marxists' logic of recuperation, nineteenth-century anarchists typically responded with a logic of substitution. Thus, as early as 1846 Pierre-Joseph Proudhon replied to Marx's request that he participate in an international network of socialist correspondents by cautioning Marx against falling into "the contradiction of your compatriot Martin Luther, who, having overturned Catholic theology, set about in a great flurry of anathema and excommunications to institute a Protestant theology" (57). Elsewhere, with an apodictic assurance that came to be characteristic of anarchist discourse, Proudhon glossed his claim that "communism has simply turned property's artillery against the army of property" (we can hear Marx interjecting here: "Precisely so!") by remarking that "the slave always apes his master" (cited by Guérin, 22). Bakunin would later take up this notion of a slavish mimicry, inscribed as it were in the very nature of political power, when he complained of Marx and the other "doctrinaire revolutionaries" that "they are enemies only of the existing authorities, because they want to take their place, enemies of the existing political institutions because these preclude the possibility of their own dictatorship" (cited by Schatz, 160).

I would trace the simplistic, even caricatural nature of these arguments (on both sides of the polemical divide) to that specifically modern notion of revolution as absolute renewal with which I began. Faced with the injunction to remake society anew—and this in the wake of the apparent failures of the revolutions of 1830, 1848, and 1871 (to take just the example of France)—the nineteenth-century revolutionary tended to parry the threat of revolutionary failure by splitting off an authentic revolutionary ideal (guaranteed by history's dialectic or by the spontaneous, eruptive force of popular instincts) from a purely contingent cause of failure. The only way to save the revolution from that regression or repetition that inhered within it (historically as well as etymologically) was to project the threat of repetition outwards onto a figure whose role was that of failure incarnate—onto a degraded, even buffoonlike double of authentic revolutionism. Engels exemplified this mechanism nicely when, in an 1882 letter to J. Becker, he interrupted his reflections on the strike at the Montceau coal mines to remark, "Incidentally, I have got so used to these anarchist buffoons that it seems quite natural to me to see alongside the real movement this clownish caricature" (Marx, Engels, and Lenin, 170).

The effect of this miscognitive tactic was ultimately to institutionalize a dialogic structure between revolutionary rivals, each of whom clearly recognized in the other precisely that which he refused to recognize in himself. A reading of Marx's 1875 "Notes on Bakunin's Book *Statehood and Anarchy*" (see Appendix) reveals an elaborate castration drama played out between polarized rivals, each attributing to the other (as his own degraded double) those recuperative and repetitive threats, that risk of revolutionary "castration," that necessarily plays through all modern revolutionary practice. The apparent disjunction of the logics of recuperation and substitution along the battle lines drawn in the Marx/Bakunin polemics is thus effectively undermined by their common insertion within a paranoid dialogue where all utterances are reducible to the formula, popularized by Lacan: "I am nothing of what happens to me. You are nothing of value [*Je ne suis rien de ce qui m'arrive. Tu n'es rien de ce qui vaut*]" (*Écrits*, 20; *114*).

I have chosen to begin with this brief (and perhaps surprising) detour through the nineteenth-century prehistory of our contemporary logics of substitution and recuperation because it is the polemical confrontation of these traditional logics that ultimately confirms the most common logic of substitution in recent French theory. I have in mind here a logic of repetition through specular doubling that entered the theoretical vulgate through the work of Jacques Lacan—more specifically, through two papers from the late 1940s in which Lacan linked narcissistic aggressivity and paranoia to the constitution of the ego in what he called the "mirror stage"—"The Mirror Stage as Formative of the Function of the I as Revealed in Psychoanalytic Experience" (1949; first version, 1936) and "Aggressivity in Psychoanalysis" (1948).

In these papers Lacan speaks of the child's *moi* (self) as constituted "in a fictional direction" through a series of libidinal relationships with images that increasingly alienate the child from him- or herself (*Écrits*, 19, 2; *113, 94*). The so-called mirror stage is crucial in this respect, for the alienation attending to the infant's jubilant assumption of the complete body image(s) she sees in the mirror prepares the way, first, for a secondary (or "transitivistic") identification with the imago of a playmate; second, for the formation of the child's ego ideal; and finally, for her full constitution as a subject through entrance into the necessarily apersonal order of language.

But resolution of the Oedipus complex and entrance into the Symbolic order by no means preclude the continuing function of imaginary structures in adult psychic life. Thus, in "Aggressivity in Psychoanalysis" Lacan analyzes the paradoxical doubling effects characteristic of political rivalry as remnants of infantile "transitivism," that "structural ambivalence" whereby the child who beats will come to identify with the child who is beaten, and vice versa (*Écrits*, 19; *113, 180*). Likewise, he traces adult aggressivity (and specifically political aggressivity) to a "miscognitive function" underlying what he sees as the *moi*'s fundamentally paranoid structure (*Écrits*, 22, 6; *117, 99*). Set up as a constellation of alien imagoes, and thus irreducibly fictional, the *moi* denies its constitutive absence of self-identity through the sort of paranoid aggressivity exemplified in the phrase "I am nothing of what happens to me. You are nothing of value" (*Écrits*, 2, 20; *94, 114*). It is precisely the narcissistic fiction of a self both whole and autonomous, in other words, that determines an aggressivity Lacan finds "in any relation to the other," but most notably in "the especial delusion of the misanthropic '*belle âme*', throwing back on to the world the disorder of which his being is composed" (*Écrits*, 6, 20; *98, 114*).

According to the Lacanian logic of specular doubling, it is only by introjecting the imago of the adversary that the rebel attains what passes for success. But this alienating identification, constructed on the basis of an ontological rift that structures the subject as a rival with itself, necessarily provokes the paranoid violence of narcissistic miscognition. Writing in an era when the diatribes of the Stalinists and the Trotskyists conspicuously repeated the *Tu quoque* (you too) structure of the Marxist/anarchist polemics, Lacan would speak of illustrating his version of Hegel's *schöne Seele* by evoking "the fate which leads the old revolutionary of 1917 to the defendant's table in the Moscow trials" (*Écrits, 175*). The step from Lacan's explorations of the pathological effects said to follow from the modern cult of the whole and autonomous ego to a far-reaching denial of the concept of revolution as total renewal has proven, we shall see, a short one indeed.

In the theoretical *Doxa* of the late 1960s and early 1970s, this Lacanian logic of repetition through specular doubling was habitually complemented by a series of recuperative dynamics that owed much of their persuasive force to the perceived failures of May '68. In the work of Deleuze and Guattari, Kristeva, and others, one finds an evident fascination with advanced capitalism's uncanny capacity to regenerate itself through the reincorporation and restructuring of specifically destructive (or "deterritorializing") energies.[1]

But such accounts do not necessarily fall under the rubric of a "logic" of recuperation. They do so only when power is made to appear monolithic or purely repressive, when the concepts of mastery and the law are denied all dialectical suppleness, or when historical analysis gives way to a simple venting of eternal verities. Rarely were these preconditions met with such essentializing zeal as when the New Philosophers wrote in a specifically Lacanian idiom, as witness the following passage from Bernard-Henri Lévy:

> Insofar as a project of revolt passes into discourse, it will necessarily be relayed by the discourse of the Master. . . . Insofar as [it] touches on what is called power, the power it institutes will bring back the figures of mastery. So long as revolutionaries, in other words, fashion their dreams in the forms of this world, they will never give birth to anything but the semblances [*semblants*] of revolution. (Cited by Aubral and Delcourt, *27*)

There are clearly passages in Lacan's texts after May '68 to support Lévy's absolutist reading of a recuperative power inherent in the so-called *discours du Maître*.[2] To the extent that Lacan saw all discrete signifiers as bearing the traces of a desire for Oneness characteristic of psychic functioning in the imaginary, the very use of language was said to reinforce the primacy of the phallus as symbol of an impossible, yet preeminently desirable, totalization. This would be one reason why, as Lacan insisted in *Television*

(1974), any denunciation of the capitalist's discourse serves only to reinforce and perfect that discourse (14; *26*).[3] In a similar vein, Lacan ended his riotous 1969 confrontation with the students of Vincennes by yoking his claims for the necessary recuperation of what he took to be the student rebels' liberationist ideology—encapsulated in the wall slogan *Jouissez sans entraves* (Fuck without hindrance)—to the prospect of a historical repetition ostensibly guaranteed by human experience:

> If you had a little patience, and if you were willing for our impromptus to continue, I would tell you that the aspiration to revolution has but one conceivable issue, always, the discourse of the master [*ça n'a qu'une chance d'aboutir, toujours, au discours du maître*]. That is what experience has proved. What you, as revolutionaries, aspire to is a Master. You will have one. ("Impromptu," 126; *24*)

But "No Thing is All," Lacan had insisted, and least of all the master's recuperation (124; *23*). If the liberationist rebel incarnates that surplus value of *jouissance* that Lacan called the *plus-de-jouir*, a surplus value whose ultimate function was to be recuperated by and for the master, that recuperation itself was never total.[4] In Lacan's work one finds evidence of a crucial asymmetry between the logic of specular doubling, which tends to function as a true impasse, and accounts of a recuperative mechanism, often inherent to language itself, that rarely fails to leave a significant remainder.[5] This perceived openness on the side of language's recuperative function was itself a commonplace of the post-May period. Barthes's use of paradox to block a nauseating solidification of meaning, Derrida's verbal sleights of hand to undercut the metaphysics of presence, Cixous's writing in a paronomastic idiom deemed unacceptable to masculine rationality—each of these tactics testifies to the possibility of blocking a process of recuperation seen to follow from the necessary implication of speaking subjects within the power relations inherent to language itself.[6] For in many of the theoretical projects of *l'après-Mai*, as I shall show throughout this study, language was at once the agent of a bind and the promise of an escape, the promise of a third term beyond any specular or structural concordance between contestatory and contested forces.

In an effort to capture the specificity of what I have called the logics of recuperation and specular doubling, it is helpful to consider what these logics are not. Certain formulations of the logic of specular doubling, it is true, hint at their author's familiarity with prior analyses (by Castoriadis, Baudrillard, and others) of Marxist theory's tendency to reproduce specifically capitalist forms of rationality (see Chapter 2). Similarly, the commonplace logics of recuperation tend to resonate with Sartre's argument—in his *Critique of Dialectical Reason*—that the necessity of organizing the revolutionary fused group so as to preserve individual liberty ultimately leads to the loss of precisely that reciprocity of recognition that binds the group together; "the group, whatever it may be, *contains in itself* its reason for relapsing into the inert being of a gathering: thus the disintegration of a group . . . has an a priori intelligibility" (1: 349; *1: 452–53*).

Where the logics of specular doubling and recuperation most obviously part company with analyses such as these, I would suggest, is in their essential resistance to contextualization within a complex, historical account of the difficulties inherent in the process of institutionalizing a revolution (the difficulty, for instance, of reconciling the often contrary demands of individual autonomy and collective solidarity). In their most univocal formulations, the logics of failed revolt meticulously occult the incremental advance, that specifically historical remainder that makes a difference. That is to say, they are grounded in an essentialist tautology whereby failure is presumed to equal failure (and nothing else), whereby the social system that returns on the far side of a revolutionary episode is deemed the same as that against which revolution was brought ("revolution is always impossible because the same always returns in the opposite"); whereby Power or the Master are always at one with themselves (and hence absolutely noxious). An account of revolution as repetition becomes a "logic," in short, when it is founded on an identitarian or tautological circularity (e.g., the conception of power as one and self-identical) and when it is subject to an "all-or-nothing" standard.[7]

Against those who would attribute the supposed failure of May '68 to the workings of a fundamentally tautological "logic of power" (the New Philosophers come to mind), Castoriadis suggests a valuable corrective. The May events, he concedes, bear witness to "that dimension of *failure* until now apparently indissociable from modern political movements: the enormous difficulty involved in extending critique of the existing order in practical and positive ways, the impossibility of assuming the goal of an autonomy that is at once individual and social by establishing collective self-governance" (*Brèche, 194*). But this "dimension of failure," Castoriadis continues, has haunted modern revolution since the defeat of the Roundheads and the ascension of Cromwell. And the failure has only rarely been total. Like the Paris Commune of 1871, May '68 and the revolutionary movements that gave rise to it left "profound marks" on French mentalities and patterns of behavior (*195*).

Castoriadis astutely attributes this occulting of a significant historical remainder to a "modern political image-repertory [*imaginaire*]" hopelessly wedded to antinomic models and unable to disengage itself from "the representation of politics—and of the institution—as a fiefdom of the State, and of that State itself (which continues, even in the most modern of societies, to incarnate the figure of power by divine right) as entirely its own master" (*195*).

At the root of the anxiety-laden mistaking of relative failure for failure itself, in other words, Castoriadis finds a double anachronism. With a fine sense of historical paradox, he links the specifically quietistic effects of those logics of revolutionary failure that were in common circulation after

May '68 to the contemporary intellectual's continuing visceral attachment to the simple moralistic dichotomies (truth/error, justice/injustice) and rigorously bipolar world-view (capitalism or communism, right or left) under the aegis of which the "intellectual" as such had known its finest hours (the Dreyfus Affair, the struggle against fascism under the Popular Front, etc.).[8] To this he adds a more radical anachronism, the continuing subservience to a fetishistic deification of Power and the State—alibis (one may suspect) for the forms of an advanced capitalism that wants nothing better than thus to be misread in feudal terms.

To this point we have considered three propositions toward a working definition of the logic of failed revolt. Such a logic depends on (1) a fetishistic essentializing of that margin of failure endemic to the modern project of revolution, coupled with (2) a corresponding occultation of all positive (if often unforeseen) historical effects. The argumentative vehicle of choice for such logics is (3) a strictly nondialectical usage of Hegelian oppositions (same/other, master/slave, inside/outside, etc.).

To these I would add a fourth and final proposition, one that is entirely consonant with the denial of historical or institutional analysis—namely (4) a tendency to shift the burden of proving such a logic onto an unspecified body of common experience. To Lacan's adduction above of "what experience has proved," let me add for the moment these passages from Jean-François Lyotard's *The Postmodern Condition*:

> These "moves" necessarily provoke "countermoves"—and everyone knows that [*tout le monde sait d'expérience que*] a countermove that is merely reactional is not a good move. Reactional countermoves are no more than programmed effects in the opponent's strategy; they play into his hands and thus have no effect on the balance of power. That is why it is important to increase displacement in games, and even to disorient it, in such a way as to make an unexpected "move" (a new statement). (16; *33*)

> In any case, there is no question here of proposing a "pure" alternative to the system: we all know now [*nous savons tous*], as the 1970s come to a close, that an attempt at an alternative of that kind would end up resembling the system it was meant to replace. (66; *107*)

Side by side with these direct appeals to shared experience, often signaled by such formulas as *tout le monde sait que . . . , on sait que . . . , nous savons tous que . . .* , or *comme chacun le sait . . .* , one finds a remarkable proliferation of metaphors whose purpose, I would argue, is to articulate the various logics of failed revolt while grounding them in everyday experience. Thus, to cite three examples analyzed in Chapter 6, Hélène Cixous speaks of woman's liberation as disrupting the volleyball game of patriarchal power: "She foresees that her liberation will do more than modify power relations or send the ball over to the other side [*camp*]" ("Laugh," 253; *45*); Roland Barthes imagines that Sollers's texts escape this painterly aporia: "Normally, in order to scour, you need a scouring language, which in its turn becomes a new coat of paint" (*Writer Sollers*, 76; 57); and Julia Kristeva speaks of fascism and Stalinism as "two antinomic systems . . . which, like an eternal couple, can send the elevators back and forth to one another for evermore" ("Why the United States," 274; 4).

I suspect that this proliferation of experiential metaphors must ultimately be read as symptomatic of the (properly unspeakable) suspicion that the logics of failed revolt were themselves not wholly adequate to experience. But this inadequacy is, on one level, clearly beside the point. For what counted in these logics was not so much their truth value, their capacity to account for the complex grounds for specific revolutionary setbacks, as the secondary gains that accrued to those who uttered them: their status as a symptom, for example, or as one element of a strategy.[9] Received ideas, they were mythic in the sense that the ritual act of their repetition lent coherence to a theoretical community whose institutionalized mythic system had since 1956 undergone a slow and painful dismantling (a process whose milestones include Khruschev's de-Stalinization, the invasions of Hungary and Czechoslovakia, the apparent failure of May '68, the slow demystification of Mao's Cultural Revolution, and the publication of Solzhenitsyn's *Gulag Archipelago*).[10] In so doing, they also served to displace the conception of the political native to that mythic system. It is this double destiny of the logics of failed revolt—their function both as symptom and as element of a strategy—that I pursue in Chapter 2.

CHAPTER 2

May '68 and the Revolutionary Double Bind

Society took to the skies, not as a bomb does when it explodes, but like a crepe expertly flipped so as to reveal its underside.

— Alain Touraine, *The May Movement*

Nothing has changed. Everything has changed.

— Edgar Morin, *Mai 68: La Brèche*

There is a curious historical irony in the fate of the leftist review *Socialisme ou Barbarie.* Founded in 1949 by a group of former Trotskyists centered around Cornelius Castoriadis and Claude Lefort and shrouded in obscurity for most of the 1950s, the review reached the height of its influence and prestige in 1968, three years after it ceased publication.

This posthumous authority was clearly readable in the manifestoes of the March 22nd Movement—in their conception of revolution as the spontaneous explosion of creative energies, as well as in their demands for a democratic self-management of the workplace by councils of elected (and fully revokable) representatives. In their introduction to *Obsolete Communism* (1968), Daniel and Gabriel Cohn-Bendit would speak of aspiring to be "no more than plagiarists of the revolutionary theory and practice of these last fifty years," popularizers of the best texts to have appeared in such reviews as *Socialisme ou Barbarie, l'Internationale situationniste,* and *Noir et rouge* (18). Indeed they single out a body of work that I shall be discussing in the pages that follow—the analyses of the May uprising published by Edgar Morin, Claude Lefort, and Cornelius Castoriadis under the title *Mai 68: La Brèche* (May '68: The Breach).

More significant, however, than any matter of theoretical influence are the ways in which the events of May themselves dramatically confirmed the analyses of the *Socialisme ou Barbarie* group. For the very outbreak of a revolutionary movement in a time of low unemployment and rapidly increasing disposable income demonstrated that revolution under modern capitalism need not be triggered by the so-called iron law of pauperization or by crises of overproduction, both more characteristic of the capitalism Marx knew than of its modern counterpart. Likewise, the movement's origins within relatively privileged sectors of French society—among students, media professionals, professors, and the like—confirmed *Socialisme ou Barbarie*'s insistence that revolution could be provoked by a radical alienation plaguing all sectors of contemporary consumer society, such that the progressively shrinking proletariat must no longer be seen as the "privileged bearer of the revolutionary project" (*Brèche*, *136*; Castoriadis, *Writings*, 1: 24). Against such an alienation, Castoriadis had advocated a process of perpetual, nonviolent recovery of that objectified human activity that is the social world, to be achieved through a fully cultural revolutionism going beyond the political "in the traditional sense of the term" (*Writings*, 1: 305, 1: 24). "The process of challenging capitalist relations and their 'rationality' in the domain of work and of power," he would write, "is inseparable from their being put into question in the domains of the family and of sexuality, of education and of culture, or of daily life" (*Writings*, 1: 17).

In the essays of Edgar Morin and Claude Lefort in *Mai 68: La Brèche*, it is typically a logic of failed revolt that justifies this extension of the political to encompass the full range of everyday activities. More precisely, the recourse to an explicitly cultural politic follows from a logic of structural repetition that brands "all the substitute political powers, including the Federation of the Left and the Communist Party" as simple variants on a bureaucratic capitalist theme (Morin in *Brèche*, *65*). In a text written in late May "under the influence of the events," Claude Lefort articulates the need to reposition the political outside its repetitive impasse:

> The political *groupuscules* who, for the most part, thrive on the condemnation of the Communist Party, live only from the desire to be its equal, to appropriate its image. Here and there they mimic the rituals of adult organizations; they restore what the so-called parties of betrayal had forsaken: *good* organization, *good* discipline, *good* positions; they define their territorial limits, their zones of competence, and the proper place of each and every member; they succumb to the same mechanisms of identification that assure the reign of a Law above all contestation, and hence the legitimacy of the position of authority and the sacralization of the group.
>
> Now it is against this system that the *enragés* [the militants of the March 22nd Movement] strike a decisive blow. Not only do they know that nothing is to be expected from Power [*le Pouvoir*: the authorities, the Powers that be], nor from those parties and unions that feign to combat it, but who, were they compelled to take power, would do so only to make it serve new interests, to displace the chess pieces of exploitation and oppression. They know too that, closer by, the *groupuscules* are locked in repetition. There is no need to look elsewhere for the grounds of their [the *enragés*'] success: they appear in student circles to be radically different from those who sur-

> round them and who clamor on about their revolutionary will. They are cut loose from the old constraints [*Ils sont en rupture de ban*]. In a society saturated by discourses and organizations, where speech and action are assigned residence, where one must have one's place and state one's identity before having the right to speak or to act, they create a new space. Or better, they hollow out a non-place [*non lieu*] where the possible is reborn. (*48–49*)

This is already, in many respects, familiar ground. Lefort's passage deploys two related logics of revolution as repetition, both justified by a certain wisdom of experience ("not only do they know . . ."). In the first of these, a logic of specular doubling, Lefort's account of the repetition that plagues those splinter groups of the extreme left known as the *groupuscules* takes on a Freudian, indeed Lacanian, tenor. In claiming that the *groupuscules'* denunciation of the French Communist Party masks a more fundamental identification with, or introjection of, that rival's image, Lefort clearly draws on Lacan's analysis of the constitution of the subject's *moi* through the appropriation of alien imagoes, and more specifically on his linkage of the attendant paranoia and narcissistic aggressivity to the Möbius logic of Freud's *Verneinung* (denial, negation), where "no" means "yes" and rejection appropriation.[1]

What is particular to Lefort's analysis, however, is the way it yokes this neo-Lacanian account of a paranoid territorialization, a rigorous division of the political universe into authentic and inauthentic domains ("they restore . . . *good* organization, *good* discipline, *good* positions"), to that repetitive scenario for which the *Socialisme ou Barbarie* authors are best known, their analysis of the Soviet system as a form of "bureaucratic capitalism." According to this analysis, the reproduction of class exploitation within a state that had abolished private property must be attributed to Marxist theory's whole-scale adoption of bourgeois values and techniques (the work ethic, the ideology of production, rationalist policing of the workplace, and so on), and the resultant incarnation of these in a bureaucracy. Or, as Castoriadis would write, one who puts into service techniques that are, "from beginning to end, the material incarnation of the capitalist universe . . . only reproduces capitalist 'rationality,' thus remaining prisoner of the universe that one claimed to be combating" (*Writings*, 1: 17). A hierarchical division between directors and executants, between those who "know" and those who "do"; the rationalization of this division in the name of organizational "efficacy"; the subjection of the executants to "a collective form of discipline"; the conception of "the worker as molecule, . . . object without resistance of capitalist 'rationalization' "—these are the ideological and practical structures that the analyses of *Socialisme ou Barbarie* had found to characterize capitalism in both its "private"—i.e., Western—and "bureaucratic"—Soviet—varieties (Castoriadis, *Writings*, 1: 303, 1: 18).

But it is precisely these structures that Castoriadis and Lefort would find reproduced within those *groupuscules* of May '68 that were organized on the Bolshevik model:

> In all organizations, a minority of directors is split off from the mass of executants; information withdraws into the space of power; hierarchies (manifest or latent) buttress administrative apparatuses; sectors of activity are partitioned off; the principle of efficacy governing the division of labor and of knowledge passes for a reality principle; thought congeals within the party platforms it settles into, and which assign the limits of what one is allowed to do and to think. (Lefort in *Brèche,* 47)

> These *groupuscules* reproduce at their very heart the division of directors and executants, the split between those who "know" and those who "do not know," the separation between a scholastic pseudo-"theory" and life itself. Likewise, they want to establish this division or split between themselves and the working class, whose "directors" they all aspire to become. (Castoriadis in *Brèche,* 105)

For Castoriadis as for Lefort, the specific charge that the *groupuscules* wanted little more than to take the place of those Party directors whose images they introject—the claim, in other words, that their actions were subject to a logic of specular doubling—becomes the corollary to a more general logic of organizational or structural repetition whereby even that "revolutionary vanguard" that is the Leninist party is seen to reproduce essentially capitalist forms of rationality.[2]

Behind Lefort's earlier allusion to the institutions of French communism as mere pseudo-rivals to the Gaullist regime ("nothing is to be expected from Power, nor from those parties and unions that feign to combat it"), therefore, we must hear the analyses of organizational repetition first elaborated by Castoriadis as early as the late 1940s. But these analyses would be strikingly reconfirmed in the May uprising itself—specifically, by the reluctance of both the PCF (*Parti communiste français*) and the CGT (*Confédération générale du travail*) to play the revolutionary role their mythology demanded.

In the damning litanies of counter-revolutionary acts subsequently rehearsed by critics of the CGT, one typically hears of the union's attempts, prior to the first wildcat strike at Renault (Cléon) on May 15, to block the spread of the students' revolt to the factories, and most especially of the leadership's timidity in the negotiations of the Grenelle accords. Likewise, critics of the Communist establishment rarely fail to mention the remarkably defensive position staked out in May by a Communist Party reluctant to put at risk its hold on the "red suburbs," still struggling to consolidate the Federation of the Left, and hesitant to call for revolutionary insurrection against a regime whose foreign policy had long been looked on favorably by the party bosses in Moscow (Joffrin, 175; Aron, *Revolution*, 22; 33).

For Edgar Morin, again writing in *Mai 68: La Brèche,* what ultimately confirmed the "official left"'s role as double and pseudo-rival to the Gaullist regime was its will to recuperate the revolutionary ferment of the student movement for specifically reformist purposes.[3] "At the end of its march to power," he writes, "the student avant-garde will find its way blocked by the unions and the great oppositional parties, who will absorb the movement to boost their own project of social reformism, to rid the movement of all revolutionary ferment, or to allow the revolutionary cohorts to go to their slaughter so as the better to commemorate them in the future" (26).

I have argued that, for Claude Lefort, the paranoid specularity of the generational rivalry that pits the revolutionary *groupuscules* against the father figures of the PCF must be read as the effect of a common reliance on an organizational rationality whose ultimate provenance is bourgeois. Behind that logic of specular doubling that pertains within the communist hall of mirrors, in other words, Lefort will find the very premise that allows for the repetitive chess game between the bourgeois order and its astonishingly loyal opposition: "They know that nothing is to be expected from Power, nor from those parties and unions that feign to combat it, but who, were they compelled to take power, would do so only to make it serve new interests, to displace the chess-pieces of exploitation and oppression" (*Brèche*, *48–49*).

But the ultimate function of these conjoined logics of specular doubling and structural repetition is to serve as an argumentative alibi, as a pretext (in both senses of that word) to the revolutionary festivity of the student militants "cut loose from the old constraints." Lefort sets the stage for the enunciation of an explicitly revolutionary position, in other words, through the gesture of dismissing back to back the practices of specular rivals whose fall back into reformism is seen as guaranteed by their common desire to pour new wine into the old, rationalist bottles. Or, more precisely, since it is the will to territorialize that characterizes the domain of revolution as repetition ("where speech and action are assigned residence, where one must have one's place"), Lefort will use the logics of repetition as foils not to a revolutionary position per se, but to the advocacy of a new atopian space, of that "non-place" where, as he writes, "the possible is reborn." This practice of constructing the political as a specular impasse in order ultimately to justify the vision of a revolutionary *non lieu* was itself, as we shall have ample occasion to verify, a commonplace (a *lieu commun*) in theoretical discourse of the period centered around May '68.

The irony of history would, however, quickly recreate a certain impasse around those disalienating cultural politics whereby the *Socialisme ou Barbarie* group and their New Left disciples sought to escape the paranoid doublings of traditional revolutionary culture. Viewed in light of the formal dissolution of *gauchiste* organizations on June 12, 1968, and of de Gaulle's massive victory in the referenda of June 23 and 30, the events of May were bound to appear as yet another repetition of a cycle of extreme political advance followed by extreme regression that, according to Lefort himself, had been played out so many times in French history since the Revolution (*Brèche*, *87*).

In retrospect, it was the very refusal to organize the forces of revolution that would seem to have guaranteed the failure of May as a revolutionary moment. "The minority in the May events," Castoriadis writes in a 1986 essay, "could perhaps have become a majority if it had gone beyond proclamations and demonstrations. But that implied a different sort of dynamic, into which it clearly neither wanted nor was able to enter" ("Mouvements," *186*). Renouncing the Leninist conception of a disciplined revolutionary vanguard charged with the dissemination of correct "Social-Democratic" consciousness, the revolutionaries of May chose to rely on a spontaneous contagion of the revolutionary virus fostered by exemplary acts of illegality in public squares (Lenin, "What Is to Be Done," 22). In order to avoid that fall back into hierarchy and seriality that Sartre had theorized as the necessary result of attempts to organize the revolution, they refused that organizational force, that Archimedean lever, by which alone a system of *autogestion* might have been implemented.

If all strategic action implies turning elements of an established system back against that system, taking off one's gloves (in Régis Debray's metaphor) to enter into struggle with "the prose of the world," the student revolutionaries opted rather to keep "their hands clean—just enough to get them cut off. Deliberate purity, more suicide than accident" (*Modeste Contribution*, *28*). The students chose to articulate, in short, a powerful utopian vision whose force as an anticipation of revolutions to come lay in close proximity to an ultimately suicidal refusal of strategic action. "The May Movement," Alain Touraine concluded shortly after the events, "was creative only in what prevented it from succeeding, its spontaneity" (*May Movement*, 62; 52).

If the action committees of May had thus broken with "Robespierre and the long, tragic history of revolutions" by refusing to become, in the words of Mark Poster, "obsessed with the threat of old authority," the apparent disintegration of the movement's libertarian wing—and the subsequent passing of the heritage of May into the hands of such *groupuscules* as the Trotskyist Jeunesse communiste révolutionnaire and the Maoist Gauche prolétarienne—would ultimately bring that obsession back with a vengeance (*Existential Marxism*, 394). I would argue that the remarkable hegemony of Marxist discourse within French theoretical circles for the nearly five years that followed May '68 largely reflects this renewed obsession with the threat of old authority and a heightened sensitivity to the sort of recuperative analysis that we find the PCF already trotting out, in its most time-worn and simplified guise, during the period of the Grenelle Accords (May 25–27):

> More and more clearly, the Communist Party accused the leftists of having knowingly played into the government's hand, and of being agitators [*agents provocateurs*] who wanted nothing more than to defeat the party of the working class by bringing down upon it the weight of a deceived public opinion and a hostile government. (Touraine, *May Movement*, 234; *203*)

> There were no tactics on the leftist side. Street battles were improvised day by day, which proved a stroke of luck for the forces of order. (Maurice Grimaud, cited by Debray, *Modeste Contribution*, 27)

Here then is the impasse that the irony of history would appear to reconstitute around the experience of May '68. New Left political theory had argued that the logics of specular doubling and structural repetition apply to those who, like the hard-line *groupuscules*, pursue a conscious strategy of organized political action. But May itself seemed to justify a logic of recuperation. By refusing organized action, it was commonly thought, the *gauchistes* had assured that their revolt would be at best irrelevant, at worst a pretext to the consolidation of established power.[4] Taken together, these logics constitute a revolutionary double bind *within or against which* theory in the wake of May '68 would habitually proceed, whether to anguish over its stricture (the New Philosophers), to dismiss it as a mere anxious fantasy (their Marxist critics) or, most interesting, to turn the impasse against itself in an effort to displace the political question (as Derrida, Barthes, Kristeva, and others would do).

This double bind is clearly an ideal type. Rarely will its constituent logics be so simply formulated or their conjunction appear so seamless as in Michael Ryan's summary of the New Philosophy: "The Master can never be altogether eliminated because to oppose him is merely to reaffirm his power. And whatever alternative is set up in opposition to the Master will be yet another Master" (Spivak and Ryan, 76). What this simplicity in fact suggests is that the bind itself is a construct, a constative pretext to real work that takes place elsewhere. Thus, in the texts of the New Philosophers, the revolutionary double bind is typically linked to a process of mourning whereby a repetitive hypercathexis of one's lost revolutionary illusions leads to a definitive detachment from those illusions (see Chapter 5).

But we also find traces of this bind in theoretical contexts largely free of this work of mourning. In the course of subsequent chapters, I shall argue that the revolutionary double bind serves to a wide range of cultural, even writerly politics, such as Barthes's advocacy of a spiralling movement of fictional imposture he calls "semiotropy" or Kristeva's apologies for avant-garde artistic practices operating on the margins of capitalist society.

The brief example I would propose here comes from the work of Jacques Derrida, where the revolutionary double bind can be seen to function as that absent question to which Derrida's conception of a "double" or "bifurcated" writing is meant to respond. In his work of the late 1960s and early

1970s, Derrida spoke repeatedly of "a kind of *general strategy of deconstruction*" entailing that "double gesture" of overturning existing hierarchies (speech/writing, presence/absence, etc.) and of "releas[ing] the dissonance of a writing within speech" (*Positions*, 41–42; 56–57). It is, I would argue, the commonplace logics of specular doubling and structural repetition that Derrida has in mind when (in a sentence curiously omitted from the English translation of *Positions*) he speaks of the "phase of overturning" as a tactical moment that "we have perhaps too quickly sought to discredit."[5]

In choosing violently to overturn existing hierarchies, Derrida runs the risk of a certain repetition so as ultimately to forestall recuperation. Or, more precisely, he risks repetition in order to debunk the properly liberal notion of a free competition among rival discourses (what he calls the myth of the "peaceful coexistence of a *vis-à-vis*") while at the same time staving off that threat of impertinence, of an absence of critical purchase, that attends to the dream of an immediate passage beyond hierarchies of power:

> Therefore one might proceed too quickly to a *neutralization* that *in practice* would leave the previous field untouched, leaving one no hold on the previous opposition, thereby preventing any means of *intervening* in the field effectively. We know [*On sait*] *what always have been the practical* (particularly *political*) effects of *immediately* jumping *beyond* oppositions, and of protests in the simple form of *neither* this *nor* that [dans la simple forme du *ni/ni*]. (*Positions*, 41; 57)

At the other edge of the interval traced within bifurcated writing, in the phase of what he calls "a positively displacing, transgressive, deconstruction," Derrida will locate the "irruptive emergence of a new concept": the play of those now-familiar quasi-concepts that are the *pharmakon*, the supplement, the hymen, spacing, and so on (*Positions*, 66, 42; 89, 57). Where the phase of overturning had sought to operate a (necessarily historical) displacement of established hierarchies of value so as to forestall a premature neutralization in the form of the neither/nor, the phase of "positively displacing" deconstruction rejoins the neither/nor so as to preclude the simple repetition that haunts strategies of inversion in their traditional Marxist guise: "the *pharmakon* is neither remedy nor poison, neither good nor evil, [etc.]"[6]

If various logics of failed revolt thus serve as the pretext to Derrida's apology for bifurcated writing, this apology will function in turn to displace the habitual implications of those logics. Built into the logic of failed revolt, one typically found a back-to-back dismissal (*renvoi dos à dos*) of the powers that be and their none-too-oppositional pseudo-rival(s) in the interest of a "third way" or "third term" whereby the very displacement of the political ultimately leads to recovery of that oppositional project betrayed by the pseudo-rival(s) (see Chapter 6). We want neither the Gaullist regime, Claude Lefort suggests, nor those "parties and unions that pretend to combat it," but rather the authentic revolutionism of the student revolutionaries "cut loose from the old constraints." But Derrida effectively deconstructs this neither/nor/but structure (with its residual proximity to the dialectic) by insisting that the twin operations of conceptual overturning and transgressive displacement be seen as necessarily conducted "in a kind of disconcerting *simul* [at once, together], in a movement of the entire field that must be coherent, of course, but at the same time divided, differentiated, and stratified" (*Dissemination*, 6; *12*).

On the strength of examples such as this, I would argue that the tactical usefulness of the revolutionary double bind for displacing the political field—toward the cultural in general and toward specifically transgressive forms of writing in particular—opens more fruitful lines of inquiry for the study of French theory as a cultural-historical phenomenon than does its evident, symptomatic role in the process of binding a traumatic loss. But in both cases, it should be noted, we are dealing with a theoretical construct, the very nature of which is to present the perils of revolutionary action in radically simplified, ahistorical terms.

One last word on recuperation. As Castoriadis reminds us, that "dimension of failure" to which the May events bear evident witness should not blind us to their profound (indeed in some sense revolutionary) effects on French society. The general sense of defeat that many felt in the immediate aftermath of May, on which the New Philosophers would continue to construct their metaphysical edifices over a decade later, presumes that the immediate signs of the movement's success or failure must be found in that specifically political arena in which the student revolutionaries had thought to act (even while rejecting its fundamental premises). If there is a point of essential agreement among the commentators on May—and there have been hundreds of them, representing wildly divergent political perspectives—it is that the real results of the events bear little fundamental resemblance to the announced political intentions of their participants.[7] More precisely, it has become commonplace to read May '68, with its refusal of modernity couched in the languages of nineteenth-century radicalism (Marxism as well as anarchism), as an alibi for hidden aspirations to a modern (we would now say post-modern) world.[8] The events would be recuperated, but in a way that effectively revolutionized the prior order.

In his now-classic *The May Movement* (1968), for example, sociologist Alain Touraine tracks the events for signs of both a movement toward and reaction against an emergent technocratic society, a postindustrial society based on information technologies, nonhierarchical decisionmaking, and the transformation of education into a force of production. To Touraine's reading, the archaic discourse of a utopian antisociety, with its emphasis on spontaneity and unstructured sociability, ultimately served as an "indirect agent of modernization" in its sweeping away of outworn hierarchies in both enterprise and academia (67; *57*). "They are making history," Touraine writes of the student leaders, "but not the history they think they are making" (47; 36).

Ten years later, in a text entitled *Modeste Contribution aux cérémonies officielles du dixième anniversaire,* Régis Debray would likewise insist on the role played by the ideologies of emancipation and the defense of "difference" (individual, sexual, racial, and so on) in the breaking down of traditional barriers to "the extension of commodification to the entire social field" (*14*). The effect of that ruse of developing capitalism called May '68 was thus to liquidate Lenin "in the mind" and De Gaulle "in fact," to issue overdue marching orders to the

> France of stone houses amid fields of rye, of the apéritif and the local schoolmaster, of yes-Papa yes-boss yes-dear . . . so that the France of software and the supermarket, of the news and industrial planning, of know-how and brainstorming [*du software et du supermarché, du news et du planning, du know-how et du brain-storming*] could display its good deals and speculations in the comfort of its own home. (*41, 13*)

Most interesting for our purposes, Debray accounts for effective implementation of this process of radical modernization by likening advanced capitalism to a complex homeostatic system, one whose very vitality depends on its capacity constantly to recuperate disruptive impulses:

> The organization assimilates its phases of disorganization, not as an expense incidental to its development, but as elements of its motor force. That which is excluded completes, that which perturbs stabilizes, that which attacks reinforces. . . . In the fully developed capitalist system, crisis is a state of normalcy, a sign of the system's good health, the very mainspring of its progress. It is order that would be the system's death. (*Modeste Contribution, 24*)

The 1980s saw the emergence of a neo-Tocquevillean reading of May exemplified in the work of Luc Ferry, Alain Renaut, and Laurent Joffrin. While agreeing with Debray's assessment of May as a step in the development of bourgeois individualism, the Tocquevilleans have been inclined simply to laud the resultant social-democratization of French society. May thus comes to appear neither as a failed revolution nor as a ruse of capitalism, but as "a great reformist revolt, a democratic insurrection" (Joffrin, *321*). "May '68," write Ferry and Renaut, "has not been a political movement that failed, but rather, quite obviously, a social movement that succeeded even beyond all prediction" (*Itinéraires, 56*). In short, the function of the May events was to assure the spread of technocracy, a continued extension of "consumer society," and the standardization of mass culture. As for the ideologies of individual emancipation, they sanctioned the growth of a hedonistic individualism, and thus set the stage for a massive return to liberal ideology in the mid-1970s.

Was the revolution itself recuperated? Of course. It is awareness of this fact that would seem to have motivated a hypersensitivity to, even a fetishization of, the problem of recuperation in the theoretical environment of *l'après-Mai*. "Whether this rupture is in complicity with the law," Kristeva writes at one point in *Revolution in Poetic Language* (1974), "or constitutes a point of departure for still more profound modifications: that is the problem" (494). In the wake of May and in the face of modern capitalism's unrivaled recuperative power—itself increasingly inscribed into what Serge Quadruppani has called the "catalogue of French ready-to-think since 1968"—the necessity of distinguishing between the profoundly revolutionary and the simply complicitous became all the more acute; "that is the problem," Kristeva writes. And yet as this need to distinguish increased, so the very possibility of doing so in a stable and satisfying manner tended to diminish. Complicity *or* renewal: the simple disjunctive would become progressively less tenable as French society moved from the antinomic poles that had defined the postwar political field ("Lenin" and "De Gaulle," for example, in Debray's formulation) toward a consensual centrism whose boundaries could encompass the politics of both Giscard and Mitterand.

In the transition from that logic of recuperation whose role was to set the authentic revolutionary off from his or her degraded double to the cybernetic model of capitalism as a relentlessly recuperative system, what tended to emerge was a heightened sense of the intellectual's necessary complicity with established power, a sense more faithful to the intellectual's actual role in modern liberal-democratic society than a deep-rooted mythology of intellectual as rebel brigand would allow us to think.[9] The ultimate function of the logics of failed revolt in the theoretical discourse of *l'après-Mai*, I will argue, has been to move politics outside the notion of political desire as desire for an impossible, total revolution—and hence outside that oscillation between despair and hope so brilliantly theorized by, and enacted in, the work of Jacques Lacan (to which we turn in the following chapter)—and towards a variety of effectively possibilist (or better: transgressive *and* interventionist) forms of cultural politics grounded in methods of "subtle" or "discrete" subversion.

PART II

Politics as Tragic Impasse

CHAPTER 3

The Tragic Ear of the Intellectual: Lacan

> A: "My politics? / My skin binds Tick? [*Ma peau lie Tique*]. . . . Answer: milk that binds the Bre knows the tax target of the without white. That's why one is born screwed. Because the dice, which bind the Bre, are those without sky . . ." *
>
> B: "Your politics tell me nothing of value. It's just as we thought. Your politics don't arm us for struggle; they disarm."
>
> — Dominique Grisoni, "Politique de Lacan"

Jacques Lacan never tired of insisting that his teaching and writings were not made to be understood. Indeed, it has often been noted, the primary function of Lacan's infamous graphs and algorithms, his rigorously polyvalent concepts (the Other, the *objet a*, the real), and his allusive, aphoristic style was to *produce* misunderstandings—in French, *des malentendus*.[1]

There was plainly method to this madness. Lacan took as his starting point Freud's discovery that the truth of the psyche could only be *malentendu*, heard in those gaps of discourse where meaning fails, where the struggle between the unconscious and censorship allows evil (and "illness": *le mal*) to be heard, but of necessity to be heard badly (*mal entendu*). If this were so, he reasoned, then the truth of desire, indeed truth itself, can never be wholly spoken; "words fail" (*Television* 3; 9). But it is precisely through

* This passage plays to parodic effect on the late Lacan's nearly unbridled taste for outrageous puns. In translating A's discourse, I have sought to capture a quality of gibberish inherent in the original French: "Ma peau lie Tique? . . . Réponse: lait qui lie Bre sait l'impôt cible du sans blanc. C'est pourquoi on naît foutu. Parce que les dés, et qui lie Bre, sont les sans ciel." Reading this passage aloud, however, yields another arch Lacanian meaning, which one might render into English as follows: "My politics? . . . Answer: equilibrium is the impossibility of the *semblant*. That's why one is (born) screwed. Because it is the moments of disequilibrium that are essential."

this material failure, this lack of material, that the truth participates in the "real." The great originality of Lacan's project lay in the lengths to which he would go to mimic this lack, reproducing the equivocation and indirection of unconscious discourse in a style, both analytic and pedagogical, that he called "mid-speak" (*le mi-dire*). He was ruthless, in short, in his desire to be misunderstood, and his readers have been happy to oblige.

There have been few areas where Lacan would appear to have been more consistently (and symptomatically) misconstrued than in the matter of revolutionary politics. In this chapter, and again in Chapter 5, I shall have occasion to examine the various arguments by which Lacan sought to portray the revolutionary project as a repetitive and/or recuperative impasse. And yet the political and theoretical history of post-May France testifies again and again to the ease with which the field mapped out by Lacanian theory could be recharted in explicitly political, even revolutionary, terms. Looking back to *l'après-Mai*, one finds past and present followers of Lacan's seminar playing critical roles in the women's movement (Antoinette Fouque, Luce Irigaray, Michèle Montrelay), in French antipsychiatry (Félix Guattari) and French Maoism (Jacques-Alain Miller, Judith Miller [née Lacan]), as well as in the realm of "textual theory" (Philippe Sollers, Julia Kristeva).

At best, each of these projects involved a selective hearing of the Lacanian lesson. To be a Lacanian in the Maoist Gauche prolétarienne, for instance, meant hearing echoes of the Maoist dictum that "the One divides into Two" in Lacan's critique of that falsely unifying knowledge he calls the *semblant*. It meant seeing the essential elements of Maoist self-criticism in the nominally self-authorizing ritual—the so-called *passe*—through which the Lacanian École freudienne de Paris (EFP) designated its highest ranking members.[2] Above all, it meant living the adventure of Mao's China, as an ostensibly democratic society under the shadow of a larger-than-life rebel leader, from within the confines of Lacan's School.

Most decidedly, there was nothing in Lacan's work to countenance either the extreme voluntarism of Maoist political thought or the Maoist's faith in spontaneous revolution. Amidst the revolutionary fervor of the May events, however, such points of essential disagreement paled beside Lacan's remarkable ability to catalyze revolutionary aspirations. His young followers may have known better than to give credence to the rumor, subsequently reported in *The New Yorker*, that it was Lacan who (in late May of 1968) had smuggled student leader Dany Cohn-Bendit across the German border into France, in the back of his Jaguar.[3] But more than anything it was their desires, their symptomatic misunderstandings of Lacanian theory, that served to perpetuate the commonplace image of Lacan as leftist radical this rumor so clearly expresses.

As the revolutionary ardor of May cooled, the temptation was great among Lacan's critics to insist on the essentially counter-revolutionary import of his work. Within their (superficially incontrovertible) arguments, however, there was once again a significant tendency toward misunderstanding.

Consider Dominique Grisoni's introduction to her 1977 "Politique de Lacan"—the witty send-up of a conversation in which a haggard disciple asks Lacan to commit himself to Giscard or Mitterand, only to be treated to a barrage of equivocation and obfuscation. In her opening remarks, Grisoni attempts to define Lacan's politics as a form of "radical pessimism" grounded in the fatalistic belief that "the die is cast . . . hence politics is only a game *upon* the real, to which consequently it does not accede" (25).

But Lacan's so-called politics are singularly resistant to any exercise in definition that would erase their status as a textual effect. And *were* they reducible to a punctual position, it would clearly not be this one: "For want of being able to change *what is*, better to opt for administring *what is* as best one can" (Grisoni, 25). For the tail Grisoni would pin on the Lacanian donkey—that of a "manager" of souls—is precisely that which Lacan had pinned for years on an American ego psychology for which analysis was little more than a process of conformist adaptation. In other words, so as to turn against Lacan a critique of psychoanalysis that PCF theorists had begun parroting back in the late 1940s, Grisoni must forget that it was Lacan's lifelong concurrence with the terms of that critique that, among other factors, had led the Communist Party in 1970 to recognize his work as the only acceptable form of psychoanalysis.

We find a similar insistence on the essentially counter-revolutionary thrust of Lacanian theory in Castoriadis's blistering review of Luc Ferry and Alain Renaut's *French Philosophy of the Sixties* (1985). In the course of this review, Castoriadis attributes the increased visibility of Lacan, Foucault, Derrida, and Deleuze/Guattari after May '68 to the supposed failure of the events. What these "French ideologues" furnished retroactively, he argues, is

> a legitimation of the limits . . . of the May movement: "You did not try to take power (you were right)." "You did not try to institute oppositional forms of power [*des contre-pouvoirs*] (again you were right, because oppositional forms of power are power themselves, etc.)." With this went a legitimation of retreat and renunciation, of non-commitment or of a localized, moderate commitment: "In any event, history, the subject, and autonomy are only Western myths." ("Mouvement," *192–93*)

Nothing could be more mistaken, Castoriadis argues against Ferry and Renaut, than to see such theoretical topoi as "the death of the subject, of man, of truth, of politics, etc." as expressing the ethos of May.[4] The function of these topoi, like that of a logic of structural repetition that Castoriadis himself had unwittingly helped to ritualize ("oppositional forms of power are power themselves"), was rather to camouflage a movement of retrenchment on the part of those who had participated in the May events. Or, more precisely, "the French Ideology" allowed former militants to rationalize a massive retreat into the private sphere, while it provided them with the illusion of a radical sensibility (*193*). Inasmuch as Castoriadis repeatedly places Lacan in the role of pied piper to this movement of self-deluded reactionism, he suggests that the malaise of contemporary political culture comes not from having misunderstood Lacan, but from having understood him all too well.

In order to reach such a stable understanding of how Lacan has historically been understood, Castoriadis (like Grisoni) has to belittle a certain desire for revolution that Lacan had been prone to take quite seriously. That is to say, he has to flatten out the profound ambivalence or duplicity of Lacanian theory's take on revolutionary politics, a duplicity made manifest by Lacan's paradoxical ability to catalyze the very aspirations he had seemingly worked to debunk. The remarkable ambivalence of the historical record around the question of the revolutionary or counter-revolutionary import of Lacanian theory suggests that we would do well to track that ambivalence back to the Lacanian text, specifically as it bears the traces of a psychoanalytic pedagogy in which the transferential bond was necessarily at play.

There is a moment of apparently egregious misunderstanding in Castoriadis's text that in fact helps to open up this project. I have in mind his astonishing claim that, insofar as Derrida, Foucault, and the other authors discussed by Ferry and Renaut occult analysis of the institution in general, and the distinction between de facto and de jure power in particular, they "draw essentially upon the authority of Lacan" ("Mouvement," *192*).

Behind this massive overstatement lies a rich and fascinating institutional history. A practicing analyst since 1974, Castoriadis had joined in 1969 with François Perrier, Piera Aulagnier, Jean-Paul Valabrega, and other former members of the École freudienne de Paris (EPF) in founding what is variously known as the Quatrième groupe or OPLF (Organisation psychanalytique de langue française). Beyond their commitment to theoretical pluralism and to the notion that psychoanalytic doctrine must be proofed in clinical practice, the members of the Quatrième groupe were united in their suspicion of a transferential conformism they saw to be built into the institutional structure of the EFP. Their experience of Lacan's School had been that of an institution in which a statutory (de jure) democratism was radically undermined by a transferential fixation on Lacan as de facto "monarch" (the term is Elisabeth Roudinesco's).[5]

Castoriadis clearly overestimates Lacan's authority in what he sees as a widespread tendency to occult the sort of institutional analysis that might account for such discrepancies of de facto and de jure power. But the very terms of his error help us to look beyond his earlier claim that Lacanian theory conveys the illusion of radicalism without its real risk to the more fundamental question of why the *effect* of Lacanian discourse was so often to create precisely the sort of self-mystification that Lacan was in principle so intent on exposing. They suggest that, rather than simply dismissing Lacan's work as the vehicle of a duplicitous bad faith, we must examine a duplicity inherent to Lacan's transmission of psychoanalytic knowledge—a divorce between intents and effects that appears to have everything to do with transference love.

"It has been the endless paradox of Lacan's position," Jacqueline Rose has argued, "that he has provided the most systematic critique of forms of identification and transference which, by dint of this very fact, he has come most totally to represent" (Mitchell and Rose, 53). The essential ambivalence of the Lacanian example for revolutionary politics in the post-May period reflects a similar Möbius logic. It was precisely because Lacan formulated a radical critique of the human aspiration to unity—and, most especially, to the one and complete Revolution—that he came to focalize the desire for the One (Revolution).[6] "From 1968 on," writes François Roustang, "an exorbitant belief in Lacan as the keeper of some great secret became widespread [among Lacan's students at the École Normale]: He was the one who would be able to build, or rebuild, the unity of knowledge" (*Delusion*, 7; *12*). Lacan was fond of citing Cardinal Mazarin to the effect that "politics is politics, but love always remains love" (*S* VII, 324; *374*). But his own (paradoxical) virtuosity in the self-styled role of "subject presumed to know" guaranteed that, in the Lacanian universe, politics was never simply politics nor love simply love.

I have borrowed the title of the present chapter, "The Tragic Ear of the Intellectual," from one of the most eloquent of witnesses to the cultural phenomenon that was Lacanian psychoanalysis. To that question I have been asking thus far—What does the modern French intellectual hear (or mishear) in Lacanian theory?—Catherine Clément responds by evoking Lacan's propensity toward the tragic:

> Lacan is steeped in Greek hubris, impossible exorbitance and deadlock [*absence d'issue*]. The Greek hero, the tragic hero, of which Lacan is a perfect stylistic and theoretical model, is situated beyond all forms of distance. . . . He has forgotten the lesson of myths, which are, as Lévi-Strauss tells us, lessons of "appropriate distance." Keeping the right distance between yourself and the madness of impossible desire, between yourself and the real: but this distance actually exists—it is regulated on all sides by the multiple codes of so-called everyday life. As described by Lacan, psychoanalytic practice consists, on the contrary, in *exacerbating distance*. Let there be no misunderstanding, you wretched souls: your desire is forever cut off from its object, which is lost, and will always be undermined in the most agonizing separations. And then there are those sublime sentences of his, which catch the tragic ear of intellectuals, always willing to allow themselves to be seduced wherever the impossible is proposed as such; those sentences, whose lulling rhythm panders to a delight in the loss of the lost paradise. (Cited by Roustang, *Delusion*, 15; *20*)

It is the very suggestiveness of a phrase like "the tragic ear of intellectuals" that ultimately necessitates a testing of its limits. What is the historical or political specificity of the intellectual who sports a "tragic ear," and how did Lacan speak to such an organ? Is the "tragic ear" indeed simply "tragic"? Or does it not imply other modes of hearing? It is to the last of these questions that I now turn, reserving the matter of historical and political specificity for Chapter 5.

Tragedy and Comedy

Since Freud wrote, in a letter to Wilhelm Fleiss dated October 15, 1897, that the "riveting power of *Oedipus Rex*" lay in its seizing on "a compulsion which everyone recognises because he feels its existence within himself," the process of psychoanalysis has consistently been theorized as a confrontation with the tragic meaning that all human subjects bear within (*Standard Edition*, 1: 265). Countless references to the Oedipus cycle, to Electra and the *Oresteia*; countless readings of *Hamlet, Lear, Medea*, and *Phèdre* all corroborate Lacan's claim that "tragedy is in the forefront of our experiences as analysts."[7]

Lacan discussed the exemplary role of tragedy for a rigorous understanding of the analytic experience in his 1959–60 seminar on the ethics of psychoanalysis. The aim of analysis as he saw it was to bring the patient (or *analysand*) to confront the question of human existence ("What am I there?") as it is posed in that space of Law and buried *jouissance* he called the Other (*Écrits*, 194; *549*). Thus the analysand mimics the tragic hero to the extent that he passes beyond the anxiety characteristic of the ego functions to the level of a certain primordial horror governed by the conjoined mysteries of procreation and death. Like tragedy, analysis points to an ethical field beyond the self-interested pursuit of pleasure, beyond any concern for utility or consequent focus on instrumentality, beyond even the desire for a localisable object—to an ethical field, in short, beyond all utilitarianisms. Its aim is *catharsis*, understood not as "discharge" or "purgation"—concepts central to Freud and Breuer's account of the abreaction of psychic trauma in the early *Studies on Hysteria*—but rather as a form of ritual "purification" (244–45; *286–87*). Against those who would reduce psychoanalysis to a strictly therapeutic process of uncovering and working over repressed psychic material, Lacan will advocate a tragic purification of desire through the subject's assumption of what he calls, following Heidegger, "true being-for-death" (309; *357*).

To exemplify the process of tragic purification, Lacan turns to the figure of Oedipus—not to the beleagured King of Thebes, but to the wizened and wittily defiant hero of Sophocles' *Oedipus at Colonus*. Wandering in a state of suspended suicide beyond all worldly "goods," in a zone between patricide and the death drive Lacan speaks of as "between two deaths" (*l'entre-*

deux-morts), Oedipus at Colonus attains the "tragic liberty" of the hero who freely consents to his malediction "on the basis of the true subsistence of a human being, the subsistence of the subtraction of himself from the order of the world" (305–6; *352–53*).

In accordance with the first and foremost of Lacan's four propositions on the ethics of psychoanalysis—"the only thing one can be guilty of is giving ground relative to one's desire"—Oedipus remains "unyielding right to the end, demanding everything, giving up nothing, absolutely unreconciled" (321, 310; *370, 358*).[8] His only passion (but it is an all-encompassing one for Lacan) is the passion for knowledge—or, more specifically, "the desire to know the last word on desire" (309; *357*). The disfigured Oedipus thus proves himself a consummate practitioner of that *entrée-en-Je* (coming into subjecthood) proposed as an imperative by Freud's *Wo Es war, soll Ich werden* (Where it was, the I must come to be), that strictly impossible imperative to accede to the truth of one's desire that grounds what Lacan calls "Freudian ascetic experience" (7; *15–16*).

In shouldering the curse that weighs on the race of the Labdacidae, Oedipus comes to emblematize a tragic paradox at the heart of Lacanian theory, whereby the *entrée-en-Je* (the advent of subjecthood) always entails recognition of a prior *entrée-en-jeu* (a putting into play)—recognition, in other words, of the fact that the subject as subject (as *Je*) is always already engendered by that "play of symbols" (*jeu des symboles*) into which he or she is born (*S* II, 198; *232*). Lacan writes:

> Symbols in fact envelop the life of man in a network so total that they join together, before he comes into the world, those who are going to engender him "by flesh and blood"; so total that they bring to his birth, along with the gifts of the stars, if not with the gifts of the fairies, the shape of his destiny; so total that they give the words that will make him faithful or renegade, the law of the acts that will follow him right to the very place where he *is* not yet and even beyond his death; and so total that through them his end finds its meaning in the last judgement, where the Word absolves his being or condemns it—*unless he attain the subjective bringing into realization of being-for-death.* (*Écrits*, 68; *279*; emphasis added)

Paradoxically, the only means of attaining true being is through the tragic realization of a death that Lacan sees, for reasons I shall discuss in a moment, as attendant on the double entrance into subjectivity and signification.

In many respects, Lacan reads Antigone in the very same terms he does her father. Refusing to compromise on her desire to bury the rotting body of her brother Polyneices, and thereby entering into the zone "between two deaths," Antigone gains tragic stature through her (criminal) assumption of the familial *Atè* (bane, ruin; reckless impulse). Indeed, even more clearly than her parricidal father, Antigone represents that tragic paradox whereby the subject's conquest of his or her "own law," his or her *entrée-en-Je*, always means "acceptance of something that began to be articulated before him in previous generations, and which is strictly speaking *Atè*" (300; *347*).

But Antigone quite literally eclipses Oedipus. In his reading of Sophocles' drama *Antigone*, Lacan insists again and again on a fascination that hangs upon her blindingly brilliant visual image:

> In effect, *Antigone* reveals to us the line of sight that defines desire.
>
> This line of sight focuses on an image that possesses a mystery which up till now has never been articulated, since it forces you to close your eyes at the very moment you look at it. Yet that image is at the center of tragedy, since it is the fascinating image of Antigone herself. We know very well that over and beyond the dialogue, over and beyond the question of family and country, over and beyond the moralizing arguments, it is Antigone herself who fascinates us, Antigone in her unbearable splendor. She has a quality that both attracts us and startles us, in the sense of intimidates us; this terrible, self-willed victim disturbs us.
>
> It is in connection with this power of attraction that we should look for the true sense, the true mystery, the true significance of tragedy. (247; *290*)

For the spectator, the moment of Antigone's definitive passage into death-in-life, her realization of the horror that is *Atè*, is marked by the "intolerable brilliance" of a beauty whose paradoxical function is both to pose a realm of *jouissance* beyond earthly goods (here: beyond that conflict between family and fatherland central to Hegel's reading of the play) and to bar access to that realm. In other words, the violent luminosity of Antigone's tragic beauty constitutes a barrier that situates the spectator before "the unspeakable field of radical desire that is the field of absolute destruction," while it operates on that spectator an "essential blindness" (216, 281; *256, 327*). By realizing what Lacan calls "a beauty that musn't be touched" (*un beau-n'y-touchez pas*), tragedy thus repeats the structure of the phantasm (239, *280*; cf. 298, *345*).

Lacan refers to the strictly unnamable locus of apocalyptic desire and buried *jouissance* beyond the phantasmatic barrier as "the analytical Thing [*la Chose analytique*]" (203; *239*). Derived from Freud's term (*das Ding*) for the first external element around which the infant orients his explorations, Lacan's Thing designates the space of the quintessential lost object: "the absolute Other of the subject, [which] one is supposed to find again" (52; *65*). In the life of the child, the Thing comes into being in several stages, beginning with that moment of "primary repression" at which the infant finds himself unable to articulate as demand his desire to recapture an original, unwilled *jouissance* with the mother (as paradigm for the "absolute Other") (*Écrits*, 286–87; *690–91*).[9]

The empty site delimited by this first experience of the Other as inaccessible takes on a more definitive form with the decline of the Oedipus complex. Lacan will speak of the act that disrupts the imaginary dyad of mother and child as an eviction of the "phallic signifier"—the signifier of the child's desire to *be* the phallus the mother desires—by the "paternal signifier" or *Nom-du-Père*.[10] The resulting absence of a primal signifier—the phallic signifier or "signifier of the *désir de la mère*"—from that chain of signifiers that constitutes the subject as living subject of desire reinforces a splitting (*Spaltung*) begun with the primary repression. Thus, as the Thing develops into a negative space hollowed out around the repressed signifier of the *désir de la mère*, the subject finds himself increasingly decentered along the lines expressed in Lacan's *Cogito*: "I am not, there where I am the plaything of my thought; I think about what I am, there [in the space of the Other] where I do not think to think" (*Écrits*, 166; *517*). Among other things, "the phallus" is Lacan's name for that which bars the desire of the Other (as locus of the subject's being), and so reinforces his existence in the mode of "lack-of-being" (*manque-à-être*).

In the intolerable brilliance of Antigone's tragic beauty—"beauty in all its shining radiance, this beauty that has been called the splendor of truth"—we see recreated the apocalyptic splendor of that Oedipal moment at which the phallus had barred the (phallic) signifier of the mother's desire, and so constituted the subject as "literally at his beginning the elision of a signifier as such, the missing signifier in the chain" (217, 224; *256, 264*). Here is Lacan, paraphrasing Paul's Epistle to the Romans (7:7):

> But even without the Law, I was once alive. But when the commandment appeared, the Thing flared up, returned once again, I met my death. . . .
>
> The dialectical relationship between desire and the Law causes our desire to flare up only in relation to the Law, through which it becomes the desire for death. (83; *101*)

Lacan leaves little doubt that Antigone's exemplarity as tragic heroine is inseparable from the rigor with which she bears within herself, "miraculously," a "signifying cut"—that which both constituted her as a subject (as subject to death) and barred that desire of the (m)Other in which the secret of her being resides:

> Yet she pushes to the limit the realization of something that might be called the pure and simple desire of death as such. She incarnates that desire.
>
> Think about it. What happens to her desire? Shouldn't it be the desire of the Other and be linked to the desire of the mother [*désir de la mère*]? (282–83; *328–29*)

There follows from this (specifically tragic) relation to being a radical suspension of "every cycle of being," a calling into question of "everything that has to do with transformation, with the cycle of generation and decay or with history itself" (236, 285; *277, 331*). The tragic heroine's approach to the limit of the pure desire for death as such implies a suspension of temporality, and a consequent interruption of the process of desire as the infinite quest for an impossible satisfaction.

But the subjective realization of being-for-death is properly untenable;

Atè, Lacan writes, "designates the limit that human life can only briefly cross" (262–63; *305*). It is in fact the death drive that tells us why, for Lacan, desire will always return on the far side of the experience of apocalyptic annihilation. For the death drive is fundamentally ambivalent with respect to an essential temporality. Revealed and veiled in the resolutely atemporal brilliance of tragic being-for-death, the death drive also serves as "the matrix of desire," since it provides the energy necessary for the primal repression (Lemaire, 167).

To speak of the death drive as "matrix of desire" is to recall that which the death drive institutes in primal repression—namely, the (maternal) Thing. As the impossible space of a buried goodness—specifically, of that bliss that had come from serving as object to the mother's desire—the Thing serves as both the cause and the aim of desire.[11] Constituted through phallic barring, it harbors the very origin of a signifying chain whose unfulfillable mandate is to effect the return to a henceforth impossible experience of satisfaction. It is both the product of that which institutes the desire for death and the matrix of a "creation *ex nihilo*" (213–14; *252–53*).

Like the death drive, therefore, the Thing implies a Möbius-spiralling linkage of the radically atemporal desire for death as such with desire as a form of temporal slippage. This linkage serves, in turn, to point out the limitations of tragedy in the constitution of a psychoanalytic ethic. Lacan defines the tragic action at the heart of such an ethic as the triumphant assumption of being-for-death through an act of negation identical to the subject's entrance into signification (313; *361–62*). In other words, tragedy implies absolute acceptance of a fatality arising from the fact that the child-subject is born into a network of symbols so total as to shape her destiny up to and beyond her death.

But the Symbolic order is ambivalent along the lines suggested by my discussion of the death drive. Locus of the paternal Law, it is also, ineluctably, the locus of a desire capable of forestalling the specifically tragic annihilation of the forces of life. Here is what we read immediately after Lacan's evocation of a "subjective bringing into realization of being-for-death" in the "network of symbols" passage from "The Function and Field of Speech and Language in Psychoanalysis" (the so-called Rome Discourse): "Servitude and grandeur in which the living being would be annihilated, if desire did not preserve its part in the interferences and pulsations that the cycles of language cause to converge on him, when the confusion of tongues takes a hand and when the orders contradict one another in the tearing apart of the universal work" (*Écrits,* 68; *279*). If the first of Lacan's four ethical propositions—the injunction not to yield on one's desire—plainly fosters a breakdown of history and natural transformation in that archetypically tragic act of assuming one's death, his fourth and final proposition brings us back to desire as a metonymical slippage from signifier to signifier driven by the lack of an object: "There is no other good than that which may serve to pay the price for access to desire—given that desire is understood here, as we have defined it elsewhere, as the metonymy of our being" (321; *370–71*).

It is just this ambivalence that allowed Lacan, in the final week of his Ethics seminar, to pose comedy and tragedy as opposite, but not incompatible, dimensions of human experience. Both are certainly defined by the alienation of desire attendant on the subject's entry into the Symbolic order. But whereas tragedy implies an attitude of lucid confrontation with the field of radical destruction, an arresting of historicity in the name of an essential purity, comedy resides in the perpetual flight of desire, an endless slippage of life: "[It] is not so much the triumph of life as its flight, the fact that life slips away, runs off, escapes all those barriers that oppose it, including precisely those that are the most essential, those that are constituted by the agency of the signifier" (314; *362*).

Lacan's insistence that the phallus "is nothing more than a signifier, the signifier of this flight" should be read to suggest that the "comic" here entails in no simple way that overcoming of external, and specifically paternal, opposition habitually associated with comic emplotment (Frye, 143). Having spoken at much length on the privileged role of tragic lucidity in the advent of a psychoanalytic ethic, Lacan in fact concludes his seminar with a brief (and at first sight surprising) claim for the exemplarity of what he calls "tragicomedy":

> The pathetic side of this [comic] dimension is, you see, exactly the opposite, the counterpart of tragedy. They are not incompatible, since tragicomedy exists. That is where the experience of human action resides. And it is because we know better than those who went before how to recognize the nature of desire, which is at the heart of this experience, that a reconsideration of ethics is possible, that a form of ethical judgment is possible, of a kind that gives this question the force of a Last Judgment: Have you acted in conformity with the desire that is in you? (314; *362*)

In his *Metahistory*, Hayden White has written cogently on that common ground of tragedy and comedy implicit in this argument. Unlike romance, he suggests, drawing on the work of Northrop Frye, both modes "tak[e] seriously the forces which *oppose* the effort at human redemption" (10). And yet they also reveal "the possibility of at least partial liberation from the condition of the Fall and provisional release from the divided state in which men find themselves in the world" (9). White continues:

> In Comedy, hope is held out for the temporary triumph of man over his world by the prospect of occasional *reconciliations* of the forces at play in the social and natural worlds. . . . In Tragedy, there are no festive occasions, except false and illusory ones; rather, there are intimations of states of division among men more terrible than that which excited the tragic agon at the beginning of the drama. Still, . . . there has been a gain in consciousness for the spectators of the contest. And this gain is thought to consist in the epiphany of the law governing human existence which the protagonist's exertions against the world have brought to pass. (9)

Lacan's work clearly situates itself within that space, common to tragedy and comedy, where the prospect of a partial release from self-division intersects with the full awareness of all that opposes human redemption. But within this space it plainly oscillates, at times promoting the epiphany of knowledge proper to tragedy, at others holding out the hope of reconciliation characteristic of comedy.[12] I have shown how Lacan's ethic of psychoanalysis entails both a facing up to the desire for death as such and a giving way to desire as a process of infinite substitution; in short, how it exploits a fissure within the concept of desire itself. I would argue that this ethic is properly tragicomic insofar as it presupposes a differential rhythm running throughout the Lacanian text—a rhythm of death and life, apocalyptic annihilation and desiderative metamorphosis, absolute despair and groundless hope.

Lacan's name for that nodal point of the tragic and the comic that allows for such a differential rhythm is none other than "the phallus," defined in "The Signification of the Phallus" as "the privileged signifier of that mark where the share of the logos is conjoined with, or wedded to, the advent of desire" (*Écrits*, 287; *692*).[13] Not a dialectical synthesis, but rather that point at which an absolute lack of meaning passes immediately into the promise of Meaning itself, the phallus signifies, in the words of Slavoj Žižek, an "oscillation between lack and surplus meaning [that] constitutes the proper dimension of [human] subjectivity" (*Sublime Object*, 223; *Looking Awry*, 91). That this process of infinitely crossing and recrossing the phallic mark might itself prove an impasse is a prospect I address in Chapter 5. In the pages that follow, I focus primarily on the tragic side of the phallic equation, showing how, as early as the mid-1950s, Lacan used demonstrably psychotic forms of intellectual rigor in an effort to debunk the liberationist presuppositions common to both American and Soviet ideologies, and thus to dismiss "back to back" the parties to the Cold War.

A Trial in Rigor

Few are born into accursed, noble races. For this reason, and because it is in the very nature of contemporary culture to paper over the (to Lacan unavoidable) fact that our desires are fated to remain unsatisfied, Lacan found himself in the position of having to reconstruct those radical impasses productive of tragic knowledge on the level of his theory. No study of the specific repercussions of Lacan's work in *l'après-Mai* can fail to account for that essentially ethical gesture whereby Lacan, as transferential "subject presumed to know," sought to compel his students' consent to the fundamental accursedness of human desire.

His instrument for provoking this epiphany of tragic insight was "logic," defined in the 1975 "Peut-être à Vincennes" (Perhaps at Vincennes) as "the science of the real because it places access to the Real in the mode of the impossible" (cited by Marini, 243; *251*). From the logic of specular doubling in Lacan's work of the 1940s and 1950s to the mathemes of the 1970s, there is a consistent linkage, I would argue, between the "logical" and the specific aims of Lacan's tragic ethic.

No single word better captures the intimacy of this linkage than one whose centrality to the work of both Lacan and Althusser would have a decisive impact on Marxist (and specifically Maoist) theory in the post-May period—that is, the word "rigor" (*la rigueur*).[14] In promoting an ethic of psychoanalysis that conjoins the requirement of logical exactitude with injunctions to ascetic self-denial, the assumption of one's fate, and even passage to a limit, Lacan points to a remarkable coherence of meaning lying beneath this term's apparent polyvalence. Here (in translation) is the *Petit Robert*'s definition:

> *Rigueur*, s.f.: *1*° Severity, extreme harshness. . . . Especially: severe, harsh morals. "Catholic by birth . . . , he took long breaths of a mountain air infused with the remnants of Protestant rigor" (Romains). . . . *Tenir rigueur à quelqu'un*, not to pardon s.o., to bear s.o. a grudge. . . . *2*° (Plural) Act of severity, cruelty. By extension: *Les rigueurs du sort*, the hardships of fate. . . . *3*° Exactness, precision, inflexible logic. . . . *La rigueur d'un raisonnement, d'un calcul*, the exactness of a piece of reasoning, of a calculation. . . . *4*° *(Etrè) de rigueur*, to be compulsory, obligatory by virtue of custom or regulation. . . . *5*° *A la rigueur*, . . . Modern: in a case of absolute necessity, to go to the limit of what is possible or acceptable (Cf. *Au pis aller*, if the worst comes to the worst).

If there is a single experience at the heart of Lacan's conception of rigor, however, it is that of listening—or, more specifically, of listening to human desire. In his 1954–55 seminar on the role of the *moi* in Freudian theory, Lacan spoke of desire as a "point" at which "one can say almost anything. But this anything isn't just anything, in the sense that whatever one may say, it will always be rigorous to those who know how to listen" (*S* II, 221; *259*). Rigor is thus a quality of attention in the act of facing up to that question of human existence ("What am I there?") as it continuously poses and reposes itself—fascinating, horrifying, never fully answerable—in the space of the Other. "The role of the analyst," Elie Ragland-Sullivan writes, "is not to 'understand' the patient, . . . but to surprise the liberty which resides in nonsense; to see how the analysand debates with his or her *jouissance*; to ascertain to what primitive discourse effects the analysand is subjected" (122).

It is on the basis of this conception of analytic listening, enjoined on analyst and analysand alike, that Lacan operates an almost seamless conjunction of those logical and ascetic senses of the word "rigor" that a secular empiricism must read as essentially disparate. For Lacan, exactitude in the cognizance of those figures through which desire is articulated in the analysand's discourse proves to be fundamentally inseparable from an ethical severity grounded in an awareness of the essentially criminal nature of human desire, a severity that Lacan's own references ask us to liken to that of Saint Paul, Luther, the Cathares, and the Jansenists (*Écrits*, 192, *549*; Marini, 83, *90*). "Rigor" implies a faithful attention to, and structural transcoding of, the quintessentially ethical passage to a limit in "the domain and the level of the experience of absolute disarray . . . a level at which anguish is already a protection" (*S* VII, 304; *351*).

As the example of a Lacanian concept whose function is precisely to catalyze such an experience of absolute disarray, consider what Lacan calls the Real.[15] Strictly unrepresentable, demonstrable only through its effects on desire, Lacan's Real is "this something in front of which words stop," an inaccessible realm given over to the death drive and its attendant forms of destructive expenditure (cited by Marini, 71; *79*). The Real is a domain of missed encounters—"the encounter in so far as it may be missed [*manquée*], in so far as it is essentially the missed encounter"—whose traumatic prototype is weaning from the mother (*S* XI, 55; *54*). Thus it often appears as a menacing yet productive lack specifically figured by the feminine body: it is "'the little girl's slit' in the painting *Las Meninas*, the 'gap [*béance*] in which there is *nothing to see*' but 'where *it* [ça] *looks* at you' " (Marini, 71; *79*). Or—in that apodictic shorthand that predominates in Lacan's later work, allowing for the assimilation of such heterodox conceptions of the Real as the unrepresentable, the traumatically unattainable, or the oppressively intolerable: the Real is "the impossible" (*Écrits, 68*).

In many respects, of course, Lacan's Real is coextensive with that always-barred realm of buried *jouissance* he called the Thing. It is the Thing he has in mind when he speaks of the need to articulate the question of a psychoanalytic ethic "from the point of view of the location of man in relation to the real" (*S* VII, 11; *21*). And yet Lacan's conception of the Real plainly exceeds that of the Thing whenever he speaks of the Real as entertaining a privileged relation with logic and mathematics—whenever the Real serves as a vehicle, in short, for Lacan's scientific pretensions.

In his provocative book *The Lacanian Delusion* (1986), François Roustang has sought to deflate those pretentions by arguing that Lacan's Real derives from an unwarranted universalization of the psychotic's particular inability to assume his castration.[16] Before considering this argument, I should like to recall the principal features of Lacan's work on psychosis, and specifically the concept of "foreclosure" (*forclusion*, after Freud's *Verwerfung*).

The Lacanian reading of psychosis begins with the essentially orthodox claim that the psychotic's hallucinations, often centered around castration, result from a failure of the primal repression and a subsequent blockage in the assumption of castration that resolves the Oedipal conflict. Transposed into the idiom Lacan developed in support of his insistence on the linguistic basis of unconscious functions, this is to say that psychosis issues from an abolition of the "paternal metaphor," a radical absence of the *Nom-du-*

Père as anchor to the Symbolic order.[17] Lacan likens the metaphoric "inadequacy" triggered by this foreclosure of the *Nom-du-Père* to a hole in the place of the Other. Such a hollowing out of the Symbolic provokes a corresponding hole "at the place of phallic signification"—that is, in that imaginary domain where the post-Oedipal subject is constituted through identification with the phallus (*Écrits*, 201; *558*). Paradoxically, the psychotic's foreclosure of the *Nom-du-Père,* and his resultant failure to constitute himself as a subject through entrance into the Symbolic order, results in his living at the mercy of a certain symbolic—a symbolic shorn of its signifying function (through foreclosure's blockage of the judgment of existence) and experienced in psychotic delirium as the Real. In short, the foreclosure of castration founds a certain repetitive logic whereby *"that which has not come into the light of the symbolic, appears in the real"* (*Écrits, 388*).

Roustang's account of the slippages whereby Lacan derives his conception of the Real as impossible begins as a gloss on a passage such as the above:

> Everything that is refused in the Symbolic order, since all assumption of castration by an *I* has for him become impossible, reappers in the Real. Or, more succinctly: What cannot be symbolized reappears in the Real. Or again: The Real is constituted by what it is impossible to symbolize. And, if "impossible" is changed from an adjective into a substantive, the result is: The Real is the impossible—meaning, implicitly, the impossible-to-symbolize. (*Delusion*, 71; *75*)

Through a series of generalizations from the specific fact of the psychotic's (pathological) impotence to symbolize the real, in other words, Lacan will arrive at an essence of the Real as that which precludes all symbolizations. Clearly disturbed by a glorification of symbolic impotence that he reads as an inversion of the analyst's mandate to bring repressed materials back into symbolic play, Roustang argues that it is the need to consolidate psychoanalysis as a science that ultimately forces Lacan to abandon his earlier conception of the analytic cure as "the assumption of his history by the subject, in so far as it is constituted by the speech addressed to the other" (*Écrits*, 48; *257*). "But this initial view has to be rejected," Roustang writes, "since if the Symbolic is appropriated, it will no longer appear in the Real, and so there will be no science" (*Delusion*, 73; *77*).

The evident value of Roustang's book lies in the care with which he tracks the various "confusions," "equivocations," and "obfuscations" imposed on Lacanian theory by the discovery, announced in Lacan's 1953 Rome Discourse, that the unconscious is structured like a language. Having thus set off on a "wrong road" through "a glaring blunder in reasoning"—a confusing of the object of psychoanalytic inquiry with its instrument—Lacan, Roustang claims, fell back into a "triumphalism of deadlock" whereby the impasses occasioned by his initial false step were repeatedly transformed into cornerstones for subsequent theorization (*Delusion*, 110–12, 57, 120; *108–10, 61, 117*). It is precisely in this triumphalism of deadlock that Roustang would locate the seductiveness of Lacanian discourse:

> Finally, one of the most powerful elements in Lacan's seductiveness lay in the fact that he pushed the contradictions and paradoxes of psychoanalysis to the limit. In his research, the more he encountered impossibilities and impasses, the more he claimed to make them the very cornerstones of his system. This exorbitance, together with a keen sense of the tragic, made him irresistible for French intellectuals. (14–15; *20*)

To lay the groundwork for my discussion (in Chapter 5) of this crucial linkage between theoretical impasses, the tragic ethos, and the beguilement of a certain politics of the worst, I should like to return here to the question of psychosis, and specifically to some remarks Lacan made in a 1975 lecture at Yale:

> Psychosis is a trial in rigor. In this sense, I would say that I am psychotic. I am psychotic for the sole reason that I have always tried to be rigorous.
>
> This plainly takes us quite far, since it implies that logicians, who tend toward this goal, as well as geometricians, would in the final analysis share in a certain form of psychosis. ("Conférences," *9*)[18]

With this clearly provocative view of the logician and mathematician as practitioners of a psychotic "trial in rigor," Lacan aimed to radicalize Freud's perception, in his 1915 essay on the "Unconscious" (150), of an "unwelcome resemblance" between philosophical abstraction and "the schizophrenic's way of thinking." I have shown that, for Lacan, foreclosure of the *Nom-du-Père* as signifier of castration leads the psychotic to deliriously live that "paternal metaphor" as the Real. Rereading the case of Daniel Paul Schreber, the subject of Freud's "Psycho-Analytic Notes on an Autobiographical Account of a Case of Paranoia," Lacan shows how the foreclosed Name-of-(God-)the-Father reappears in a delusional genealogy that Schreber constructs for his doctor, Paul Emil Flechsig, from the names of his own ancestors: Gottfried, Gottlieb, Fürchtegott, and Daniel (*Écrits, 580*; Macalpine and Hunter, x–xi). The psychotic lives the real, in other words, through a heightened attention to signifiers, or to what Lacan calls "the letter" (*la lettre*). But what is this exercise in psychotic abstraction, he would reason, if not an analog to those logical and mathematical practices that refer to the real—rigorously—through formulae "expressed by means of little letters" ("Conférences," *26*). Might we not define psychotic delirium in the very terms we use to define science—as "that which holds itself together, in its relation to the real, thanks to the use of little letters" ("Conférences," *26*)?

Such an attention to the letter helps, in turn, to account for a dual gesture of inclusion and exclusion proper to the Lacanian "trial in rigor." Roustang speaks of Lacan's equivocations around a series of radically polyvalent concepts such as the Real and the Other as fostering "an assimilation of the most disparate elements"—unwarranted traversals of historical and disciplinary boundaries whose effect was to suggest that Lacan's work had gathered within itself "the totality of human knowledge" (*Delusion*, 116–17; *114*). That is to say, in less polemical terms, that Lacan's texts mimic schizophrenic discourse to strategic effect by subjecting words to the same process of condensation and displacement to which dream-thoughts are subject in the dream work; "a single word, which on account of its manifold relations is specially suitable, can come to represent a whole train of thought" (Freud, "Unconscious," 145).

To complement this assimilationist movement proper to psychotic delirium—"since, for [the psychotic], everything is a sign of . . . how well-founded his thought is, as well as an opportunity for him to add to it"—Roustang will find in Lacan's text a second, and equally delirious, tendency to exclude all evidence that might threaten the coherence of its theoretical construction (*Delusion*, 117; *115*).

It is of course in the very nature of the scientific discipline to be founded on an exclusionary delimitation of its field of inquiry; Saussurian semiology, it has often been remarked, is all the more powerful, all the more scientific, for its bracketing of the problem of reference. Still, there is nothing inherently "psychotic" about Saussure's highlighting of the signifier as a means of delimiting a coherent field for linguistic study. Lacan plainly inflects Saussurian semiology in the direction of a psychotic rigor when he moves, in a 1955 gloss of Saussure, from the relatively uncontroversial claim that "signification is realized only on the basis of a grasp of things in their totality" to the more radical assertion that "*the signifier alone* guarantees the theoretical coherence of the whole as a whole" (*Écrits*, 126, *414*; emphasis added). For this phrase conjoins the two component principles of psychotic rigor as Lacan would practice it—namely, attention to "the letter" and the quest for an impossible (logical) coherence.[19]

Catherine Clément has written incisively about Lacan's lifelong fascination with psychotic style and his use, in the later work, of "the incommunicable strangeness of the delirious text with calculated effect." Into the most hermetic, even hallucinatory of passages, Clément notes, Lacan invariably slipped "a limpid sentence or two" (*Lives*, 59; *73–74*). On the one hand, therefore, Lacan used a psychotic style to militate against "the reactionary principle operant in the duality of the sick and the healer" (*Écrits*, 115; *403*). To be rigorous in the Freudian sense, he insisted, was to erase the line demarcating psychic normalcy from psychic pathology, to practice a necessary complicity. "By revealing itself as akin to a whole gamut of disorders, [psychoanalysis] throws light upon them" (*Écrits*, 119; *407*). On the other hand, this complicity was itself strategically motivated. Unlike the psychotic, in other words, Lacan never lost sight of the dialogic situation into which his utterances would fall.

Lacan's critics have been quick to point out the theoretical advantage to be derived from a textuality that mimes psychotic logic. It is not just that his arguments are traversed by what Malcolm Bowie once called "weighty and unargued personal predilections" ("Jacques Lacan," 148). Rather, these predilections remain impervious to critique insofar as the theory itself operates a radical exclusion of the very terms in which such a critique might be framed. By mimicking a psychotic rigor that was both radically assimilationist (to the point of apparent universality) and radically exclusionary (to the point of foreclosing critique), Lacan gave rise to an analytic theory that was, as he himself insisted, "to be taken or left" (reported by Marini, 87; *94*). Alongside his remarkable capacity for analytic "rigor," understood as a mode of listening to the truth of desire as articulated in the Other, we find a no less remarkable denial of that specifically collective form of "rigor" that is founded on a process of proposition and response—a denial, in short, of theoretical answerability.

By way of illustrating the psychotic coherence of a theorization that can only be "taken or left," I should like to return to Lacan's equation of the "real" with the "impossible." That there is something unavoidably circular about the discourse this equation generates is a point few readers will have missed. For example, it is the essential circularity of Lacan's definitions of the primary process and the real—both are fundamentally impossible—that will make it so difficult for readers to determine which exactly he is defining here: "the primary process encounters nothing of the *real* other than the *impossible*, which remains, from the Freudian perspective, the best definition one can give of it" (*Écrits, 68*). Lacan will repeatedly define truth (that is, the truth of the Real) as that which cannot be wholly spoken. At the same time, however, the fact that it is materially "impossible" to speak the truth—"words fail"—is said to demonstrate that truth depends on the real: "Yet it is through this very impossibility that the truth holds onto the real" (*Television*, 3; *9*). Finally, notice how much more overtly circular the following definition of the unconscious becomes by virtue of Lacan's substituting "such that in consequence" (*pour que de ça*) for a more banal "insofar as" (*en tant que*): "The unconscious . . . is only a metaphorical term designating the knowledge that only sustains itself by presenting itself as impossible, such that in consequence it can conform by being real (that is, real discourse)" (cited by Marini, 66; *73*).

This circularity is never more problematic than in those instances where Lacan seeks to reconcile the apparently heterodox senses of the real as radical impasse on the one hand and as a suprasensible reality formulated by mathematical and physical laws on the other. One would like to know, for instance, if the privilege of logic and mathemes in the later Lacan should be read as a consequence of our inability to inscribe the real *except* as an impasse: "The real only manages to be inscribed through an impasse of formalization. That is why I have thought to be able to sketch out a model of it by taking mathematical formalization as my point of departure" (*S* XX, *85*). Or does logic's value lie rather in its ability to retranscribe the real *as* an impasse, as Lacan suggests in "Peut-être à Vincennes," where he defines logic as a "science of the real because it places access to the real in the mode of the impossible" (cited by Marini, 243; *251*)?

It is Lacan's tragic ethic that shows why, for Lacan, these very questions would be misplaced. For they tend to divorce two moments of that ethic that Lacan, thinking of the teaching analysis, would see as essentially linked: the epiphany of tragic knowledge (the real can be inscribed only as an impasse) and the exemplification of that knowledge for another (the real reinscribed as an impasse). Strictly, I would argue, those circular arguments by which Lacan would (re)constitute the real as impossible have little sense apart from that pedagogical process whereby analysts are produced; "the aim of teaching has been and still is," he remarked in 1964, "the training of analysts" (*S* XI, 230; *209*).

The precise function of theoretical circularity within this pedagogical process was to counter what Althusser once spoke of as the "vicious circle" of ideological miscognition.[20] By deploying a circularity that served to reinforce the specifically psychotic coherence of a theory that could be only "taken or left," Lacan sought to incite his students to an asymptotic approach to that limit of absolute disarray characteristic of the true psychotic. Or, more precisely, the function of Lacan's theorizations in the mode of the all or nothing was to provoke an epiphany of tragic insight that would approximate psychosis to the extent that it followed a breakdown of those adaptive ego functions Lacan accused his contemporaries of overvaluating, to ironically pathological effect. In short, Lacan's psychotic "trial in rigor" was meant to put ego psychology on trial, and with it that underlying ideology of happiness and personal liberation he associated with "the American Way of life":

> However we regulate the situation of those who have recourse to us in our society, it is only too obvious that their aspiration to happiness will always imply a place where miracles happen, a promise, a mirage of original genius or an opening up of freedom, or if we caricature it, the possession of all women for a man and of an ideal man for a woman. To make oneself the guarantor of the possibility that a subject will in some way be able to find happiness even in analysis is a form of fraud.
>
> There's absolutely no reason why we should make ourselves the guarantors of the bourgeois dream. A little more rigor and firmness are required in our confrontation with the human condition. That is why I reminded you last time that the service of goods or the shift of the demand for happiness onto the political stage has its consequences. The movement that the world we live in is caught up in, of wanting to establish the universal spread of the service of goods as far as conceivably possible, implies an amputation, sacrifices, indeed a kind of puritanism in the relationship to desire that has occurred historically. (*S* VII, 303; *350–51*)

Here as elsewhere, Lacan chides the ego psychologists for conceiving analysis merely as a process of adaptation to the ever more generalized society of goods. To these "managers" of the soul—Lacan uses the English term—therapy means little more than the production of "imagoes" (i.e., imaginary representations of interpersonal relationships) that are wholly complicitous with the commodity structures and political myths of modern bourgeois society (*Écrits*, 116; *403*). In repudiating or failing to recognize that "radical excentricity of the self to itself with which man is confronted," in having recourse to a (quintessentially liberal) notion of compromise that Freud is said to have evoked "as supporting all the miseries that his analysis assuages," ego psychology shows itself to be founded on an ideologically driven miscognition of "the truth discovered by Freud" (*Écrits*, 171; *524*).

But all such miscognitions, Lacan writes, "suppose a recognition"; failure to acknowledge the self's necessary inscription within that dialectic whereby desire "burns only in relation to the Law" results, paradoxically, in desire's sacrifice on the pyre of the Law (*Écrits, 165*). What emerges from the post-Revolutionary universalization of the "service of goods"—the advent of an order grounded in self-interest, acquisition, and the aspiration to happiness—is a paradoxical (and puritanical) "amputation" of human desire. Ego psychology's founding act of *méconnaissance* (miscognition) results in nothing less than an inversion of its official aim—the attainment of happinesss.

It is this (miscognitive) amputation of desire pursuant to the post-Revolutionary "shift of the demand for happiness onto the political stage" that motivates Lacan's perception of American capitalism and state communism as structural doubles. In the Ethics seminar he speaks of the "communist horizon" as subsuming "everything that has to do with the relationship of man to desire" to the service of goods—as repeating, in other words, the "bourgeois dream." Like "the American Way of life," communism simply perpetuates "the eternal tradition of power, namely, 'Let's keep on working, and as far as desire is concerned, come back later' " (*S* VII, 318; *367*). That an ideology of liberation should work to precisely inverse effect is an argument whose vicissitudes I examine in the next section, which focuses on Lacan's various pronouncements on the subject of May '68.

The Perils of Liberation

For Lacan, as for Bataille, it is axiomatic that "transgression in the direction of *jouissance* only takes place if it is supported by the oppositional principle, by the forms of the Law" (*S* VII, 177; *208*). With her desire to know "what's at the bottom of desire," the tragic heroine seeks insight into the ways her being is shaped by a recuperative dynamic inherent to this dialectic of desire and the Law.[21] What she learns is that human *jouissance* depends on a transgressive movement that ultimately reaffirms the very laws, social norms, or taboos against which it is directed.

Strictly speaking, what I have called the logic of recuperation begins on the near side, the all-too-human side, of this tragic insight. It begins with a liberationist flight from tragic knowledge whose effect, Lacan shows, is to aggravate the very alienation of desire it attempts to deny. The logic of recuperation begins, in other words, where the recuperative movement inherent to transgression meets that logic of *Verneinung* where "no" means "yes" and miscognition recognition.

There is a moment in Lacan's *Television* where he appears to advance the now-widespread notion that modern capitalism is uniquely capable of appropriating contestatory impulses for the consolidation of its hegemonic power:

> All the less so because, in relating this misery [the misery of the world] to the discourse of the capitalist, I would denounce the latter.
>
> I would only point out that I cannot do this in all seriousness, since in denouncing it I reinforce it—by normalizing it, that is, perfecting it. (13–14; 26)

Within a Freudian frame, however, the principal model for conceptualizing the process whereby normative structures are perfected through the recuperation of transgressive tendencies is the superego in its double role as both the agent and the product of repression. The eternalist logic of a formulation like "since in denouncing it I reinforce it" clearly owes more to this model than to more historically grounded analyses of capitalist hegemony in the Gramscian mold.

The superego's centrality to Lacan's thinking on the subject of recuperation becomes apparent later in *Television*, with his critique of the hedonist detour of "sexo-leftism" (Deleuze/Guattari, Lyotard, et al.) (31; 52). It is not just that liberationist ideology falsely presupposes the original innocence of a natural desire antedating cultural and familial repression, whereas Lacan will insist that the birth of desire is strictly contemporaneous with repression. "Sexo-leftism" actually redoubles "the curse on sex" to the extent that it mistakes for liberating an injunction whose true origin is the superego: "The superego is fucking articulated as an imperative: *Fuck* [*Jouis*]!" (*Television*, 31, 52; *S* XX, *10*). If liberationist ideology's founding act of miscognition thus renders it particularly susceptible to recuperation by the order of culture (call it advanced capitalism if you will), this is because, in repeating the master's injunction, displacing (and hence effectively effacing) the real locus of enunciation, liberationist ideology veils the master's power, thereby fulfilling the foremost precondition to its continuing function as power.

Lacan had made a similar argument in his 1969 "Impromptu at Vincennes" when he accused the student militants of playing the role of Spartican slaves to the Pompidou regime: "You don't know what that ['helots';

in French, *ilotes*] means either? The regime puts you on display; it says: 'Watch them fuck' [*Regardez-les jouir*]" (128; *25*). The liberationist rebel incarnates the *plus-de-jouir*—a surplus value of *jouissance* whose function (like that of its Marxian homologue) is to be recuperated by and for the master.[22] Like the hysteric, moreover, on whose contestations psychoanalysis had first constituted itself as a master discourse, the rebel pits his *jouissance* against the social order, but does so in the name of a higher law with which he unwittingly identifies (Kristeva, *Polylogue, 523*). Though Lacan was careful to insist that the master's recuperation of the *plus-de-jouir* is never total, we find him ending his "Impromptu at Vincennes" by calling on human "experience" to vouch for the inevitable recuperation of revolutionary desires and for the master's eternal return: "If you had a little patience, and if you were willing for our impromptus to continue, I would tell you that the aspiration to revolution has but one conceivable issue, always, the discourse of the master. That is what experience has proved. What you, as revolutionaries, aspire to is a Master. You will have one" (126; *24*).[23]

This incident has a well-known epilogue from *Television*. Responding to Jacques-Alain Miller's contention that his claims for the recuperative effect of revolutionary aspirations dishearten his young listeners ("Frankly, you are discouraging the young"), Lacan says:

> They got on my back, which was the fashion at the time. I had to take a stand.
>
> A stand whose truth was so clear that they've been crowding into my seminar ever since. Preferring my cool, after all, to the crack of the whip [*De préférer, somme toute, à la trique ma bonace*]. (32; *53*)

That Lacan would speak of the revolutionaries of May as coming to prefer his *bonace*—literally, the calm of the sea before or (as in this case) after a storm—to the cudgels of the French security police, the C.R.S., clearly illustrates that quest for the least malevolent of masters that Jambet and Lardreau would associate with Freudian political realism (*L'Ange, 51*). But Lacan's response also plays on the adjective *bonasse*: "excessively good, simple-minded"; in the "Impromptu" itself, he had provoked laughter with the unlikely, yet coherent pronouncement, "But I am simplistic!" (122; *23*).

In this homonymous conjunction of a placid, reflective surface with dumb simplicity (both mute *and* obtuse), I would read an allusion to that "pure mirror of an unruffled surface" to which Lacan had likened the analyst-pedagogue as that bearer of transferential love he called the "subject presumed to know" (*sujet supposé savoir*) (*Écrits*, 15; *109*). The militant's love for the analyst-pedagogue, Lacan implies, depends on the latter's functioning as the "*objet a* incarnate"—that is to say, on his standing in for the Other as that space where "it [*ça*] is known," or, in this case, where the truth of revolutionary desire is supposed to reside. It is not enough to insist that knowing the truth of such desire means knowing the lack that dooms it to a relentless flight after an impossible satisfaction. Lacan's point here is a corollary of this universal structure of desire: that the knowledge of a fully self-present and potentially consummate revolutionary moment, which the militant originally supposes of the Other, can only be a narcissistic illusion, an inverted reflection of the revolutionary's ego ideal in the placid mirror of the subject presumed to know.

Let us pause for a moment to consider the place of the Other in the act of revolt, seen as a narcissistically driven process of *méconnaissance*. Insofar as it is modeled on the Oedipal father, the Other serves as the lynchpin of a cultural order (Lacan's Symbolic) founded on desire's essential lack. As such, it long occupied the crucial role of an impersonal third term, disrupting imaginary I/you dyads (mother/child, analyst/patient, etc.) and throwing both partners to the imaginary relationship "onto the axis of the symbolic" (Rose in Mitchell and Rose, 36).

By the early 1970s, however, Lacan had largely abandoned this insistence on the Symbolic's power to counteract the narcissistic effects of imaginary doublings. One effect of this development was a heightened attention to the fundamental ambivalence of the Other, whose position as guarantor of culture seemed increasingly inseparable from its function as a divisive (and hence disutopian) third party to all interhuman communication. But this, in turn, meant finding narcissistic specularity within that very dialogue with the Other that was originally thought to constitute a partial break from the Imaginary. Juliet Flower MacCannell describes this conception of the Other with exemplary clarity:

> But this mutuality [of shared desire], existing perhaps only as an hypothesis, yields immediately, because of the individuated narcissistic notion of the two needed to share, to a monologic "pseudo-dialogue" with the Other, the inverse model of the ego. The subject, now isolated within his own ego, "gives up" or sends his desire to the system, and expects, in exchange, an increase—the same kind of surplus value communal work in the interhuman is supposed to yield: he demands the *love* seemingly promised by the system. . . .
>
> But the Other does not respond. And in the place of the love demanded, gives nothing. Or rather it gives desire back in inverted form, as an image of love. (68)

No existence in human culture can escape this relation to the Other as "an inverted image of the self" and the idealizing (or ideologizing) of the "narcissistic mode of relationship" on which it is founded (MacCannell, 71). Yet it is the rebel-slave, the *ilote*, who realizes this essentially narcissistic rapport with the Other most acutely. For the very intensity of the revolutionary desire that the rebel sends into the communal system comes to repeat itself, on the far side of the Other's lack of response, in the rebel's love *for* that Other, seen by Lacan as the specular image of the rebel's ego ideal. It is the radicality of the rebel's expectation of a surplus value conferred by the system, his demand for love in the form of a confirmation of his revolutionary hope, that causes his demand to rebound most intensely as a surplus value recuperable by the Other as guarantor of the order of culture.

What this analysis suggests is that the recuperative and repetitive effects Lacan attributes to political revolt must be traced back to the intense (though not atypical) narcissism of the rebel's relation to the Other. Consider in this respect Lacan's account of the failures of that "naturalist liberation of desire" advocated by the libertines or *libre-penseurs*, Enlightenment precursors of the contemporary "sexo-leftists" (*S* VII, 3; *12*). Likening the libertine's transgression to the *ordál*, that medieval mode of trial by subjection to fire, boiling water, or scalding iron (and the root of our modern "ordeal"), Lacan speaks of the summoning of God, as author of nature, to account for "the extreme anomalies whose existence the Marquis de Sade, Mirabeau, and Diderot, among others, have drawn our attention to. . . . He who submits himself to the ordeal finds at the end its premises, namely, the Other to whom this ordeal is addressed, in the last analysis its Judge" (*S* VII, 4; *12*).

It is this recourse to God as Other and thus as ultimate judge that signals a reaffirmation of the Law at the heart of the Sadean inversion: "The defense of crime only pushes him into a displaced recognition of the Law. The Supreme Being is restored in and through maleficence" (*Écrits*, *790*). Such a recuperative reaffirmation of divine Law will in turn find its origin in a narcissism constitutive of the human subject's relation to the Other, but heightened in the libertine—specifically, in the structure of the Other as an "inverse mirror-image of the narcissistic ego ideal" (MacCannell, 69). The libertine is exemplary to the extent that his actions go beyond Hegelian recognition, whereby "man's desire finds its meaning in the desire . . . to be recognized by the other," to that desire, as Anthony Wilden writes in another context, "to TAKE THE PLACE of the Other in desire" (*Écrits*, 58, *268*; *System*, *22–23*). The libertine's folly lies not in the self-alienating desire to desire through the Other, which is coextensive with human existence, but rather in his manifesting that desire *while believing he has had done with God*. Lacan ultimately debunks this narcissistic dream of radical self-sufficiency by evoking a logic of repetition—by arguing for the reemergence of the divine, Paternal edict within the libertine's discourse to his victims.

In Chapter 1 I spoke of the logics of failed revolt as degraded or truncated dialectics. The following section further explores that status by returning to the neo-Hegelian dynamics of Lacan's early work, and specifically to his rewriting of Hegel's *schöne Seele* in the 1946 "Propos sur la causalité psychique" (Remarks on psychic causality).[24]

Toward the Beautiful Soul

Near the end of "Aggressivity in Psychoanalysis" (1948), Lacan speaks of the modern cult of the ego, and the "utilitarian conception of man that reinforces it," as culminating in "an isolation of the soul ever more akin to its original dereliction" (*Écrits*, 27; *122*). The "neurosis of self-punishment" characteristic of "the 'emancipated' man of modern society" reveals, and is revealed by, an "original splitting" (*déchirement*) through which "at every moment he [that is, 'man' in general] constitutes his world by his suicide" (*Écrits*, 28; *124*). Living his subjectivity not as a *Je*, but as a *moi*, through a series of imaginary fixations that cause him to mistake the truth of his desire, so-called emancipated man repeats to the point of folly what Lacan calls a "primordial Discord between the *moi* and being," an ineluctable *béance* (opening, gape, rent) whose earliest lived manifestations include birth trauma, the effects of that physiological "prematurity" characteristic of the human newborn (lack of motor coordination, etc.), and the subsequent trauma of severance from the mother (*Écrits*, 14, *187*; *96*).

Lacan had spoken to these issues two years earlier in a lecture at the Bonneval hospital entitled "Propos sur la causalité psychique." In this text, Lacan attempts to refute the organicist pathogeny of Henry Ey—and specifically Ey's conception of delirium as indicative of an individual's failed adaptation to reality—by tracing the causality of madness back to the primordial *béance*. We pick up Lacan's argument immediately after a passage in which he has used Freud's death drive as an associative pivot by which to move, quite vertiginously, from the primacy of visual recognition and the will to suicide in the Narcissus myth to the traumata of separation, and finally to the spool game by which Freud's grandson replayed these in a "liberating repetition":

> At the beginning of this process of [psychic] development, therefore, we find a linkage between the primordial, essentially alienated *moi* and the essentially suicidal act of primitive sacrifice—that is to say, the fundamental structure of madness itself.
>
> Thus the primordial discord between the *moi* and being would be the keynote whose overtones would reverberate throughout the various phases of psychic life, the function of which would be to resolve that discord by developing it.
>
> Any resolution of this discord through an illusory conflation of reality with the ideal would resonate to the depths of the imaginary nexus of narcissistic, suicidial aggression. (*Écrits*, *187*)

It may go without saying that the threshold between the "essentially suicidal" repetitions of the death drive in the *Fort/Da* game and that narcissistic self-aggression attending the illusory attempt to realize the ideal is both narrow and shifting. This passage plainly sets the suicidal and narcissistic confusion of real and ideal off from the more canny strategy of resolving the primordial discord "by developing it"—a strategy common, as I shall argue later in this chapter, to Freud's grandson and Lacan alike. But in Lacan's text the proof of the death drive as primitive sacrifice, as the structuring principle of primary masochism, falls to that same Narcissus myth that motivates his critique of those unwitting masochists who take ideal illusion for reality. What is the status of a critique of narcissistic self-aggression, one is tempted to ask, that would appear to assume the inevitability of such aggression in the form of the death instinct?

My analysis, several pages back, of Lacan's recourse to the logic of recuperation suggests one answer to this conundrum. Lacan would reserve his critique for those who, in the frenzy of their quest for a free and self-sufficient subjectivity, tend actively to aggravate that miscognition endemic to the formation of the ego—for those whose words and deeds obey the logic of *Verneinung*. His critique of Sartrean existentialism clearly operated along these lines: "But unfortunately that philosophy grasps negativity only within the limits of a self-sufficiency [*self-suffisance*] of consciousness, which, as one of its premises, links to the *méconnaissances* that constitute the ego, the illusion of autonomy to which it entrusts itself. . . . Existentialism must be judged by the explanations it gives of the subjective impasses that have indeed resulted from it" (*Écrits*, 6; *99*).

From his reading of Hegel, and particularly from the dialectic of labor in the master-slave relation, Lacan will take the conviction that true liberty is possible only in dialectical relation with servitude:

> The very being of man must effect, through a series of crises, the synthesis of his particularity and his universality, to the point of universalizing that particularity itself.
>
> This is to say that, in the movement that leads man to increasingly adequate self-consciousness, his liberty becomes inseparable from the development of his servitude. (*Écrits, 182*)

If Lacan's later work tended to avoid the Hegelian diction and paradigms of the 1946 "Propos," it would nonetheless remain faithful to the underlying premise that human liberty, such as it is, depends on a decisive passage through the other, epitomized by the therapeutic of crisis that is the analytic situation. Lacan's life-long critique of narcissism is coherent, in other words, to the extent that it defines the narcissist as one who denies that his desire, and ipso facto his liberty, is necessarily mediate.

But this critique is ambivalent nonetheless. Lacan could be merciless in his contempt for the modern ideologies of the self and their contribution to what he once called "the 'great winged hornet' of narcissistic tyranny" (*Écrits*, 27; *122*). But if the narcissist is thus the product of a specific historical moment—the age of bourgeois democratism—he is also seen to epitomize that all-too-human madness of attempting to rid human existence of the necessary mediations under which it labors. Lacan would in fact play this second, eternalist form of narcissism off against its more historically and culturally bound counterpart. Thus, in the "Propos" he deliberately ventures the card of ancient wisdom against Henry Ey's bourgeois-liberationist conception of mental illnesses as affronts to, and shackles on, human liberty: "Finally, I believe that in attributing the causality of madness to that unfathomable decision whereby the human being understands or fails to recognize his liberation, to that snare of fate that deceives him about a liberty he has not in fact won, I am formulating nothing other than the law of our becoming as expressed in the ancient phrase Γέγοι', οἷος ἐσσὶ [become such as you are]" (*Écrits*, 177).

In this, Lacan's eternalist mode, the risk of madness—that is, of narcissistic self-aggression—appears as nothing less than coextensive with the human experience inasmuch as that risk must be measured by the seductive power of those imaginary identifications on which "man stakes both his truth and his being": "Far from being contingent upon the fragile nature of his organism, madness is thus the permanent virtuality of a fissure opened up in his essence. . . . And not only can the being of man not be understood without madness, it would not be the being of man if it did not bear madness within itself as the limit of its liberty" (*Écrits*, 175–76).

On the one hand, as Lacan would argue against Sartre, to conceive the human project as that of fully realizing personal liberty is properly mad. But on the other, there can be no liberty, indeed no human value, *except* on the margins of madness. Revolutionary desire, to take the case of most interest to me here, may be pure folly. But folly of this sort is the necessary condition for "the being of man." Between these two poles, corresponding to those of tragic insight and comic flight, there is no place for the stable critique, only for an endless oscillation between the critical and the complicitous, a self-conscious playing of the limit between madness and liberty that Lacan equates with the taking of risks.

This ambivalence is particularly acute in Lacan's analyses of those scenarios of paradoxical self-punishment that he variously refers to, conflating two moments of the Hegelian dialectic of Spirit, as the "law of the heart" (Hegel's *Gesetz des Herzens*) or the "beautiful soul" (*belle âme*; in Hegel, *schöne Seele*). Whatever element of critique we must read into Lacan's reference to the Moscow trials as an instance of narcissistic self-aggression —"I could have . . . looked for the law of the heart at work in the fate that leads the old revolutionary of 1917 to the defendant's table in the Moscow trials" (*Écrits*, 175)—must therefore be counterbalanced by his insistence throughout the "Propos" on reading the "heart"'s infatuated identification with an ego ideal thought to be wholly unmediated "as the human being's relationship to the very best in him, since that ideal represents his liberty" (*Écrits*, 172).

If Lacan developed the most rigorous modern critique of that narcissistic presumption, or "frenzy of self-conceit," that attends to the workings of the "heart"; if he elaborated a tragic ethic presupposing an awareness of the necessarily mediate nature of human desire, achieved through a "synthesis of [the subject's] particularity and universality"; it is nonetheless true that, both in his dealings with the institutions of psychoanalysis and through the madness of his style, he repeatedly sought to recast himself in the ostensibly unmediated role of the outcast rebel. "He was alone," Catherine

Clément writes, "like the hero whose destiny he tried to explain, hero of both the law of the heart and the insanity of presumption: the rebel brigand, the Robin Hood of psychoanalysis" (*Lives*, 109; *127*). It is with this ambivalence in mind that I turn to a closer examination of Lacan's appropriation of the Hegelian paradigm.

In Hegel's *Phenomenology of Spirit*, "the law of the heart and the frenzy of self-conceit" finds its place in a dialectic whereby rational self-consciousness raises itself from mere self-certainty to the level of truth through its own practical activity. More specifically, it represents the negative or miscognitive moment in the dialectical movement from the pure singularity of the pleasure-seeker to that true consciousness of universality that is the realization of Virtue.

The specific story Hegel tells is that of a sentimental, universalist reformer who is both oppressed by the "violent ordering" of a world that contradicts the dictates of his own heart and cognizant of the sufferings of "a humanity that does not follow the law of the heart, but is subjected to an alien necessity" (221). To demonstrate the excellence of his nature while promoting the welfare of mankind, the individual seeks to impose the law of his heart as a universal ordinance, as the law of all hearts. But his attempt fails when "others do not find in this content the fulfillment of the law of *their* hearts, but rather that of someone else" (224). Although born in reaction to the pure individuality of the hedonist (more precisely, to the paradoxical loss of individuality in the hedonist's enslavement to pleasure), the heart's project of sentimental reform therefore ends up repeating a sterile individualism to the extent that it mistakes its own being-for-self for a universal law: "Individuality is not yet dislodged from its seat, and the unity of both has not been brought about by the mediating agency of the individuality itself, has not yet been achieved by discipline" (222).

At the same time, however, consciousness learns from this experience the nature of reality as a vivified, universal ordinance; it "attains to being the alienation of itself" (224–25). As a result, consciousness finds itself athwart a contradiction: what is real and essential for consciousness in general is plainly not so for the heart. The law of the heart therefore "reveals itself to be this inner perversion of itself, to be a deranged consciousness which finds that its essential being is immediately non-essential, its reality immediately an irreality" (225). Madness begins, in other words, with the collision of two forms of essentiality, with the perception of an intolerable contradiction between reality for consciousness in general and reality for the heart:

> The heart-throb for the welfare of humanity therefore passes into the ravings of an insane self-conceit, into the fury of consciousness to preserve itself from destruction and it does this by expelling from itself the perversion which it is itself, and by striving to look on it and express it as some-

> thing else. It therefore speaks of the universal order as a perversion of the law of the heart and of its happiness, a perversion invented by fanatical priests, gluttonous despots and their minions. . . . It is the heart, however, or the individuality of consciousness that would be immediately universal, that is itself the source of this derangement and perversion, and the outcome of its action is merely that *its* consciousness becomes aware of this contradiction. . . . This its law ought to have reality; the law, then, is for it *qua* reality, *qua* valid ordinance, its own aim and essential nature; but reality, that very law *qua valid ordinance,* is on the contrary immediately for it something which is not valid. (226)

With this portrait of a consciousness that would impose its law as a universal, but that ultimately loses contact with reality through the outward projection of its inner perversion, Hegel anticipates later Freudian work on the mechanisms of defense typical to paranoid delirium.

The rebellious and self-certain Spirit exemplified by the heart reappears later in the *Phenomenology* in the guise of that base, judgmental consciousness Hegel ironically dubs the *schöne Seele.* Hard-hearted and misanthropic where the heart was sentimental and philanthropic, far more inclined to vaporous, impotent abstractions than to grand reformist syntheses, the beautiful soul nonetheless shares with the heart an overriding will to maintain the purity of its being-for-self: "It lives in dread of besmirching the splendour of its inner being by action and an existence; and, in order to preserve the purity of its heart, it flees from contact with the actual world, and persists in its self-willed impotence to renounce its self which is reduced to the extreme of ultimate abstraction" (400).

It is this flight into the desert of "self-willed impotence" that ultimately drives the beautiful soul into madness: "The 'beautiful soul', lacking an *actual existence,* entangled in the contradiction between its pure self and the necessity of that self to externalize itself and change itself into an actual existence . . . is disordered to the point of madnesss, wastes itself in yearning and pines away in consumption" (407).

I would argue that Lacan's tendency to conflate those two negative moments in the dialectic of the Spirit that are the law of the heart and the beautiful soul derives from the way each links a certain delirious self-certainty in the face of contradiction to a miscognition whose recuperative and/or repetitive effects Hegel plainly delineates. Just as the heart's mistaking of his own pleasure for universal law caused his reformism to repeat the sterile individualism of the pleasure-seeker, so does the beautiful soul's critique of the "hypocrisy" of the active consciousness fall into "the hypocrisy that wants its judging to be taken for an actual deed, and instead of proving its rectitude by actions, does so by fine sentiments" (403). This repetition, endemic to the beautiful soul's denunciation of the other's hypocrisy, works in turn to recuperative effect. For in failing to transcend its purely individual basis, such a denunciation legitimates the (ostensibly hypocritical) law of the other:

> In denouncing hypocrisy as base, vile, and so on, it [the universal consciousness of the beautiful soul] is appealing in such judgement to its *own* law, just as the evil consciousness appeals to *its* law. For the former comes forward in opposition to the latter and thereby as a *particular* law. It has, therefore, no superiority over the other law, rather it legitimizes it. And this zeal does the very opposite of what it means to do; for it shows that what it calls true or genuine duty and which ought to be *universally* acknowledged, is something *not* acknowledged; in so doing it concedes to the other an equal right to be *for itself*. (402–3)

Here, after this brief excursus into Hegel, is how the law of the heart appears in Lacan's "Propos":

> This miscognition reveals itself in the act of revolt, through which the madman seeks to impose the law of his heart upon what appears to him to be the disorder of the world—an "insane" endeavour . . . insofar as the subject fails to recognize in this worldly disorder the very manifestation of his actual being. What he feels to be the law of his heart is in fact nothing but the inverted, virtual image of that same being. He thus fails to recognize it doubly, and precisely in order to divide actuality from virtuality. Now he can only escape his actuality through this virtuality. His being is thus caught in a circle, unless he breaks out of that circle through some act of violence in which, striking a blow at what he takes to be disorder, he strikes himself by means of a social counter-blow.
>
> Such is the general formula for madness as one finds it in Hegel. (*Écrits*, 171–72)

The madman seeks to break out of the actuality of his disordered being, which he mistakes for the disorder of the external world, through his recourse to the law of the heart. But this virtual law is nothing less than the mirror image of his actual disorder, as the madman obscurely recognizes when, with the lucidity of folly, he strikes at his own being through the intermediary of a castigating and vengeful society.

On the following page, Lacan returns to this striking linkage of specular doubling and masochistic effect—now under the aegis of the *belle âme*—in a discussion of that most implacable of French cultural icons, Molière's Alceste:

> The fact is that Alceste is mad and Molière portrays him as such—quite deservedly since, within his beautiful soul, Alceste does not recognize the extent to which he himself contributes to the disorder against which he revolts. . . . Alceste is beside himself on hearing Oronte's sonnet because he recognizes in it his own situation . . . and that fool who is his rival appears to him as his own image in the mirror. The madman's remarks to which he then gives vent clearly reveal that he seeks to strike out at himself. For that matter, each time one of their counter-blows shows him that he has managed to do so, he suffers its effect with great delight. (*Écrits*, 173–75)

Lacan frequently links the self-aggression of the "misanthropic *belle âme*" to the narcissism endemic to post-Revolutionary, utilitarian culture.

Thus, in the Rome Discourse, he speaks of the *moi* of modern man as having taken form "in the dialectical impasse of the *belle âme* who does not recognize the very reason of his being in the disorder he denounces in the world" (*Écrits*, 70; *281*).[25] Once again, however, Lacan's critique of narcissism proves fundamentally ambivalent. For it is precisely in his discussion of Alceste that Lacan speaks of "madness" as "the permanent virtuality of a fissure opened up in [man's] essence"; the "being of man," you will recall, would not be the "being of man" if it did not bear within itself madness—exemplified since Hegel by the *belle âme*—as "the limit of its liberty" (*Écrits*, *176*).

To gauge the full extent of Lacan's rewriting of Hegel, we need examine the ways in which his insistence, first on the specularity of the *belle âme*'s relations with a supposedly disordered world, and second on the ultimately masochistic effect of those relations, elaborates on suggestions within the Hegelian text, while nonetheless blocking the latter's dialectical movement. I have shown that, in Hegel, the beautiful soul's denunciation of the hypocrisy of the active consciousness has the paradoxical (and potentially recuperative) result of conceding "to the other an equal right to be *for itself*." In the so-called logic of failed revolt, such a demonstration of recuperative effect would mark a rhetorical *coup de grâce*.

But Hegel's dialectical machine marches relentlessly onward: "This judgement has, however, at the same time another aspect from which it becomes the way to a resolution of the antithesis confronting it" (*Phenomenology*, 403). In denouncing the other's hypocrisy, the passive, universal, and judgmental consciousness of the beautiful soul "places itself . . . *alongside* the first [active, individual, evil] consciousness, and the latter, *through this likeness*, comes to see its own self in this other consciousness" (403). Specifically, in remarking that the passivity of the judgmental consciousness places it "in contradiction with itself as the absolute will of duty," the active consciousness sees its own obtuseness to duty as reflected in an other for whom "the side of reality is [likewise] distinct from the words uttered" (403). By seeing itself in the mirror of the other, consciousness paves the way for the universalization of its particularity, for the discovery of its true destination within a social community governed by the consciousness of duty as a universal. For Hegel, the specular moment marks a crucial step in the preparation of the dialectical *Aufhebung*—that movement whereby an initial difference is at once preserved, and transcended.

Much the same can be said of that moment in the *Phenomenology* that authorizes Lacan's analysis of the masochism underlying the heart's oblique solicitation of society's punishment.[26] Whereas for Lacan the force of society's backlash against the heart's mad remarks expends itself in the "delight" of the heart's submission to it, Hegel specifically sees a dialectical form of recuperation growing out of collective resistence to the law of the heart: "The established laws are defended against the law of an individual, because they are not an unconscious, empty and dead necessity, but a spiritual universality and Substance, in which those in whom this spiritual substance has actuality live as individuals, and are conscious of themselves" (227).

I would argue that Lacan's refusal of such a dialectical movement, his reading of the beautiful soul scenario as a "dialectical impasse," must be seen to follow from the privileged role he accords to psychotic *méconnaissance*, in the formation of the ego as in his theory as a whole. In a gloss of Lacan's claim that madness objectifies the subject "in a language without dialectic," Anthony Wilden has spoken to the extraordinary, yet surreptitious, privilege of the psychotic model in founding that oscillatory movement characteristic of life in the "dialectical impasse": "For Lacan, the Language 'without dialectic' is to be found in schizophrenic or psychotic language, where a 'regression' to treating words like things leaves the speaker in the grip of an uncontrollable shifting between opposites in which binary differential elements (for example, inside, outside; good, bad; O, A) are not 'anchored' to the '*points de capiton*' supposed by Lacan's theory of the paternal metaphor" (*Language*, 129).

The Hegelian dialectic avoids the multiplication of impasses by focusing neither on the self that carries out an action nor on the particular form of its act, but rather on a movement of Spirit driven by the endlessly renascent dialectic of the particular and the universal. As the result of an *Aufhebung* initiated by a reactive movement on the part of the unhappy consciousness's dialectical counterpart—the active consciousness for the *belle âme*, the hedonist for the heart—the sufferings of unhappy consciousness are ultimately taken back into Spirit itself; "the wounds of the Spirit heal, and leave no scars behind" (*Phenomenology*, 407). But mediating between the particular and the universal, seeing an overarching sameness at the heart of the other's difference, is precisely what the psychotic, who has a libidinal stake in maintaining his absolute difference, can never do. In the "dialectical impasse" that is the Lacanian *belle âme*, all wounds resemble Amafortas's, condemned to being eternally reopened in the impotent expectation of divine grace.

The Fool and the Knave

I began this chapter by attributing a striking divergence of opinion on the political import of Lacanian theory to Lacan's paradoxical ability to inspire those same revolutionary desires whose impasses he persistently delineated. This ambivalence of effect proved consistent with the terms of a psychoanalytic ethic that foresaw the return of a specifically comic flight of desire on the far side of tragic being-for-death; the intellectual "ear" to which Lacan spoke was thus not "tragic" so much as "tragicomic."

Following discussion of the ways Lacan sought to compel assent to the accursedness of human desire by mimicking psychotic rigor, I turned to his critique of a series of liberal and/or liberationist flights from rigor. Most notably, I showed how Lacan traced the various repetitive and recuperative effects he attributed to the liberationist project to a narcissism endemic to modern, post-Revolutionary culture. Indeed, it was the liberationist rebel's demand for a confirmation of his revolutionary hope that came to epitomize that narcissistic relation to the Other characteristic of the modern, hypertrophic ego. At the same time, however, Lacan read the narcissistic self-aggression of the rebellious *belle âme* as exemplifying a madness that was both the realization of a primordial *béance* and the limiting condition of human liberty. Human value, he suggested, resides on the margins of such a madness.

I shall return to this final paradox in Chapter 5, where I show how Lacan's reading of the *belle âme* inspired the revolutionary *jusqu'au-boutisme* (bitter-endism) of two of his self-professed disciples, Christian Jambet and Guy Lardreau. To conclude the present chapter, I shall turn once again to the Ethics seminar, and specifically to that moment in which Lacan speaks of giving "some clarification of the political meaning of this turning point in ethics for which we, the inheritors of Freud, are responsible" (*S* VII, 182; *214*). Exemplary to my argument in multiple ways, this passage speaks particularly to the question of a certain duplicity inherent to the Lacanian position on transference love, and hence to that narcissistic bond uniting the would-be revolutionary to the analyst-pedagogue as "subject presumed to know."

The passage I have in mind begins with Lacan's borrowing two terms from Elizabethan theatre, the "fool" and the "knave," in order to say some "categorical," but nonetheless "illuminating," things about (political) "intellectuals":

> The "fool" [English in the original] is an innocent, a simpleton, but truths issue from his mouth that are not simply tolerated but adopted, by virtue of the fact that this "fool" is sometimes clothed in the insignia of the jester. And in my view it is a similar happy shadow, a similar fundamental "foolery" that accounts for the importance [*fait le prix*] of the left-wing intellectual. (*S* VII, 182; *215*)

The "knave"—again he uses the English—Lacan likens to what Stendhal's *Lucien Leuwen* had dubbed *le coquin fieffé* (the arrant rogue). Figure for the right-wing intellectual, the knave is Everyman with an extra dash of resolve, he who will not shrink before the consequences of "what is called realism—namely, the ability to admit (when necessary) that he's a crook [*canaille*]" (*S* VII, 183; *215*).

Having thus presented the types of the left-wing and right-wing intellectual, Lacan proceeds: "After all, a crook is certainly worth a fool, at least for the entertainment he gives, if the result of gathering crooks into a herd did not inevitably lead to a collective foolery. This is what makes the politics of right-wing ideology so apt to produce despair" (*S* VII, 183; *215*).

A certain number of the young psychiatrists in Lacan's audience at the

Hôpital Sainte-Anne, we can be sure, would have been pleased with this apparent wave of the left hand. For them, Lacan quickly follows with the right: "But what is not sufficiently noted is that by a curious chiasma, the foolery that constitutes the individual style of the left-wing intellectual gives rise quite nicely to a collective knavery, a collective black-guardism" (*S* VII, 183; *215*). We can only imagine the frustration of those who, having anxiously waited for the master to show his political hand, would have discovered themselves in the face of a chiastic impasse.

Neither left nor right. Neither foolery (which results in collective knavery) nor knavery (which breeds foolery). By 1960 this neither/nor structure had long been associated with a series of (primarily leftist) attempts to think one's way outside political bipolarities, most recently by such forerunners of the French New Left as Cornelius Castoriadis and Claude Lefort.[27] But it could be argued that dismissing the parties to the Cold War back to back, as Lacan would explicitly do later in this same seminar, was also at the time an eminently Gaullist gesture.

Ultimately, however, the neither/nor structure implicit in Lacan's chiastic impasse is only indirectly political. First and foremost, it is a reflection of Lacan's principle of neutrality or nonintervention, his renunciation of all prescriptive therapeutics; "*ne uter*," Catherine Clément reminds us in evoking this principle, means "neither one nor the other" (*Lives*, 141; *164*). Behind Lacan's apparent refusal to cast his lot for the fools or for the knaves, we must read that mistrust of analytic power that had led him to stress the analysand's quest for the truth of his or her desire over the analyst's power to effect a cure (Clément, *Lives*, 142; *165*).

But the chiastic doubling of fools and knaves proves unstable precisely on account of its inherent stability; the chiastic impasse exists to be conjured away. No sooner has Lacan formulated his suggestion of analytic neutrality than he shifts to a more personal, almost confessional, mode of address. In the unruffled surface of the analyst as mirror, weekly magazines appear:

> What I am proposing here for you to reflect on has, I don't deny, the character of a confession. Those of you who know me are aware of my reading habits; you know which weeklies lie around on my desk. The thing I enjoy most [*Ce qui me fait le plus jouir*], I must admit, is the spectacle of collective knavery exhibited in them—that innocent chicanery, not to say calm impudence, which allows them to express so many heroic truths without wanting to pay the price. It is thanks to this that what is affirmed concerning the horrors of Mammon on the first page leads, on the last, to purrs of tenderness for this same Mammon. (183; *215–16*)

Lacan spoke these words in 1960, at a time of leftist self-criticism—Edgar Morin's influential *Autocritique* had appeared in March of 1959—as well as of growing disillusionment with a Communist Party compromised by its chronically weak opposition to the Algerian war. Lacan, who was never a leftist, confesses to privileging the knavery of collected fools over the foolery of assembled knaves. Specifically, he finds a certain *jouissance* in the spectacle of a collective duplicity traceable to what he would later analyze as the communist subservience to the (liberal, bourgeois) "service of goods."

But the leftist spectacle is in fact doubly privileged. Alongside the communists' repetition of the "bourgeois dream" one finds the spectacle of that individual fool who, in not yielding on his political desire, proves far more seductive than the realist knave; out of the mouths of fools, Lacan remarks, operative truths are known to come.

The apparent unreadability of Lacan's "politics" derives from a certain "monstrous" coupling underlying this double predilection for the leftist spectacle. If Lacan is drawn to the leftist fool out of respect for the truth of revolutionary desire, he is no less the proponent of a knavish realism that allows him to hear the left-wing collectivity's tender "purrs." What Lacan will call a "step-by-step" approach implicit to the psychoanalytic ethic accepts a measured dose of knavish realism so as not to fall into the metaphysical knavery of those contemporaries who, "under the guise of the truth about truth, [let] a great many things by which truly ought not to be let by" (*S* VII, 184; *216*).

His realism is thus strategic, but at the same time it is the condition of his *jouissance*. Strictly, Lacan's bliss resides neither in the spectacle of individual desire nor in that of collective duplicity, but in the gap or fissure that splits the subject caught between foolish desire and knavish realism. To those enmeshed in what Lacan sees as the narcissistic aggressivity endemic to a polarized political sphere, such a blissful coupling can only appear perverse. This would, of course, be precisely right, if by "perversity" one understands (with Roland Barthes) an erotic intermittence deriving from the very structure of the split subject as Lacan himself had theorized it.[28]

In her *Jacques Lacan* (1986) Marcelle Marini has argued that, of Lacan's many verbal styles, the most beautiful and forceful is the preacherly one: "He harangues his listeners, painting pictures that strike their imaginations so as the better to convert them; he apostrophizes, calls down curses, and then, at just the right moment, lets flicker in the distance the fleeting glimmer of a hope" (90–91; 97). I would make this point in terms of the erotic gap between foolish desire and knavish realism. In his Seminars as in the *Écrits*, Lacan will repeatedly *textualize* the fissure between desire and realism—or, if you will, between revolutionary hope and revolutionary despair—in a manner intended to impress on his addressees the truth of desire itself as a perverse, tragicomic oscillation, one that temporalizes (and textualizes) the paradox of desire as an endless quest for a way out of the very impasse that constitutes it. Lacan's politics (such as they are) are unthinkable outside of such a specifically textual, vacillatory movement.

A relatively simple form of this tragicomic oscillation appears in Lacan's remarks on the question of revolutionary change from his 1969 lecture at Vincennes. When a student suggests that Lacan's project bears no resemblance to the student militants' "will to change society and, among other things, to destroy the University," Lacan insists otherwise ("Impromptu," 125; *24*). But, having spoken of interrupting his seminar during the May events "to show my sympathy for what was astir and which continues . . . moderately," Lacan follows with this warning: "Contestation makes me think of something that was invented one day, if my memory is right, by my (late) good friend, Marcel Duchamp: 'the bachelor makes his chocolate by himself.' Watch out lest the demonstrator make chocolate of himself [*que le contestataire ne se fasse pas chocolat lui-même*]" ("Impromptu," 119; *22*).

This rhythmic conjuring of impasse structures (again, in all senses of the word "conjuring") will in fact punctuate even the most highly written of Lacan's texts. After speaking (in the Rome Discourse) of the modern self as taking form "in the dialectical impasse of the *belle âme*," Lacan writes, "But a way out is offered to the subject for the resolution of that impasse in which his discourse raves. Communication can be validly established for him in the common task of science and in the posts that it commands in our universal civilization" (*Écrits*, 70; *281–82*). As one reads on, of course, it becomes clear that Lacan is being ironic; the function of that "profuse culture" that gives modern man detective novels and group therapy "will give him the wherewithal to forget his own existence and his death, at the same time to misconstrue [*méconnaître*] the particular meaning of his life in communication"—to block, in short, the eventual epiphany of tragic knowledge (*Écrits*, 70; *282*). Not only is the participation in culture not a "way out" of the psychotic impasse, it actually repeats it. For, like psychotics, the "hollow men" of modern culture—Lacan cites here the opening lines to Eliot's poem—do not speak, but are spoken by, language.

With this claim of repetition, the cycle begins anew:

> This is not to say, however, that our culture pursues its course in the shadowy regions beyond creative subjectivity. On the contrary, creative subjectivity has not ceased in its struggle to renew the never-exhausted power of symbols in the human exchange that brings them to the light of day. . . . And another look, probably no less illusory, would make us accentuate this opposing trait: that its symbolic character has never been more manifest. It is the irony of revolutions that they engender a power all the more absolute in its exercise, not because it is more anonymous, as people say, but because it is more reduced to the words that signify it. And more than ever, on the other hand, the strength of the churches resides in the language that they have been able to maintain. (*Écrits*, 72; *283*)

Here, as before, Lacan follows the promise of an escape from confinement—in madness, in culture, in language, and so on—with a reaffirmation of that confinement justified by a logic of repetition or (as in this case) recuperation. In the subsequent paragraph, Lacan then circles back to science, and particularly to his own hope of formalizing psychoanalysis so as to "assure our discipline its place among the sciences."

To read Lacan's text with an ear to its tragicomic rhythms is, admittedly, a crude way of proceeding—one that perforce misses the subtle particularities of Lacan's highly calculated argumentative meanders. In the passage just cited, for instance, Lacan's general statement on the "irony of revolutions"—revolutions engender a power all the more absolute for being reduced to the words that signify power—alludes specifically to the reduction of Freud's "Copernican Revolution" in those "churches" that were the established psychoanalytic societies.[29] However questionable its strictly hermeneutic merit, however, this form of reading has a serious stake. For it allows us to see how Lacan mimics, as a sort of argumentative ground bass, an oscillation built into the very structure of the desiring subject.

In his Four Fundamental Concepts seminar Lacan spoke of a certain exercise in "alienation" in which a process of "endless repetition" manifests "the radical vacillation of the subject" (*S* XI, 239; *216*). He could have been referring to the experience of hearing the tragicomic rhythms of the Lacanian text; in fact, he was speaking of the *Fort/Da* game. In that game, you will recall, the child's gesture of expulsion (*Fort*) serves to constitute the object (the mother, as figured by the spool) as other, external to the pleasure-ego, "lost"—in short, as an object of desire. As Juliet Mitchell reminds us, any satisfaction the child may subsequently attain from that object "will always contain this loss within it" (Mitchell and Rose, 6). The function of Lacan's tragicomic rhythms, I would suggest, is to place his readers in the position of Freud's grandson, expelling and retrieving their hopes for a "way out" of the cultural bind, endlessly repeating (in a specifically temporalized form) the Möbius logic of a human desire that is constituted only through the impossibility of its satisfaction.

It was such an experience of repetition that Lacan had in mind when, in his "Propos sur la causalité psychique," he counterposed a suicidal confusion of the real and the ideal (characteristic, he thought, of the revolutionary intellectual) with the more canny strategy of resolving the primordial *béance* "by developing it" (*Écrits, 187*). Human desire is an impasse, specifically a tragicomic one. But as an impasse desire opens out onto the infinite process of its unfolding through the production of what Lacan called, in another context, "impasse-bound detourings" (*S* XX, *16*).[30] The only true "solution" to the impasse that is human desire, in other words, was to "supplement" or "develop" it through deployment of specific impasses endlessly conjured forth and conjured away—in the process of training future analysts or, as Lacan would insist in the final years, in writing. It is in this sense that one could say of politics what Lacan said of sexual relations, that "insofar as it doesn't work, it works nonetheless" (*S* XX, *34*).

In an argumentative coda destined to uncover the "utility" of his "crude" or summary reflections on the fool and the knave, Lacan recounts the dream of one of his friends and patients. In this dream, which bears the traces of "some yearning or other stimulated in him by the formulations of this seminar," someone cries out, referring to Lacan, "*But why doesn't he tell the truth about the truth?*" (*S* VII, 184; *216*). Having noted that his patients and students often express such an "impatience," Lacan concludes: "I am content to tell the truth of the first stage, and to proceed step by step" (*S* VII, 184; *216*).

As an example of what he calls *un pas vrai*—an (un)true step; a "true" step in "mid-speak"—Lacan then refers back to that argument that had served as a bridge between the dream anecdote and his earlier "confession" of personal bliss—namely, his characterization of Freud as an antiprogressive humanitarian:

> Freud was perhaps not a good father, but he was neither a crook nor an imbecile. That is why one can say of him two things which are disconcerting in their connection and their opposition. He was a humanitarian—who after checking his works will contest that?—and we must acknowledge it, however discredited the term might be by the crooks on the right. But, on the other hand, he wasn't a simpleton, so that one can say as well, and we have the texts to prove it, that he was no progressive [*progressiste*]. (*S* VII, 183; *215–16*)

Having conjured away the neither/nor structure implicit in the chiastic doubling of fools and knaves with a story of personal bliss, Lacan had thus revived that structure in reference to Freud. Neither (rightist) crook nor (leftist) fool, Freud occupies the puzzlingly oxymoronic space of the antiprogressive humanitarian. As such, he calls attention to the narcissistic underpinnings of a post-Revolutionary leftist mythology (stunningly practiced, for example, by Jules Michelet) that had ritualized the linkage of humanitarian concern with the notion of historical progress.[31]

Lacan's excursus on the "political sense" of that ethic entrusted to Freud's heirs leads him, therefore, to the neutralizing practice of telling the truth "step by step" so as to avoid the metaphysical knavery of those who would tell the truth about truth. And yet it is a "yearning" for just such a truth, left in Lacan's patient "by the formulations of this seminar," that had prompted Lacan's reflections on metaphysical knavery. In the opening of this chapter I suggested that it was Lacan's relentless critique of the demand for the One (truth, meaning, system, Revolution, etc.) that caused him to focalize the desire for the One; Lacan became the "subject presumed to know," in other words, by virtue of his attempts to undermine the image of the analyst as one who knows.[32] That he was in fact fully aware of this specific instance of Möbius logic is clear from the present passage. For, by framing his critique of metaphysical knavery with the tale of a metaphysical thirst inspired by his seminar, Lacan effectively rehearsed that paradoxical process whereby the analyst's critique of imaginary totalizations (specifically, political ones) gives rise to the equally imaginary supposition that the analyst possesses total (political) knowledge.

In his first seminar at the École Normale, just one year after an ad hoc commission of the International Psychoanalytic Association had accused him of manipulating the transference love of his students and patients, Lacan asked what is meant by the phrase, "to liquidate the transference." Since that relationship between subject and Other that drives the transference is properly interminable, he concluded, this can only mean liquidating that "deception by which the transference tends to be exercised in the direction of the closing up of the unconscious" (*S* XI, 267; *241*). The aim of analysis, in other words, is to move beyond that "narcissistic relation" whereby the analysand makes himself lovable so as to draw the analyst as Other "into a mirage relation in which he convinces him of being worthy of love" (267; *241*). Analysis moves toward that moment at which a fracturing of the *moi*'s imaginary unity turns the analysand's love for the analyst into hatred. Desupposing the analyst's knowledge, seeing the analyst once and for all as fundamentally abject, the analysand thus "passes" into an unmediated relationship with his Other (*S* XX, *64*).

There is a curious moment in the Four Fundamental Concepts seminar at which Lacan ends a reflection on transference love by recalling the legend of Actaeon surprising Diana and her nymphs at their bath: "The truth, in this sense, is that which runs after truth—and that is where I am running, where I am taking you, like Actaeon's hounds, after me. When I have found the goddess's lair, I shall no doubt change myself into a stag, and you can devour me, but we still have a little way to go yet" (*S* XI, 188; *172*). Not the least of the many oddities in this allegory of the passage beyond the transferential supposition of knowledge is the apparent absence of Diana and the nymphs. But in fact Diana is here in at least two guises. First, Lacan has simply transformed the naked goddess of myth into her cave as the site of a truth to be approached at great cost. In the language of the Ethics seminar, she has become the Thing as locus of a creation *ex nihilo*. Second, Diana's presence is latent in that central act of the mythical drama that Lacan here appropriates for himself in the role of Actaeon—that is, the metamorphosis of the young hunter into a stag. As Lacan rewrites the story, it is not a vengeful Diana who causes "old stag antlers" to sprout on Actaeon's head, rendering him both abject and mute ("Now say you saw me undressed!" she cries, "if you can!"); it is Actaeon (Lacan) himself.[33]

The implications of this usurpation for a specifically gendered reading of Lacan's "hommosexual" allegory are clear. In one striking respect, however, this may not be the most relevant usurpation. For if we follow Lacan's allegory in relation to his theory of the "pass," it is neither Diana nor Actaeon who should effect the latter's transformation into the stag, but the dogs themselves. Desupposing the knowledge of that master who had led them on a hunt for "truth," "Actaeon's hounds" would come to see the master's fundamental abjection, in the very moment they devoured him.[34]

In the wake of May '68, I have suggested, Lacan's critique of the demand for one Truth and one Revolution perpetuated the narcissistic illusion that knowledge of a fully self-present revolutionary moment was indeed possible, and that Lacan himself was the bearer of that knowledge. Whether, and in what sense, Lacan may have actually "wanted to remain the one who was supposed to know," as François Roustang has argued, is a question we need not attempt to resolve (*Delusion*, 8; *14*). In his letter of January 5, 1980, dissolving the École freudienne de Paris, however, Lacan would speak of his School as a Borromean knot, in which "it be enough for one to go away for all to be free" ("Letter," 129). Only the master could change himself into the stag. Only Lacan, "me in the role of Lacan," could cut the ring that bound all others (*S* XI, 188; *172*).

CHAPTER 4

Rigorous Dialectics: Althusser

Marx based his theory on the rejection of the myth of the *homo œconomicus*; Freud based his theory on the rejection of the myth of the *homo psychologicus*. Lacan has seen and understood Freud's liberating rupture. He has understood it in the fullest sense of the term, taking it rigorously at its word and forcing it to produce its own consequences, without concessions or quarter. It may be that, like everyone else, he errs in the detail. But he has given us the *essential*.

— Louis Althusser, "Freud and Lacan"

In January 1964, having been appointed *chargé de conférences* at the École Pratique des Hautes Études through the good graces of Claude Lévi-Strauss and Louis Althusser, Lacan transferred his seminar to the École Normale Supérieure on the rue d'Ulm, where it would remain until his exclusion from the École Normale in June of 1969. The effect of Lacan's institutional proximity to Althusser (*directeur d'études* for philosophy at the rue d'Ulm), coupled with Althusser's Marxist reworking of Freudian concepts ("overdetermination," "symptomatic reading," "mirror recognition," etc.), was to help focus the theoretical agenda of the late 1960s and early 1970s on the political (indeed, often specifically Marxist) implications of Lacanian theory. Although most noticeably exemplified by the work of the *Tel Quel* group, an uneasy coexistence of Lacanianism and Marxism-Leninism also characterized the work of certain Maoist intellectuals, from the young Althusserians of the École Normale's Cercle d'épistémologie to segments of the Maoist UJCml (Union des jeunesses communistes marxistes-léninistes) and Gauche Prolétarienne. It has been suggested, in fact, that Althusser's students at the École Normale turned to Maoism in quest of a political orientation whose rigor would match that they had found in Althusserian theory (Bensaïd, Krivine, and Weber, 44).

Addressing the (undeniably fascinating) question of how one might trace such a preoccupation with rigor both to the historical objectives of the École Normale as an institution and to the specific power dynamics at the rue d'Ulm in the mid-1960s is a task whose complexity precludes my pursuing it here.[1] Nor do I intend fully to detail the subtle shifts imposed on the work of both Lacan and Althusser through the passage of students from one seminar to another.[2] My aim in this short chapter, rather, is to explore two specific repercussions of that exigency of theoretical rigor so central to the Lacan/Althusser nexus. First, in Althusser as in Lacan the effort rigorously to neutralize an ideological circularity characteristic of reigning humanisms (ego psychology for Lacan, philosophical Marxism for Althusser) meant putting into play a certain *conceptual* circularity, the risk of which was theoretical psychosis. But second, Althusser's work (like Lacan's) can also be read as pointing the way to those theoretical structures by which theorists of *l'après-Mai* conjured the very "impasse" into which that work so deliberately falls. In this sense its example, like that of Lacanian theory, would prove fundamentally ambivalent.

In the previous chapter I showed how Lacanian rigor presupposes what Lacan called "Freudian ascetic experience"—a stripping-away of the imaginary miscognitions constitutive of the ego so as to reveal that core of human experience where the subject comes face to face with the death inherent in her relation to the Symbolic order. In that act of listening so vital to the Freudian project, rigor thus meant hearing the truth of desire as it is expressed in the fissures and blanks of the analysand's discourse, surprising sense in the very articulation of nonsense. In Lacan's pedagogical practice, moreover, it meant pushing his interlocutors to the brink of a certain psychosis, where a heightened (and ostensibly scientific) attention to the "letter" found its place within the theoretical quest for an impossible logical coherence. Ultimately, the function of Lacan's psychotic "trial in rigor" was to thwart a revisionist conception of the analyst as simple guarantor of the "bourgeois dream" through the recovery of what Althusser called the "liberating rupture" of the Freudian *Urtext*—specifically the books on dreams (1900), parapraxes (1901), and jokes (1905) ("Freud and Lacan," 195; *17*).

In its most fundamental, technical sense, "rigor" for Althusser implied recognition of the determinative role played by those complex, internally contradictory thought structures he called, in the spirit of Gaston Bachelard, "problematics." As the system of unarticulated, often conflicting questions governing the answers a given text both can and cannot propose, as the structural condition of what it can and cannot see, the problematic manifests itself primarily in textual gaps or silences, and thus can be uncovered only through Althusser's answer to the rigor of Lacanian listening, the practice of "symptomatic reading." In his analysis of wages (*Capital*, chap. 19), Althusser argues, Marx read the work of Smith and Ricardo symptomatically, such that Marx's own concept of labor power (and ultimately his theory of surplus value) was shown to reside in the blank spaces hollowed out in classical political economy's discussions of the value of labor (*Reading*, 22–24; *1: 20–23*).

What political economy does not see is what it *does*: its production of a new answer without a question, and simultaneously the production of a new latent question contained by default [*portée en creux*] in this new answer. . . . Far from knowing it [had produced a new problem], [political economy] remained convinced that it was still on the terrain of the old problem, whereas it had *"unwittingly changed terrain."* (*Reading*, 24; *1: 23*)

In a second moment, Althusser reads Marx himself symptomatically by tracking the necessity within his work of an (unarticulated) concept of structural causality—"the concept of the effectivity of a structure on its elements"—not fully theorizable in the terms of Marx's age (*Reading*, 29; *1: 31*).[3] Implicit within this new answer, then, is what is arguably the central question of Althusser's theoretical project—the requisite but absent question of the specific difference of Marx's dialectic from Hegel's (*Reading*, 33; *1: 35*). To read the Marxian *Urtext* rigorously, in short, is to theorize the necessity of a conceptual "change of terrain" going far beyond Marx's own claims (in his Afterword to the second edition of *Capital*) to have unleashed the materialist power of Hegel's dialectic by "inverting" it. For simply to reverse speculative philosophy, as Ludwig Feuerbach would have done when he gave "different answers, but to the same questions," is to remain its "unconscious prisoner" (*For Marx*, 72, 90; *69, 88*).[4] A rigorous reading of Marx must thus read him against the grain, showing how the absence of a concept behind the word "inversion" points to a change of theoretical base that would only come into focus nearly a century later, in the work of the Althusserians themselves.

Behind this insistence on conceptual rigor lay a serious ideological stake. For just as the rigor of Lacanian listening presupposed the refusal to sanction an analytic revisionism complicit with the bourgeois society of goods, so will the concept of symptomatic reading prove inseparable from Althusser's uncompromising critique of Marxist revisionism. Althusser repeatedly chastised the 20th Congress of the Soviet Communist Party (1956)—and most especially Khruschev's antimaterialist denunciation of the Stalinist "personality cult"—for having unleashed "a wave of *bourgeois* ideological and philosophical themes" within communist circles—a petty exaltation of the Rights of Man, "the first of which are *liberty* and its converse, *alienation*" (*Réponse*, *65, 67*). Recapturing the rigor of Marxist historical materialism, returning Marxism to the purity of its "liberating rupture," meant rejecting an existentialist or *gauchiste* revisionism that derived its neo-Hegelian focus on alienation and self-realization from the reading of Marx's *1844 Manuscripts*.

Indeed Althusser's lifelong insistence on an epistemological break separating the subjective neo-Hegelianism and Feuerbachian humanism of Marx's pre-1845 writings from the dialectical materialism of his maturity must be read as a radical attempt to purge Marxist theory of an atavistic Hegelianism whose political effects would, he argued, always prove counter-revolutionary. Thus, of Sartre's assumption that "man is essentially a *revolutionary animal* because he is a *free* animal," he wrote: "The rest of us, communist philosophers, know that this old philosophical tune has always had political effects" (*Réponse, 21*). The more militant, less "theoreticist" tone characteristic of Althusser's work after 1967 leaves no doubt but that Marxist-Leninist rigor implies the sort of consciously "dogmatic" defense of orthodoxy exemplified by

> the great struggles of Engels and Lenin against . . . the invasive idealism of Dühring and Bernstein, both of them declared humanists and neo-Kantians, and whose theoretical revisionism served as an alibi for political reformism and political revisionism.
>
> Let J. Lewis reread the opening pages of "What Is to Be Done?" (*Réponse, 62–63*)

I shall return to this Leninist conception of rigor in a moment. So as to move beyond the evident analogies traced thus far between the Lacanian and Althusserian conceptions of rigor, I would turn here to the Lacanian borrowing of Althusser's most central to the concerns of this book—namely, his analysis of the "vicious circle" that is "the mirror relation of ideological recognition" (*Reading*, 53; *1: 63*).[5]

In the opening essay to *Reading Capital*, Althusser justifies a seemingly scandalous assimilation of Hegelian idealism to an empiricist conception of knowledge on the grounds that Hegelianism and empiricism both tend to confuse the real object with the object of knowledge, real processes with the processes of knowledge. Hegelianism, to be sure, reverses empiricist valuations, subsuming object to subject, practice to theory, historical order (the chronological unfolding of phenomena) to logical order (the deduction of categories). But Hegelian idealism and empiricist pragmatism are equally ideological to the extent that they seek to abstract a pure essence of the real object from its unessential dross, eliminating the latter together with all traces of the abstraction process itself (*Reading*, 36; *1: 40*). Both are inevitably led into that lack of scientific rigor that characterizes ideology for Althusser—emblematizable here as a common refusal of Spinoza's warning not to confuse the *idea* of the circle (as *object* of knowledge) with the circle as *real object*—through their frenzied quest for epistemological *guarantees*:

> By what *right* do you tell us that practice is right? says idealism to pragmatism. Your right is no more than a disguised fact, answers pragmatism. And we are back on the wheel, the closed circle of the ideological question. In all these cases, the common rule which permits this action [*ce jeu*] is in fact the question of the *guarantees* of the harmony between knowledge (or Subject) and its real object (or Object), i.e., the ideological question as such. (*Reading*, 57; 1: 69)

The particular genesis of this argument is not difficult to trace. The quarrel of idealism and pragmatism endlessly repeats what Althusser elsewhere calls, in the spirit of Lenin's *Materialism and Empirio-criticism*, "the eternal null inversion for which philosophy is the garrulous theater, the inversion of the fundamental categorial opposition of matter and mind" (*Lenin*, 57; *45*). Writing shortly after his article on Lacan, Althusser borrows Lacan's (neo-Hegelian) analysis of the aggressivity that attends to specular rivalry in the Imaginary order as the vehicle for a specifically Leninist vision of philosophy as the domain of a pure tendential struggle leading nowhere.[6] Likewise, in the following passage Althusser's extension of the specular metaphor to encompass the tautological posing of theoretical questions as the "exact reflection" of desired ideological answers couches Lenin's insight on the tautological nature of ideological constructions in terms of the imaginary recognition structures that subtend Lacan's analysis of ego formation:

> In the theoretical mode of production of ideology . . . , the formulation of a *problem* is merely the theoretical expression of the conditions which allow a *solution* already produced outside the process of knowledge because imposed by extra-theoretical instances and exigencies (by religious, ethical, political or other "interests") *to recognize itself* in an artificial problem manufactured to serve it both as a theoretical mirror and as a practical justification. (*Reading*, 52; *1: 62*)

Althusser's antidote to theories of knowledge that tailor questions and problems to the precise measure of desired ideological answers or solutions is a practice of symptomatic reading attentive to the way texts produce new answers to questions not yet posed, and new questions in the very hollow of those answers. Against the closed circle of that "mutual mirror-recognition structure" in which the ideological characters of "Subject and Object" necessarily move, Althusser poses the rigorously open structure proper to scientific knowledge, "the circle perpetually opened by its closures themselves, the circle of a well-founded knowledge" (*Reading*, 55, 69; *1: 66, 1: 85*).

While recognizing (with Engels and Lenin) the practical necessity of the ideological battle, where one parries the enemy's blows by turning his ideological concepts back against him, Althusser seeks to avoid the repetition endemic to ideology's "vicious circle" through what he calls "the sole theoretically founded flight [*fuite*]—which is precisely not a *flight*, since flight is always committed to what it is fleeing from, but rather the radical foundation of a new space, a new problematic that allows the real *problem* to be posed, the problem misrecognized in the recognition structure in which it is ideologically posed" (*Reading*, 38, 53; *1: 43, 1: 64*). It is in fact only from within a scientific problematic geared to uncover the specific mechanisms by which the production of the object of knowledge produces in turn the cognitive appropriation of the real object—"the real *problem*"—that one can hope properly to situate the reasons for the necessary "unreason" (*déraison*) of ideological struggle (*Reading*, 34; *1: 37*).

Far from constructing a scene of closure as the pretext to a flight into "openness," in other words, Althusser insists that scientific rigor is possible only when an object or problem is put to the test from within the already-structured field of a given theoretical problematic. No truly dialectical conception of "well-founded" knowledge as a "circle perpetually opened by its very closures" can fail to grasp the necessary circularity of knowledge production as a process of transforming "something which in a sense *already exists*" (*Reading*, 34; *1: 37*).

Althusser's emphasis on knowledge as production is, of course, crucial. His hermeneutic is plainly not a historicist exercise in interpretive model building aimed at progressively recovering an original meaning—an authorial intent, sociocultural context, or empirical concrete "richer-and-more-living-than-theory"—presumed to be objectified in a subject text (*Reading*, 117; *1: 148*). It implies rather a process of dialectical (self-) refinement involving both the theoretical problematic governing the reader's interpretations and that which governed the production of the text, limiting the questions it could pose and the concepts it could articulate, and thereby determining its ideological fissures.

A truly Marxist hermeneutic, in other words, implies "the dialectical circle of the question asked of an object as to its nature, on the basis of a theoretical problematic which *in putting its object to the test puts itself to the test of its object*" (*For Marx*, 38, *31*; emphasis added). In Althusser's work this typically meant that the development of a (still embryonic) Marxist philosophy presupposed rereading the historical materialism of *Capital* in dialectic with a theory of epistemological history—based on concepts like the "problematic" and the "epistemological break" said to be "present and active in Marx's scientific thought"—that Althusser equated with Marxist philosophy itself (*For Marx*, 32; *24*):

> May I sum up all this in one sentence? This sentence describes a circle: a philosophical reading of *Capital* is only possible as the application of that which is the very object of our investigation, Marxist philosophy. (*Reading*, 34; *1: 37*)
>
> That this operation in itself constitutes an indispensable circle in which the application of Marxist theory to Marx himself appears to be the absolute precondition even of the constitution and development of Marxist philosophy, so much is clear. (*For Marx*, 38; *30–31*)

Unconvinced by the supposed clarity of this operation, Althusser's critics have spared no effort in detailing the problems raised by such claims. Here, for instance, is one of the best, Alex Callinicos:

> If the mechanism of the epistemological break appeared mysterious, more mysterious still is the fact that this break involved the covert emergence of a distinct theory, Marxist philosophy, the theory of theoretical practice. If the problematic of Marxist science required a symptomatic reading for it to be extracted from Marx's texts, how much more so will the problematic of Marxist philosophy, whose principles in some strange ("dialectical") form are present in these same texts. Yet, since the notions of symptomatic reading and problematic are categories of Marxist philosophy, how do we come

> to possess these albeit provisional principles of Marxist philosophy, since they are necessary in order to initiate the circular motion described in Althusser's work? (74)

Notice how, in order to interrogate the supposedly indispensable circularity of Althusser's method, Callinicos is forced to appeal to a question of origin (how does the circular motion begin?). Moments later, however, he will claim to have caught Althusser *in flagrante delicto* "invoking the familiar philosophical concept of *origin*, whose function, as [Althusser himself] says . . . , 'is to summarise in one word what has not to be thought in order to be able to think what one wants to think' " (75).

I would phrase the critique in slightly different terms. Strictly speaking, there is nothing of an origin in the "dialectical" circle whereby a theoretical problematic simultaneously proofs its object and proofs itself by that object. But nor is there any of that aggressive circularity so characteristic of Althusser's formulations of his epistemological project. That aggressivity pertains not to the dialectical mechanism of Althusser's hermeneutic, but to his uncompromising quest for what he calls (in the immediate context of the "indispensable circle" passage above) "a definition of the irreducible specificity of Marxist theory" (*For Marx*, 38; *30*). This "irreducible specificity" is partly a function of the dialectic that prevails, within Althusser's reading of *Capital*, between Marx's insight into the differential development of theoretical formations, as "the object of Marxist philosophy," and that comprehension of the mechanisms of the capitalist mode of production attained through what Althusser calls "the identification and knowledge of the specific difference of the object of *Capital* itself" (*Reading*, 74–75; *1: 90*). But this formulation in turn suggests a more restrictive locus. The specificity of Marxist theory resides in the ostensibly scientific problematic of Marx's mature work, a problematic structured by such concepts as "mode of production, forces of production, relations of production, infrastructure-superstructure, ideologies, etc." (*Réponse*, *52*).

That Althusser's theory of the "epistemological break" readily lends itself to a certain mythification of an origin is most evident perhaps in his discussion of Marx, Nietzsche, and Freud as " 'natural' children," each condemned to the necessity of constituting the very theoretical space in which his discoveries might be situated, to the necessity (as he says of Freud) of being "himself his own father" ("Freud and Lacan," 196; *18*).[7] In Althusser, as in Lacan, there are manifest overtones of that interpretive drive to retrieve an original sacred meaning, long since forgotten, that Ricoeur calls "positive hermeneutics" (discussed by Jameson, *Marxism*, 119). Yet it is neither hagiography nor hermeneutic exegesis that motivates the apparent mythification of an originary moment in both Althusser and Lacan so much as the shared conviction that science has an origin by virtue of the fact that it has an object.[8]

It follows, therefore, that scientific rigor can arise only through a disciplined affirmation of the irreducibility of that theoretical object:

> Lacan's first word is to say: in principle, Freud founded a *science.* A new science which was the science of a new object: the unconscious.
> A rigorous statement. ("Freud and Lacan," 198; 20)

> Does not the difficulty Marx seems to have felt in thinking in a rigorous concept the difference which distinguishes his object from the object of Classical Economics, lie in the *nature* of his discovery, in particular in its fantastically *innovative character*? . . . And in this case, does not Marx's scientific discovery imperiously demand that we pose the *new* philosophical problems required by the disconcerting nature of its *new object*? (*Reading,* 75; *1:* 90)

In short, the aggressive circularity of Althusser's reading of *Capital*—where seeing Marxist philosophy is said to presuppose Marxist science, which in turn presupposes Marxist philosophy—is largely a function of a demand to maintain the essential purity of a nascent science's radically new theoretical object. It is thus one strategy, though a privileged one, in a battle against theoretical revisionism that Althusser conceives as the practical equivalent of war:

> It is here that Lacan intervenes: he defends the irreducibility of analysis against these "reductions" and deviations, which dominate most contemporary theoretical interpretations; he defends its irreducibility, which means *the irreducibility of its object.* That this defense requires an uncommon lucidity and firmness, sufficient to repulse all the voraciously hospitable assaults of the disciplines I have listed, cannot be doubted by anyone. ("Freud and Lacan," 203; 24)

In the essays collected in *For Marx* and *Reading Capital,* Althusser attempts to draw a clear distinction between the theoretical modes of production of science and ideology (specifically theoretical ideology). In the latter, as I have shown, he finds theoretical problems to be formulated solely in view of desired, extratheoretical solutions. Or, in Hegelian/Lacanian terms, they function as mirrors within which preexistent solutions are brought (as if miraculously) to recognize themselves. What Althusser calls "the impasse of . . . analytico-teleological critique" is structured by the coupling of this theoretical teleology with two further presuppositions (*For Marx,* 67; 64). These are, first, that "any theoretical system and any constituted thought is *reducible to its elements,*" which can then be compared with similar elements from other systems; and second, that ideas are "auto-intelligible," since their history is bred only of itself (*For Marx,* 56–57; 52–53).

Where ideology proves constitutively incapable of self-analysis and self-transformation (its circle is fully closed), science draws strength from the "extreme attention" it pays to the points of its own theoretical fragility; its circle is open, because "perpetually opened by its closures themselves" (*Reading,* 30; 1: 31). Or to catch the early Althusser making the same point in a more obviously Leninist mode, "We know that a 'pure' science only exists on the condition that it be incessantly purified; that a science free in the very necessity of its history exists only if it is incessantly liberated from the ideology that occupies it, haunts it, or lies in wait for it" (*For Marx*, 170; *171*).[9]

But the openness characteristic of this rigorously self-critical scientific practice is paradoxical, since—like the conception of "theoretical practice" that Althusser would theorize on its model—it is fundamentally self-validating. This point would have been of particular importance to the Althusser of 1965, for if scientific practice is capable of validating "the quality of its product" on the basis of "definite protocols" contained within that practice, without recourse to a "pragmatist criterion" of truth, then the same can be said "of the science which concerns us most particularly: historical materialism. It has been possible to apply Marx's theory with success because it is 'true'; it is not true because it has been applied with success" (*Reading*, 59; *1: 71*).

What this particular conjunction of arguments suggests, to this reader at least, is that the very move that allows for the most powerful, "rigorous" self-critique—science's self-reflexive attention to its points of theoretical fragility—bears within itself the potential for a phantasmatic theory building deriving its power from its coherence and unity of purpose, its expulsion or nonrecognition of recalcitrant "impurities"—the potential, in short, for "psychotic" theorization. To prove this point fully would take me far afield—to the thorny question for Althusser of theory's articulation with the real, to the selectivity of Althusser's reading of the Marxian *Urtext*, and to the play of hallucination and reality within Althusser's autobiographical writings (*Avenir*, *74*). If I decline to make these detours here, it is because Althusser himself, with characteristically self-critical rigor, all but concedes the point:

> The reader should realize that I am doing all I can to give the *concepts* I use a strict meaning [*sens rigoureux*], and that if he wants to understand these concepts he will have to pay attention to this rigour, and, *in so far as it is not imaginary* [emphasis added], he will have to adopt it himself. Need I remind him that without the rigour demanded by its object there can be no question of *theory*, that is, of theoretical practice in the strict sense [*au sens rigoureux*] of the term? (*For Marx*, 164; *164*)

Matters shift a bit after Althusser's recanting of his "theoreticist deviation" and his progressive rapprochement with the PCF. In particular, the attempt to sharply distinguish science from ideology gives way to a more orthodox focus on science's ideological effects. Reading Althusser's 1968 essay on "Lenin and Philosophy" one is struck by his interest in the delicate balancing act through which Lenin attempted to maintain science's distinction from ideology as a domain of open dialectical inquiry while nonetheless insisting on science's unmistakable ideological import. Of the distinction between relative and absolute truth, Lenin wrote:

> It is sufficiently "indefinite" *to prevent science from becoming a dogma in the bad sense of the term,* from becoming something dead, frozen, ossified; but at the same time it is sufficiently 'definite' to enable us to *draw a dividing-line in the most emphatic and irrevocable manner* between ourselves and fideism and agnosticism, between ourselves and philosophical idealism and the sophistry of the followers of Hume and Kant. (*Materialism,* 153; cited by Althusser, *Lenin,* 60–61, *49*; emphasis Althusser's)

Althusser's gloss on this passage takes the form of an elaborate theoretical dance. The function of philosophical intervention, he writes, "consists of 'drawing a dividing-line' between ideas declared to be true and ideas declared to be false, between the scientific and the ideological." But this gesture, by functioning (ideologically) to distinguish between the scientific and the ideological, itself has effects in both the scientific and the ideological domains: "The effects of this line [*tracé*] are of two kinds: positive in that they assist a certain practice—scientific practice—and negative in that they defend this practice against the dangers of certain ideological notions: here those of idealism and dogmatism" (*Lenin,* 61; *49–50*).

The extraordinary usefulness of the word "rigor" in the wake of Lenin has stemmed largely from its ability to encompass both scientific and ideological senses at once. Or, more precisely, to speak of the "rigor" of open scientific inquiry, constantly engaged in proofing itself through examination of its weaknesses, has meant evoking ipso facto that act of "drawing a dividing-line" that serves to guarantee a purity of purpose against revisionist temptations. This slippage, this *Wortspiel,* is clearly at work prior to Althusser's break with "theoreticism"; witness the passages I have quoted from his 1964 essay "Freud and Lacan." But it is never more clearly exemplified than in Althusser's February 1968 interview with Italian Communist Maria Antonietta Macciocchi. Asked why he attaches "a great deal of importance to rigour, including a rigorous vocabulary," Althusser responds:

> A single word sums up the *master* function of philosophical practice: "*to draw a dividing line*" between the true ideas and false ideas. Lenin's words.
>
> But the same word sums up one of the essential operations in the direction of the practice of class struggle: "*to draw a dividing line*" between the antagonistic classes. Between our class friends and our class enemies.
>
> *It is the same word.* A theoretical dividing line between true ideas and false ideas. A political dividing line between the people (the proletariat and its allies) and the people's enemies. (*Lenin,* 21; *Positions, 53*)

What the defense of this "dividing line" might look like if pushed to its psychotic limit will be the subject of my next chapter. To bring the present chapter to a close, I should like to look back at some issues briefly raised in Chapters 1 and 2, and fully elaborated upon in Chapter 6. In theoretical texts of the post-May era, I have suggested, the metaphor of mirror recognition served most commonly to designate a relationship of rivalry among homologous double figures, a relationship given to paranoia and narcissistic aggressivity and whose very closure became the impetus to the staking out of a radically decentered theoretical space. In Chapter 6 I show how this argumentative logic served to rationalize various forms of pluralistic "oppositionality," from micropolitical practice (Cixous et al.) to the "triumphant plurality" of the text itself (Barthes).

In a curious way, Althusser's work of the mid-1960s appears to anticipate this development. In the opening essay to *Reading Capital*, just after his discussion of the "closed circle" of idealism and pragmatism, Althusser evokes "the pair of 'contraries' theory and practice constituting the two terms of a mirror field" (57–58; *1:* 69–70). Even when the theory/practice opposition is used in the service of "a revolutionary vision which exalts the workers' cause," he argues, it functions as an "ideological myth"; Marxism's traditional criterion of practice inverts, but does not undo, "the social division of labor . . . between power (political, religious, or ideological) and oppression (the executors who are also the executed)" (58; *1:* 70).

On the far side of this specular deadlock of the ideological operators "theory" and "practice," Althusser finds just what he put that deadlock there to find—namely, an ostensibly "scientific" conception of practice. Or, to borrow Marx's metaphor, the "change of terrain" called forth by Althusser's rhetorical (and fundamentally teleological) construction involves a reconception of the social formation as the complex articulation of a series of distinct, relatively autonomous *practices* (economic, political, ideological, technical, and scientific/theoretical), each of which is determined only "in the last instance" by economic practice (58; *1:* 71).

Insofar as the aim of this "plural solution" (Barthes) would be to justify a certain margin within established institutions—specifically here, the place of theoretical practice within the theretofore hostile climes of French Marxism—it is comparable to those discussed in Part III of this study. Yet there can be no question here, as there would be in the work of Barthes, Kristeva, Cixous, and others, of leaving the Leninist "dividing line" behind. For it is precisely in this context that Althusser, going on to discuss the criteria specific to scientific and theoretical practice, makes his claims (discussed above) for the self-reflexive, self-validating nature of that practice. And, as this chapter has amply demonstrated, there was never but a small step from Althusser's refusal of pragmatist validation to his claims for scientific self-purification ("a 'pure' science only exists on the condition that it be incessantly purified"), and hence back once again to that scientific/ideological dance he would come to theorize under the name of Leninist "rigor."

CHAPTER 5

The Castration Drama of the Maoist Intellectual: Jambet and Lardreau

Intellectuel(le) (adj.): That which is purely spiritual, which has no body. Angels and the Blessed are intellectual substances. The reasoning soul is also said to be an intellectual power.

— Furetière's *Dictionnaire* [1690]

Thus, if we are sufficiently cruel to ourselves to incorporate the father, it is perhaps because we have a lot to reproach this father with.

— Jacques Lacan, *Seminar VII: The Ethics of Psychoanalysis*

The subject of this chapter is one of the more curious documents of an intellectual "affair"—that of the so-called New Philosophers—already better known for its curiosities than its intellectual substance. *L'Ange*, by Christian Jambet and Guy Lardreau, is an exceptionally dense and self-conscious piece of philosophical mysticism, whose Lacanian subtitle, *Pour une cynégétique du semblant* (Toward the hunt after semblances), speaks of nothing so clearly as its authors' common formation at the École Normale. And yet the book is known to have sold a remarkable 15,000 copies in the two years following its February 1976 publication (Ory, *Entre-deux*, 230).

It would be easy to dismiss the *L'Ange* phenomenon—and indeed the New Philosophy as a whole—as the mere product of a publicity machine named Bernard-Henri Lévy; Lévy's essay consecrating this philosophical "new wave" appeared in a June 1976 number of *Les Nouvelles littéraires*. It would be easier still to mock the overwrought confessional tone in which Jambet and Lardreau, like so many other New Philosophers, prefigure their definitive abandonment of revolutionary hope, the collapse of their faith in what the French called *les lendemains qui chantent* (lyric tomorrows). In many respects their book is a hodgepodge of New Philosophical ingredients: two parts hysterical confession to one part overestimation of "the Master," copiously seasoned with references to the lessons of Solzhenitsyn's *Gulag Archipelago* and the "failure" of May '68, and shot through with absolutist logics of a thoroughly comic rigidity: "Like two simpletons, Jambet and Lardreau have worshipped windmills; thus, everything becomes a windmill!" (Aubral and Delcourt, *47*).

But all is not ridicule in the world of the Angel. Or rather, however assiduously Jambet and Lardreau's work might appear to court derision, it remains of interest nearly two decades later on at least two grounds. First, it is an important attempt to come to grips with the specifically counter-revolutionary implications of Lacanian theory. And second, it is a privileged symptom of that mythological crisis undergone in the mid-1970s by Third World revolutionism in general and French Maoism in particular. Indeed, it is the sense of loss imposed by that crisis, and worked over in the dialogue with Lacan, that makes of Jambet and Lardreau's book a mirror onto that specifically tragic mode of listening that Clément associates, provocatively, with the intellectual as such: "And then there are those sublime sentences of his, which catch the tragic ear of intellectuals, always willing to allow themselves to be seduced wherever the impossible is proposed as such; those sentences, whose lulling rhythm panders to a delight in the loss of the lost paradise" (cited by Roustang, *Delusion*, 15; 20).

In the pages that follow, I read the experience of loss or separation to which Clément's "intellectuals" bend their "tragic ear" on three levels of decreasing historical specificity—the first involving the breakdown of the revolutionary model in the mid-1970s, the second a series of contradictions endemic to the role of the revolutionary intellectual, and the third a nostalgia implicit in the very mandate of the "intellectual" as such. I then go on to explore how Jambet and Lardreau's conception of cultural revolution would lead them actively to embrace the *belle âme* scenario as Lacan had earlier defined it. After a brief analysis of the repetitions plaguing Jambet and Lardreau's attempt to affirm a specifically dualistic, paranoid worldview, I conclude by returning to the question of how Lacan's work both evokes and effectively parries the folly of the *belle âme*.

Maoism Eclipsed

Born in 1963 as the result of a splitting of the world Communist movement into Chinese and Soviet camps, French Maoism set out to save Marxism-Leninism from a revisionism it saw to be rampant in the organizations of the Soviet sphere, most notably the PCF and the CGT (Hess, *8*). In the years that followed, a drive toward doctrinal purity led Maoist groups to denounce the PCF's failure of revolutionary resolve on the Algerian question, to chastise both the PCF and the Trotskyites for failing to arrive at "an accurate estimation of Stalin," and to protest the CGT's unanimous revocation (in the wake of May '68) of that clause in their charter that called for an "abolition of the division between bosses and wage-earners" (cited by Hess, *84, 92*). In the 1970s, at a time when the communist parties of Europe tended to advocate a peaceful transition to socialism through communist participation in established parliamentary structures, the Maoists urged strict fidelity to the Leninist conception of the revolutionary party, and especially to a "dictatorship of the proletariat" line that had fallen into disfavor after the Soviet Union proclaimed itself a "State of the Whole People" in 1956.

Above all, therefore, what Maoism promised its French adherents was the return to a purity of revolutionary purpose, a Marxist-Leninist rigor, that had been progressively corrupted by a spirit of compromise permeating and buttressing the capitalist order. Pursuant to this aim, the Maoists sought to restore an "organic unity of theory and practice" lost to Western Marxism since the generation of Lenin, Trotsky, and Luxemburg, and yet realized anew in the person of Mao Zedong (Anderson, *Considerations*, 29). In an interview from his Maoist phase, Sartre spoke of the practice of encouraging Maoist intellectuals to work in French factories as serving to "simplify" their language, to transform them into "new men" through daily contact with the working class ("Ami," *464*).

But Maoism would not have weighed heavily on a considerable portion of the French left were it not for a tension, inherent in Maoist doctrine, between the insistence on an absolute and disciplined subservience to the will of the people on the one hand and an antiauthoritarian, even neoanarchist, faith in spontaneous action on the other. What sympathetic note such a tension might have struck within a French psyche given to oscillating between conformist adaptation to hierarchical social structures and outbursts of libertarian revolt is not a question I would pose here.[1] Rather, I would simply note that this tension allowed French Maoism to play a significant role on both sides of that ideological divide that traverses the revolutionary map of *l'après-Mai*. If Jambet and Lardreau epitomize the Maoist mainstream in conforming to what Morin calls the "Marxist-Leninist-religious" heritage of May, a significant number of self-proclaimed Maoists—including the most prominent members of the *Tel Quel* collective—pursued a more "libertarian-communitarian" line. Indeed, one historian of French Maoism has gone so far as to trace the origins of the MLF to a special number of the Maoist biweekly *Tout* devoted to the liberation struggles of women and gays (Hess, *167*).

In the following chapter I shall examine how, in the absence of concrete details, Mao's Cultural Revolution came to serve as a screen for the projection of French cultural-political fantasies, especially among proponents of a new, revolutionary *écriture*. But the Cultural Revolution served a second imaginary function. Presented in France as both a hotbed of radical cultural democracy *and* the privileged site of strict fidelity to Marxist-Leninist doctrine, it allowed a significant number of Maoist militants to fantasize a squaring of one of twentieth-century European Marxism's most troublesome circles: its inability to reconcile the demands of revolutionary discipline with those of democratic, grass-roots participation in the revolutionary process.

Perhaps the phantasmatic edifice of French Maoism was destined to collapse of its own accord. But its demise was clearly hastened by a series of revelations exposing the sordid underside of that apparent paragon of antibureaucratic, antireformist Communism that was Maoist China—revelations first of the sufferings inflicted by the Red Guards in the name of Cultural Revolution, then of the mysterious death of Mao's chosen successor, Lin Biao (September 1971), and finally of the bitter succession crisis acted out, in the three years prior to Mao's death (1976), between the Gang of Four led by Jiang Quing and the reformist faction of Deng Xiaoping. Like all of the other revolutionary models rejuvenated in the immediate aftermath of May, moreover, Maoism fell victim (in the mid-1970s) to a mounting perception that reformist evolutionism offered a surer means of effecting social change than revolutionary upheaval and that the vocabulary of class struggle was but a poor instrument for analyzing a social order in which power was increasingly fractured and diffuse.

Introducing a chapter of *L'Ange* entitled "Lin Piao comme volonté et représentation" (Lin Biao as will and representation) Guy Lardreau acknowledges the phantasmatic quality of the Maoist adventure with remarkable candor:

> It was not about China, or Mao, or even the great Cultural Revolution, but the fact that we took all of this to be a new gospel, a premonition of the Angel.
>
> What we saw represented was an effect of our will, our desire—quite simply, a fantasy [*un phantasme*].[2]

And yet Jambet and Lardreau had by no means been won over to the camp of those who, like Derrida and Barthes, advocated complicitous subversion over pure revolutionary opposition; *L'Ange* was in fact a radical attempt to salvage the ideal of "absolute purity" from the wreckage of a Cultural Revolution fought under its banner (*110*). Asked in a May 1976 interview why for them militancy was henceforth out of the question, Jambet and Lardreau would respond, "We came to realize at a certain point that the masses had gotten all they could get out of us, that intellectuals had nothing left to give to them. Everything we had done had passed over into the masses themselves. Witness the events at Lip. It was becoming clear that there was no longer any sense in militancy" ("L'ange, entre Mao et Jésus," *57*). From the workers' occupation of the Lip watch factory in the summer of 1973, and their reorganization of production according to the principles of workers' self-management, Jambet and Lardreau concluded that the Maoist intellectual had actually been too successful for his own good.

What is perhaps most astonishing about this (inherently remarkable) claim is the way it denies a sense of loss that plainly haunts the pages of *L'Ange*. Or, more precisely, it denies all evidence of a political paradigm shift that my reading of *L'Ange* will suggest triggered this sense of loss. What I have in mind here is the generalized breakdown of a political bipolarity whose mark on modern French culture had never been stronger than in the three decades preceding May '68—the so-called *Trente glorieuses*. Various rightist revivals notwithstanding—from the "New Right" of the late 1970s (Alain de Benoist, Louis Pauwels) to Jean-Marie Le Pen's Front national—the general tendency of French politics in the post-May era has been resolutely centrist. One correlative of this tendency, I would suggest, was an increasing reliance on modes of micropolitical subversion that effectively moot the Maoist's assumption that an intellectual's militancy must show itself under the aegis of a revolutionary party.

As an instance of how this unarticulated paradigm shift ultimately shapes the argument of *L'Ange*, consider Lardreau's exposition of the book's project:

> We have put to the test an experience of conversion, a cultural revolution whose moral has yet to be articulated, but the rudiments of which will be found here. We emerged from it broken by a failure which, in fact, as we tried to think it through in terms of the thoughts that had led us astray, we did not understand. We thought we had touched bottom. It was one of those moments when everything gives out, when whole nights are spent sobbing quietly over a past beyond remedy. . . .
>
> We retired to the desert, where our demons told us sneeringly that *nil novi sub sole*. To decide among [*trancher dans*] the legions of thoughts that endlessly assailed us, we would have needed the discriminatory tact of Evagrius Scholasticus; and we understood that nothing was more difficult without the gift of grace [*sans charisme*]. We found ourselves victims of a deplorable system of note-taking whereby all the somewhat new ways we thought up to shatter this world were immediately accompanied by a burst of laughter: "That's'n old one" [*zavons déjà entendu ça*]. One thing however was certain: we didn't want to let ourselves be Schreberized. We had to find the rock on which to shatter the evil spirit.
>
> Furthermore, we knew that duplicity had to be rejected; there are only two paths, each one loathsome to the other. It wasn't a matter of renouncing our principles, but of going yet further along the path of our unfinished conversion. Against all the powers and dominions, it was a question of maintaining our hope that, despite everything, another world was possible.
>
> To designate this possibility, no other image came to us but that of the Angel. (*10*)

In the splendid isolation of their personal desert, two anchorites do battle with a multiplicity of demonic Sandmen whose message—"there is no new thing under the sun" (Ecclesiastes 1:9)—is a (reformist) assault on their hope for revolution as absolute renewal.[3] The surprising lesson they draw from the failure of their Maoist "conversion" is the need to persist ("going yet further") in that very endeavor whose irremediable loss they had previously wept. This means affirming duality against duplicity, opposing "oppression's eternalist arguments" (and especially the Hegelian fusion of the Two into One) through a form of "Manichaean provocation" derived from the Maoist dictum that "One divides into Two" (45). It means conceiving of history not as a dialectical play of contradictions—Marx's "Manichaeanism" is said to be "incomplete"—but as an eternal dual between the Master and a Rebel whose independence from that Master can be asserted only through the radically disincarnate figure of the Angel (33, 230). Jambet and Lardreau's insistence that "there are only two paths, each one loathsome to the other" implies, in other words, a radically antidialectical take on the Leninist model of history as epic struggle.

But the paradigm that Jambet and Lardreau go so far in asserting is also quite explicitly a paradigm in eclipse, no longer able to account for the failure of the political actions whose necessity it demonstrates ("as we tried to think it through . . ."). Their anchorites suffer accordingly from the absence of any principle of selection, any generalized belief system, that would allow them to "decide among" (*trancher dans*: literally, to "slice into") their demonic thoughts. More precisely, what they lack is the very basis of Marxist-Leninist rigor as we saw Althusser define it in the previous chapter—as the capacity "'*to cut a dividing line*' [*trancher*] between the true ideas and false ideas," as well as between "our class friends and our class enemies."

"The Angel" is Jambet and Lardreau's name for that which would fill this void:

> The Angel must come. . . .
> I see no other way to hold on to the hope of revolution. (36–37)

Unnamable or many-named, the Angel is strictly articulable only in negative metaphors, the object of a negative theology. Neither divinity, symbol, nor icon, it is rather a rigorously intangible principle of rebellion. Or, better, it is a "necessary illusion," modeled on the Maoist notion of the "masses," holding out to intellectuals in crisis the possibility of a revolt leading to "another world": "Here, it is only the requirement that intellectuals not delude themselves on the question of ethics. The masses don't need the Angel, for they are it. The Angel is a necessary illusion, whose purpose is to point out to those who speak rebellion's conditions of possibility" (79). Like all millenarian thinking, Jambet and Lardreau's is fundamentally nostalgic. More acutely than to the Christian heretics on which it tends to dwell, I would argue, their book casts a longing glance backward to the figure of the communist writer-militant in the golden age of the French leftist intellectual—an age that began in 1932, with the Komintern's mobilization of a wide spectrum of leftist writers and thinkers in the struggle against fascism, and ended in 1956 with the fracturing of the left in the wake of the invasion of Hungary (Ory and Sirinelli, 96).

L'Ange functions nostalgically, in other words, by recreating, in the guise of a modern Manichaeanism, a polarization whose prominence on the political landscape of twentieth-century France is traceable first to the application of a Leninist model of history to the struggle against fascism and later to a postwar reinvigoration of that model by a PCF glorified for its role in the Resistance. Just as the Angel functions as a golden lie allowing the Maoist intellectual to maintain his hope for revolution in the face of evidence that the Master invariably prevails, so does a radical dualism derived from Plato, Mao, and the Christian heretics serve phantasmatically to recreate the "lost paradise" of that bipolar political field that had come to be the natural habitat for intellectuals of the *après-guerre*.

In his preface to *For Marx*, Althusser writes of communist action in the era of the Stockholm Appeal (1950) and the (communist-led) Mouvement de la paix with a mixture of nostalgia for youthful enthusiasms and wariness at the violence that has been done to the Marxist movement by the practice of treating science as "merely the first-comer among ideologies":

> In our philosophical memory it remains the period of intellectuals in arms, hunting out error from all its hiding-places; of the philosophers we were, without writing of our own, but making politics out of all writing, and slicing [*tranchant*] the world with a single blade, arts, literatures, philosophies, sciences with the pitiless cut [*coupure*] of class—the period summoned up in caricature by a single phrase, a banner flapping in the void: "bourgeois science, proletarian science." (22; *12*)

Caught in the throes of their unhappy consciousness, attempting to reaffirm a dualism that they can experience only in the mode of separation or loss, Jambet and Lardreau never attain this complexity of tone. Their affirmation of duality can only be absolute, because they envision what is lost as the very precondition of the rebel's existence; "there must be Two worlds," Jambet writes, "for rebellion to have meaning" (*46*).

The Knave-Driver

It is here, in the face of a double breakdown of revolutionary hope and political bipolarity, that Jambet and Lardreau, our modern-day St. Michaels, enter into struggle with Jacques Lacan: "If the gadflies bother us, it is because they obscure the only true debate, that desperate, one-way debate we carry on in our heart of hearts with the only one who thinks today, the only one who never lies, Lacan, the knave-driver [*le chasse-canaille*]" (*12*). Lacan is the Angel's natural adversary to the extent that he questions the very possibility of revolution "in the most arduous and rigorous of terms" ("L'ange, entre Mao et Jésus," 57). I have shown (in Chapter 3) how Lacan works to undercut the mobilizing potential of the right/left polarity by arguing for a complex, chiastic doubling in the process of political collectivization; the foolery of collective knaves, he suggests, is matched only by the knavery of collective fools. In this respect, Lacanian "rigor" actively subverts its Leninist counterpart.[4] Moreover, on the question of a revolutionary hope that his own text will alternately conjure forth and conjure away, Lacan nonetheless insists on its properly suicidal effects:

> I just want you to know that more than once I've seen hope—what they call lyric tomorrows [*les lendemains qui chantent*]—drive people I've valued as much as I value you to kill themselves, period.
>
> And why not? Suicide is the only act that can succeed without misfiring. (*Television*, 43; *66–67*)[5]

But Lacan's position as the Angel's privileged interlocutor is fundamentally ambivalent. Theorist of those dialectical impasses by which the revolutionary project works to repetitive or recuperative effect, Lacan also lays the groundwork for the *cynégétique du semblant* (hunt after semblances) of *L'Ange*'s subtitle. It is to Lacan, in other words, that Jambet and Lardreau look for guidance in ferreting out those imaginary (and ideological) unifications, derived from the ego's penchant for conciliation and compromise, that serve to camouflage the Master's despotism by masking the fundamentally conflictual nature of history.[6]

But this means they must use Lacan against himself. For the Angel—defined in neo-Lacanian terms as "the only position left from which to hunt out the *semblant* on behalf of the rebel"—also represents a last-ditch attempt to avoid the reformist complicity inherent in the ostensibly "Freudian" quest for "the least evil of possible masters" (77, *51*): "[*L'Ange*] was written to open a breach, to push the logic of rebellion to its bitter end, its point of crisis [*jusqu'au bout, jusqu'à un paroxysme*], which Lacanian realism compelled us to do. An endeavor that was desperate [*désespéré*], in the etymological sense of that word" (*13*). Or, to speak in the language of Lardreau's introduction, the pursuit of an "ethics of revolt" means using Lacanian categories irreparably enmeshed in the "duplicity" of "Freudian" political realism so as paradoxically to affirm a revolutionary duality, the "two paths" of the age-old struggle of Master and Rebel (*51, 10*). Any eventual failure of this duplicitous strategy could only mean a resigned assimilation into the Freudian fold:

> I do not say that it is possible to pursue the discourse I am sketching out here. I only say I will do everything to do so, since I see no other answer. And if this doesn't take, I'll have to become a Freudian. In that case revolution would be impossible, at least such as we have understood it since the promises of the Cultural Revolution, and several of us will thus have lost our reason to think. (*34*)

In their efforts to salvage the revolutionary model, Jambet and Lardreau are brought to negotiate the most paradoxical of terrains. They seek to effect a Cultural Revolution, "an inversion of all values," while avoiding that inherently recuperable gesture of negation that Freud referred to as *Verneinung* (*87*). They espouse paranoid specularity, maintaining their absolute difference as Rebels from a "Master" defined as specular counterpart, while nonetheless refusing psychotic delirium on the Schreberian model ("we didn't want to let ourselves be Schreberized").[7] So as to salvage that "single blade" with which they might slice the world once again with a Leninist rigor, Jambet and Lardreau take the properly desperate step of risking the eternal wounds of Lacanian miscognition, even to the point of effecting a certain cut "upon" themselves.

There is, in fact, a castration drama running throughout *L'Ange*. Worked out largely in relation to the theoretical impasse structures of the Freudian fathers, this drama takes its impetus from the historical decline of the revolutionary model, as well as from a self-loathing to which Maoist doctrine tends to condemn the Maoist intellectual. In the face of those contradictions that had plagued their being as Maoist intellectuals in an apparently postrevolutionary age, Jambet and Lardreau respond by assuming (as it were) their own castration, running the risk of that self-directed violence that Lacan, after Hegel, attributed to the *belle âme*.

Unhappy Consciousness

The immediate focus of Jambet and Lardreau's critique in *L'Ange* is the "ideological" revolution, defined as the passage "from one mode of production to another, from the master to the master" (92). Against all those theories of revolution—be they orthodox Marxist or liberal-bourgeois—that insist on the germination of the new within the field of the old, Jambet and Lardreau posit an eternal rebellion, loosely modeled on the Chinese Cultural Revolution and animated by the desire to refuse mastery as such:[8] "In cultural revolution, mastery itself is at issue. It has no other 'material basis' than oppression *as such*; the very mechanism of its causation is captured entirely by the formula: 'Where there is oppression, there is resistance.' . . . Throughout all of history there runs a rebellion that refuses the Master" (92).

In his essay on Lin Biao, Lardreau speaks of his critique of ideological revolution as growing out of an already developed critique of the Marxist concept of production, a concept "which gave us a revolution just like all those other revolutions from which it inherited" (91). What he has in mind are works such as Baudrillard's *The Mirror of Production* (1973), where the Marxist fetishism of production is shown to mirror that of capitalism itself, or the recently rediscovered analyses of the *Socialisme ou Barbarie* group; a two-volume collection of Castoriadis's writings for that journal (*La société bureaucratique*) appeared in 1973, just two years prior to the composition of *L'Ange*. But Jambet and Lardreau's argument in fact recalls nothing so much as nineteenth-century anarchist theory, which had likewise tended to mobilize an absolutist understanding of power and a logic of revolutionary repetition in the service of a radically ahistorical, dualist vision of human experience as epic struggle.[9] Ironically, in other words, Jambet and Lardreau's fetishizing of the absolutely "new" places them on one of the best-trodden of revolutionary terrains.

I have argued that the most immediate experience of loss or separation behind Jambet and Lardreau's penchant for hearing the world with a "tragic ear" was the mid-1970s bankruptcy of the Marxist revolutionary model and the French left's corresponding drift into the political center. In Clément's formulation, however, the tragic ear was not the specific province of disillusioned revolutionaries in *l'après-Mai* so much as an attribute of the intellectual class as a whole. If an argument on this level of generality is defensible, it is so only in light of the specific history of the term "intellectual" in its contemporary nominative sense. For inasmuch as French usage still understands *l'intellectuel* restrictively—as one who employs abstract concepts such as truth, power, and justice within a logical and totalizing critique of the existing social order—it implicitly bears witness to the late nineteenth-century codification of the intellectual's role, not only around a series of Enlightenment values, but also within an artistic and political milieu for which anarchism was a dominant reference.[10]

It may well be, however, that the intellectual's mandate to the global critique of existent society (or, at its most extreme, of power itself) was nostalgic from the outset. I would suggest, without arguing the point here, that the seductive power exercised by the intellectual's aspiration to such a critique, and his corresponding taste for global solutions, developed in proportion to the *unavailability* of such solutions through developments in late industrial capitalism and bourgeois republicanism that effectively laid to rest the theological-monarchical model of power incarnate.[11] Such an analysis would help account for the "intellectual"'s particular susceptibility to the pathos of modernist "agonism," defined by Renato Poggioli as a taste for "sacrifice and consecration: a hyperbolic passion, a bow bent toward the impossible, a paradoxical and positive form of spiritual defeatism" (66). It would of course also account for a tragic ear eternally receptive to the seductions of an "impossible" that proposes itself "as such" (Clément).

More immediately useful to the examination of Jambet and Lardreau's particular brand of unhappy consciousness, however, is a third possible determinant of the intellectual's tragic ear—namely, an experience of the contradictions inherent in the subjectivity of the modern revolutionary intellectual as "intellectual." Jean-Paul Sartre explored these contradictions on several occasions, most notably in a series of lectures delivered in the fall of 1965 under the title "Plaidoyer pour les intellectuels" (In defense of intellectuals). In the first of his three talks, Sartre portrayed the modern "technician of practical knowledge" as a "potential intellectual," a virtual example of "what Hegel called 'Unhappy Consciousness' " (396). Torn between the universalist implications of his scientific method and his "surreptitiously particularist" ideology, between his commitment to a humanistic egalitarianism and the fact of his personal privilege, the technician of practical knowledge embodies that "single contradiction" that is the fact of bourgeois domination (*391–92*). He becomes an intellectual (that "monstrous product of monstrous societies") when he refuses the self-censorship or "mutilation" native to his condition as technician of practical knowledge, turning the technician's methods of rigorous inquiry to the specifically dialectical task of grasping his contradictions in society and society's contradictions in himself (*401–2, 397*). In so doing, the intellectual manages to transform that "contradictory being that has been allocated to him" into a "harmonious totality" (*401*). Sartre, like Hegel, thus plainly insists on the dialectical destination of the Unhappy Consciousness (*396*).

But for the revolutionary intellectual of the postwar era, the road to such an overcoming of inherent contradictions was paved with still other contradictions, other modalities of unhappy consciousness. In the second lecture of his "Plaidoyer," Sartre spoke of the intellectual who serves "the movement of popular universalization" as a "consciousness in tatters, impossible to sew up" (*422*). Traitor to the bourgeoisie, mistrusted by the popular classes "on account of the very culture he puts at their disposition," this "*bungled* product of the middle classes" is condemned to a process of perpetual self-criticism so as to combat his tendency to reproduce bourgeois ideology and petty-bourgeois sentimentality (*423, 404*). At the same time, moreover, he must live out a contradiction between his allegiance to the organizations of popular revolution and his mandate to defend the people's historical goals "*against all forms of power*—including the political power expressed by mass parties and the organizations of the working class" (*424*).

Sartre's "Plaidoyer" antedated both the Chinese Cultural Revolution and Sartre's own Maoist militancy. And yet, with its portrayal of the intellectual as a monstrous superfluity (*un homme de trop*) condemned to "perpetual self-criticism" if not to "martyrdom," the "Plaidoyer" plainly anticipated the unhappy consciousness of the Maoist intellectual. On the far side of a Cultural Revolution that had condemned its intellectuals as "freaks and monsters," as the "stinking ninth category" of Chinese society, Jambet and Lardreau speak of the Maoist intellectual as torn between knowledge and salvation, between the desire for knowledge as constitutive sin of "our eternally learned minds" and a desire to be assimilated into the masses (Link, 40; Holley, 5; *L'Ange, 132*). Indeed, they explicitly equate the Christian doctrine of original sin with Mao's insistence on an endless process of reeducation to combat the bourgeois tendencies inhabiting all subjects of the socialist state (*137*).[12] What he does not make explicit is an articulation between Maoism and the Lacanian ethic whose effects permeate *L'Ange* nonetheless. For it is precisely the Maoist tendency to portray the intellectual as emblematic repository of counter-revolutionary values, as the locus of a perpetual struggle against an always already criminal desire, that explains the Maoist intellectual's seemingly irresistible attraction to what Lacan called "Freudian ascetic experience"—that process of tragic purification whereby the conquering of one's own law means consenting to the malediction of one's race.

For Jambet and Lardreau, however, the intellectual is subject to a double curse. Bearer of the corrupting germs of the dominant culture, he is also condemned to play a specifically recuperative role, and this in at least two senses. First, he acts from a position of marginality that has proven highly suited to providing that dominant culture with the sort of reformist leverage it cannot attain on its own. If one grants Lardreau's absolutist definition of the "Master," it is all but inevitable that French Maoism and its successor movements would have served as "a point of leverage through which the master assures his own reform" (*152*).[13] Second, the intellectual's oppositionality is said to be shadowed by an "abject submission to Authority's thought" (*135*).[14] Looking back on the experience of a Cultural Revolution in which the intellectual's humility before the masses served as the simple alibi for submission to Chairman Mao himself, Lardreau concludes that

> in the end, Rebellion turns back entirely into Obedience. The sorry end to which monasticism leads the Rebel is such that, kneeling to his own bloodless shade, he recites the merits of submission. (As for the Rebel himself, one must imagine that he has already set out again elsewhere, and that, leaving this history through which he passed in all his fury, he has returned to his own history, where he does not cease to foment cultural revolution.) (*134*)

A History Without Desire

The figure of the Angel must be read as a response, itself curiously ambivalent, to the essential ambiguity of this portrait of a Rebel at once inevitably cowed into obedience and eternally escaping into the transcendent realm of "his own" history, where the spirit of Cultural Revolution lives on in an essential purity. On the one hand, the Angel is explicitly the product of what one might call a transcendental swerve. If sexuality and the ways of the flesh represent "the mode of being of the body as subject to sin, and thus to the Master," then the project of refusing Mastery as such, as Jambet and Lardreau reason by an "easy deduction," must imply a swerve outside the realm of sexuality: "Let us thus simply state that our Angel . . . is endowed with a body—that ethereal, luminous, spiritual body that the first Fathers bestowed upon it. . . . The Angel . . . is not an asexual being. Nor is it anything that can be marked by a sex. . . . Sexuality is not pertinent where the Angel is concerned" (*L'Ange, 36*; "L'Ange, entre Mao et Jésus," *55*).

On the other hand, this transcendental swerve is itself dictated by a self-conscious strategy of inversion, indeed precisely that sort of inversion whose repetitive (and hence strictly nontranscendent) effects Lacanians have detailed under the logic of *Verneinung*:

> Here is the only possible opening:
>
> One must do precisely the opposite [*le juste inverse*] of what the discourse of liberation suggests; one must totally sever sex from rebellion.
>
> One must postulate the following—that the perpetuation in Freud of that which is relates not to unhappy sexuality, but to sexuality in general. (*34*)

To understand why Jambet and Lardreau would risk embracing the essentially conservative logic of *Verneinung* so as to posit the Angel as a figure of revolt entirely independent of sexual predication—that is, as neither sexual nor asexual—we need turn briefly back to Lacan. When Lacan wrote, in *Television*, "that One occurs, perhaps, only through the experience of the (a)sexed [*l'(a)sexué*]," he made two related claims (40; *63*). First, he correlated the experience of the One, as an asymptotic approach to the limit of a mythical "universal fusion," to a notion of being derived through an operation of specifically linguistic subtraction, a form of symbolic castration mimicking the essential impossibility of sexual relations (*S* XX, *15*). The absolute "being" of traditional ontology, he had remarked two years earlier in the *Encore* seminar, "is only the fracturing, the breakage, the interruption of the phrase, 'sexed being' [*être sexué*], insofar as the sexed being has an interest in *jouissance*" (*S* XX, *16*). And second, through the parenthetical play of "the (a)sexed," he drew attention to the dual role of the woman as "not-all" (*pas-toute*) in the genesis of the mythic Oneness ascribed to the love relation: that is, the woman as barred "la" (the empty signifier driving the infinite play of language as phallic exchange) and the woman as *objet a* (bearer of the male's totalizing fantasy).

The point I would make here concerns the second of these claims, and specifically the role of the *objet a* in delimiting the *béance* that serves to evoke the totalizing fantasy. To the extent that Jambet and Lardreau aspire to a radical dualism, one should not be surprised to find them distinguishing, where Lacan in fact did not, between the "asexual" as bearer of a myth of universal fusion and an interruption of sexual predication that allows for duality ("Nor is [the Angel] anything that can be marked by a sex").

But their refusal of the "(a)sexual" is further determined, I would argue, by a specific denial of the analyst as the *objet a* incarnate. Behind Jambet's contention that the power the analyst derives from his essential abjection renders him the most dependable of relays to Hegelianism, seen (far too univocally) as a pure discourse of mastery, there is the fear that the analyst's embodiment of the object that falls from the Other serves the dangerous function of mimicking the *béance* or "not all" (*pas tout*) on which the rebel has traditionally founded his hope (*74–75*). Jambet invokes this second point while arguing that the liberationist's injunction to untrammeled bliss represents a capitulation to the *objet a*: "It is clear that the semblance of rebellion acts only on the authority of a preference for *jouissance*, that it submits to the (*objet a*)" (*76*).

Throughout *L'Ange*, however, one finds traces of the suspicion that the structural correspondence of revolutionary hope to transferential love threatens Jambet and Lardreau's own work as well. Most telling in this respect is their enthusiastic espousal of Pierre Legendre's conclusion that it is the Master's ability to inspire love that serves, in the Western tradition, to ground "an endless science of power" (*24*). In Lacan's analysis, as I have shown in Chapter 3, the rebel demands love from the Other in the form of a confirmation of his revolutionary hope. But the Other does not respond; indeed, as a narcissistic fiction, the Other cannot respond. In the face of this silence, the rebel submits to the *objet a* that falls from the Other, thereby setting into motion a recuperative mechanism that Jambet and Lardreau work out explicitly in their critique of Lyotard and Deleuze/Guattari. But it is fear of this mechanism that plainly underwrites their own transcendental swerve, which they conceive as "a supreme denial of the (a), from which we turn away in order to affirm rebellion." For "Lacan is not lying when he speaks of the lie as inevitable, and then hunts out the inevitable lie. Let us assert that it is possible not to lie, which presupposes that one add: outside desire, in another history" (*79*).

The Rebel as Beautiful Soul

This absolutist refusal of Lacan's conception of language as instrument of the lie that is human desire is but the last in a series of gestures suggesting that, as heralds of Cultural Revolution, Jambet and Lardreau come quite deliberately to assume the madness of the *belle âme*. *L'Ange* opens with the tale of a metaphorical flight from the actual world that plainly echoes Hegel's analysis of the beautiful soul's renunciative quest to preserve its essential purity.[15] More important, the act of conceiving the Angel appears to unfold in accordance with that play of the actual and the virtual that Lacan found in the workings of the *belle âme*.

To escape the actuality of the rebel as "bloodless shade," as an essentially submissive figure implicated in a process of historical evolution that relentlessly compromises the purity of all acts of rebellion, Jambet and Lardreau posit its virtual inversion—an unbowed, transcendent rebel fully at home in that "other history" where the eternal project of Cultural Revolution remains impervious to the recuperative mechanisms of actual history. In a passage that bears an ultimately deceptive resemblance to the first, critical moment of Derrida's "double gesture,"[16] Lardreau writes:

> Before conceiving itself as a "new culture" . . . the cultural revolution puts itself forth as an anti-culture, a deliberate and systematic inversion of all the values of this world. . . . Within this radical inversion, the image of madness necessarily comes to the fore. The very soul of the cultural revolution is the *belle âme*, as Lacan described it after Hegel. While the *belle âme* assumes what it knows to be its own madness in the eyes of this world, it knows too that, in truth, it is the other's wisdom, and this very world, that are themselves mad. (*87–88*)

Citing texts from the *Journal of Lei Feng* to the opening of Paul's First Epistle to the Corinthians, Lardreau argues that, if saintliness is but madness in the eyes of the world, then Cultural Revolution's injunction "to make oneself mad, to make oneself simple of mind" can only take the form of a "deliberate, systematic inversion" of worldly values (*135, 148, 155*). The voluntarism of this injunction to a mad simplicity is of course fully consonant with the (often excessive) faith in subjective determinants characteristic of Maoist doctrine; it is nonetheless absent from both the Lacanian and Hegelian accounts of the beautiful soul. It is significant in this regard that the "Hegel" whom Lardreau evokes as theorizing the saint's "willful madness" sounds like no one so much as Pascal, who wrote, "Men are so necessarily mad that it would be mad, by another twist of madness, not to be mad."[17]

I have argued that, for Lacan as for Hegel, the dramas of the heart and the beautiful soul lead necessarily to "dialectical impasses" when envisioned strictly from the perspective of those figures themselves. Pascal becomes useful for Jambet and Lardreau in helping to unlock such impasses, in authorizing a rewriting of the *belle âme* scenario in such a way that it is the rebel's lucid assumption of what the world deems mad, his assenting to a "senseless wager" on the eventual triumph of the heretofore always defeated Angel, that forms the basis of the rebel's own revolutionary hope (*152*).

According to the beautiful soul scenario inherent in the argument of *L'Ange*, what the revolutionary as *belle âme* fails to recognize in the disordered spectacle of a rebel eternally cowed into submission would be the manifestation of the actual submissiveness of his own disordered being (more on this in a moment). That which he takes to be the law of his heart would in turn be a virtual inversion of this disorder: here, the image of the Angel as transcendent Rebel.

Lacan's analysis goes on to speak of the *belle âme* as resorting to an act of self-victimization in order to break out of that circular bind whereby only an inversion of his actual disorder can promise escape from that disorder: "striking a blow at what he takes to be disorder, he strikes himself by means of a social counter-blow" (*Écrits, 172*). We find traces of this masochistic mechanism in the way *L'Ange* lingers over the dissevering of sex and rebellion in the Christian heretic's act of self-castration. After having claimed that sexuality is entirely irrelevant to the fully transcendent Angel, Jambet and Lardreau go on to speak of castration as that fine, razorlike line separating the orthodox monk, whose castration is merely symbolic, from the heretic saint (*100*). Thus of Origen's self-mutilation Lardreau writes, "Indeed there was something essential to early Christianity in these lunatic practices, something carried out in all rigor, and which makes Christianity of a piece with cultural revolution" (*105*).

Knowing what to make of this scenario that begins with the spectre of eternal obedience and ends in a fantasy of revolutionary self-castration supposes that we can locate that particular or actual experience of submissiveness that spurs the miscognitive mechanism into action. In the true psychotic, this experience would be the object of foreclosure. In Jambet and Lardreau, who would embrace psychosis tactically (hence voluntaristically), it becomes the matter of ample commentary.

What I have in mind are those pages, drenched in pathetic self-pity, in which Lardreau evokes the compunction of Maoist intellectuals torn between their thirst for knowledge and their desire to become one with the masses they serve. If the will to culture is the original sin of an intellectual still libidinally attached to his role as guardian to the "treasures of the past," then only deliberate "intellectual fasting," only the calculated desire for "a supreme amnesia," can guarantee the radical innocence required of Cultural Revolution as bearer of the absolutely new. While suffering under the demands of a faith that would ask him to trample on the *Timaeus*, the former *normalien* speaks of aspiring to the pure, infantile faith of the Red Guards and to a reading of *Capital* as crude and naive as that which the anthropomorphites had given the Bible (*132–34*): "We yearned for humility. The saint, with whose abject status as rubbish or muck the intellectual found himself more naturally in accord—*that* was what we were aiming for" (*133*). They would even have torched the Bibliothèque Nationale, Lardreau writes, "to suffer properly" (*133*).

In formulating the Maoist intellectual's drive to humility, Lardreau might appear to mimic an abjection that Lacan attributes to the analyst-saint in the role of the *objet (petit) a*.[18] But the abjection of the Maoist intellectual ultimately lacks the sort of calculated, dialectical effect on the desire of another that motivates the Lacanian analyst's incarnation of the *objet a*. The most immediate purpose of the Maoist intellectual's self-humiliation, like that of the Christian ascetic, is rather to call down the charity of a quasi-divine grace.[19] It is interesting, therefore, that Lardreau formulates this will to abjection as the intellectual's glorious assumption of a grievance that has traditionally stigmatized his kind as the scourge of humanity: "If they had had a more cultivated group of police, one would have seen raised against us the old reproach of *odium generis humani* [object of hatred to the human race]. . . . Therein lay our greatness, which many will never understand" (*134*).

In choosing to occupy "this necessary role of *héautontimoroumenos* [self-torturer] . . . within the cultural revolution," in other words, the Maoist intellectual plays the Lamb of God, taking upon himself a violence said to have plagued his fellow "intellectuals" since ancient times (Lardreau repeatedly uses the word "intellectual," anachronistically, to refer to the heretic saint).

It is here, with the image of the intellectual as expiatory self-tormentor, that we rejoin *L'Ange*'s exemplification of the *belle âme*:

> If the cultural revolution is first of all an anti-culture in the strictest sense, as an inversion of all values, then it is first carried out against those who support, transmit, and incarnate culture, who give it their body and blood —namely, intellectuals. If intellectuals are to make themselves heralds of the cultural revolution, they must burn themselves, since the fires of cultural revolution burn for everything of which they are made. (*131*)

The *belle âme* scenario played out in *L'Ange* begins, therefore, with the Maoist intellectual's submission to the contradictions of his status *as* Maoist intellectual, passes through an externalization of this actual submission (the eternally obedient Rebel) and the positing of its virtual counterimage (the Angel), and ends with the fantasized self-castration of the earthly rebel (Origen et al.).

Inasmuch as we can speak of the Maoist intellectual as himself submitting to a form of intellectual castration, this scenario folds relentlessly back on itself: in breaking the "circle" of virtual and actual rebellion, the masochistic violence of the heretic saint's self-castration ironically returns us to the actual experience of a Maoist intellectual *en contradiction perpétuelle.*[20] But since the Maoist and Freudian dramas so plainly double one another here, it also serves to revisit Jambet and Lardreau's experience of "Freud" as castrating father. Thus Jambet speaks of desperately reiterating their wager on another world, "but without being able to proceed beyond this sole proposition: 'The Angel must come.' A neutral subject [*sujet neutre*]: as soon as we try, uncritically, to develop its predicates, Freud [read "Lacan"] is there to reduce them to ashes" (70).

The Phallic Comedy

Paradoxically, this vicious circle of masochistic violence represents a break from Lacanian theory precisely to the extent that it theorizes the impossibility of breaking with Lacan as castrating father. It was Lacan's great originality to have driven a wedge between the real, biological father or his imaginary substitutes—all more or less "deficient," more or less impotent—and the Symbolic father or *Nom-du-Père.* Salvation, he argued, depends on the "exquisite character" of the son's love for the father—not for the real father; nor for the imaginary or ideal father, castrating or otherwise; but for the bodiless Father as pure signifier, a Father who is all the more radically present for being absence itself. In his various readings of Pascal's wager, most particularly in the 1968–69 *Séminaire XVI: D'un autre à l'Autre* (From an other to the Other), Lacan characterized this Symbolic father as "a rift that remains wide open in my discourse" and that can be known only through an act of faith since there is no "Other of the Other" to guarantee it (cited by Marini, 216; 225).

When Jambet and Lardreau speak of laying their bets on the radically disincarnate figure of the Angel, they would situate that figure in the very gap that is the *Nom-du-Père*. Yet they compromise the purity of their angelic signifier by inscribing it into the narcissistic self-aggression of a *belle âme* scenario acted out explicitly under the aegis of the imaginary father (be it Mao or Freud/Lacan). Their Angel is ostensibly the object of a pure faith, like that which motivates both the Pascalian and Lacanian wagers, but as a "necessary illusion" designed to salvage the Maoist intellectual's faith in revolution while veiling his fundamental self-division, its status is patently, indeed militantly, imaginary.

I would clarify this point by referring to a concept that, like so many others in Lacan, stands in a relation of variable equivalency to the ever-protean "phallus." What Lacan called the *signifiant-maître* (S_1 in the pseudo-scientific algorithms of Lacan's late work) is that signifier, predominant in the discourse of the master, that assures the unity of the barred subject's ($) "copulation" with the signifying chain (S_2) as locus of "a knowledge that does not know itself" (it is the very essence of the master, Lacan strenuously insisted, not to know what he wants) (*S* XX, *130*; *S* XVII, *34–35*). A signifier without a signified, a symbol of the very breakdown of meaning (and in these respects quite close to the phallus), the master-signifier is the incarnation of "the One" in language (*S* XX, *74*).[21] As such, it serves to establish a relationship between subjects—or in Lacan's jargon, "to represent a subject for all other signifiers" (*S* XVII, *101*).

The status of master-signifier is by no means a fixed one; all signifiers, Lacan insisted, are potentially master-signifiers. In the modern era, however, this status has been most plainly emblematized by a series of political shibboleths—"communism," "democracy," "freedom," "the people," etc.—that border on nonsense by virtue of their radical polyvalence. Insofar as the "copulation" of subject and knowledge instituted by such signifiers forms collectives modeled on that "little master" that is the *moi*, the function of the master-signifier—unlike the more radically ambivalent phallus—is largely imaginary (*S* XVII, *32*).[22] Or, more precisely, what the master-signifier emblematizes in the later Lacan is an imaginary potential inherent in the Symbolic itself.

Consider Lacan's algorithm for the discourse of the master, the first of those "four discourses" whose schemata he introduced in the *Envers de la psychanalyse* seminar (1969–70):

$$\frac{S_1}{\$} \rightarrow \frac{S_2}{a}$$

In one of many competing glosses he would give to this schema over the years, Lacan stated, "In sending itself forth toward those means of *jouissance* [the *objet a* as *plus-de-jouir*] called knowledge [S_2], the master-signifier [S_1] not only induces, but also determines, castration [the bar of S]" (*S* XVII, *101*; terms added). As *L'Ange* suggests, such a castration is by and large imaginary, easily reducible to the castrating gesture of the idealized father. Thus Lardreau plainly links the function of the Maoist "masses" as master-signifier to that recuperative dynamic whereby revolt is transmuted into submission to the father as ego ideal:

> Because, for us, the Masses had always been but a pure signifier, the master-signifier, we rediscovered in the depths of our own humility an obedience to their place-holders [*tenant-lieu*], in whom we too found our religious superiors [*nos abbas*]. (*136*)
>
> Always *named*, [the masses] are only a pure signifier, precisely identical to the name of the Chairman. Thus, to fight for the people, for communism, is to fight for Chairman Mao. (*150*)

By modeling the "Angel" on a master-signifier (the Maoist "masses") whose recuperative power they so evidently fear, Jambet and Lardreau effectively assure the perpetuation of that power. What forces them into this most desperate of binds is a specularity inherent in their definition of the Rebel himself. For their Rebel is nothing more than the specular double of an eternal Master, defined (tautologically) as that force that invariably channels cultural revolution into ideological revolution.[23] To question the inevitability of recuperation would thus be to question the very existence of the Rebel himself, which Jambet and Lardreau are plainly not prepared to do.

As a narrative of self-realization centered on the conflict between a Messianic hero and his demonic antagonist, *L'Ange* plainly aspires to the mode of romance (Frye, 186–87; White, 9). For what is at stake here is the possibility of transcending the self-divisions proper to the world of lived experience—the self-divisions specific to the Maoist intellectual, as well as those that haunt postlapsarian humanity as a whole. I have shown how, consistent with the law of the heart, the Angel represents the inversion of a disorder that plagues Jambet and Lardreau's being as desiring agents. Its purpose is to transcend sexual desire—said to be entirely of and for the Master, "du Maître"—while having done with that passage from master to master that is "ideological revolution" (*35, 91*).

Yet the Angel's effect—indeed, the raison d'être of its curious (non-) existence—is to maintain desire, specifically "our desire for the masses" ("L'ange, entre Mao et Jésus," *56*). And there is no shortage of anecdotal evidence to suggest that, for Jambet and Lardreau, it was precisely the will to have done with the passage from master to master that motivated their own repetition of that passage. Or, to put this another way, since "there is no love but that which is of the master [*du maître*, again in both senses]," it was their will to transcend their love for the master that ultimately provoked their frantic flight from old loves to new:[24] "If [Jambet] has jumped from Tel Quel to Derrida, then to Althusser, then to Lenin and Mao, then to Plato and a certain John of Ephesus, setting fire each time to that which he had worshipped three months earlier (I have seen him do it), this is because he is moved by a true passion for truth" (Philippe Némo, cited by

Aubral and Delcourt, *47–48*). The extraordinary passion with which Jambet and Lardreau throw themselves into the quest for truth suggests that they unwittingly subscribe to that belief for which they roundly chastise their liberationist adversaries—the belief that, on some level, "desire can overcome castration" (77).

This formulation of the repetitive effect of Jambet and Lardreau's project leads to yet another, which can serve here to anticipate issues addressed in Chapters 8 and 9. With their self-conscious reworking of Lacan's *belle âme* scenario, their grandiose and paranoid fantasy of a history traversed by the struggle against "the Master," and their desire to have the "last word" on the matter of revolution, the authors of *L'Ange* plainly aspire to a form of tactical psychosis. They do so, I would suggest, in an effort to foreclose a certain hysteria—specifically, a hysterical dependency on those fabrications of their own desire to know that are "Lacan" and "Mao" (*S* XVII, *36*).[25] It was Lacan's position, after all, that May '68 had represented a hysterical revolt, "a provocation intended to be refused" (Žižek, *Sublime Object*, 112). But the absolute demand inherent in Jambet and Lardreau's project is such that their refusal of hysterical dependency itself gives rise to a distinctively hysterical haste. "To a hysterical neurotic," Slavoj Žižek has written in another context, "the object procures *too little* enjoyment; à propos of every object, his experience is how 'this is not that,' which is why he hastens to reach, finally, the right object" (*Sublime Object*, 192).

In the end, however, the crucial question for any reading of *L'Ange* is perhaps not "Is there repetition here?" Jambet and Lardreau are themselves painfully aware of the "trap" of *Verneinung*, woefully conscious that theirs is a hopeless attempt to disprove the Lacanian axiom that "not to want to desire and to desire are the same thing" (*S* XI, 235; *213*). There is little to be gained, moreover, in showing that Jambet and Lardreau's critiques of their "enemies" rebound on themselves. For their fervid attempt to put forth a fundamentally dualistic and paranoid world-view leads them actively to embrace the sort of narcissistic specularity that Lacan spoke of as determining such transitivistic effects. What a reading of *L'Ange* might best demonstrate, rather, is how the various repetitions into which the book falls serve as a foil or countermodel to Lacan's tragicomic play with the impasses of human desire.

In the previous chapter I argued that Lacan's paradoxical ability to catalyze those same revolutionary aspirations he was so zealous in debunking derived from an essential double gesture. On the one hand, he advocated a tragic ethic whereby the analysand is brought to assume a "signifying cut" that the analyst as tragic hero appears to bear within himself. On the other hand, he was assiduous in producing "impasse-bound detourings" whose specifically comic function was to eternalize the analysand's thirst for knowledge (*S* XX, *16*).

I suggested, moreover, that this double gesture be linked to a duplicity inherent in the phallus as Lacan understood it. In his role as *objet a* (cause and aim of the other's desire), the cross-dressing analyst dons the luminous mantle of Antigone—sign of that phallic barring of a phallic signifier (the signifier of the *désir de la mère*) that serves to constitute all post-Oedipal subjects as the original "elision of a signifier." But insofar as the formulations of his seminar leave his listeners crying out for the "truth about truth," the analyst sets in motion a "flight" of "life" above the barriers constituted by phallic barring, a slippage signified by the phallus itself.

In their search for a romantic resolution of the impasses of revolutionary desire, Jambet and Lardreau do mimic (albeit literal-mindedly) the tragic heroine's assumption of phallic barring. In the process, however, they come to act out themselves that paradigm for comedy that Lacan put forth in the Ethics seminar:

> However little time I have thus far devoted to the comic here, you have been able to see that there, too, it is a question of the relationship between action and desire, and of the former's fundamental failure to catch up with the latter. . . . It is not so much the triumph of life as its flight, the fact that life slips away, runs off, escapes all those barriers that oppose it, including precisely those that are the most essential, those that are constituted by the agency of the signifier. (*S* VII, 313–14; 362)

The Lacanian lesson Jambet and Lardreau choose to ignore, in other words, is that the act of assuming the "signifying cut" is properly nonsensical when not linked to the production of textual detours that develop, and cause others to develop, the impasses of human desire. Lacan's tragicomic ethic cannot be separated from the didactic process within which his work so clearly (even necessarily) situates itself; the Lacanian analyst acts out the *objet a*, and causes others to cry out for truth, so that they in turn will act out the *objet a*, and cause still others to cry for truth.

In a fine analysis of how Lacan's late work effectively radicalized Lévi-Strauss's analogy between magical and mathematical symbols, Mikkel Borch-Jacobsen has argued that behind the "little letters" of Lacan's algorithms there lay "nothing less than a new 'scientific myth,'" whose purpose was to institute a new "Religion of the Symbolic" in our ostensibly postsacred societies (*Lacan*, 163). "Taken literally," Borch-Jacobsen writes, Lacan's project was ultimately that "of extension to society as a whole of that 'scientific delirium' psychoanalysis—an elegant solution to the problem of madness [the problem of the individual cure], since it amounted to dissolving that problem in the establishment of a society that was itself delirious (or, according to Freud, religious)" (166).

I would suggest that it was precisely insofar as Lacan managed to catalyze the transferential dynamic at the root of this mad imperial scheme that he was able to parry the specific madness of the *belle âme* (166). I have argued that there is an appeal to tactical psychosis in both the tautological circularity of Jambet and Lardreau's apology for the "Rebel" and the theoretical circularity through which Lacan sought to counter the vicious circles of ideological miscognition. Both projects, moreover, are radically (and self-consciously) "fictive" or "mythic." Yet only in the case of Lacanian theory was the very nature of modern community both programmatically and pragmatically put into play.

In the following chapter I turn to the cult of "writing" in French theoretical work of the early to mid-1970s. Without wanting fully to address the problematic of writing as it appears in Lacan's roguishly vatic *Encore* seminar, I would like to end the present chapter by quoting something he said in that context about the writing of "little letters."[26] Likening the *écrit* to that "piece of textual work that comes out of the spider's belly, his web," Lacan noted:

> It is a truly miraculous function: as surface itself emerges from an opaque point of this strange being, one sees the trace of these writings take form, in which one can grasp those limits, those points of impasse or dead-end, which show the real acceding to the symbolic.
>
> This is why I don't find it useless to have come to a writing of the *a*, the $, the signifier, the *A*, and the ϕ. (*S* XX, *86*)

The ostensible purpose of the *Encore* seminar was to interrogate a feminine *jouissance*, a *jouissance* of being itself, "beyond the phallus."[27] It is therefore curious that, at the very moment at which Lacan would seem to call into question a life's work of teaching on the ineluctability of the phallic signifier, he effectively resituated the phallic pivot of his tragicomic ethic within the gossamer tracery of a spider's web. If Malcolm Bowie is right (and I think he is) to see *jouissance* as the "central redeeming notion" of Lacan's late work, then it is specifically in the echoes of a spider's *jouissance* that one must hear both the inevitability of phallic return and the mad ambition of Lacanian community (*Lacan*, 156).

PART III

Conjuring the Impasse

CHAPTER 6

Third Terms: Barthes, Kristeva

By *subtle subversion* I mean, on the contrary, what is not directly concerned with destruction, evades the paradigm, and seeks some *other* term: a third term, which is not, however, a synthesizing term but an eccentric, extraordinary term.

— Roland Barthes, *The Pleasure of the Text*

Neither Right nor Left, but Ahead.

— Slogan of the Green Party (U.S.)

In that period of relative stability between the March 1962 armistice in Algeria and the events of May 1968, the institutional focus of French intellectual life underwent a significant shift. Rapid growth in enrollments on the university level—from fewer than 140,000 students in 1950 to 570,000 in 1967—led to a marked increase in the professoriate. The new (and more overtly academic) discourses of the *sciences humaines* came to replace philosophy and literature as the vehicles of choice for intellectual interventions; Lévi-Strauss, Foucault, and Barthes (all future members of the Collège de France) appeared to have sent Sartre into a definitive eclipse. Readers learned of a new "structuralist" methodology not in literary reviews—whose cultural predominance had dated back to the early days of the *Nouvelle revue française* (*NRF*)—so much as in the pages of the increasingly popular newsweeklies (*L'Express, Le Nouvel Observateur*). In short, the magnetic centers of the French intelligentsia shifted away from the literary review, and the figures of editor and *littérateur*, and toward the twin poles of the university (universités, grandes écoles, C.N.R.S. [Centre national de la recherche scientifique]) and the mass media.[1]

But at the very moment in which these sociocultural developments conspired to rob the work of writing of its long-held status as "sacralizing mark of the intellectual" (Foucault), there emerged a series of theoretical paeans to *écriture*, and they emerged precisely among those "structuralists" and (soon to be) "post-structuralists" whose rise to preeminence had signaled the decline of the novelist (or novelist-philosopher). With a fine sense of historical irony (and indeed with no less self-irony), Foucault would speak in 1977 of this "relentless theorization of writing," typified by certain passages of his own *The Order of Things* (1966), as "doubtless only a swansong" for the political privilege theretofore enjoyed by the writer as intellectual figurehead (*Power/Knowledge*, 127).[2]

It would be a mistake, however, simply to dismiss the theorizations of *écriture* as mere exercises in nostalgia. For they allow us to register a significant double development—one that is directly attributable, I suspect, to the increasing integration of the intellectual within the pedagogical and ideological structures of Fifth Republic France. On the one hand, largely through their insistence upon the inescapability of the power relations inscribed in (and transmitted by) language, the ideologies of writing typically reinforced the assumption that effective oppositional practice presupposes a "fatal complicity"—the expression is Derrida's—with the systems and structures to be dismantled.[3] On the other hand, and indeed *often in the same texts*, writing served as the vehicle for a compensatory utopianism, for the dream of voyages *ailleurs* (elsewhere), to utopian (or, as Barthes would say, "atopian") spaces. It is precisely this constitutive tension between the quest for a writerly elsewhere and the recognition of a necessary complicity that I track in the present chapter's readings of texts by Roland Barthes and Julia Kristeva.

Neither / Nor / But

It will have been apparent from the discussion in Chapter 2 that the logics of recuperation, specular doubling, structural repetition, and the like share a common tripartite structure. Each typically begins with the uncovering of a pseudo-opposition between the principles or structures of the established social order and an oppositional force whose action is found to be deeply complicitous with those principles or structures (repeating them and/or being recuperated by them). The back-to-back dismissal (*renvoi dos à dos*) of the parties to this pseudo-opposition then serves as a pretext for articulating a "third way" or "third term" whereby the political is displaced and a certain force of oppositionality recovered. Taken as a class, in other words, the logics of failed revolt commonly give rise to argument in the mode of the neither/nor/but—neither the Gaullist establishment, nor its Communist pseudo-rivals (the PCF and CGT), suggests Lefort, but May's authentic revolutionism; neither the anticommunist stereotypes of bourgeois economism, echoes the manifesto of *Tel Quel*'s June 1971 movement, nor the "dogmatico-revisionism" of the PCF ("the best of all possible repressive repetitions"), but a true "proletarian cultural revolution" animated by "Mao Zedong Thought" ("Déclaration," *134*).

The history of this neither/nor/but schema is of course deeply intertwined with that of a specifically modern tendency to polarize the political sphere. In past moments of intense bipolar pressure (during the Dreyfus Affair, the Popular Front, or the Cold War, for example), the schema could be found playing both sides of the bipolar divide. In their 1938 "Manifesto: Towards a Free Revolutionary Art," for instance, André Breton and Diego Rivera (with help from Trotsky) spoke of "the currently fashionable catchword: 'Neither fascism nor communism!' " as a "shibboleth" to those who would cling to "the tattered remnants of the 'democratic' past" (117). And yet from 1932 to 1939, the communist movement as a whole won widespread support among French intellectuals precisely by dismissing back to back the crisis-stricken principle of liberal democracy and the rising tides of fascism. Trotsky himself would complete the logic, in *The Struggle Against Fascism in Germany*, by analyzing fascism as the expression of the tendencies toward totalitarian organization contained within monopoly capitalism.

But if the neither/nor/but schema has frequently worked to solidify existing partisan polarities, it has just as often served to call such polarities into question—by recasting the bipolar struggle, by laying the groundwork for a consensual centrism, or by rationalizing a large-scale retreat from the political.[4] Rarely distinct, yet never exactly equivalent, the impulses to centrism and to political disengagement were in fact closely allied in the cultural climate of late-1970s France, marked as it was by a widespread disenchantment with the political legacy of May '68, by a corresponding return to liberal values (as evidenced by the rediscovery of Tocqueville and the rehabilitation of Raymond Aron), and by a creeping sense of moral and intellectual vacuity reflected in such titles as *Le Comble du vide* (The height of vacuity), a special number of *Critique* (1979), and *L'ère du vide* (The vacuous era) by Gilles Lipovetsky (1982). Few gestures were in fact more characteristic of the period than the back-to-back dismissal. Thus, as Pascal Ory notes, "Songwriters, always good indices of the general tone of public opinion, tried to outdo one another with back-to-back dismissals (François Béranger, *Magouille(s) Blues*; Herbert Pagini, *Ni Marx ni Jésus*; Michel Sardou, *Je vous accuse*; Henri Tachan, *Ni droite ni gauche*; and all of Renaud's work)" (*L'entre-deux-Mai, 233*).

In his provocative analysis of the "new mediocracy" (*nouvelle médiocratie*), Régis Debray has linked the back-to-back dismissal of left and right, the refusal of a Manichaean world-view, to the domestication of intellectual life by capital. At the root of the modern mass media's tendency to reduce all distinctions between truth and falsehood to a simple difference among equally admissible (and hence worthless) points of view, Debray finds the specifically economic imperative to maximize one's audience. "A mediocrat is overjoyed," Debray writes, "when he can dismiss the left and the right back to back: this is his guarantee, certifying that he is on the path not only of human nature and of sound reason, but also of maximum profitability" (*Teachers*, 93; *110*).

Debray's critique is a powerful one, particularly when applied to the highly theatricalized pseudo-debates engineered around the New Philosophers. But to attribute the extraordinary prominence of the neither/nor/but model in theoretical work of *l'après-Mai* solely, or even principally, to the growing mediatization of French intellectual life is to risk closing off the sort of productive inquiry that might uncover its radical overdetermination.

I would argue, in fact, that we need first understand this prominence in the context of a specifically twentieth-century quest for an independent, leftist third way—a quest to revive an authentic oppositional alternative to established, bipolar rivals. Seen from the perspective of post-May theory, the major players of this third way tradition include, in the 1930s, the so-called nonconformists (especially Bataille and the *Contre-Attaque* group); in the 1950s, Sartre (and the short-lived Rassemblement Démocratique Révolutionnaire), the leading authors of *Socialisme ou Barbarie* and *Arguments* (Castoriadis, Lefort, Morin, Lefebvre, Axelos, et al.)—indeed, the *nouvelle gauche* as a whole; and, in the 1960s and beyond, the *gauchiste* leaders of May '68, various Maoist factions, and the Eurocommunist movement.[5] (As late as 1981 the Italian Communist Party would signal its break with Moscow over the suppression of the Polish labor union Solidarnösc by announcing the opening up of a *terza via*).

To gauge the extent to which the neither/nor/but structures of post-May theory might be said to draw on this specifically leftist tradition, consider the work of Roland Barthes. Even in his early, neo-Sartrean period Barthes suffered from a visceral aversion to the rampant stereotypy of political language. Yet one of his most pronounced argumentative tics—his tendency to construct "mechanical" oppositions in the interest of what he variously calls a "third form" or "third term"—was itself quite patently a political stereotype. In a 1973 essay on Sollers's *H*, Barthes speaks of the novel as putting the Sentence on trial, both for an inherent religiosity and for complicity in the "tyranny of the signified":

> And yet what is substituted for the Sentence is not its mechanical opposite, a babbling or a jumbling up of words [*le babil, la bouillie*]. A third form is making its appearance, keeping the powers of seduction which the sentence has in language, but avoiding the way it cuts up and closes down [*sa découpe, sa clôture*]—that is to say, in short, *its power of representation.* (*Writer Sollers*, 80; *62–63*)

The full genealogy of this ritual quest for a "third form" in Barthes would need to account for his (often unspoken) dialogue with Sartre—especially in *Writing Degree Zero*—for his part in propagating *Tel Quel*'s reading of Bataille, and for his role in the founding in 1956 (with Edgar Morin and Konrad Axelos, among others) of a review, *Arguments*, whose mandate was precisely to elaborate a post-Stalinist critique of capitalist society.

I would argue that the political overtones in Barthes's 1973 account of a "third form" that would break with the seductive, but ultimately confining Sentence—and by extension with the project of representation—derive from his earlier tendency to equate Stalinism with the closure of a specifically axiological "definition" whereby facts are always already values and descriptions always already judgments. Or as he wrote in the 1953 *Writing Degree Zero*:

> In the Stalinist world, in which *definition*, that is to say, the separation between Good and Evil, becomes the sole content of all language, there are no more words without values attached to them, so that finally the function of writing is to cut out one stage in the process: there is no more lapse of time between naming and judging, and the closed character of language is perfected, since in the last analysis it is value that is given as explanation of another value. (24; *21*)

In several crucial respects, however, third way thinking in the period defined by the events of May '68 would part company with that of previous generations. In the generation of Sartre and Castoriadis, for instance, the third term scenario habitually served to designate a position to be constructed. It justified as necessary the solution of definite social or political dilemmas in the light of a precise historical situation. Thus Sartre would find the catalyst to the unveiling of an (essentially historical) "third term" in the act of choice attendant to human practice in the world. "An outcome is invented," he writes in *What Is Literature?*, "And each one, by inventing his own outcome [*issue*; also "way out"], invents himself. Man must be invented each day. . . . The historical agent is almost always the man who in the face of a dilemma suddenly causes a third term to appear, one which up to that time had been invisible" (235–36; *290–92*).

For Sartre the writer's commitment begins with the impossibility of choosing between the bourgeoisie and the Communist Party, with a double refusal to prepare for war with either the Soviet or the Anglo-Saxon bloc (*263–64*). The heretofore invisible third term that this commitment serves to uncover is socialist democracy, conceived in *What Is Literature?* as the objective, concrete realization of the Kantian "City of Ends": "that chorus of good wills . . . which thousands of readers all over the world who do not know each other are, at every moment, helping to maintain" (218–19; *268*).

We can certainly quarrel with Sartre's faith in literature's eventual capacity to transform the individual reader's aesthetic intuition of belonging to a community of fellow readers, each exercising an essential liberty, into the specific will to take concrete action toward the reshaping of society on just such a model (222; *273*). We can be suspicious, moreover, when he argues that the separatist tendency apparently inherent to the act of reading can be overcome without resacralizing reading as a form of "mystical communion" (a style of reading characteristic, Sartre notes, of churches and parties) (221; *271*). There is, one might say, a healthy dose of the utopian in the central political argument of *What Is Literature?* But there is nothing particularly escapist about this utopianism; the project Sartre announces through the neither/nor/but model may be impossible per se—the more directly political commitment of his later years certainly implies as much—but it is just that, a project.

In the work of a Sartre, therefore, the utopian moment of the third term scenario serves to revive a genuine political option (in this case, socialist democracy) in the face of a pseudo-dilemma such as that offered by the rivals of the Cold War. An analogous will to reaffirm meaningful political choice motivates Castoriadis's early essay, "The Problem of the USSR and the Possibility of a Third Historical Solution" (1947). In an interesting permutation on the commonplace tripartite structure I have uncovered thus far, Castoriadis's essay begins with the recognition of Stalinism as a "third historical solution, beyond the dilemma of capitalism or socialism." Insofar, however, as the "historical meaning" of this putative solution "would be that of a fall into an unprecedented modern barbarism," its positing allows Castoriadis ultimately to reaffirm Trotsky's "Socialism or Barbarism?" dilemma, to argue that the "socialist solution" remains "the only progressive [one]" because "choos[ing] between bureaucratic barbarism [i.e., Stalinism] and ultraimperialist barbarism [capitalism] has no meaning for us." The existence of a historical solution corresponding to "the proletariat's potential revolutionary bankruptcy" serves to demonstrate "that socialism is neither fated nor inevitable." It is rather "simply possible," and as such an incitement to "revolutionary action itself" (*Writings*, 1: 50, 1: 45–46).

Where the "third term" scenarios of Sartre and Castoriadis had sought to recenter political practice, those of *l'après-Mai* were often, as Barthes put it, self-consciously "eccentric" (read "ex-centric" [*excentrique*]).[6] In the work of Cixous and the late Barthes, for instance, the neither/nor/but scenario is predicated on the need to escape a vicious circularity said to plague *all action* in the pre-existing space of the political (at a time, ironically, when the bipolar nature of that space was far less evident than it had been for Sartre's generation). Indeed, where the third term had once named a project, it increasingly named a destination, an "elsewhere" or "non-place" (Lefort) that was too disembodied to serve as a surrogate homeland (as the Soviet Union had done for two generations of Western Marxists), and yet still somehow home to the "revolutionary" idea. Where it had once issued an invitation to the overcoming of a practical aporia through recognition of socialism's possibility, it now issued an *invitation au voyage*. But, here again, it is writing that was both the agent of this displacement and its ultimate beneficiary.

Invitations au voyage

> Life is elsewhere.
> — Wall slogan, May '68

> It is a singular land, a land of milk and honey as they say, that I dream of visiting with an old friend. A singular land, drowned in the mists of our North, and which could be called the Orient of the West, the China of Europe, so freely has warm, capricious fantasy acted on it.
> — Charles Baudelaire, "L'invitation au voyage"

To open up the question of writing's capacity to provoke the revolutionary excursion, I would turn to another essay Barthes devoted to the work of Philippe Sollers, a review of *Logiques* and *Nombres* entitled "The Refusal to Inherit." First published in the *Nouvel Observateur* on April 30, 1968, just four days before the police touched off the events of May by entering the Sorbonne to evict the assembled militants, this essay begins, ironically, "The revolutionary idea is dead in the West. From now on, it is *somewhere else* [*ailleurs*]. For a writer, however, the political whereabouts of this *somewhere else* (Cuba, China) matter less than its form" (*Writer Sollers*, 69; *47*).

Sollers's work, Barthes continues, situates itself in that "*far distance* of the revolution" occasioned by the "dispossession" of the West, the ouster of the Western subject from its position of imperialist centrality. To the "structuralist" critique of the Cartesian subject, in other words, Sollers would join a specifically writerly *tiers-mondisme* (Third-Worldism). The "migration" onto new forms of revolutionary writing retraces (albeit always with a certain formalist detachment) that prior exiling of revolutionary aspirations away from the collaborationist reformism of the PCF and CGT, and towards the ostensibly purer revolutionism of Third World liberation struggles, in which the proletariat was seen as remaining faithful to its traditionally "redemptive" role (Ory and Sirinelli, *211*).

The "refusal to inherit" of Barthes's title refers to Sollers's obligation to unwrite—or, better, to rewrite "in a contradictory, 'scandalous' manner"—both the political language of the leftist "fathers," "absorbed for the last twenty years by the anti-Stalinist struggle," and "the traditional anti-formalism of Communist intellectuals" (70; *48*).[7] "Annulling" the two terms of this Western impasse "one by the other," Sollers pursues the impossible project of inheriting "the uninheritable," by which Barthes means the intertextual practice of writing, especially when that writing incorporates Chinese ideograms, as Sollers's does in *Nombres* (70; *49*).[8] "Immediately," Barthes writes, "another language then appears possible, one which is revolutionarily justified"; the back-to-back dismissal of two positions said to share "the same blithe lack of interest in the responsibility of forms" thus serves to justify the revolutionary decentering of writing's representational project through a reconception of the real as "a continuous flow of different kinds of writing stretching out to infinity" (70–71; *49, 51*).

The monumental irony of this argument lies in the way it dismisses the "political language" of the anti-Stalinist "fathers" while massively appropriating that neither/nor/but model that was their most characteristic argumentative form. Barthes then goes on to deploy a specifically structuralist variant of that logic of structural repetition that "fathers" such as Castoriadis had (in this respect, quite unwittingly) helped popularize. "What is the point of copying the real," he asks, "even from a revolutionary point of view, since that would be to have recourse to the essence of bourgeois language, which is, above all else, a language which copies?" (*Writer Sollers*, 73–74; *53*).

Barthes's response to this repetitive dilemma arising from the unifying closure of linguistic representation underscores his (and indeed his generation's) Oedipal break.[9] Writing, he argues, is the privileged expression of a revolutionism of "the final difference, *the difference which has no resemblance*":

> What can pass from the revolution into literature is subversion, is a fire (the image with which *Nombres* opens) or, if you prefer to speak in specific, positive terms, what can make this move is *plurality* (different forms of writing, quotations, numbers, masses, mutations). What Sollers represents, as a continuation and a beginning at one and the same time, is this way out of the West's narcissistic game, the arrival of an absolute difference—which politics will certainly take it upon itself to present to the Western writer, unless he makes the first move. (*Writer Sollers*, 74; *53–54*).

On the one hand, Sollers's work marks a "continuation" in that, like Lefort's, it would recapture an authentic spirit of revolution by escaping the narcissistic specularity that pits organized communisms against their capitalist doubles, and against one another. On the other hand, it marks a new "beginning" by conceiving of revolution as "the arrival of an absolute difference"; the puzzling slippage in Barthes's first sentence from revolution to incendiary riot and a "positive" plurality measures the breadth of this displacement. While this uncanny return of an (eminently Western) sense of the "plural" does indeed signal a break from the leftist fathers, it also reminds us that (as Barthes well knew) any radical migration in the quest for a nonnarcissistic other must ultimately entail a retrieving of the same otherwise.[10]

This gesture of using the repetitive "aporia" of traditional revolutionary strategies as pretext to the call for a "plural solution" recurs frequently in Barthes's work of the 1970s. In the essay "Over Your Shoulder" (1973), for example, he speaks of Sollers's *H* as "scour[ing] almost all languages clean":

> The aporia, the logical contradiction, which it avoids is that normally, in order to scour, you need a scouring language, which in its turn becomes a

new coat of paint. Hence the plural solution: using the cracks of language to produce on the wall (the screen, the page) of representation, a number of multiple stains, bizarre sketches, cracking (is it not said that Chinese writing was born of the cracks appearing on tortoise shells which had been heated white-hot?). (*Writer Sollers*, 76–77; *57*).

Likewise, in his inaugural address to the Collège de France, Barthes will muse, "If I were a legislator (an aberrant supposition for someone who, etymologically speaking, is an an-archist, far from imposing a unification of French, whether bourgeois or popular, I would instead encourage the simultaneous apprenticeship to several French forms of speech, of various function, promoted to equality" ("Inaugural Lecture," 466; *24*).

We want neither a unified bourgeois language, Barthes implies, nor its proletarian double (which by the very fact of its unification, and thus its grounding in a principle of power [*arkhè*], could only be the negation of bourgeois language). What we need rather is a third term outside this structural repetition—or, better, since any particular third term is destined to be recuperated in time, a new textual *economy* outside the commercial logics of exchange and substitution, an economy that would thwart the coercive subjection inherent to language (to nomination, representation, and linguistic propriety) through the radical plurality of its constituent elements.[11] What we require, as Barthes had written in *S/Z*, is a disseminative textuality that would disperse all criticism, all metalanguage, all centered meaning, "within the field of infinite difference," a productive, nonrepresentational textuality to open up "a circularity in which no one (not even the author) has an advantage over anyone else [*n'a barre sur personne*]" (5, 98; *11, 105*).[12]

In one of his *Mythologies* (1957), Barthes had dismissed that very "neither-norism" (*ninisme*) by which *S/Z* sets the stage for a "triumphant" plurality as "on the whole a bourgeois figure, for it relates to a modern form of liberalism" (153; *241*). In *S/Z*, however, he claims that the "triumphant plural" of a textuality "unimpoverished by any constraint of representation" requires a mode of interpretation that is "in no way liberal" (5–6; *11–12*). While I would reject (for reasons outlined above) the early Barthes's reading of "neither-norism" as "on the whole" a trope of modern liberalism, I would also contest his absolute refusal of the liberal moniker for the theory of textuality worked out in *S/Z*.[13] It is surely the case that Barthes's work in that text calls into question several of the concepts most central to classical liberalism—the individual (and by extension the novelistic character as "a moral freedom endowed with motives and an overdetermination of meanings"), responsibility (specifically authorial responsibility), representation, and property/propriety (94; *110*). Moreover, his work as a whole mounts a sustained attack on the very notion upon which the liberal order is founded: the notion of consensual thinking.[14]

But in moving away from the individual as liberal monad, Barthes moves interpretation toward what might be called a "postliberal" textuality—an essentially plural textuality that is productive by virtue of its capacity to enact, or invite, an infinite play of interpretive desire.[15] The thrust of Barthes's work in *S/Z* is to displace the "representative model" of reading, grounded in the metaphoric act of "legal substitution," in favor of an essentially metonymic "step by step method . . . whose very gradualness would guarantee what is productive in the classic text" (12, 216; *19, 221*). By opening up the plurality of the classic text, multiplying its points of entry and its "zones of reading"; by insisting that "the meaning of the text can be nothing but the plurality of its systems, its infinite (circular) 'transcribability' " (*S/Z*, 120; *126*); in short, by grounding his theory in the specifically metonymical play of critical desire, Barthes incorporates as it were that preeminent product of liberal "in-difference"—the modern academic institution—into his critical antisystem: "We shall not set forth the criticism of a text, or the criticism of *this* text; we shall propose the semantic substance . . . of several kinds of criticism (psychological, psychoanalytical, thematic, historical, structural); it will then be up to each kind of criticism (if it should so desire) to come into play, to make its voice heard, which is the hearing of one of the voices of the text" (*S/Z*, 14–15; *21*).

To dream of new (and specifically "productive") textual economies as an escape from the liberal-bourgeois economy of representation, to affirm plurality as an escape from narcissistic specularity, to go East to escape the West—these are decentering moves that run an inordinately high recuperative risk. Barthes's variable awareness of that risk, and his equally variable insistence upon parrying it theoretically, will be subjects of discussion in the final segment of this chapter. My path for the moment leads back to *le tiers-mondisme.*

The Other Mao

"What can be addressed, in the consideration of the Orient," Barthes writes in *The Empire of Signs*, "are not other symbols, another metaphysics, another wisdom (though the latter might appear thoroughly desirable); it is the possibility of a difference, of a mutation, of a revolution in the propriety of symbolic systems" (3–4; *10*). The intensity of this desire for a specifically symbolic revolution accounts in part for the binocular vision of Mao Zedong in and after May '68. Where groups like the UJCml and the Gauche prolétarienne saw in Mao the sole remaining champion of revolutionary practice, doctrinal purism, and Leninist party discipline, the literary Maoists (including the best-known members of the *Tel Quel* group) focused on Mao as the author of "On Contradiction" (with its insistence on the possible leading role of superstructural practice), as the apologue for modes of practice grounded in the immediate experience of "a subjectivity that has become the place of the 'highest contradiction' " (Kristeva), and above all, as the instigator of a Cultural Revolution that would long remain sufficiently enshrouded in mystery to be a blank screen for the projection of anarcho-libertarian fantasies.[16]

But this long-standing tendency to fetishize the antiauthoritarian and populist aspects of Maoist doctrine, and thus to look to the Cultural Revolution as a true antibureaucratic revolution, as "a hope for libertarian socialism," would ultimately prove untenable in the face of what Kristeva calls "the Cultural Revolution's fall back into a nationalist and socialist variant whose point of reference remains the land of the Soviets" ("Mémoire," *52*; cf. Hess, *105*). Her attempts, in the conclusion to *About Chinese Women* (1974), to salvage something of these fantasies from the reality of Chinese political life seen firsthand are nonetheless indicative of the mythopoeic pressure to which both Mao and Maoist doctrine were long subjected. Nothing could be easier (or more justified), Kristeva admits, than to see Mao as "a feudal lord," to see Chinese ideology as "a flat and restrictive positivism" or the Chinese Communist Party (CCP) as "an offshoot of dogmatism" (200; *227*). But by focusing on the Chinese family and the role of Chinese women as the bases of a social ethic, she continues,

> it can appear as if it were a question there of creating a society where power is active, but not symbolized by anyone: no one can appropriate it for himself if no one—not even women—can be excluded from it. . . . There would be no more *instance* of the Law in itself, if each individual, man and woman, took it upon himself to remake it by permanently confronting it with his/her practice, in his/her discussions with others. (201; *228*)

Looking back in 1983, however, on *Tel Quel*'s Maoist phase (1970–77, suggests Michel Condé), Kristeva would conclude: "Our Maoism was an antiorganizational, antipartisan antidote, an unadulterated utopia that had nothing to do with the parties of the left" (Condé, *22*; "Mémoire," *51*). She continues, "I believe I can say, however, that for the majority of those who made the voyage to Peking and back . . . this long and circuitous trip, which from the outset was more cultural than political, ultimately inaugurated a massive return to the only continent we had never left, that of inside experience [*l'expérience intérieure*]" ("Mémoire," *53*).

Significantly, this rediscovery of the dark continent of *l'expérience intérieure*, of a fascination with "our own strange, foreign, feminine, and psychotic side," did not signal an end to the age of theoretical grand tourism ("Mémoire," *52*). The impetus to "migration" as an instrument of cultural disorientation would by and large survive the effacement of its Third World referents, as indeed Barthes's insistence that the political locus of the "elsewhere" matters less than its form had suggested it should. Thus where Kristeva, Sollers, and company had once traveled to China in an effort to anticipate "this impossible phenomenon [*cet impossible*] that is attempting to assert itself in our society, and of which the avant-garde, women's struggles, and the battle for socialism are merely symptomatic on various levels," they would soon hop the plane to New York (*Polylogue*, 520–21).

"Why the United States?"

In French theory of *l'après-Mai*, I have argued, the absolutist formulations underlying the logics of revolution as repetition served a primarily *tactical* function: they defined an impasse (the contemporary neither/nor) as the pretext to a displacement, translation, or reinscription—the "migration" (in Barthes's words) toward an "ex-centric" third term. It was not uncommon, moreover, for the third term to name both a plural solution and a touristic destination. The journey or exile that disoriented ethnocentric meaning commonly entailed a heightened attention not so much to difference (an inexpugnable narcissism served to limit this), but to a programmatic multiplicity—of languages, styles, meanings, desires, political positions, erotic sites, and so on. One common species of third term scenario exhibited this double role with exemplary (albeit paradoxical) concision: that which looked to the United States as a privileged site of plural oppositionality.

As I noted in my Introduction, the early years of the post-May period were witness to the massive abandonment of a conception of politics centered around an organized party seeking to elucidate and totalize the world historical aspirations of an oppressed class. Political energies found their way henceforth into local struggles in the defense of "difference" (both public and private). This micropolitical shift would in turn play a crucial role in defusing an anti-Americanism that had long been characteristic of the French left. The specific enthusiasm of a Jean-Paul Sartre for American music (jazz, blues) or American novelists (Faulkner, Dos Passos) had never blunted, for instance, his deep hostility to the America of the arms race, "the plague Ridgway," and the Rosenberg trials.[17]

The 1970s, by contrast, saw the publication of works such as Edgar Morin's *Journal de Californie* (1970), promoting the conception of a "youthful cultural revolution," California style, whereby the dominance of the white, adult, First World heterosexual male would be dismantled "to the benefit of an open-ended pluralism in which young people, women, homosexuals, and Indians all proclaimed, within their very demands for equality, their difference and not their identity" (*Brèche*, 155). Régis Debray, no great admirer of either American oppositional culture or French micropolitics, would nevertheless write in 1978, "The MLF next to Woman's Lib, the FHAR next to the gay power movement, our communes next to California's, our Occitans beside the Chicanos, our 'marginal' press beside the Free-Press, Larzac next to Woodstock. . . . Fine copies no doubt, but the originals are still better" (*Modeste Contribution*, 49).

But it was only in the mid-1970s, at a time when economic malaise and internal dissensions (e.g., in the MLF) had combined to blunt micropolitical fervor in France, that American oppositional practice commonly found its way into the third position of the neither/nor/but scenario. In the passage that follows her likening of traditional class struggle to a repetitive volleyball game, for instance, Hélène Cixous links the very possibility of subversive action to an inevitable upheaval, already perceptible in the United States, in the ways in which the gendered individual gets produced as such:

> She foresees that her liberation will do more than modify power relations or send the ball over to the other side [*camp*]; she will bring about a mutation in human relations, in thought, in all praxis: hers is not simply a class struggle, which she carries forward into a much vaster movement. Not that in order to be a woman-in-struggle(s) you have to leave the class struggle or repudiate it; but you have to split it open, spread it out, push it forward, fill it with the fundamental struggle so as to prevent the class struggle, or any other struggle for the liberation of a class or a people, from operating as a form of repression, pretext for postponing the inevitable, the staggering alteration in power relations and in the production of individualities. This alteration is already upon us—in the United States, for example, where millions of old moles [*taupes*] are in the process of blowing up [*faire sauter*] the family and disintegrating the whole of American sociality. ("Laugh," 253; *45*)

We could certainly tax Cixous with naiveté (confident that we would not be the first). It would be easy, moreover, to construe the metaphorical slippage from "old mole" to landmine in her final sentence ("des millions de taupes sont en train de faire sauter") as an ideological alibi, to insist that the rhetoric of explosion serves as a compensatory myth whose purpose is to convey an aura of radicalism to what is patently a fall back into reformism. Or one could ask, as I shall have occasion to do in Chapter 8, how the rhetoric of the anarchist deed—Cixous's explosive texts demand to be read as such—might point to effective, strategic options within the so-called new mediocracy.

To better exemplify the complex issues at stake in this commonplace species of third term scenario, however, I would turn here to a long passage from "Why the United States?", the roundtable discussion between Kristeva, Sollers, and Marcelin Pleynet that introduces *Tel Quel*'s special number on the United States (73, *71*; Fall 1977). Kristeva opens the discussion by speaking of having crossed the Atlantic on three occasions, moved by the same "desire for discovery and a change of scene [*dépaysment*]" that had brought her from Bulgaria to Paris in late 1965:

> I also tried to experience such a change through my interest in China, which I viewed as an anarchist outbreak within Marxism. But the trip to China finally made me realize that this was a re-run, somewhat revised perhaps, of the same Stalinist or let's say Marxist-Stalinist model. It was therefore out of curiosity and the desire to discover some other solution to the impasse of the West that I flew off twice to the United States, and then finally a third time for a longer stay. . . .

> I seemed to perceive in the economic and political logic of America a new way of dealing with the Law [*la Loi*], with the increasingly brutal economic and political constraints which are inevitable in any society, and all the more so in a technocratic system. The question is to know "how to deal with" this economic and political constraint. In both Western and Eastern Europe, our way of doing things, inherited perhaps from a certain religious and state tradition, consists of "dealing with" a constraint by confronting it with its antithesis. But as everyone knows [*comme chacun le sait*], to invert Spinoza's phrase, every negation is a definition. An "opposing" position is therefore determined by that to which it is opposed. And in this way we arrive at two antithetical systems which introject one another and reflect each other's properties [*qui s'intériorisent réciproquement et se renvoient les qualités*]: on the one hand, a government, the conservative and established System; on the other hand, an opposition that ultimately has the same statist, collectivist and totalitarian flaws. All this has culminated in those twentieth-century dramas that are Fascism and Stalinism, which, like an eternal couple, can send the elevators back and forth to one another for evermore [*qui peuvent se renvoyer les ascenseurs à n'en plus finir, comme un couple éternel*].
>
> In America, though, it seems to me that opposition to constraint is not unique, isolated and centralized, but is *polyvalent* in a way that undermines the law [*effrite la loi*] without attacking it head on.
>
> It can be said that this polyvalence, that is, the multiplicity of social, ethnic, cultural and sexual groups, of various forms of discourse . . . ends up by "ghettoizing" the opposition, since for each opposition an enclave is created where it stagnates. . . . But there is also a positive aspect, which is precisely that it avoids the paranoiazation of the system, the confrontation [*face à face*] of two laws, each equally sure of itself but fascinated by, and internalizing the other. ("Why?" 273–74; *3–4*)

For my purposes, the founding moment of this argument comes when Kristeva appeals to an ostensibly common body of knowledge and experience ("as everyone knows") to ground her claim that "every negation is a definition."[18] The lines that follow develop a logic of specular doubling whereby those "two antithetical systems" that are bourgeois capitalism and Stalinist communism constitute themselves, as individual rivals had for Lacan, through a process of mutual introjection ("which introject one another and reflect each other's properties"). It is the image of a specular bind created by the paranoid *face à face* of two laws sharing the same "statist, collectivist and totalitarian flaws" that serves rhetorically to set up that apology for the polyvalence of American oppositional practice to which the argument tends.

Once again, in other words, absolutist formulations serve to define a logical bind as the pretext to a displacement that is also a "migration." Kristeva's talk of Stalinism and Fascism as an "eternal couple" suggests that the logic of repetition, as a logic, is only conceivable outside history. Any historical or institutional contextualization would undo the imaginary stasis on which the reciprocally defining oppositional couple is predicated. Such an inherent antipathy to historical contextualization should tip us off to the logic's function as an ideological pretext.

Likewise, our perception of the specifically constructed nature of Kristeva's "impasse of the West" is heightened by a rhetorical slippage from "the Law" ("la Loi") to "the law" ("une polyvalence qui effrite la loi"). The idealistic residues of "the Law" work to solidify the argument *as a logic*, but must then be conjured away to allow for a displacement of the paranoid impasse. Inversely, the resistance that the relative, and hence essentially contextual, notion of "the law" must put up to the formulation of any logic of failed revolt demands that such a notion be occulted until such time as the logic itself has fulfilled its tactical purpose. Kristeva's argument works, in other words, by avowing *and* disavowing the ineluctable nature of "the Law"—not fetishistically (for fetishism implies a true splitting of the subject), but rather as a deliberate ideological ruse.

But the most crucial argumentative slippage in this particular neither/nor/but scenario occurs when the structural repetition pertaining between the bourgeois, capitalist "System" and its communist counterparts gives way to the well-oiled routine of fascism and Stalinism, sending the elevators back and forth "like an eternal couple." A certain margin of American capitalist society thus finds its way outside that society's habitual place in the first position of the neither/nor/but structure, and into the privileged third.

The three years that separate *Revolution in Poetic Language* (1974) from "Why the United States?" (1977), it has often been noted, mark a major shift in the explicit focus of Kristeva's work. Where she had once sought to open up semiotics to the revolutionary "materialism" of avant-garde literary practice, she came increasingly to address specific problems of femininity and motherhood in conjunction with "the psychoanalytic adventure" (she became a mother in 1976, a practicing analyst in 1979) ("Mémoire," 53). Simply put, her texts of the late 1970s speak of "dissidence" and "ethics" where those of 1972–74 had spoken of "revolution" and "politics"; the United States and Eastern Europe supplant China as privileged points of reference. Indeed, of the trip to China she later wrote: "This was for me a good-bye to politics, feminism included" ("Mémoire," 52).

On one level of analysis (superficial perhaps, but inescapable), Kristeva's reflections on the United States must be situated within the context of that massive turn from Marxism of which the New Philosophy was only the most visible of symptoms. As if to lead the general dash to ring the death knell of a revolutionary ideal whose position of intellectual hegemony in France dated back to the Liberation, Sollers remarks in "Why the United States?", "The United States is 1776, something that doesn't belong to the Jacobin model of the French Revolution" (279; *8*).[19] In the sentence immediately preceding the above-cited passage from that text, moreover,

Kristeva categorically refuses the very fear of recuperation that had traditionally haunted revolutionary practice:

> First, I feel that American capitalism—which everyone agrees is the most advanced and totalizing in the world today—far from undergoing a crisis (and yet this was during crisis periods, notably that of the Yom Kippur war, the energy crisis, the Watergate crisis, the crisis of the presidential election last autumn) is a system of permanent recuperation, of patching-up of crisis [*de replâtrage de crise*]. Here I don't mean to be pejorative,[20] but rather want to convey a sense of the most livable possibility of survival [*un sens de possibilité de survie des plus vivables*]. ("Why?" 274; 3)

Looking back on the Orientalism of the late 1960s and early 1970s from the perspective of 1978, it would become possible to argue that the *voyage en Orient* had stood in for a transatlantic journey that remained unthinkable to a European intellectual class strongly marked by the cultural fallout of the Cold War.[21] Or more precisely, the argument went, the Orient served as an alibi for that for which the United States was itself only an alibi—namely, economic modernization. By conjoining the touristic and pluralistic displacements habitual to the neither/nor/but scenario of *l'après-Mai*; by looking beyond the bounds of the heretofore "exceptional" French nation for the signs of new "economies" based on the "infinite (circular) transcribability" (Barthes) of meaning, desire, or social power; the ideologies of writing would have effectively prepared the way for the economic internationalism that emerged under Giscard d'Estaing in the period between 1975 and 1977.[22] Such, transposed into the terms of our analysis, is the reading of Régis Debray. Playing on Columbus's belief that he had reached the East when he had in fact landed in the New World, Debray writes, "In France, all the Columbuses of modernity, following Godard, thought to have discovered China in Paris when they had actually landed in California. . . . As travelers well know, voyages in space are also voyages in time. To change continents is to change centuries" (*Modeste Contribution*, 35–36).

This analysis is doubtless too neat by half. Highly plotted, and therefore prone to the fallacy of mistaking sequence for consequence (*post hoc, propter hoc*), it stands as a classic instance of that essentially paranoid drive to "political interpretation" that functions, in Kristeva's terms, as "the apogee of the obsessive quest for A Meaning" ("Psychoanalysis," 304). Moreover, Debray's argument is constitutively blind to those very postrecuperative subversive residues that his own perception of advanced capitalism as a complex recuperative system would imply are our best hope for social opposition. If, as Debray suggests, the recuperation of oppositional forces is inevitable under advanced capitalism, the critical question becomes one of guaranteeing a subversive potential within the very process of recuperation, of learning (as it were) to coopt cooptation. As I show in the following chapter, it is precisely because capitalism allows for a heterogeneous, contestatory margin that is neither fully subversive nor fully recuperated—a margin variously emblematized in Kristeva's work by the avant-garde artist or by the globe-hopping European intellectual ("Why?")—that Kristeva would come to speak of it as offering "the most livable possibility of survival."

So as not to miss the particular challenge of Kristeva's work, I would argue, one must resist the impulse to chase down ideological valences in the hope of pinning Kristeva to one or several political positions. America, she is careful to insist, is neither a model to be identified with nor a surrogate homeland nor even a destination (a place of destiny); "the woman traveler [*la voyageuse*] seeks no native hearth, no land of her own, no familial shelter" ("Why?" *15*; *Polylogue, 495*). Through the specifically dissident act of exiling herself from proper, naturalized meaning ("Exile is already in itself a form of *dissidence*"), from the belief that life has "a Meaning guaranteed by the dead father," Kristeva's analytic *voyageuse* interrogates American culture as a rigorously open question posed to European intellectuals on the site of shared cultural crises ("Dissident," 298; 7).[23]

What one can miss by reading Kristeva's remarks on the United States in the context of a massive turn from revolutionism among French intellectuals of the mid-1970s, I would suggest, are the profound continuities—both theoretical and political—beneath Kristeva's apparent shifts in the prevailing winds of political fashion. It is with an eye to just these continuities—her emphasis on the specifically ethical function of transgressive practice, her insistence on an anticipatory or utopian moment within such practice, and her complex, dialectical assessment of capitalism—that I shall reread (in the following chapter) that central body of Kristeva's work in and around *Revolution in Poetic Language*. To conclude the present chapter, however, I would return to the work of Roland Barthes, and specifically to his argument for fiction as the ultimate of third terms.

Trickery, Utopia, Fiction

> Everyone knows that a place exists that is not economically or politically indebted to all the vileness and compromise. That is not obliged to reproduce the system. That place is writing. If there is an elsewhere that escapes infernal repetition, that elsewhere lies where it [*ça*] writes itself, where it dreams, where it invents new worlds.
>
> — Hélène Cixous, *The Newly Born Woman*

> The most consistent nihilism is perhaps *masked*: in some way *interior* to institutions, to conformist discourse, to apparent finalities.
>
> — Roland Barthes, *The Pleasure of the Text*

When we come to write the intellectual history of France in *l'après-Mai*, it will be apparent that the strategies, dilemmas, and anxieties attending the intellectual's effort to guarantee a subversive margin from within specific pedagogical and ideological institutions will have been played out and worked over largely in relation to language.

Roland Barthes's address inaugurating the Chair in Literary Semiology at the Collège de France provides an exceptional case in point.[24] Barthes opens his remarks by underscoring his status as academic outsider; he is "a fellow of uncertain nature" [*un sujet incertain*], prone to interrogate his pleasure where others pursue rigorous scholarship, "disciplined invention." He follows with a meditation on the Collège de France as a space "outside the bounds of power" (*hors-pouvoir*) ("Inaugural Lecture," 458; *9*).

On one level, as Barthes well knows, this vision of a site *hors-pouvoir* is strictly impossible: "power (the *libido dominandi*) is there, hidden in any discourse, even when uttered in a place outside the bounds of power" (459; *10*). And yet, paradoxically, election to that ultimate institution that is the Collège de France frees the professor from those very "supplemental constraints" (Lyotard) that typically differentiate institutional exchange from simple discussion.[25] The Collège is "power's untouched portion" because inquiry under its aegis is unchecked (or so Barthes muses, thinking of Michelet) by those scientific, metalinguistic, and ascetic exigencies that allow academic institutions to brand certain utterances (for example, the phantasmatic, the corporeal, the "perverse") as inadmissible. "A professor's sole activity here is research: to speak—I shall even say to dream his research aloud—not to judge, to give preference, to submit to controlled scholarship" (458; *9–10*).

Having thus posed the Collège as largely free of those mechanisms by which institutions typically distinguish between acceptable and unacceptable modes of inquiry, Barthes goes on to find analogous mechanisms in the grammatical structures of language itself. As a speaker of French, he writes, "I am obliged to posit myself first as a subject before stating the action which will henceforth be no more than my attribute. . . . I must always choose between masculine and feminine, for the neuter and the dual are forbidden me. . . . I must indicate my relation to the other person by resorting to either *tu* or *vous*; social or affective suspension is denied me" (460; *13*). By realizing in the act of utterance that system of potential expression that French designates as *la langue*, one activates a whole range of intrinsic distinctions, classifications, and hierarchies of value, each with its specific effects of power. In language, Barthes continues, one cannot avoid subjecting others and being subjected by them; "servility and power are inescapably intertwined"; "human language has no exterior." Short of the "impossible" escape offered by "mystic singularity" (Kierkegaard) or by Nietzschean affirmation, "there is no exit" (461; *15*).

But much as the evocation of academic norms had provoked a reverie on the Collège as the exceptional space of their suspension, so this reflection on our necessary confinement through the power relations inherent in language will rebound as a subversive tactic. In the rhetorical structure of Barthes's "Inaugural Lecture," it is literature that comes to realize—perpetually, yet no less tactically—that dream of an impossible outside held forth by the Collège:

> But for us, who are neither knights of faith nor supermen, the only remaining alternative is, if I may say so, to cheat with language, to cheat language. This salutary trickery, this evasion, this grand imposture [*Cette tricherie salutaire, cette esquive, ce leurre magnifique*] which allows us to understand language *outside the bounds of power,* in the splendor of a permanent revolution of language, I for one call *literature.* ("Inaugural Lecture," 462; *16*)

In a well-known passage from *The Pleasure of the Text,* Barthes speaks of Flaubert as having elevated rhetorical discontinuity (specifically, asyndeton and anacoluthon) to a structural principle; "a generalized asyndeton," he writes, "seizes the entire utterance, so that this very readable discourse is *underhandedly* one of the craziest imaginable: all the logical small change is in the interstices" (9; *18*). Not surprisingly, recent work on the typescript of *Plaisir* by Armine Kotin Mortimer has revealed that Barthes's own revisions frequently involved a deliberate suppression of logical connectives. My reading of the late Barthes in the conclusion to this chapter will take the form of an extended meditation on the seeming absence of logical continuity, the apparent effects of contradiction, in the phrase "this salutary trickery, this evasion, this grand imposture."[26] Can we in fact read in the interstices of Barthes's asyndeton the sort of "logical small change" that would allow for a relatively coherent theoretical trajectory from "trickery" to "evasion" and to "imposture"? Or are we faced here with a mix of multiple, incompatible voices on the part of a self-described "echo chamber" of theoretical vocabularies (*Roland Barthes,* 74; *78*)? To what degree does Barthes's later work subscribe to that model of tactical transgression that gained theoretical currency through rereadings of Bataille by Derrida, Sollers, Kristeva, and others? To what degree is it frankly utopian? What "voyage" does it invite? What do "fiction," "perversity," and "permanent revolution" have to do with such questions?

Few gestures were more characteristic of that body of theory that is the subject of this study than the pursuit of a tactical duplicity. As the title of Part III is meant to suggest, the act of conjuring away a theoretico-political impasse depended on the prior act of conjuring forth its founding conditions; the displacement of the paranoid dynamics proper to the bipolar political sphere (the identification of a degraded double, the foreclosure of internal division and difference, the quest for One Meaning, etc.) presupposed a localized (and purely tactical) *aggravation* of those dynamics.

In the feminist work of Irigaray and others, for instance, theoretical formulations grounded in the binarism of same and other give impetus to a displacement of theory outside the masculinist (and "paranoid") logic fostered by that binarism. In Kristeva and Foucault, tactical formulations of a monolithic conception of power or "the Law" set up a micropolitical fracturing of that conception (Kristeva's "polyvalence that undermines the law"). In Derrida, recourse to logics of revolution as repetition lays the groundwork for an attempt to undermine the Logos itself. Indeed, as Kristeva's use of the specular metaphor ("le face à face de deux lois") serves to remind us, the rigid antinomies common to most formulations of the logics of failed revolt (the antinomies of same/other, inside/outside, etc.) must *themselves* be analyzed as the products of a paranoid projection tending to mask an underlying, structural indifferentiation between the parties to imaginary struggle. The very act of constructing an impasse is thus itself both locally and tactically paranoid.

Despite Barthes's acute sensitivity to the effects of power attendant to binary thinking, we should thus not be surprised to find him employing binarisms "duplicitously," and to specifically tactical effect, in the "Recuperation" fragment of *The Pleasure of the Text*:

> Art seems compromised, historically, socially. Whence the effort on the part of the artist himself to destroy it. . . .
>
> Unfortunately, this destruction is always inadequate; either it occurs outside the art, but thereby becomes impertinent, or else it consents to remain within the practice of art, but quickly exposes itself to recuperation (the avant-garde is that restive language which is going to be recuperated).
>
> The awkwardness of this alternative is the consequence of the fact that destruction of discourse is not a dialectic term *but a semantic term*: it docilely takes its place within the great semiological "versus" myth (*white* versus *black*); whence the destruction of art is doomed to only *paradoxical* formulae (those which proceed literally against the *doxa*): both sides of the paradigm are glued together in an ultimately complicitous fashion: there is a structural agreement between the contesting and the contested forms.
>
> (By *subtle subversion* I mean, on the contrary, what is not directly concerned with destruction, evades the paradigm, and seeks some *other* term: a third term, which is not, however, a synthesizing term but an eccentric, extraordinary term [*un terme excentrique, inouï*]. An example? Perhaps Bataille, who eludes the idealist term by an *unexpected* materialism in which we find vice, devotion, play, impossible eroticism, etc.; thus Bataille does not counter modesty with sexual freedom but . . . with *laughter*.) (54–55; 86–87)

Barthes's argument begins with a classic instance of that all-or-nothing logic proper to the logics of failed revolt. Envisioned with a bit of historical rigor, the avant-garde's "destruction of discourse" cannot help but be a "dialectic term" in Barthes's minimal sense, for even the purest of destructions will exert a constructive effect by virtue of its entering into contradiction with existing artistic practices or sociohistorical structures. To historical analysis, in other words, all destructions of discourse necessarily function, in precisely differentiable ways, both "outside" and "within" existing practices and structures. But by subsuming this destruction to the disjunctive either/or logic characteristic of the semantic paradigm (destruction is either outside or inside, "impertinent" or "recuperated"), by assimilating the phenomenon to its agonistic mythification, Barthes actively aggravates the very antithetical logic by which the *Doxa* habitually proceeds. "It is necessary to posit a paradigm," he explains in *Roland Barthes by Roland Barthes*, "in order to produce a meaning and then to be able to divert it [*le dériver*]" (92; *96*). Posing the antitheses of inside/outside and impertinence/recuperation, together with the paradigmatic complicity (or structural repetition) of "the contesting and the contested forms," Barthes seeks to "emerge" from that antithesis and that complicity through the "subtle subversion" of what he elsewhere calls a "deportative" (or "translational") third term (*un troisième terme [de déport]*)—in this case Bataille's unexpected materialism, his laughter (*Roland Barthes*, 138; *142*).[27]

What is extraordinary about this third term scenario is certainly not its duplicitous construction. Nor is it the fact that Barthes looks to laughter as an (ostensibly unexpected) "other term"; by the mid-1970s, the mode of Bataille and the laughing Nietzsche had long since ritualized the insistence on laughter's capacity to disrupt repetition.[28] In arguing that "women among themselves" use laughter to exceed a phallic "seriousness of meaning," for example, Luce Irigaray writes: "To escape from a pure and simple reversal of the masculine position means in any case not to forget to laugh" (*This Sex* 163; *157*). What is most unexpected in Barthes's third term scenario is rather the hesitancy with which he puts forward the Bataillean example ("perhaps Bataille").

In Bataille's work "transgression" served to denote a rare "double experience"—an experience of the interdiction *and* its violation, an overstepping of social limits that nonetheless maintains those limits for the purposes of *jouissance*. Transgression, as Bataille's formula would have it, "*suspends the interdict without abolishing it*" (*Erotism*, 36; *42*). Predicated thus on "the profound complicity of law and the violation of law," the movement of transgression proper to erotism (and to religious experience more generally) serves to actuate an essential "duplicity" (Bataille's word); the subject "is torn" along the fault line of "two irreconcilables"—the anxiety founding the interdiction and the desire to transgress it; the world of rational work and the world of sacred violence (36, 40; *43, 46*). Erotism and religious experience, Bataille insists, are thus comprehensible only through an "inside experience" (*expérience intérieure*). What is missed by the radical separation of observing subject from observed object posited by positivist science is the profound continuity, which Bataille further explores in *The Accursed Share*, between the excedentary movement proper to erotism and that which governs biological, social, and political life. In short, erotism must be envisioned as "the stirrings of life within ourselves" (*Erotism*, 37; *44*).

Barthes was never more faithful to this model of transgression than in *The Pleasure of the Text*, where he speaks of Sade's monstrous coupling of a conformist, canonical language with a subversive "edge of violence" as instituting an essentially modern erotic "duplicity": "Neither culture nor its destruction is erotic; it is the seam between them, the fault, the flaw [*la faille*] which becomes so." However much a certain modernism might privilege that "mobile" or "blank" edge "where the death of language is glimpsed," culture itself, Barthes writes, always "recurs as an edge" (6–7; *14–15*). It is this fault line, this interval, that serves to realize that erotic intermittence of the split subject that Barthes calls "perversion." Of the reader who both "enjoys the consistency of his selfhood (that is his pleasure) and seeks its loss (that is his bliss)," Barthes writes, "He is a subject split twice over, doubly perverse" (14; *26*).

Curiously, however, it is in the context of a specifically tactical (as opposed to erotic) duplicity that Barthes comes to cite Bataille's formula on transgression's capacity to lift interdictions without abolishing them. In textual theory of *l'après-Mai*, it was common to look to transgression as the basis for subversive strategies undertaken in full cognizance of the fact that, as Barthes put it, "human language has no exterior." Barthes's critique in "Inaugural Lecture," of those who would conceive of semiology as a metalanguage—"I cannot function *outside* language, treating it as a target, and *within* language, treating it as a weapon"—applied equally to those more politically minded theorists who failed to realize that language's capacity to serve as instrument of the Law's transgression could never be wholly divorced from its status as locus of the Law itself (473; *36*). Because the neopositivist dream of a position at once outside and within language had proven impossible, it was commonly argued, oppositionality must issue from a subversive margin, an externality within. What Barthes called a "masked" nihilism must take the form of an endless process of transgression, implying a "profound complicity" (Bataille) with existing institutional and discursive structures.[29]

A primary function of the logics of failed revolt, it would seem, was to rationalize such a tactical complicity by showing that it served to preclude far more insidious variants. Most typically, the process of transgressive subversion was seen to forestall an unwitting complicity proper to that relation of specular doubling said to link the Law's guardians with those who would disavow it. "In the last resort," Barthes remarks in *Writer Sollers*,

> language is the only place in which Bataille's recommendation, defended by Sollers in *Logiques*, can be put into practice. Language, in other words, is the only place in which we can *suspend interdicts without abolishing them*. . . . It is this *internal externality* (raising the bar of the Sentence while still keeping his eyes fixed on it) which is equally displeasing to the guardians of the Law and to its negators. (94, *82–83*; cf. *Pleasure*, 38, *62*)

For Barthes, as for Sollers and Kristeva, it was "literature" or "fiction" that best disclosed a play of transgression capable of thwarting the repetitive dynamic inherent in the act of political negation (*Verneinung*).

Yet Barthes was reluctant to follow Derrida, Kristeva, Sollers—and indeed a certain Bataille—in insisting on the capacity of the transgressive act actively to displace historically defined cultural limits. His conception of "salutary trickery" left little place for what Sollers had called, in an essay on Bataille, "the inevitable trickery [*tricherie*] [that] consists in repositioning, displacing the limit" (*Logiques, 193*).[30] Whatever homage Barthes paid, in other words, to the (quintessentially Telquelian) notion of a perpetual transgression undertaken from a position of "internal externality," he ultimately resisted the interventionist implications of this notion sketched out so strongly by Derrida in the following passages, from interviews by Henri Rouse (1967) and Julia Kristeva (1968) respectively:

> By means of the work done on one side and the other of the limit the field inside is modified, and a transgression is produced that consequently is nowhere present as a *fait accompli*. One is never installed within transgression, one never lives elsewhere. Transgression implies that the limit is always at work. (*Positions*, 12; *21*)

> Doubtless it is more necessary, from within semiology, to transform concepts, to displace them, to turn them against their presuppositions, to reinscribe them in other chains, and little by little to modify the terrain of our work, and thereby produce new configurations. . . . Epistemological breaks are always, and fatally, reinscribed in an old cloth [*tissu*] that must continually, interminably be undone. (*Positions*, 24; *35*)

Barthes's motives for refusing to cast his semiology in the actively interventionist role of eternal reweaver of political meaning were many and complex. The most prominent of these, I would suggest, was his relative unwillingness to counter the violence of language and the social order with specifically violent tactics. The evident utopian pressure in Barthes's text takes form, I shall demonstrate, as a movement of infinite regress from an evaluative violence that keeps returning within the utopian project itself.

Here again the comparison with Derrida is instructive. As I showed in Chapter 2, the first phase of Derrida's "double gesture" entails an "overturning"—itself necessarily violent—of the "violent hierarchy" embodied in all classical philosophic oppositions (*Positions*, 40; *56*). Deconstructive practice thereby risks a certain repetition in order to forestall the practical inefficacy (the impertinence) of all premature neutralizations in the form of a neither/nor. Deconstruction, Derrida insists, "is not *neutral* [*neutre*: neuter, neutral; from the Latin *neuter*: neither]. It *intervenes*" (93; *129*).

Barthes was by no means averse to overturning established hierarchies of value. In accordance with a "two term dialectic" he variously identifies as the dialectic of "meaning" or of "value," he repeatedly counters the accepted with the paradoxical, the stereotypic with the new, the rule with its exception.[31] At the same time he takes great pleasure in passing what he calls his "knife of Value" between cognate words, or across the joints of single words; thus he is "for" figuration, but "against" representation; "for" a Baudelairean (antinatural) artifice, but "against" mimetic artifice (*Roland*

Barthes, 127–28; *131*). As the ostensibly violent response to the "true violence . . . of the self-evident," however, Barthes's "knife of Value" rings false. The image resonates fully (indeed *too* fully) with the castrating cut, as well as with that "insidious heroism" Barthes complained of in Bataille; it reminds us that this is a critic who found textual bliss in "a sudden obliteration of the warrior *value*" (*Roland Barthes*, 85, *88*; *Pleasure*, 30; *50*). The "scandalous truth about bliss," Barthes suggests in *The Pleasure of the Text*, is "that it may well be, once the image-reservoir of speech is abolished, *neuter*" (16; *28*).[32]

No apologist for the exceptional, the paradoxical, and the new has been more cognizant than Barthes of the entropic and recuperative pressures to which these are subject.[33] He writes, "A *Doxa* (a popular opinion) is posited, intolerable; to free myself of it, I postulate a paradox; then this paradox turns bad, becomes a new concretion, itself becomes a new *Doxa*, and I must seek further for a new paradox" (*Roland Barthes*, 73; *75*). Barthes's ever-increasing conviction that even the most duplicitous and paradoxical of languages traces an inexorably entropic path toward an ultimately nauseating consistency of meaning led him repeatedly to "abjure" his previous work, to "shift" theoretical "ground" in the interest of pleasure ("Inaugural Lecture," 467–68; *25–26*). Jonathan Culler has captured this movement in a striking formulation: "Barthes," he remarks, "is a seminal thinker, but he tries to uproot his seedlings as they sprout" (*Barthes*, 12).

But Barthes had a second tactic for combatting what he saw as the inexorable densification of meaning, the "doxification" of paradox—a tactic less reactive than abjuration and more perverse. If paradox inevitably breaks down in the irreversible time of history, it can be made to persist as oscillation in the reversible time of the text. "What else is paradox," Patrizia Lombardo asks, "if not a circular syntax (the *also*), a figure of reversal or inversion, which abolishes logical contradiction in writing, and founds writing (and reading) on a continual oscillation and transformation?" (139). In issuing forth as textual oscillation, paradox gives birth in turn to a specifically amoral, perverse intellectual subject—a split subject who, by oscillating among contrary gestures, comes to thwart the formation of that image that is the modern intellectual's warrant of authenticity, and the ultimate guarantor of his or her responsibility (*Writer Sollers, 89*).

Paradox, in other words, serves to realize that "back-and-forth . . . amoral oscillation" that Barthes equates with the "neutral" or "neuter" [*le neutre*] (*Roland Barthes*, 132; *135*). Here is what Barthes writes of his own work (in *Roland Barthes by Roland Barthes*) under the rubric "Oscillation of Value":

> On the one hand, Value prevails, determines, separates good from bad ("*neuf*"/"*nouveau*," *structure/structuration*, etc.): the world signifies in the strong sense, since everything is caught up in the paradigm of taste and distaste.

> On the other hand, every opposition is suspect, meaning exhausts, he wants a rest from it. Value, which armed everything, is disarmed, absorbed into utopia: no more oppositions, no more meanings, no more Value itself, and this abolition leaves nothing over [*est sans reste*].
>
> Value (and with it, meaning) thus unceasingly oscillates. The work, in its entirety, limps between an appearance of Manichaeism (when meaning is strong) and an appearance of Pyrrhonism (when its exemption is desired). (*Roland Barthes*, 139–40; *142–43*)

Initially intended to distance the (overtly theatrical) struggle in Barthes's early work between "a *pseudo-Physis* (*Doxa*, the natural, etc.) and an *anti-Physis* (all my personal utopias)," the "neutral" is Barthes's (extraordinarily plastic) term for a superior, "delectable" suspension of meaning and value, as well as of a theatricality inherent in the exercise of power, linguistic or otherwise.[34] Barthes's catalogue of "Figures of the Neutral" in *Roland Barthes by Roland Barthes* reads as the resumé-in-drift of his utopian visions—from *Writing Degree Zero*'s anticipation of a new "Adamic language" and the *Michelet*'s penchant for the "smooth" and the "seamless" to *Pleasure*'s apologies for "drift" and "pleasure in its ecstatic aspect." The "neutral," Barthes writes in summation of this catalogue, is "whatever *avoids or thwarts or ridicules* ostentation, mastery, intimidation" (*Roland Barthes*, 132, *135–36*; emphasis added).

We rejoin here the issue of Barthes's refusal of an interventionist rhetoric and the comparison with Derrida. For where Derrida uses the "phase of overturning" to subvert traditional associations of political responsibility with individual autonomy and moral integrity, and yet ultimately to think responsibility otherwise, Barthes makes the more scandalous move of neutralizing responsibility entirely.[35] The effect of Barthes's association of the neutral with the action of a perverse, amoral (morally vacant) subject is to moot that question of political responsibility (present or absent?) that underlies our sense of a meaningful distinction between "thwarting" and "avoiding" (or, as in the passage from "Inaugural Lecture," with which I began, between "trickery" and "evasion"). Curiously, what one finds in the examples of Barthes and Derrida are two incompatible glosses on the French expression *renvoyer dos à dos*. Where Derrida opts to "dismiss back to back" the responsibility of the liberal, Cartesian subject and the absolute irresponsibility of a premature neutralization in the interest of a new responsibility of effective intervention, Barthes "dismisses unsuited" the question of political responsibility ("to dismiss unsuited" is the specifically juridic sense of *renvoyer dos à dos*).

But what are we to make of the third elements of Barthes's seemingly parallel formulations—the notion of a "grand imposture" (in "this salutary trickery, this evasion, this grand imposture") or that of "ridicule" (in "avoids or thwarts or ridicules")? I would approach this question by noting a certain drift in the very structure of the "neutral" itself. Reading Barthes, one is often hard pressed to decide whether the "neutral" should be taken to name a utopian disarming of value (and as such to occupy the second position in the "oscillation of value") or to designate the movement of oscillation itself.[36]

The solution to this apparent difficulty, I would argue, lies with the realization that the utopian disarming named by the neutral serves to institute an oscillation—or better, a spiraling movement—by virtue of a paradox inherent in the very notion of a utopian suspension of value. For in the act of suspending the two-term "dialectic of value" (*"I like / I don't like"*), the neutral necessarily inscribes itself as a value.[37] By positing itself as a position beyond struggle, in other words, the neutral enlists itself in a new struggle, a struggle against struggle itself; "[the neutral] is, *at another link of the infinite chain of language*, the second term of a new paradigm, of which violence (combat, victory, theater, arrogance) is the primary term" (*Roland Barthes*, 132–33; *136*). It is precisely because the utopia of insignificance is itself hypersignificant—"What is a utopia for?" Barthes asks; "to make meaning"—that Barthes's texts will be impelled endlessly to reposit utopia at another turn of the spiral, to make utopia return, but otherwise (*Roland Barthes*, 76; *80*).

Barthes's name for this spiraling motion of utopian return without repetition is fiction. In a meditation on the opening of Marx's *Eighteenth Brumaire* entitled "Le retour comme farce" (Recurrence as farce) he remarks, "On the spiral's trajectory, everything recurs, but in another, higher place: it is then the return of difference, the movement of metaphor; it is Fiction. Farce, however, recurs lower down; it is a metaphor which leans, fades and falls (slackens)" (*Roland Barthes*, 89; *92*). Like metaphor, fiction and farce bring the same back otherwise. What separates them—and what likewise separates literature as "grand imposture" (*leurre magnifique*) from the neutralizing discourse that "ridicules" ostentation—is the active play of an image system, the textualization of singular phantasms.

On the far side of the "neutral"'s suspension of power's theatrical ostentation, we find the notion of a semiology partaking in what Barthes calls "literature's third force," its capacity "to *act* signs rather than to destroy them . . . to institute, at the very heart of servile language, a veritable heteronomy of things" ("Inaugural Lecture," 468–69; *28*). Such a semiology, Barthes writes in the "Inaugural Lecture," rests neither on "'semiophysis,' an inert naturalness of the sign," nor on "'semioclasty,' a destruction of the sign." Its basis lies rather in what Barthes calls "semiotropy": "turned toward the sign, this semiology is captivated by and receives the sign, treats it and, if need be, *imitates it as an imaginary spectacle*" (475–76, *39*; emphasis added).

The semiologist tropes signs as literature itself tropes knowledge ("literature displaces [*fait tourner*] the various kinds of knowledge, does not fix or fetishize any of them"); he "plays with signs as with a conscious decoy [*leurre*] . . . as with a painted veil, or again, a fiction" ("Inaugural Lecture," 462, 475; *18, 39–40*). For Barthes, in short, it is the spiraling movement of semiotropy, a tropic movement of return without repetition opened up by the play of a fictional "imposture," that best allows language to be understood "*outside the bounds of power*, in the splendor of a permanent *revolution* of language" (462, *16*; emphasis added). And it is just this movement that Barthes has in mind when, in the late work, he speaks of a "translational" or "deportative" third term:

> In him [that is, Barthes himself], another dialectic appears, trying to find expression: the contradiction of the terms yields in his eyes by the discovery of a third term, which is not a synthesis but a *translation* [*qui n'est pas de synthèse, mais de déport*]: everything comes back, but it comes back as Fiction, i.e., at another turn of the spiral. (*Roland Barthes*, 69; *73*)

CHAPTER 7

Tracking the Heterogeneous Contradiction: Kristeva

. . . but all of this together and infinitely, furious with intelligence.
— Julia Kristeva, *Revolution in Poetic Language*

First produced to be submitted for the French *doctorat d'Etat,* Julia Kristeva's *Revolution in Poetic Language* (1974) is a massive (and massively difficult) piece of work, a book as breathtaking in its synoptic ambition as it can be maddening in its relentless shifts of theoretical perspective. Two decades after its original publication, Kristeva's "materialist" account of a disruptive ("revolutionary") power inherent in poetic language remains very much an enigma. The subject over the years of several excellent short commentaries, it has only recently begun to receive the sort of sustained *collective* assessment that one of its first (and best) readers would suggest it demanded.[1]

The present chapter aims to further this process of critical appraisal by focusing on Kristeva's complex rewriting of the third term model outlined in Chapter 5. How does the notion of "heterogeneous contradiction" allow Kristeva to return to the neither/nor/but scenario, but to return to it otherwise? How does her apology for the transgressive practice of what she calls the *sujet en procès* (the subject in process/on trial) inform her critique of those "new paranoid systems" that are fascism and Stalinism (*Polylogue, 518*)? What are the aims, and the limitations, of a politico-theoretical project explicitly formulated in the time of an anterior future? These are but the principal questions to be addressed in the pages that follow.

Semiotic/Symbolic

Kristeva's case for a "revolution in poetic language" begins, it is well known, with a reconception of the "speaking subject" as constituted by the dialectical relation of two signifying modalities she calls the "semiotic" and the "symbolic." Indissociable yet heterogeneous moments of a single signifying process (*le procès de la signifiance*), the semiotic and the "symbolic" are separated by a "threshold" that Kristeva names, after Husserl, the "thetic phase" (*Revolution*, 48; *46*).[2] In the interest of clarity and concision, I have found it useful to begin the following brief outline of the concepts central to Kristeva's argument with a discussion of the thetic phase.

Initiated with the separation in the mirror stage of an "imaged ego" from the world of objects, and fully realized through the discovery of castration, the thetic moment is that which posits the subject as separate (from objects, from the maternal body), and hence as signifiable. The thetic phase culminates thus in the resolution of the Oedipus complex: with the final severance of dependence upon the mother, with the constitution of the Other through the displacement of incestuous and autoerotic drives, and finally, with the opening up of that *béance* between signifier and signified that Lacan saw as the precondition of all desire (*Revolution*, 47; *45–46*).

What is instituted in the thetic phase, therefore, is a subject at once split and unified, which Kristeva names the "unary subject" (*sujet unaire*) (*Polylogue*, 55).[3] Product of the Oedipus, the unary subject is split insofar as it is determined by the *manque à être*, that impossible longing for fusion with the All (*le Tout*) that Lacan speaks of as fueling desire's endless metonymic flight. And yet the unary subject is also unified because it is established in the Oedipus through a specifically homosexual identification with a same-sexed parent under the aegis of that law of the One, that "logically thetic identificatory unity," that Lacan calls the *Nom-du-Père* (whose function, Kristeva reminds us, may be realized by any power-wielding entity—father, mother, State, family, etc.) (*Revolution* 176, *158*; *Polylogue*, 55).

Kristeva frequently portrays the semiotic and symbolic as respectively preceding and succeeding (both "logically and chronologically") the positing of the subject in the thetic phase (*Revolution*, 41; *40*).[4] Prior to spatial intuition, representation, signification, and Law, what Kristeva calls the semiotic *chora* names a preverbal "rhythmic space" of vocal and gestural motility, an ever ephemeral, "nonexpressive totality" formed (and unformed) by a play of oral and anal drives oriented around the maternal body (*Revolution*, 26; *23*): "The semiotic is articulated by flow and marks: facilitation [*frayages*], energy transfers, the cutting up of the corporeal and social continuum as well as that of the signifying material, the establishment of a distinctiveness and its ordering in a pulsating *chora*, in a rhythmic but nonexpressive totality" (*Revolution*, 40; *40*).

The symbolic, by contrast, typically refers to a modality of language governed by the normative functions of grammar, syntax, semantics, and pragmatics, and thus ultimately by paternal Law. Constructed through an arresting of semiotic motility in the thetic phase, the symbolic designates those linguistic features attributable to the particular functions of a separate or "punctual" ego—judgment, signification, predication, positioning, and the like.

When Kristeva comes to define the Symbolic—a.k.a. the Symbolic order—she speaks of it as containing within itself, dialectically, the very scission between the semiotic and the symbolic I have just outlined. Playing on the Greek *súmbolon* (sign of recognition, tessera), she characterizes the Symbolic as an "always split unification that is produced by a rupture [the thetic break between signifier and signified] and is impossible without it" (*Revolution*, 49; *46*).

To ground this vision of the Symbolic (order) as a perpetually cleaved unification, one must look beyond the obvious yet pertinent analogy to the unary subject; "the subject never *is*," Kristeva insists later in *Revolution*; "the *subject* is only the *signifying process*" (*Revolution*, 215; *188*). Specifically, we must look to a complex, developmental dialectic that is seen to link the semiotic and the symbolic as "two heterogeneous operations that are, reciprocally and inseparably, preconditions for each other" (*Revolution*, 66; *65*).

On the one hand, the symbolic presupposes the semiotic since it constitutes itself through a parasitical arresting of semiotic motility: "the subject, finding his identity in the symbolic, *separates* from his fusion with the mother, *confines* his *jouissance* to the genital, and transfers semiotic motility onto the symbolic order" (*Revolution*, 47; *45*). Elsewhere Kristeva will speak of the symbolic functions of logical negation and linguistic predication as "stoppages" or "knottings" of the mobility specific to semiotic negativity (*Revolution*, 124; *114*). Thus, while the constitution of the unary subject plainly depends on the paranoid suppression of a certain "heterogeneous other" (the alienating *imago* in the mirror stage, the maternal body and *chora* in the Oedipus), this paranoia is nonetheless said to lie "in close proximity" to the schizoid fragmentation (*morcellement*) characteristic of the semiotic, "camouflaging its secret even while drawing on its energy" (*Revolution*, 134; *123*).

But if the semiotic is thus a precondition to the symbolic, it is discoverable only after the thetic break through the symbolic's transgression; "the semiotic that 'precedes' symbolization is only a *theoretical supposition* justified by the need for description" (*Revolution*, 68; *67*). Kristeva's work clearly refuses that nostalgic longing for a return to an original semiotic and maternal space that certain critics have tried to read into it. As a mobile space modeled by the drives, and particularly the death drive, the semiotic *chora* is inconceivable outside that process—which Kristeva variously calls "negativity" or "rejection" (*le rejet*)—whereby the (postsymbolic) subject is perpetually engendered *and* negated: "The semiotic *chora* is no more than the place where the subject is both generated and negated, the place where his unity succumbs before the process of charges and stases that produce him. We shall call this process of charges and stases a *negativity* to distinguish it from negation, which is the act of a judging subject" (*Revolution*, 28; *28*).

The semiotic can no more escape the symbolic than the symbolic the semiotic for the reason that negativity can be discerned only through the irruption of the semiotic's violent rhythms athwart symbolic stases and thetic positions. Indeed, the dialectical rigor with which Kristeva would think through the reciprocal implication of symbolic and semiotic, and thus the impossibility of any presymbolic utopia, comes to the fore in her work through the specifically bipedal syntax of sentences such as this: "Negativity—rejection—is thus only an *operation* [*fonctionnement*], discernible across those *positions* that absorb it and disguise it: the real, the sign, and the predicate all appear as differential moments, markers in the process of rejection" (*Polylogue, 67*).

At this precise differential point where symbolic and semiotic split inexorably back into one another, where thetic stases serve to realize the very negativity that puts them in process and on trial (*en procès*), Kristeva will locate the function of art and avant-garde textuality. Her readings of Artaud, Bataille, Lautréamont, Mallarmé, Joyce, and others invariably focus on specific textual features (portmanteau words in Joyce, enunciative shifts and semantic inversions in Lautréamont, syntactic ruptures and phonetic networking in Mallarmé) said to manifest the disruptive return of the semiotic within the very texture of language. In "Le sujet en procès" (The subject in process/on trial), for instance, Kristeva rereads Artaud for signs of the irruption within the symbolic of an "overload of pleasure" associated with the work of the sphincter muscles (sucking, expulsion, defecation, etc.) and variously attributable to the oral and anal drives (melody, harmony, and rhythm in the first case; word deformation, glossolalia, interjection, and expectoration in the second) (*Polylogue, 74–75*). All that separates the artist from the schizophrenic is the fragile equilibrium the artist maintains (although rarely so precariously as in the case of Artaud) between symbolic unification and the risk of bodily fragmentation through the violent effects of negativity (*Polylogue, 80–81*).

The reprise of the *chora* in language, in other words, presupposes that the subject is "firmly posited by castration so that drive attacks against the thetic will not give way to fantasy or to psychosis but will instead lead to a 'second-degree thetic'" (*Revolution*, 50; *47*). Between the Scylla of repressive unification ("the thetic repressing the drive") and the Charybdis of a liberationist fragmentation ("the drive effacing the thetic"), the text remains that "intermediary" that "dialectizes" the thetic and the drives "by miming the constitution and deconstitution of the subject: a subject in process/on trial [*sujet en procès*]—neither metalinguistic superego, nor projective ego, nor fall from symbolicity, but all of this together and infinitely, furious with intelligence" (*Révolution, 616*).

Transgression, Negativity, Rejection

It is here, with Kristeva's conception of the *sujet en procès*, that we return to the neither/nor/but scenario, albeit in a guise more overtly dialectical than was common in French theory of *l'après-Mai*. In an important chapter of *Revolution* on the relation of poetry to sacrifice, Kristeva suggests that the social function of art is neither to absolutize nor to deny the thetic "cut" (in this case, religious interdiction), but rather to accept such interdictions as a means of recovering what theology occults from ritual practice—namely that "trans-symbolic jouissance" whose function is to "threaten" (indeed, to transgress) "the unity of the social realm and of the subject" (*Revolution*, 80; *78*).

> Neither intransgressable and guilt-producing divine fiat, nor "romantic" folly, pure madness, surrealist automatism, or pagan pluralism. But rather a heterogeneous contradiction between two irreconcilable elements, separate but inseparable from the *process* in which they assume asymmetrical functions—such to us is the condition of the subject in the signifying process [*signifiance*].
>
> Literature has always realized this condition most explicitly. (*Revolution*, 82; *80*)

It is precisely because literature best objectifies that "heterogeneous contradiction" between the thetic and the drives constitutive of the *sujet en procès* that it manages to avoid that impasse formed by the specifically specular roles of "guardian of the law" (which Kristeva will elsewhere ascribe to "Marxism, Freudianism, Phenomenology, and various forms of empiricism") and "disavower of the law" (the "pagan pluralism" of Lyotard above, Derrida—surprisingly—elsewhere).[5]

As my reading of Barthes has already suggested, the work of Georges Bataille (or, more precisely, a certain take on that work) served as a privileged touchstone for the formulation of third term scenarios among theoreticians of the *Tel Quel* group. And yet Bataille's precursor role was arguably never more palpable than in the texts of Kristeva. Bataille's model of a transgression that maintains the interdiction as a stimulus to *jouissance*; his emphasis on modes of experience that foster a contradiction between "the subject's presence and his *loss*, between thought and its expenditure [*entre la pensée et sa dépense*]"; his postulation that matter can be "the motor-force of transgression" and bodily energy "revolutionary"; his insistence on rethinking problems of community on the basis of heterogeneity, expenditure, and the disappearance of meaning—all are the subject of significant reworking in Kristeva's revolutionary semiotics (*Erotism*, 38, *45*; *Polylogue, 119*; Richman, 65; *Polylogue, 110*).

Most important for our purposes is Kristeva's concurrence with Bataille's privileging of literature as the vehicle by which transgressive energies enter the social sphere. "Only literature," Bataille had written in *Literature and Evil*, "[can] lay bare the play of the law's transgression, without which the law would have no purpose *independent of the necessity to create order*" (25; *25*). What Bataille knew, Kristeva suggests, is that only a fictionalizing of limit experiences (erotism, sacrifice, revolution, etc.) can effectively put into question "specular and narcissistic unity, from the level of language [the "I" as enunciative position, semantic distinction, etc.] to that of ideology [fascism, in particular]"; only literature functions as "a discrete means (and yet how profound and unsettling) for the struggle against all oppressive unity—and against its opposite [*envers*], an exuberant or ghoulish nihilism" (*Polylogue, 135*). Only a literature that maintains that contradiction between self-presence and loss, binding and separation, or meaning and nonsense that Bataille had analyzed under the rubric of *l'expérience intérieure* can hope to operate the sort of "discrete" subversion that serves to avoid the specular impasse pitting the "guardians of the Law" against its nihilistic "disavowers."

In a well-known note to the sentence from *Erotism* in which he speaks of transgression as lifting the interdiction without abolishing it, Bataille writes: "There is no need to stress the Hegelian nature of this operation which corresponds with the dialectic phase described by the untranslatable German 'aufheben': transcend without suppressing" (36; *42*). Much as Derrida had done in "From Restricted to General Economy,"[6] however, Kristeva chooses to read Bataille against himself, to find in the very movement of transgression a logic more radically divisive, more resistant to the suppression of contradiction, than that of the Hegelian *Aufhebung*: "This explosion of the semiotic in the symbolic is far from a negation of negation, an *Aufhebung* that would suppress the contradiction generated by the thetic and establish in its place an ideal positivity, the restorer of presymbolic immediacy. It is, instead, a *transgression* of position, a reversed reactivation of the contradiction that instituted this very position" (*Revolution*, 69; *68*).

Refusing the idealist dialectic's implacable movement toward an "ideal positivity"—be it through a pure transcendence of the semiotic or a return to the "pre-symbolic immediacy" of the maternal *chora*—the transgressive movement of *signifiance* plays both sides of the thetic limit, maintaining the heterogeneous contradiction between its semiotic and symbolic modalities as it reactivates the contradiction that installed the thetic position. (More on this final point in a moment.)

For Kristeva, the project of reading Bataille against his expressed Hegelianism goes hand in hand with that of reading Hegel himself against the grain, of theorizing "on the basis of and despite [*à partir de et malgré*] Hegel" (*Revolution*, 112; *104*). Following Hegelian clues, Kristeva seeks to decenter dialectical "triplicity" through a neither/nor/but scenario whose third term is not the product of an *Aufhebung*, but the expression of that "*fourth term* of the true dialectic" that is Hegelian *Negativität* (*Revolu-*

tion, 113; *105*). As Lenin had done before her, Kristeva looks to Hegel's notion of negativity—defined as the logical function of that concrete movement of Becoming that produces the theses of negation and the negation of the negation, the *Aufhebung*—for the possibility of a materialist conception of the movement of objective process, a "logic of matter" (*Revolution,* 109–10, *101–2;* Hegel, *Logic,* 128). Heterogeneous to logic inasmuch as the latter implies the relational, rational capacities of the unary subject, negativity nonetheless produces logic "through a movement of separation or rejection . . . that has the necessary objectivity of a law and can be seen as a logic of matter" (*Revolution,* 112; *104*). "A materialist reading of Hegel," Kristeva writes, "allows us to think this negativity as the trans-subjective, trans-ideal, and trans-symbolic movement found in the *separation of matter,* one of the preconditions of symbolicity, which generates the symbol as if through a leap" (*Revolution,* 117; *108*).

For Kristeva, as this language implies, Lenin's reading of Hegelian negativity realizes its "materialist" potential only "with the help of the Freudian discovery" (*Revolution,* 113; *105*). Teasing out the dialectical possibilities of an ambivalence within Freud's notion of the drive—alternatively seen as a somatic representative within the psyche and as "part of the process of somatic excitation"—Kristeva comes to conceive of the drive as the dialectical limit of the mental, the biological, *and* the cultural, as that vanishing point where psychic contradiction folds into social contradiction, as well as into its corporeal counterpart.[7]

But it is the death drive in particular, such as Freud posited as underlying the repetition compulsion in the infant's game of *Fort/Da,* that ultimately allows Kristeva to think through the process whereby negativity (or better, "rejection") serves productively to reconstitute, indeed to revolutionize, the real. Kristeva uses "the Freudian discovery," I shall show in a moment, to retain an "affirmative negativity" or "productive dissolution" she sees as characteristic of the Hegelian dialectic while nonetheless ridding the dialectic of that teleological "theology" whereby Hegelian becoming erases the moments of rupture that constitute it, closing off the movement of heterogeneous matter "by the assertion of the Absolute Spirit which knows its end in its beginning" (*Revolution,* 113, *105;* Coward and Ellis, 150).[8] In deriving a theory of drive rejection (*le rejet pulsionnel*) from the concept of expulsion (*Ausstossung;* in French, *repoussement*) put forth in Freud's essay on "Negation" and in *Beyond the Pleasure Principle,* Kristeva would explicitly counter the "ideational closure" inherent in Hegel's treatment of "Repulsion" in the *Logic,* where ideal Unity is shown to depend on the One's (paranoid) "suppression of the other" (*suppression de l'être autre*) and where negativity can be posed only as "repetition of the ideational unity in itself" (*Revolution,* 159; *145*).

In psychoanalytic theory it is common to read the gesture of rejection or expulsion, variously epitomized by linguistic negation (*Verneinung*) and by the *Fort* moment of Freud's spool game, as operating a double institution. The act of expulsion serves to establish "an outside that is never definitively separate"; it consolidates the pleasure-ego as always provisionally distinguishable from the "real" (*Revolution,* 148; *135*).[9] At the same time, expulsion founds the symbolic function inasmuch as it is the separation of body and object that provides the matrix for the separation of subject and predicate in linguistic signification (*Revolution,* 123; *114*).

In his essay on "Negation" Freud has much to say about the ways in which the faculty of judgment derives from the interplay of those "primary impulses" that are "introduction into the ego" and "expulsion from the ego"; thetic distinction (to borrow Kristeva's terminology) tracks those psychic resistances and facilitations set up through a prior mapping, in accordance with the pleasure principle, of similarities and differences "in" the material world ("Negation," 216). Kristeva clearly draws on this work, while seeking to develop its "materialist" potential, when she implies that the separation and differentiation characteristic of the symbolic depend on a prior movement of separation or rejection inherent in heterogeneous matter itself—as when she speaks of negativity as "the trans-subjective, trans-ideal, and trans-symbolic movement found in the *separation of matter*" (*Revolution,* 117; *108*).

But as she pushes Freud (somewhat wishfully) toward a certain materialism, Kristeva also pushes traditional materialism toward Freud—specifically, toward a conception of the unconscious as a mnemonic record of "the scissions of matter" (*Revolution,* 160; *147*). Central therefore to Kristeva's "materialist" elaborations on Freud's claim that "negation, the derivative of expulsion, belongs to the instinct of destruction" (i.e., to the death drive) is a recognition that true "objectivity" is not to be found "within" an outside world (natural and/or social) so much as at that dialectical vanishing point between the psychic, corporeal, and cultural on which she locates the drives ("Negation," 216). Thus, if expulsion (*Ausstossung*) or repudiation (*Verwerfung*) plays a crucial role in the establishment of the thetic, it also "points toward" a repetitive rupturing of bodily unity, a manifestation of the repetitive and disintegrative force of the death drive at the dialectical limit between the body and "natural and social constraints":

> Indeed, although for Freud *Ausstossung* or *Verwerfung* posits the sign, it already functions beforehand, "objectively" so to speak, in the movement of living matter subject to natural and social constraints. . . . While establishing the sign, subject, and judgment, *Verwerfung* points *at the same time* toward the repeated scissions of a-symbolized living matter and toward the inorganic. The drive that thus takes shape operates in a trans-symbolic realm that sends the signifying body back to biological a-signifiance and finally to death. (*Revolution,* 159–60; *146*)

"Rejection" is of course Kristeva's name for this movement of expulsion that points backwards to a corporeal dislocation prior to the thetic cut—and hence to aggressivity, primary masochism, and the death drive.[10]

The process (or trial) of the subject begins with an "unburying" of the anality repressed in the Oedipus, with the recovery, *in and through the symbolic*, of the pleasure attending to bodily discharge as the "fundamental experience of separation" (*Revolution*, 151; *137*).[11] Thus Kristeva will read the glossolalia, paragrams, and interjections of Artaud's text as traces of spasmodic discharges that have reinvested themselves in language, and in the process made manifest that "pleasure underlying the symbolic function of expulsion" occulted by Freud (*Revolution*, 149; *136*).

It is in this context that one must situate Kristeva's notion that the transgressive "explosion" of the semiotic in the symbolic reactivates "against the grain" the very contradiction that had installed thetic positionality. Kristeva speaks of anal rejection as "a step on the way to" that definitive detachment from an object, that repression of the object's materiality beneath the linguistic sign, that grounds the symbolic as a modality of lack under the aegis of the superego; "preced[ing] the establishment of the symbolic, [anal rejection] is both its precondition and its repressed element" (*Revolution*, 149; *136*). The reactivation within the symbolic of the repressed prerequisite that is anal rejection infuses language with the pleasure of a "jubilant loss [that] is simultaneously felt as an attack against the expelled object, all exterior objects (including father and mother), and the body itself" (*Revolution*, 151; *137–38*).

Although fully ambivalent in its own right, this prethetic aggressivity associated with the death drive is said to trigger a dialectical positivation when it returns athwart the thetic positionality of the symbolic and the unary subject.

> Through the new phonematic and rhythmic network it produces, rejection becomes a source of "aesthetic" pleasure. Thus, without leaving the line of meaning, it cuts up and reorganizes that line by imprinting on it the path of drives through the body: from the anus to the mouth.
>
> Rejection therefore constitutes the return of expulsion—*Ausstossung* or *Verwerfung*—within the domain of the constituted subject: rejection *re*constitutes real objects, "creates" new ones, reinvents the real, and resymbolizes it. (*Revolution*, 155; 141)

In his discussions of the pleasure principle, it has been noted, Freud tended to oscillate between two conceptions of the so-called principle of constancy.[12] According to the first—formulated in *Beyond the Pleasure Principle* as the "Nirvana principle" and linked to the death drive (Thanatos)—the dominant tendency of mental life lay in the effort to reduce psychic excitation to zero. In the second—associated with the binding, preservational force of the life instincts (Eros)—pleasure lay in the maintenance of a constant level of excitation in a psychic homeostasis. Kristeva's account of the transgressive power of drive rejection in poetic language attempts to dialectize the terms of this oscillation by arguing that it is the productive reiteration of the death drive that ultimately assures "a *thresh-*

old of constancy" (*Revolution*, 160; *147*): "Although it is destructive—a 'death drive'—rejection is the very mechanism of reactivation, tension, life; aiming toward the equalization of tension, toward a state of inertia and death, it *perpetuates* tension and life" (*Revolution*, 150; *137*).

Framed in this way, Kristeva's dialectic of rejection bears a striking resemblance to that commonplace of nineteenth-century vitalist biology according to which it is the life and death of particular organisms that assures the continuity of life itself; "if life is a matter of death," Cabanis wrote in 1830, "death in turn gives birth to and immortalizes life."[13] But Kristeva parts company with the vitalist model, and rejoins a specifically ateleological dialectic of objective "historical" process, inasmuch as the movement from Thanatos to Eros, from a radical reduction of tension to its perpetuation, depends specifically on rejection's entering into contradiction with existing social, linguistic, or psychic stases; "the aim to resolve tension," Coward and Ellis write in an analogous context, "produces new tensions as it comes into contradiction with other forces, thus necessitating a further aim of destruction" (140).

Rejection becomes productive, in other words, only in practice. It is thus to the practice of the *sujet en procès*—always already pulverized, decentered, because suspended on the ostensibly dialectical limit between conflicting drives and objective contradictions—that Kristeva looks for signs of a productive rejection "that includes heterogeneous contradiction as the mainspring of an infinite dialectical—material and signifying—movement" (*Revolution*, 203; *180*):

> Nevertheless, the moment of practice dissolves the subject's compactness and self-presence. First, it puts the subject in contact with, and thus in a position to negate, various objects and other subjects in his social milieu, with which the subject enters into contradiction, whether antagonistically or not. Although an externality, the contradiction within social relations de-centers and suspends the subject, and articulates him as a passageway, a non-place, where there is a struggle between conflicting tendencies, *drives* whose stases and thetic moments (the *representamen*) are as much rooted in affective relations (parental and love relations) as they are in class conflict. Rejection, de-centering the subject, sets his pulverization against natural structures and social relations, collides with them, rejects them, and is de-posited by them. At the moment of rejection (which presupposes the phase annihilating a former objectivity), a binding, symbolic, ideological, and thus positivizing component intervenes ("we intervene," writes Hegel) in order to constitute within language, the new object produced by the "subject" in process/on trial through the process of rejection. (*Revolution*, 203; *179–80*)

In short, it is a mode of practice theorizable ("on the basis of and despite" Freud) as the objectification of the process that is *signifiance* that best serves to realize the promise inherent in Hegelian negativity as "the liquefying, dissolving agent that does not destroy but rather reactivates new organizations and, in that sense, affirms" (*Revolution*, 109; *102*). How the apology for this mode of practice ultimately inflects Kristeva's take on cultural life under advanced capitalism is the subject of the following section.

The New Paranoid Systems

It was clearly not a question for the Kristeva of *Revolution*, as it was for Barthes, of formulating specular impasses as pretexts to the quest for a post-dialectical, ex-centric term. And this for two reasons. First, the "change of terrain" (Marx) implicitly proposed by such impasses in her work entails the recovery of a dialectic, albeit an ateleological one—a dialectic whereby the determinants of the impasse are not evaded but infinitely transgressed.[14] The concept of negativity, for example, implies no escape from judgment (or from desire as fueled by lack, or from the paranoid "suppression of the other")—no escape, in short, from the unary subject. Rather, Kristeva writes, the concept of negativity leads "the indelible trace of the judging subject's presence . . . elsewhere [*dans un ailleurs*]," to a place where both trace and presence "are produced by a struggle of heterogeneous antitheses [*contraires*]" (*Revolution*, 118; *109*).

Second, as this example suggests, the acts of negation constituting Kristeva's specular impasses (the relation of doubling, for example, between "guardians" and "disavowers" of the law) are readable only in light of that struggle of heterogeneous contraries that produces them, and is then effaced by them. Strictly speaking, specular impasses cannot serve as pretexts for Kristeva since they are constituted through the overvaluation of a thetic positionality that enjoys no theoretical existence independent of a more fundamental negativity. It is indeed helpful to consider Kristeva's work as incessantly promoting a third term, provided we understand this "third term" exhaustively, as the transgressive practice of a *sujet en procès* that objectifies those heterogeneous contradictions (between anal rejection and thetic stases or between class interests) that drive negativity as an ateleological process of generation and negation. For Kristeva, however, specular impasses exist only through the erasure of this third term, through a refusal of transgressive practice.

We are now in a position to reread the specular bind between capitalism/fascism and Stalinism as Kristeva would formulate it, three years after *Revolution in Poetic Language*, in "Why the United States?" (see Chapter 6). Behind the ostensible commonplace that "every negation is a definition," we must surely hear Kristeva's reading of Frege in the earlier text, where she attributes the "logical solidarity" of negation and affirmation to the fact that, in the realm of judgment, all logical negations serve to affirm "the indestructible presence of the unary subject: 'I' " (*Revolution*, 260, 119; *199*, *110*). Likewise, her insistence on tracing a specifically European tendency to "deal with" constraint by confronting it with its antithesis back to "a certain religious or state tradition" clearly resonates with her analyses of the ways in which Christianity (and a monarchical system based thereon) came to sublimate their inherent negativity "in the *unity* of the subject and the supreme theological agency [*instance*]" (*Polylogue, 107*).

Kristeva sees this traditional recuperative mechanism as having been appropriated by bourgeois society in the early capitalist era. For the constitution of a rational, unified bourgeois subject, like that of its juridical corollary, the bourgeois state, depended on the repression of rejection, heterogeneous contradiction, and "*jouissance* in death" (*Revolution*, 191; *171*). In other words, capitalism's demand for the unary subject (as both agent and object of technocratic manipulation) determined a paranoid foreclosure of "the heterogeneous other" (a formula by which Kristeva variously refers to the catalysts of a "schizoid" pulverisation of the *moi*, as well as to other selves) (*Revolution*, 134; *123*). "In the State and in religion," she writes, "capitalism requires and consolidates the paranoid moment of the subject: a unity foreclosing the other and taking its place" (*Revolution*, 139; *127*). Thus capitalism comes to exemplify the "'paranoid' mark" in the path of Hegelian desire, that movement whereby self-consciousness "explicitly affirms that [the nothingness of the other] is *for it* the truth of the other; it destroys the independent object and thereby gives itself the certainty of itself as a *true* certainty, a certainty which has become explicit for self-consciousness itself *in an objective manner*" (Hegel, *Phenomenology*, 109; cited in *Revolution*, 134; *123*).

It is in the mirror of this paranoid suppression of negativity, inherent in capitalism as an ideology of desire, that Kristeva will in turn see traditional Marxism. From Feuerbach, she suggests, Marxist theory has inherited the conception of a fully conscious, atomistic subject defined by explicit "needs" and "desires," a subject that is none other than the unary subject demanded by capitalism. When the proletariat defines itself collectively on the model of the unary "man of desire and of lack," it thus renews in its negation of the capitalist order "the paranoid subject of speculative thought, the State, and religion": "The anthropomorphization, better still, the subjectification of Hegelian negativity in the form of a human unity—the man of desire and of lack—is represented in Marx by the proletariat, which is viewed as the means for realizing the total man—mastered and unconflicted; man is above all a '*master*,' a '*solution to the conflict*'" (*Revolution*, 138; *127–28*).

Kristeva then extends her critique of traditional Marxism as capitalism's specular double to the question of practice. For by hypostatizing "the *thetic moment of rejection*"—choosing to fight old theses with new ones (on the very field of representation) while at the same time offering up the image of a "dilated, inflated, tenacious ego armed with ideological and theoretical assurance"—the traditional revolutionary represses that immediate "experience" that pulverizes the *moi* and so condemns his practice to "a mere mechanical repetition of actions without any modification of real, material, signifying, objective and subjective devices" (*Revolution*, 206; *182*). Accordingly, Kristeva reserves the epithet "revolutionary" for the endlessly transgressive expenditure of a "thinking-speaking subject," for a practice of structuring and destructuring that rigorously plays that complex limit between linguistic forms, social structures, and corporeal *frayages* on which alone she would locate the "real" (*Polylogue, 16–17*).[15]

It should be apparent by now that all political problems in Kristeva's work of the early 1970s tend to revolve around a single central problem—that of giving voice to what political and religious monologism repress: "this drive semiotic [*sémiotique pulsionnel*] that is heterogeneous to meaning and the One, and that makes them go" (*Polylogue, 17*). Typically, therefore, her evaluations of modern political ideologies focus on the degree to which they sustain and/or subvert the paranoid foreclosure of the death drive instituted by early capitalism as heir to Christian monologism. In "Politique de la littérature" (The politics of literature), for example, bourgeois liberalism and Stalinism are seen to double one another insofar as they set out, simply and "naively," to impede precisely that which fascism exemplifies—the return of a (previously foreclosed) death drive within the real itself (*Polylogue, 17*). (Kristeva's point elsewhere about the societies of the Stalinist order is at least marginally true of liberalism as well: regimes "built on the illusion that the negative—death, violence—does not concern them" are necessarily prone, through the logic of foreclosure, to enacting the "negative" in themselves [*Polylogue, 175*; *Desire*, 161].)

On one level, as a long list of historical avant-gardists sympathetic to fascism would attest, fascism and the literary avant-garde share a common will to objectify the death drive. But where avant-garde textuality transgresses "paranoid closure"—and never more productively than in those moments of history in which "*the very principle of paranoid power*" is discredited (1870 and, implicitly, 1968)—fascism reconstitutes that principle through what Kristeva calls, in another context, "the *detour of negativity toward the becoming-One*" (*Revolution*, 134; *123, 401*). Both fascism and the avant-garde text find their dialectical precondition in capitalism's breaking down of such "traditional moral constraints" to the direct manifestation of the death drive as religion, the nation, and the patriarchal family (*Polylogue, 518*). Thus, Kristeva argues, rejection's capacity to destroy subjective, phantasmatic unity will be enhanced through the weakening of "homosexual" (i.e., Oedipal) identifications that follows from the dissolution of the family under capitalism (*Revolution*, 177; *159*).

But, in the case of those "new paranoid systems" that are fascism and Stalinism, this weakening of traditional subjective identifications paves the way for a massive identification with the head of state as epitome of the Feuerbachian universal man, as the unary "desiring subject . . . [that is] the basis of the authoritarian State . . . [and is] best represented by 'the head of state' " (*Polylogue, 518*; *Revolution*, 137; *126*). Fascism and Stalinism radicalize the logic of the unary subject inherent in capitalism insofar as they press the force of negativity as "heterogeneous other" into the service of the Other as a specular, narcissistic Unity, as all-knowing interlocutor and product of narcissistic demand. Between the narcissism driving the cults of personality in the "new paranoid systems" and that which Lacan had seen to be endemic to the age of bourgeois democratism, Kristeva would find both a profound continuity—subsequently confirmed by the phenomenon of Reaganism—and a no less significant difference of degree.

This difference of degree, insofar as we might account for it in Kristevan terms, would help explain the argumentative slippage of that passage from "Why the United States?" (see Chapter 6) where the specular doubling of the capitalist "System" and its communist rivals gives way to an eternal coupling of fascism and Stalinism. It would indicate, moreover, that the gesture of situating capitalist society's oppositional margin in the third position of a neither/nor/but structure must be viewed less as a symptom of the French intelligentsia's rightward migration circa 1976–77 than as the development of presuppositions already very much at work in Kristeva's texts of the *Revolution in Poetic Language* phase.

I would begin to locate such a difference of degree by examining the extent to which the supposed unity of the state, as a logical extension of the unary subject, depends on the narcissistic (and of course paranoid) "suppression of the other." Kristeva sees modern capitalism as parting company with its fascist and Stalinist progeny to the extent that it opens up a space for the transgression of the norms underlying the social unit—a space akin to what Barthes called "internal externality." In the course of the nineteenth century, she suggests, rapid developments of the means of production through scientific and technological advances served to free capitalist societies from the necessity of maintaining strict subservience to ideological and linguistic norms. Indeed, it was the ability of the capitalist mode of production in the final decades of that century to appropriate unto itself the very *mise en procès* (putting into process / on trial) of its fundamental social norms that constitutes that "new phenomenon" for which Kristeva will find evidence in the texts of Lautréamont, Mallarmé, Joyce, Artaud, and others (*Revolution*, 15–16; *13*). By thwarting this "new adjustment between the law and its transgression," fascism and Stalinism would come to exemplify (but again, as a matter of degree) the more general principle that "a (any) society may be stabilized only if it excludes poetic language" (*Polylogue, 357, 365; Desire,* 23, 31).

Kristeva's analysis of texts from the historical avant-garde under advanced capitalism invariably insists on a double movement of opposition and recuperation. By reinscribing within the very texture of poetic language the negativity repressed by the ideological and economic mechanisms of capitalist society, the avant-garde text serves to "insert, within a non-thought, . . . the violence of rejection, which is viewed as death by the unary subject" (*Revolution*, 186; *166*).

But in entering into contradiction with the capitalist system and its ideological appendages, Kristeva continues, "the text also plays into its hands; through the text, the system provides itself with what it lacks—rejection—but keeps it in a domain apart, confining it to the ego, to the 'inner experience' of an elite, and to esoterism" (*Revolution*, 186; *166*). Much of the specific textual analysis in *Revolution in Poetic Language* aims to uncover that triple gesture whereby the capitalist mode of production "produces" the forms of its contestation (e.g., a "schizophrenic" shattering of the symbolic), "marginalizes" those forms (in esoteric literary elites), and then "exploits [them] for its own regeneration" (*Revolution*, 15; *13*). Thus, the third part of Kristeva's massive study serves to illustrate the proposition that the Third Republic "finds a prop in the infinite in the guise of religion, esoteric rites [*mystère*] and poetry, and could not function without these 'margins' " (*Révolution, 380*).

What ultimately limits this mechanism of production and marginalization for recuperation, Kristeva would argue, is the specifically transgressive signifying practice of the speaking subject (*sujet parlant*). Or, more precisely, it is the practical manifestation of a blissfully transgressive excess that is attributable, dialectically, to the destructuring tendencies inherent in advanced capitalism; "with modern capitalism," she writes, "destructuring takes precedence over structure, excess gets the best of constraint" (*Polylogue, 518*):

> It is true that capitalism enjoys an extraordinary capacity to restructure the shattering [*éclatement*] that nourishes it [the breakup of the patriarchal family, of the State, etc.]. . . . But there remains a sensitive place [*lieu névralgique*] where this permanent patching-up is most difficult, if not impossible. I have in mind the speaking subject, his relations with the constraining social unit, and with a *jouissance* that hinges upon this unity, on the condition it be exceeded. (*Polylogue, 518*)

As the point of breakdown in the capitalist mechanism of "permanent patching-up," the transgressive practice of the *sujet en procès* lays the groundwork for Kristeva's conception of a specifically political ethic.

The Ethics of Transgression

In the mid-1970s, following a massive disillusionment with the political agendas of May '68 (of both "libertarian-communitarian" and "Marxist-Leninist-religious" varieties), it became common to hear talk of ethics in theoretical contexts where politics (indeed, revolutionary politics) had once prevailed. One commentator has captured the mood of these times in these laconic phrases: "Politics is a dead end. There remains only . . . ethics" (Hirsch, 199).

Kristeva, as usual, would prove more subtle, if not also more deeply equivocal. Already in her work of the *Revolution in Poetic Language* period one finds clear indications that the political and the ethical are properly inseparable, that a certain "revolution" depends on an ethics of transgression exemplified in literary (and, more especially, poetic) practice. "If literature has an ethical function," she writes in the 1973 "Politique de la littérature," "it is this: to invest language with that which monologism represses (from rhythm to meaning)" (*Polylogue, 18*). In her well-known essay on Roman Jakobson, "L'éthique de la linguistique" (The ethics of linguistics, 1974), Kristeva speaks of a "new ethical formulation" made possible by the work of Marx, Nietzsche, and Freud:

> Ethics used to be a coercive, customary manner of ensuring the cohesiveness of a particular group through the repetition of a code—a more or less accepted apologue. Now, however, the issue of ethics crops up wherever a code (mores, social contract) must be shattered in order to give way to the free play of negativity, need, desire, pleasure, and *jouissance*, before being put together again, although temporarily and with full knowledge of what is involved. (*Polylogue, 357; Desire*, 23)

Two points need be made about Kristeva's ethics of transgression and their pertinence to the question of "revolution"—poetic or otherwise. First, what Kristeva understands by "ethics" implies the "negativizing" of narcissism through practice: "In other words, a practice is ethical when it dissolves those narcissistic fixations (ones that are narrowly confined to the subject) to which the signifying process succumbs in its socio-symbolic realization" (*Revolution*, 233; *203*). When the disruptive force of the death drive is diverted into forms of specular aggressivity (the correlative, for Lacan, of narcissistic identification); when totalitarian systems turn negativity to the account of the leader as all-knowing Other (possessor of a racial memory or a logic of history); when the rejection operative in the work of a Mallarmé becomes "knotted" around the unity of the elitist *moi* or serves to reproduce the repressed fetishistic logic of the capitalist mode of production—in all these cases, as in so many others in *Revolution*, it is narcissism that defuses the revolutionary potential of a negativity that puts thetic positions in process and on trial (*Revolution*, 186; *166, 366*).

Only the negation in practice of such "narcissistic fixations" will allow for the "revolutionary" (or, as Kristeva would later say, "dissident") transgression of an established power, definable (in Lacanian terms) as "a void linking instances of narcissistic identification" (*Révolution, 510*). I would argue, in fact, that we must read what Philip Lewis has called the "perpetually self-revising, reflexive, open-ended, [and] self-validating" quality of Kristeva's texts as a sign not simply of her unfailing attention to the irreducible heterogeneity of human reality, but more particularly of her efforts to dissolve those narcissistic, imaginary identifications with the One invariably elicited by her theoretical metalanguage.[16]

My second point follows from the first. I have shown how Kristeva's ethics of transgression imply an endless practice of structuring and destructuring on the limit between the subjective and the social.[17] As a consequence, they are revolutionary and ethical precisely *because* they refuse what Bataille once called "the infantile ethical tendency of revolutionary unrest" (*Visions, 33–34*). By playing the role of "intermediary between the irruption of rejection and its new, provisional and ephemeral unification," the poetic text serves to guarantee a protracted, dialectical process of production and disruption—a process "the realization of which demands at best several centuries," and in the face of which "revolutionary impatience remains dissatisfied" (*Révolution, 612, 592, 614*).

Indeed, Kristeva's very concept of "revolution" might be said to play the limit between the senses of absolute renewal and cyclical return with which I began this study, and this to the extent that it tracks that dialectic whereby it is the repetitive return of the death drive across thetic positions that ultimately assures the continuity of life itself. Witness, for instance, the (at first sight surprising) conjunction of "revolution" and "survival" in a sentence such as this: "The theory of the unconscious seeks the very thing that poetic language practices within and against the social order: the ultimate means of its transformation or subversion, the precondition for its survival and revolution" (*Revolution*, 81; *79*).

The curious ambivalence in this conception of revolution resurfaces in the following passage, where the phrase beginning "capitalism makes its way toward" appears to pivot between a traditional dialectical reading (according to which capitalism necessarily hastens its own demise, "like the sorcerer, who is no longer able to control the powers of the nether world whom he has called up by his spells") and a more heterodox reading whereby capitalism survives as it makes its way toward a "revolution of the subject" that is in fact already in progress (Marx and Engels, *Manifesto*, 478):

> On a historical level, the very conceivability of such a subject marks the end of a historical era that is consummated in capitalism. Shaken by social conflicts, revolutions, and demands for the irrational (from drugs to madness, both on their way to being recognized and accepted), capitalism makes its way toward an *other* society that will be the achievement of a *new* subject. The *expérience intérieure* of the "sovereign subject" is one symptom of this revolution of the subject. (*Polylogue, 124*)

Intrinsic to Kristeva's concept of revolution, I would argue, is a logic of perpetual renewal—"la logique d'un renouvellement"—whose ethical stake lies not in the fact that it registers the historical stability of Western capitalism (although surely it does), but rather in the way it serves to block the recuperation, by the modern culture of narcissism, of the promise that has inhered to the word "revolution" since at least 1789 (*Revolution*, 172; *156*).[18] More precisely, Kristeva's "realist" dialectic of disruption and survival works to preclude the reproduction, in and through her theory of poetic revolution, of that oscillation between revolutionary hope and despair

I have shown to be elicited by the texts of Lacan and fully realized in the work of Jambet and Lardreau (see Chapters 3 and 5). For what sets this oscillation in motion is the fundamentally narcissistic act whereby the reader projects the knowledge of a fully self-present revolutionary moment, a world historical great red night (*grand soir*), onto a theoretical text that subsequently proves to have been nothing more than the unruffled mirror in which the reader had found the inverted image of his revolutionary ideals. Fascism and Stalinism represent the limits to an ethics of revolutionary transgression because they exemplify the demand for just such a process of narcissistic fixation, a process in which the subject comes to depend on his leader as Other for the knowledge of a "true" logic of history that is but the reflection of his own political desire.

One prerequisite to a reformulation of political ethics on a rigorously nonnarcissistic basis, therefore, is the repudiation of all systems, logics or personalities that would claim a specifically predictive insight into the movement of history (such as Karl Popper has analyzed under the rubric of "historicism"). For Kristeva, the dialectic of history tends toward no certain *telos*, no utopian state. Indeed, the settled situation of a social utopia is precisely precluded by a dialectic that finds constancy in the eternal renewal of the contradiction between rejection and existing social, linguistic, and psychic stases—by a dialectic, if you will, of permanent revolution.

There is, however, something approaching a utopian moment in Kristeva's work, and more particularly in her ethics of transgression. In texts from both before and after her so-called good-bye to politics, we find Kristeva insisting on modes of practice (poetic, political, psychoanalytic, or "semanalytic") specifically attuned to the emergence of what she calls, in "L'éthique de la linguistique" (The ethics of linguistics) "another meaning, but a future, impossible meaning" (*un autre sens, mais a-venir, impossible*) (*Polylogue*, *368*; *Desire*, 33). It is only by unpacking this (exceptionally overdetermined) notion of an impossible meaning to come that one can fully understand the ethical (or better, ethico-political) implications of Kristeva's work in the period under discussion.

A Politics of the Future Impossible

The most familiar resonances to be heard in Kristeva's evocations of a certain "impossibility" are doubtless those that bear the names Lacan and Bataille. When she speaks of the avant-garde text as drawing the signifier nearer to a "drive heterogeneity" (*hétérogène pulsionnel*) or an "impossible real" that is at once its unattainable limit and the condition of its existence, Kristeva plainly appropriates Lacan's insistence on the impossibility or unrepresentability of the death drive: "The death drive is the Real in so far as it can only be thought as impossible, that is, every time it appears right under your nose, it is unthinkable" (*Révolution*, *581*; Seminar of March 16, 1976, cited by Roustang, *Delusion*, 100; *103*). And yet, while following Lacan's lead in disjoining the traditional linkage between the moral and the possible (specifically, possible action), Kristeva will refuse that tragicomic oscillation that results from the Lacanian injunction not to yield on one's (inherently unsatisfiable) desire. Her ethics of the impossible rejoin the possible not as an effect of hope, but as the upshot of a specifically transgressive practice.

In this respect, Kristeva's ethics of the impossible bear a stronger resemblance to Bataille's. For in Bataille "transgression" serves to name both a movement beyond the "real" world of utility, science, and reason to that "impossible" realm of *l'expérience intérieure* (a realm of violence, sacrifice, sovereign play, erotic excess, and the communication of fissured subjects) *and a reaffirmation of this-worldly limits*. It is thus the very impossibility of any definitive "utopian" installation in the "impossible" that determines a return to the world of utility as realm of the possible. Bataille captures this double movement constitutive of transgression in these final lines of a preface to *L'Impossible*:

> The human race stands before a double prospect. On the one hand, that of violent pleasure, horror, and death—exactly that of poetry—and, in the opposite direction, that of science or the real world of utility. Only the useful—the real—has a serious nature. We are never in a position to prefer seduction: truth has its claims on us, indeed all possible claims. Yet we can and must respond to *something* that, not being God, is stronger than these claims. This is the *impossible*, to which we accede only by forgetting the truth of these claims, by accepting disappearance. (*Œuvres complètes, 3: 102*)

This necessary reaffirmation of the realm of science and social utility speaks in turn to the way in which Bataille, like Kristeva, ultimately dialectizes the vitalist play of death and life: "discontinuous beings that we are," Bataille writes in *Erotism*, "death means continuity of being"; "the death of one being is correlated with the birth of the other" (13, 55; *19, 62*). For the productivity of the death drive (and of a poetry that espouses its disruptive power) depends on their entering into contradiction with an existing social order: "by introducing transcendence into an organised world," Bataille contends, "transgression becomes the principle of an organized disorder" (*Erotism*, 119; *132*).

There can be no question here, as there had been for Barthes, of looking to literature as an impossible, atopian space of liberty, as that "grand imposture" that allows one to hear an impossible language outside politics and all relations of power. For Bataille as for Kristeva, rather, the poetic experience of sovereign expenditure finds its full realization in the poet's act of taking political responsibility for "the order to come":

> When disgust with a powerless liberty thoroughly commits the poet to political action, he abandons poetry. But he immediately assumes responsibility for the order to come [*à venir*]: he asserts the direction of activity, the

> major attitude. When we see him we cannot help being aware that poetic existence, in which we once saw the possibility of a sovereign attitude, is really a minor attitude. (*Literature and Evil*, 38, *41*; cited in *Revolution*, 212; *186*)

In accordance, however, with the long-standing, Saint-Simonian dream of a confluence between the political and aesthetic avant-gardes, Kristeva would precisely deny the necessity of choosing between political action and a poetic practice that she theorizes as always already political.

From the perspective of the mid-1970s, this dream of parallel avant-gardes would prove as problematic as it was desirable. If the conjunction of textual negativity with a revolutionary critique of the social order was, as Kristeva suggests, "precisely what the dominant ideology and its various mechanisms of liberalism, oppression, and defense find intolerable," it remained "also what is most difficult to accomplish" (*Revolution*, 191; *170*).

For Kristeva, as for the authors of the *Tel Quel* group more generally, the central political problem in this respect was one of address. The question with which Kristeva closes "Le sujet en procès"—"Can the artist make himself heard by subjects transforming the process of history, and if so how?"—applies doubly for the theoretical work of *Tel Quel*, the highly technical and allusive idiom of which only exacerbated that "gulf between socialist thought and the soil of popular revolution" that Perry Anderson has shown to be characteristic of Western Marxism (*Polylogue*, *106*; *Considerations*, 54).

Compounding this problem of verbal complexity was a perception that the industrial working class, as the potential addressee of a new revolutionary poetics, had massively betrayed its historical mission (see Chapter 2). The recuperation of the proletariat by the enticements of consumer society—theorized by Marcuse in *One-Dimensional Man* and thought to account for the reformist actions of the PCF and CGT in the May events—was but the most prominent of the contemporary developments that led Kristeva to suggest that "today" one can read the following analysis between the lines of the *Eighteenth Brumaire*: "Every time the revolutionary process settles in, realizes itself, and so takes form as a state structure or an ideology, this process is betrayed, reduced to local interests . . . , to preexisting ideological systems, to subjective identifications representing private property" (*Révolution*, *377*).

Tel Quel's antidote to this perceived absence in the structure of artistic and theoretical address was to speak of revolutionary practices as directed to an addressee *à venir*: to conceive of dialectical materialism, for example, as understandable only by a "new subject" who is "elusive because he *transforms* the real" (Kristeva) or to take the side of a proletariat "that does not yet exist, but remains to be constituted" (Bernard Sichère) (*Revolution*, 178, *161*; cited by Kritzman, "Changing," 417).[19] Kristeva's *Revolution* epitomizes the *Tel Quel* project to the extent that it would anticipate this new subject—free from a recuperative enclosure in subjective modes of experience, burst open by and toward "heterogeneous materiality"—and would do so specifically by reading *past* moments of rupture (Lautréamont/Mallarmé, Marx/Freud) as "massive symptoms" of a social mutation "still to come" (*à venir*) (*Revolution*, 212, 186; Sollers, *Théorie d'ensemble*, 394).

But this revolution *à venir* is properly "impossible," not simply because it is to be attributed to the transgressive practice of a subject that is "elusive," a "nonplace," because it is traversed by a negativity that is itself impossible to know or to think, but also because—from the point of view of the practice that projects it—it *will not have taken place as such*. Here again, Kristeva looks to the exemplary role played by texts of the historical avant-garde.[20] In a discussion of the reawakening of feudal mythemes in the poetry of Mayakovsky, she writes, "The irruption within the order of language of the anteriority of language evokes a later time, that is, a forever [*appelle à plus tard, c'est-à-dire à jamais*]. The poem's time frame is some 'future anterior' that will never take place [*n'aura jamais lieu*], never come about as such, but only as an upheaval of present place and meaning" (*Polylogue*, 366–76; *Desire*, 32).

Avant-garde textual practice implies a double temporality. The text remains anchored in the present to the extent that it both represents and rejects existing stases of language and ideology. But in the very movement of its negativity, "the text is always a 'future anterior': echo and precursor, outside time; a telescoping of 'before' and 'after'; a break in the series, in teleology, in becoming; the moment of a leap" (*Révolution*, 364). By instituting a shuttle-movement between "a rhythmic, meaningless, anterior memory" and a meaning announced "*pour plus tard ou jamais*" (strictly: for later, and for an *impossible* forever), poetic language serves to disrupt both the teleological movement of eternal self-presence that is the Hegelian dialectic and the obsessive linearity of empiricist historiography while it points the way toward what Kristeva calls "a monumental historicity" (*Polylogue*, 366; *Desire*, 32).

It is of course from Nietzsche's "On the Uses and Disadvantages of History for Life" that Sollers, Kristeva, Derrida, and others have derived their various conceptions of a "monumental historicity."[21] In that text Nietzsche speaks of "monumental history" as originating in the specifically life-affirming demand to envision the "great moments in the struggle of the human individual" as a single chain, a chain "unit[ing] mankind across the millennia like a range of human mountain peaks" (68). Those lofty human summits on which monumental history dwells serve an *exemplary* function; they are "models, teachers, comforters"—antidotes to resignation and paradigms of a once- and thus ever-possible greatness ("Uses," 67).

In the following chapter I shall argue for the centrality of exemplary action—defined as public political action serving to capture and catalyze the collective imagination, and thus to elicit individual acts of imitation—in the political context of May '68. Typically, the efficacy of the exemplary act, its capacity to spark a mimetic "contagion," was seen to depend on the (more or less subjective) identification of others with the act's original agent. Such, of course, was precisely the sort of identification that Kristeva found to repeat the "narcissistic fixations" buttressing advanced capitalism as we know it.

It remained the case, however, that the act of anticipating an "impossible" revolution *à venir* (while addressing an "impossible" subject, equally *à venir*) was itself a form of exemplary action. Philip Lewis is precisely right when he claims that the *Tel Quel* authors perceived their "fundamentally *exemplary* role as a historicizable force, as a present condition of the future possibility of a revolution which cannot be theorized within the mainstream of social evolution, which can be anticipated in its necessity only from a purposefully marginal position" (32).

Kristeva's (arguably untenable) response to the problem of theorizing exemplary action in rigorously nonnarcissistic terms was to speak of the identification elicited by the "monumental historicity" endemic to poetic language, which ceaselessly displaces resurgent semiotic rhythms "to an impossible time-to-come," as identification not with another subject (however life-affirming), but rather with "productivity" itself as the impossible identity of the signifying process with "objective, natural, and social laws": "To identify with the process of signifying, subjective, social identity, to identify with an impossible identity—this is precisely what it means to practice process, to put the subject and its stases in process/on trial, to make the laws of *signifiance* correspond to objective, natural, and social laws" (*Polylogue,* 90).

Reading passages such as this in the mid-1990s, one cannot help but be struck by their wishful theoreticism, their tendency blithely to square theoretical circles with little regard for considerations of actual political practice. But Kristeva's attempts to reformulate the logic of history and the practice of exemplary action in forms that resist the narcissistic drive to One Meaning or Word remain of interest, I would argue, to the extent that they imply the quest for what she calls, in the 1977 essay, "A New Type of Intellectual: The Dissident," a "new status of the *modern community*" (294; 4).

Her reading of Lautréamont's *Poésies* in *Revolution in Poetic Language* serves as a case in point. In the events of 1870—the fall of the Second Empire, French defeat in the Franco-Prussian war, and a "crumbling of national values"—Kristeva finds the historical objectification of a romantic, nihilistic rejection operative in Lautréamont's earlier *Chants de Maldoror* (*Révolution, 413*). Grasping for the positive as for a "life-buoy," Lautréamont is said to have turned to that "new signifying disposition" exemplified in the *Poésies*, where an apparently "classical" diction is put in process by a series of ironic subversions (subversions of the enunciative position, of the structure of logical opposition, and so on). In so doing, Kristeva claims, Lautréamont anticipated the Paris Commune as the sociohistorical realization of that productive movement of negativity whereby the thetic is called forth so as incessantly to be transgressed. Despite its lack of any concrete historical reference, in other words, *Poésies* foreshadows the Commune to the extent that it demands "a new legality, a new positivity, but always . . . questionable, impossible, ironized, because it is preoccupied above all with the *jouissance* procured by (the) *movement* [*le mouvement*: the political movement as objectification of the movement of negativity] and not by the *taking of power*" (*Révolution, 414*).

Two points need be made here. First, Lautréamont's *Poésies* (and the commune they "anticipate") are seen to enact that very same shuttle movement between the past and a still-impossible future to which Kristeva's own readings of Lautréamont and others lay claim: "To the historical present [the dissolution of the bourgeois order], *Poésies* responds with a still-impossible future [beyond the commune], taking the guise of an anteriority [classicism]" (*Révolution, 413–14*). Ostensibly grounded in the movement of negativity, "monumental history" as Kristeva practices it tends to collapse historical moments of revolutionary upheaval into a single "chain," held together by a common focus on that future impossible of which the moments themselves are said to be symptomatic.

One name for this future impossible—this is my second point—is the "modern community." For it is precisely to that which Kristeva sees as precluding the Paris Commune's "success" (in the traditional sense of taking hold of the reigns of power), to that *jouissance* attending to the movement of "negativity" or "rejection," that she will look for the basis of a new sociability: "A sort of *community* results from this nonetheless, no doubt on account of this thetic that is affirmed so as to be denied in the very movement of rejection: *a community sealed together by the subject articulated . . . as the process of an incessant negativity*—countering the individualistic exceptionality of the *ego* through the communal exceptionality of all" (*Révolution, 416*; emphasis added).

At the heart of Kristeva's critique of the modern politics of narcissism, I have found a paradoxical causal linkage (both logical and historical) between a defense of "the individualistic exceptionality of the ego," such as exemplified under bourgeois capitalism, and that movement, epitomized by fascism and Stalinism, whereby the demand for social unity serves to close down this exceptionality. The impossible unity and autonomy to which the bourgeois subject aspires in the full flower of his narcissism finds its highest realization, in other words, in the image of the leader of the totalitarian state as putative bearer of the "truth" of his subjects' desires.

When Kristeva returns to the question of the community in the essay on the intellectual as dissident (subsequent, therefore, to her *adieu à la politique*), she attempts to retheorize the community "sealed together" by the subject in process within an expressly nonrevolutionary setting. Specifically, she looks to the transgressive syncretism of meaning, sound, gesture, and color in the "new languages" of the avant-garde and contemporary underground culture as the basis of a nonnarcissistic ethic of subjective "singularity"—an ethic that would neither deny nor hypostatize the social group, but rather make use of the group to affirm "singularity" through the deployment of new forms of noncoercive address:

> In place of the mass meeting or the walkabout [*A la place du bain de foule ou de masse*] whose most "successful" manifestations are fascist meetings or socialist realism, these new languages use the group to interpellate singular forms of subjectivity or the unconscious. What has emerged in our postwar culture, after the wave of totalitarianism, are singular forms of speech and jouissance [*la singularité des dires et des jouissances*] serving to counteract the One equalizing Word, even when it is secular or militant. . . . Communal but singular, addressed to all and yet carried out by each alone: such is the culture of our age, when it is not an echo-chamber of the past. ("Dissident," 295; *4*)

The role of the intellectual, her "dissident function," is to "become the analyst" of that process whereby semiotic negativity fissures social, discursive, or institutional unity, thus rendering it "impossible." But in so doing she asserts the future possibility of "the Impossible"—of "another society, another community, another corporality"; of a collectivity paradoxically sutured by the openness of the dissident subject (or what Kristeva used to call the *sujet en procès*) to material, social, and corporeal negativity: "Give voice to the singularity of unconsciousnesses, desires, needs. Call into play the identities and/or languages of the individual and the group. Become the analyst of the impossibility of social cohesion, of homogeneous discourses and time-honored institutions. Assert oneself as the revealer of the Impossible" ("Dissident," 295; *4*).

In *Revolution in Poetic Language*, Kristeva had suggested that, "among all political movements, it is perhaps anarchism that corresponds most closely to [the] transversal operation of the process of signifiance" (*Révolution, 421*). As her subsequent equivocations on the matter would suggest, the very complexity of the specific relation between political anarchism and aesthetic subversion on the model sketched by *Revolution* tends to preclude all cursory treatment. It is nonetheless curious that Kristeva would return to the anarchist parallel (and indeed to the Paris Commune) in the paragraph that immediately follows her characterization of the intellectual as "revealer of the Impossible":

> Only the Paris Commune, as the first (and the only?) post-bourgeois revolution, has perhaps displayed this degree of anarchist enthusiasm in its fight against all power, beliefs and institutions.
>
> But an explosion of languages, like that of our age, has rarely produced such a clear awareness of the closed nature of society and its safety mechanisms, which range from the group (the Family, the Nation, the State, the Party) to its rational and technological forms of discourse. In this place where discursive and rational coherence is burst asunder, the intellectual,

> as the agent of discursive rationality, is the first to suffer the effects of its break-up [*l'intellectuel qui en est l'agent en subit le premier les effets*]: his own identity is called into question, his dissidence becomes more radical. ("Dissident," 294–95; 4)

These paragraphs, like those which precede them in the "Dissident" essay, pose questions remarkably similar to those I shall raise in the following chapter, which explores the complex interface between anarchism, exemplary action, and hysteria in the manifesto writings of Hélène Cixous. The efficacy of explosive speech acts addressed to all and yet carried out singularly; the creation of community through the exemplary action of a subject traversed by an "external" negativity (such as social violence); the political subject as victim of the very act by which she asserts herself as "revealer of the Impossible"—these are among the most prominent of those problematics to be explored in a reading of Cixous's "Explosive Hysterics."

CHAPTER 8

Explosive Hysterics: Cixous

> We are reliving the false-starts and illusionments of those who, as children of the nineteenth century, tried to mount a revolt against socio-symbolic unity.
>
> — Julia Kristeva, *Revolution in Poetic Language*

This chapter takes as its starting point three of Hélène Cixous's best-known texts: the 1975 "The Laugh of the Medusa," her contributions to *The Newly Born Woman* also from 1975, and a 1976 essay entitled "Coming to Writing." Like such earlier works as her novels *Neutre* (1972) and *Portrait du soleil* (Portrait of the sun, 1973), these texts explore the complex margins that separate autobiography, fiction, theory, and criticism. But they do so from a position of explicitly feminine militancy indicative of Cixous's recent engagement with the work of the collective Psychanalyse et politique.[1]

As the space of a performative writing meant to bring addressor and addressee into a relationship of "intimate collusion," each of these texts is a manifesto or partakes of the manifesto form (Perloff, 106). By raising her voice on the cacophonous floor of history, she who speaks would incite other women to raise *their* voices, to effect their "shattering entry" into a history that "has always been based *on [their] repression*" ("Laugh," 251; *43*). The unabashed purpose of Cixous's mid-1970s manifesto writings is thus to make a scene as a prelude to the constitution of new, specifically feminine forms of community. Against the Hegelian drama of recognition and a (historically masculine) form of desire grounded in the battle unto death, against a frenzy of appropriation seen to be driven by masculine anxieties of loss, these texts posit ways of being with the other that are dependent on vertiginously proliferating exchange, gift without reserve, and reciprocity without mastery (*Newly Born*, 78-80, *144–47*; "Laugh," 263–64; *52*). Beyond the tragicomic oscillation inherent in the Lacanian dialectic of desire and the Law, they dare to imagine a comic flight into a utopian realm of "pure . . . unbridled desire, immediately outside all law" (*Newly Born*, 117; *217*).

As one might expect from so masterful a discursive mimic as Hélène Cixous, the commonplaces I call the logics of failed revolt serve, once again, as rhetorical pretexts to a movement beyond the impasses they delineate. "Let us not be trapped by an analysis still encumbered with the old automatisms," she writes in the Medusa essay:

> It's not to be feared that language conceals an invincible adversary, because it's the language of men and their grammar. . . .
>
> Nor is the point to appropriate their instruments, their concepts, their places, or to begrudge them their position of mastery. Just because there's a risk of identification doesn't mean that we'll succumb. Let's leave it to the worriers, to masculine anxiety and its obsession with how to dominate the way things work—knowing "how it works" in order to "make it work." For us the point is not to take possession in order to internalize or manipulate, but rather to dash through [*traverser d'un trait*] and to "fly" (or "steal" [*voler*]). ("Laugh," 257; *49*)

Here, in the space of several lines, Cixous has managed to (1) dismiss Lacanian anxieties about the recuperative power of the *discours du maître* ("It's not to be feared . . . "), (2) warn against a repetition that she, like her sisters at Psych et po, saw to inhere to all forms of "feminist" practice that ignored the necessity of revolutionizing the Symbolic ("Nor is the point . . . "), and (3) finesse the question of specular doubling ("Just because there's a risk . . . ").

This triple gesture sets the stage for a pun on the French verb *voler* (to fly, to steal) that exemplifies a conception of discursive complicity central to Cixous's project: the only way for the newly born woman to fly, she suggests, is to steal her wings, shimmering and multiple, from the discursive fathers (Derrida, Lacan, Bataille, Kleist, Shakespeare, et al.). Or, closer to my concerns, the only way to "cut through" (*traverse[r]*) what Cixous calls the "psychoanalytic closure" would be to hijack psychoanalytic concepts so as to think them "elsewhere" or "otherwise" ("Laugh," 263; *53*).[2]

The aim of this chapter is to show how Cixous's hijacking of a concept crucial to the historical development of Freudian theory, that of hysteria, helps structure her response to the question I left hanging at the end of the previous chapter, the question of "a new status of the modern community" (Kristeva). I will argue that Cixous's work performs the political (or better, "ethico-political") task of rethinking the problem of community within what Alice Jardine has rightly diagnosed as a generalized theoretical turn "from paranoia to hysteria" (*Gynesis*, 38). Against a paranoid suppression of alterity endemic to the (historically male) subject who would be One—be it the individual (the liberal monad) or those transcendent subjects we call the state, the party, the family, or the fatherland—Cixous proposes forms of hysterical self-division that play themselves out, in an endless relation of metaphoric transfer, on the body politic, on the text as body, and on the body proper. But this play of hysterical metaphoricity proves, in turn, to be closely allied with a metaphorics of anarchist bomb throwing, a metaphorics whose untimely pertinence in the political context of post-May France I examine in this chapter's final sections.

The Hysterical Text

Cixous opens a portion of her dialogue with Catherine Clément in *The Newly Born Woman* by evoking her seduction by—even sense of election to—the hysterical "situation": "I got into the sphere of hysteria because I was drawn—called. . . . If it is only a metaphor—and it's not clear that this is so—it functions well, it has its use. I started with Dora; I read that text in a sort of dizziness, exploding over the situation presented, where at heart I found myself siding frenetically with the different characters" (147–48; *271–72*). Likewise in "Sorties," her principal contribution to *The Newly Born Woman,* Cixous writes: "The hysterics are my sisters. As Dora, I have been all the characters she played, the ones who got shivers when she cut through them [*qu'elle traverse et fait frémir*], and in the end I got away, having been Freud one day, Mrs. Freud another, also Mr. K . . . , Mrs. K . . .—and the wound Dora inflicted on them" (99; *184*). To be "drawn" or "called" into the "sphere of hysteria" is thus to mimic that same mimetic facility that Charcot had found at work in the hysteric's *attitudes passionnelles,* and which had led Freud's Dora to mime first the gastric pains of one cousin, then the appendicitis of another (*Dora,* 54, 121).[3]

Faced with intolerable circularities—those of specular doubling, of the masculine anxiety of lack, or of the "psychoanalytic enclosure" more generally—Cixous's response, like Dora's in the face of *her* family circle, is to "cut through" (*traverser*). Although specular identification with a rival clearly serves to perpetuate the Hegelian "empire of the selfsame" (*empire du propre*), Cixous by no means rejects all identification with another. The transversal strategy she shares with her hysterical "sister" leads her rather to call for "vertiginous crossings" (*traversées*) of the other, "brief, identificatory embraces" ("Laugh," 259–60; *50*). Like the "flight"/"theft" pun, the punning title of "Sorties" effectively restates the paradoxical logic of the hysteric's transversal tactic: the best hope of escape (*sortie*) from the masculine enclosure lies with the giddy mimeticism of the hysterical attack (*sortie*) (see Gallop, "Keys," 136).

But Cixous will go still further. In a series of remarkable pages from the 1976 "Coming to Writing," she speaks of her body as a medium—traversed, impregnated, and invaded by the other; capturing language and the real through its nerves and senses; working them over and recomposing them as a book ("Coming," 52, *63*; cf. Conley, *Cixous*, 146). André Breton's well-known glorification of the hysteric as medium, of that "procession of nude young women gliding along the rooftops" (*141*), pales beside Cixous's violently symptomatic descriptions of a quasidemonic possession attending her coming into writing:

> "Writing" seized me, gripped me, around the diaphragm, between the stomach and the chest, a blast dilated my lungs and I stopped breathing.
>
> Suddenly I was filled with a turbulence that knocked the wind out of me and inspired me to wild acts. . . . But in the depths of the flesh, the attack. Pushed. Not penetrated. Invested. Set in motion. The attack was imperious: "Write!" Even though I was only a meager anonymous mouse, I knew vividly the awful jolt that galvanizes the prophet, wakened in mid-life by an order from above. ("Coming," 9; *18*)

In an important article on the changing face of hysteria in the late nineteenth century, Gladys Swain has shown that the hysteric's capacity to be possessed follows from an essential (feminine) dispossession. While acting out (in more or less displaced form) the experience of being sexually possessed by a man, the hysteric also acts out the woman's dispossession to and through nature, an overcoming of her "self-preserving self" and her sense of "subjective, personal proprietorship" by the "reproductive self." As the "irruption of [a] potential to be dispossessed that serves to define the feminine condition," the hysterical attack thus reproduces "the age-old logic of feminine representation" (114, 125).

"A woman, by her opening up," Cixous writes in a similar vein, "is open to being 'possessed,' which is to say, dispossessed of herself" (*Newly Born*, 86; *159*). But dispossession is a threat, she insists, only to those practitioners of restricted economies who consign their lives to the "lack-banks" of the "father's religion" (85; *157*). For not only does the "maddening movement" of perpetual loss enacted in the "shredded woof" of the hysterical body turn that body itself into text—"Life becomes text starting out from my body. I am already text"—this textuality points in turn toward a new, specifically feminine mode of being with the other ("Coming," 52; *63*). Or, more precisely, openness to (dis)possession fosters a new (hysterical) economy functioning on that complex limit where textuality and sociability fold into one another:

> Writing is the passageway, the entrance, the exit, the dwelling place of the other in me—the other that I am and am not [*que je suis et ne suis pas*], that I don't know how to be, but that I feel passing, that makes me live—that tears me apart, disturbs me, changes me, who?—a feminine one, a masculine one, some?—which is indeed what gives me the desire to know and from which all life soars. (*Newly Born*, 85–86; *158*)

> To admit that writing is precisely working (in) the in-between [*travailler (dans) l'entre*] . . . this is first to want the two, as well as both, the ensemble of the one and the other, not fixed in sequences of struggle and expulsion or

> some other form of putting-to-death, but infinitely dynamized by an incessant process of exchange from one subject to another. ("Laugh," 254; *46*)

Rarely has writing's capacity to work (in) the in-between been explored with such persistence and fictional intelligence as in Cixous's 1973 *Portrait du soleil.* A novelistic reworking of the Dora case, *Portrait* is also a remarkable meditation on Bataille's vision of eroticism as a domain of violence and corporeal violation. For here, as in Bataille, the act of disarticulating one's lover, of opening up a wound in a being constituted as discontinuous, is seen ultimately to restore a continuity fundamental to being itself; the injunction to kill thus becomes the injunction to a certain sacred communication: "Dieubis is. I kill him [*Je le tue*]. Dieubis is. I kill him. Dieubis is. I say *tu*" (*Portrait, 15*). "The violence of the one proposes itself," Bataille had written, "to the violence of the other; on each side there is an inner compulsion to get outside the self (outside the limits of individual discontinuity)" (*Erotism,* 103; *114*). But such a pure reciprocity had foundered on Bataille's tendency to portray the woman as the primary recipient of erotic violence: "The woman in the hands of her assailant is despoiled of her being [*dépossédée de son être*]. . . . She is brusquely laid open to the violence of the sexual urges set loose in the organs of reproduction" (90; *100–101*).

Cixous's project in *Portrait du soleil,* although markedly compromised by the novel's final scene, is to rethink the model of erotic communication such that the injunction to dispossess the other "has a double sex (both male and female) and a single body, red and undelimited" (*37*). In the following passage, a female narrator who names herself Cixous reflects on an act of throat-cutting/castration in which she parries a threat of disarticulation through an equally disarticulating confusion with the object of her violence:

> One of the most beautiful forms of expenditure is that which awakens, in short order, the dizzying charm of the categorical imperative ["You must kill"], such that you can no longer turn back without being mortally torn apart. The task must be carried out, even if it entails your own death, because you are confused with your target in an extraordinary way. It is as if you *were* that target—the penis to be stroked, the body to be killed. Nothing more radically purifies the world of all that is not me: I take an interest in the round Head; I become one with the neck; I bend solicitously over [*Je me penche sur*] the penis and I am that musculature. *Schwarzer, rett'dich!* [Blacky, be off!] (*39*)

In *The Interpretation of Dreams,* Freud derives the phrase *Schwarzer, rett'dich!* from the image, in the dream of a female patient, of an unrecognizable black vegetable he interprets as a "dream combination" of asparagus—"No knowledgeable person of either sex will ask for an interpretation of asparagus"—and black (Spanish) radish (*Schwarzer Rettig*). What the phrase conceals, or so Freud fancies, is "a phantasy of my behaving in an improper and sexually provocative manner, and of the patient putting up a defence against my conduct." "If this interpretation seems incredible," he adds, "I need only point to the numerous instances in which doctors have charges of the same kind brought against them by hysterical women" (218–19).

As Freud's analysis here clearly implies, the hysterical symptom represents a particularly unstable adjoining of contraries—a volatile compromise between repressive and transgressive forces, activity and passivity, Thanatos and Eros, aggressivity and engendering. More particularly, it expresses both a revolt against the Law and an identification with that Law, whose vengeance it commonly acts out on the hysteric's own body. Witness the case that Freud cites as evidence of "the bisexual nature of hysterical symptoms," the patient who acts both roles of the seduction scene, "press[ing] her dress to her body with one hand (as the woman), while trying to tear it off with the other (as the man)" ("Aetiology," in *Dora* 151). Or, as Cixous would write in "Coming to Writing," "As myself, I was a center of passions, fear and trembling, fury and vengeance. . . . Me: the lamb. Me: the wolf" (14–15; *28*).

What hysteria clearly shares with the experience of erotic transgression, which Bataille himself links to "the anguish, nausea and horror commonly felt by young girls in the last century," is a tendency to suppose the Law as fundamental. In rewriting Bataille's theory of communication, however, Cixous pushes the ambivalent logic of hysterical identification to the point where it founds the subject on a differential play without origin—between self and other, woman and man, suffocating hysteric and sacrificial cutthroat:

> I felt the throat resist. I felt myself suffocate at the intersection of contradictions that strangled me: the one is the other is me. Cutting through this logic, as I would have had to do, would have meant cutting into myself. (*Portrait, 16*)
>
> As a cutthroat am I not the one whose throat is cut? What holds me back is that the subject has a thousand names and who knows which is the first throat. (*Portrait, 85*)

As *Portrait du soleil* unfolds, scenarios of erotic transgression increasingly give way to the slippage of subjects crossing and recrossing what Cixous calls "the line of genders" (*131*). Thus Freud, wanting to speak to Freud, speaks to Frau Freud and identifies himself as Frau Freud: "'Funny situation,' I mumbled. 'I know,' I said" (*150*). What began as a transgressive intimacy linking the narrator to a succession of "god"-lovers—"Dieubis is . . . I say *tu*"—ends in a cross-gendered play of displacement and identity grounded in the same/other structure of resemblance:

> I change places, displacing Jeor whom I am and whom I follow [*que je suis*] and whom I am not and do not follow, displacing Dieubis who is Jeor whom I am and follow, and so forth. . . . I approached myself. (*169*)
>
> Resemblance. The same difference: none all. (*120*)

In writing—or, more precisely, in "fiction"—the subject "approaches" herself through a tropological play, a movement of "spacing" or the "in-between," that Cixous will ultimately call "MetaFor" (*Portrait, 84, 176*).

What she means by "MetaFor" is clearly not the substitution of a figurative meaning for a proper one, an operation far too reminiscent of those Hegelian "sequences of struggle and expulsion" that writing, as a "working (in) the in-between," is intended to banish ("Laugh," 254, *46*; see Conley, *Cixous*, 34). Rather "MetaFor" names a movement of perpetual exchange without the repression of difference, a movement at work in language (in puns and in portmanteau words) as well as in the relation to others. In *Portrait du soleil*, for instance, the narrator's sacrificial cutting of the orange-blooded phallus/neck resonates, metaphorically, with her cutting of *l'oranje*—a blood orange whose name is itself a "metaphoric condensation" of "Oran" (the narrator's birthplace) and the first person singular pronoun, *Je*.[4]

If the narrator of *Portrait* ultimately approaches herself through the complex metaphoricity of *l'oranje*—"The oranje is my birth fruit and prophetic flower. The first time I cut up a word it was this" (5)—"The Laugh of the Medusa" will speak of the plurality of women approaching themselves through the so-called maternal metaphor:

> Text: my body—shot through with streams of song; [hear me]; I don't mean the overbearing, clutchy "mother" but, rather, what touches you, the equivoice that affects you, fills your breast with an urge to come to language and launches *your* force; the rhythm that laughs you, the intimate addressee who makes all metaphors possible and desirable; body (body? bodies?), no more describable than god, the soul, or the Other; that part of you that enters and spaces you [*la partie de toi qui entre en toi t'espace*], urging you to inscribe in language your woman's style. ("Laugh," 252; *44*)

If one restores to this passage the exhortation to "hear me" (*entends-moi*) that was left out of the standard English translation, a crucial indeterminacy comes into focus. To whom is this exhortation, and the passage as a whole, addressed? Is the addressee an "other" woman, brought into language by an "equivoice" (note the metaphoric condensation) emanating from the text that is the author's own body? Or is it rather that body/text itself, called to effect a certain self-spacing? Cixous's point, I would suggest, is that we cannot in fact distinguish. For if the mother is a "metaphor" for that gift whereby "woman gives woman to the other woman," then it designates any part of the self or other that serves to other the self, to give birth to the self as other. It names a hymenic play of inside and outside, a spacing of self and other, through which "woman" approaches herself; in a word, it names a *je(u)*: "She comes in, comes-in-between herself me and you [*Elle entre, elle entre-elle moi et toi*], between the other me where one is always infinitely more than one and more than me, without the fear of ever reaching a limit; she takes her bliss in our becoming" ("Laugh," 263–64; *53*).

Passages such as these certainly justify Gayatri Spivak's characterization of Cixous as "the most Derridean of the French 'anti-feminist' feminists" ("Feminism," 145). As both a metaphor for specific acts of womanly giving and the very possibility of a perpetual metaphoricity—"the intimate addressee who makes all metaphors possible and desirable"—Cixous's "mother" obeys a double logic analogous to that sketched out by Derrida in his reading, in "The Double Session," of the whitenesses that pervade and structure Mallarmé's text. For Cixous, to paraphrase Derrida, every specific act of the feminine gift serves to trope that spacing, that hymen, or that in-between (*entre*) that makes it possible just as, inversely, all such spacings function as tropes of that gift (see *Dissemination*, 257–58; *290*). As she strikes such Derridian notes, Cixous would have her reader believe that hysteria has been (or will soon be) left behind—indeed, left behind by the maternal metaphor itself: "You might object, 'What about she who is the hysterical offspring of a bad mother?' Everything will be changed once woman gives woman to the other woman" ("Laugh," 252; *44*). And yet it is the play of hysterical (dis)possession that, time and again in Cixous's work, allows for "writing" as the passage "in me . . . [of] that other that I am and am not"—for a textual/social economy, in short, driven by the endless becoming of "MetaFor."

The Explosive I-Woman

If we are fully to grasp what is at stake in the linkage of hysteria and metaphoricity, however, we need turn to one of the more astonishing aspects of Cixous's manifesto writings: their tendency to thematize the hysteric's contestatory potential in consistently explosive terms. In *The Newly Born Woman*, for instance, Cixous will elide the typically passive nature of nineteenth-century hysterical aggressivity by speaking of Freud's hysterics as "bombarding his mosaic statue/law of Moses [*statue mosaïque*] with their carnal, passionate bodywords" (95; *176*). Likewise Dora becomes for Cixous "the nuclear example [both central and bomb-like] of women's power to protest" and of its capacity "to burst the family into pieces" (154; *283*).

Perhaps the most telling example of Cixous's tendency to equate hysterical symptomatology with explosive fracturing comes in the following passage, in which she hijacks the punning title of Lacan's seminar on feminine *jouissance, Encore*:

> *In body/Still more* [*En corps*]: woman is body more than man is. Because he is invited to social success, to sublimation. More body hence more writing. For a long time it has been in body that she has answered the harassment, the familial conjugal venture of domestication, the repeated attempts to castrate her. Woman, who has turned her tongue [*tourné . . . sa langue*] ten thousand times seven times before not speaking, is either dead from it or knows her tongue and her mouth better than anyone. Now, I-woman am going to blow up the Law: an explosion henceforth possible and inescapable; let it be done, right now, in language [*dans la langue*]. (*Newly Born*, 95, *175*; "Laugh," 257; *48–49*)

The tense structure of this extract suggests that the hysteric's relation to the practitioner of *écriture féminine* is that of the honored precursor; "yesterday's victims of torture," Cixous writes in this vein, "anticipate the new woman" (*Newly Born*, 95; *176*).[5] Yet the pun on which the passage itself turns underscores a profound continuity. For by troping (on) *la langue* ["tongue"/"language"], Cixous effectively undermines the very distinction she is in the process of drawing—between the hysteric, who fractures her body as she "tropes" her tongue, and the I-woman who (like Cixous herself here) fractures the Law by troping in language.

This distinction is more tenuous still in the passage where Cixous speaks of being "drawn" into the "sphere of hysteria" through her reading of the Dora case: "If it is only a metaphor—and it's not clear that this is so—it functions well, it has its use [*efficacité*]. I started with Dora; I read that text in a sort of dizziness, exploding over the situation presented [*dans une sorte d'éblouissement, d'explosion de la situation présentée*], where at heart I found myself siding frenetically with the different characters" (*Newly Born*, 147–48; *271–72*).

My analysis in the previous section has suggested that the efficacy of that which is perhaps "only a metaphor"—namely, the Dora case—should be attributed to that particular metaphor's exemplary relation to metaphoricity itself. Like the "mother" in the "The Laugh of the Medusa," Dora exemplifies the womanly gift as a spacing of self and other: "What woman is not Dora / She who makes the others (desire)" (*Newly Born*, 147; *271*).

But the passage implies a good deal more than this. For what is fostered by the vertiginous play of identifications within the hysteric's explosive "situation" is a form of explosive reading (and ultimately of explosive writing) that mimics such identificatory play to specifically empowering ends.[6] The efficacy of the Dora case as a metaphor thus goes beyond the relation to metaphoricity itself, since the spacing of self and other that results from Dora's explosive example depends on a collapsing of the distance between the hysterical other and the posthysterical self. The Dora case "has its use," in other words, because those explosive hysterics that facilitate the metaphorical working of the in-between are themselves eminently contagious.

To evoke contagion in discussing Cixous's work of the early to mid-1970s is, almost inevitably, to evoke Bataille. The image of the laughing Medusa, for instance, plays on a quintessentially Bataillean linkage of contagion and intimate participation: "The contagion in question [in the sexual act] is like that of yawning or of laughter. . . . Seeing and hearing a man laugh I participate in his emotion from inside myself. This sensation felt inside me communicates itself to me and that is what laughs in me. What we know in participation (in communication) is that which we feel intimately (*Erotism*, 152–53; *169*).

Likewise the poetic force of Cixous's puns and portmanteau words—her practice of metaphoric condensation—strips language of its instrumental character, dissociates word and thing, and thus uncovers an intimacy with language that, for Bataille, is properly divine: "In poetry, we have only to forget the stone's identity with itself and talk about the moonstone [*pierre de lune*]: the stone participates henceforth in my intimacy (I slip, as I speak of it, into the intimacy of the moonstone)" (*Erotism* 153; *170*). Indeed, the very proliferation of wordplay in Cixous's novels and manifesto writings might be read as the effect of a certain "contagious" animation—a "deep-seated frenzy, a violent laying hold of an object, consuming it like fire"—that has long been implied, Bataille writes, by the words "divine" and "sacred" (*Erotism*, 180; *201*).[7]

But I will argue that Cixous's manifesto writings mark a clear break from Bataille in one crucial respect. Consider this passage from "The Laugh of the Medusa": "When the 'repressed' of [women's] culture and society returns, it's an explosive, *utterly* destructive, staggering return, with a force never yet unleashed and equal to the most forbidding of suppressions. For when the Phallic period comes to an end, women will have either been annihilated or borne up to the highest and most violent incandescence" (256, *48*; cf. *Newly Born*, 95, *175*).

Here, as so often in her work, Cixous echoes Bataille's assumption that individuals participate through their own sovereign ferment in the explosive and tumultuous movement of life (*Accursed Share*, 10, *50*; *Erotism* 59, *67*). She assumes, moreover, that the accumulation of excess energies requires sumptuary expenditure, "gloriously, or else catastrophically" (*Accursed Share*, 21; *60*). "For if we do not have the strength to destroy surplus energy ourselves . . . ," Bataille writes, "that energy destroys us; it is we who pay the price of the inevitable explosion" (*Accursed Share*, 24; *62*). This becomes a choice, for Cixous, between the catastrophic self-annihilation of the hysterical forerunner and the explosive hysterics—gloriously incandescent—of the I-woman and her text:

> A feminine text cannot fail to be more than subversive [*ne peut pas ne pas être plus que subversive* (note the double negative)]. It is volcanic; as it is written it brings about an upheaval of the old property crust, carrier of masculine investments; there's no other way. There's no room for her if she's not a he [*n'est pas un il* (cf. *isle*: island)]. If she's a her-she [*si elle est elle-elle*], it's in order to smash everything, to shatter the framework of institutions, to blow up the law, to break up the "truth" with laughter. ("Laugh," 258; *49*)

However insistently such passages may strike their Bataillean notes (the volcano, laughter, transgressive wordplay, etc.), their spirit remains foreign to Bataille's. For Cixous's manifesto writings tend to conceive of the explosive act as both instrumental in nature and endowed with a quasimagical efficacy. In Bataille, "the explosive movement of transgression" finds its true meaning in a sphere of sacred ambivalence and pure contagious violence beyond the profane world of work and purposeful activity (*Erotism*, 115; *127–28*). Ritual acts traditionally read in "magical (and utilitarian)" terms are inflected in the direction of a "religious interpretation, more in keeping with that character of supreme play that is generally the achievement of art" (*Erotism,* 75; *84*).

Although Cixous's fiction proves fully consonant with this tendency in Bataille, the performative nature of her manifestoes precludes it. Again and again one reads of the supposedly necessary efficacy of those acts of explosive expenditure that characterize the woman's libidinal economy:

> Because the "economy" of her drives is prodigious, she cannot fail, in seizing the occasion to speak, to transform [*ne peut pas en prenant la parole, ne pas transformer*] directly or indirectly *all* systems of exchange based on masculine thrift. ("Laugh," 252; *45*)
>
> Now, I-woman am going to blow up the Law: *an explosion henceforth possible and inescapable*; let it be done, right now, in language. (*Newly Born,* 95, *175*; "Laugh," 257, *48–49*; emphasis added)

Insofar as Cixous's politicized staging of the posthysterical explosive fantasy appeals to the sort of utilitarian magic thinking that Bataille consistently downplays, it finds a more precise equivalent in two by now rather untimely historical phenomena. It echoes the conversion symptom of late nineteenth-century hysteria, whereby the dragging of a once-swollen foot might serve to realize a fantasy of childbirth or a spasmodic cough that of "sexual gratification *per os*" (*Dora,* 121–22, 65). But it also repeats the magical thinking inherent in classical anarchism's justifications for "propaganda by the deed": "The old world crumbles beneath the weight of its own crimes," Octave Mirbeau once wrote in article on the anarchist bomb-thrower François-Claudius Ravachol; "he who ignites the bomb is destined to sweep it away" (1). I explore the grounds for these untimely repetitions in the following section.

Exemplary Action

To read theoretical work of the post-May period with an eye to the logics of failed revolt is to be sensitized, often to the point of nausea, to that most persistent (and reductionist) of theoretical commonplaces—the "Is it contestatory or is it conservative?" debate. Near the beginning of her essay in *The Newly Born Woman,* Clément insists (quite rightly) that the feminine roles of sorceress and hysteric are "ambiguous, at once contestatory and conservative": "*Contestatory,* because the symptoms—the attacks—revolt and shake up the public, the group, the men, the others to whom they are exhibited. . . . But *conservative* at the same time, since every sorceress ends up being destroyed, . . . every hysteric ends up inuring others to her symptoms" (5; *14*).

But this sense of an inherent ambiguity all but disappears in the "Exchange" that closes the volume. To counter Cixous's portrait of the explosive hysteric as "the typical woman in all her force," whose absolute demand ("I want it all") serves to disrupt the restricted economies surrounding her, Clément takes a classic recuperative line: "It is metaphoric, yes—a metaphor of the impossible, of the ideal and dreamed of totality, yes, but when you say 'that bursts the family into pieces' [*ça fait voler les structures en éclat*], no. It mimics, it metaphorizes destruction, but the family reconstitutes itself around it" (*Newly Born*, 155; *285*). By occupying "challenging positions foreseen by the social bodies," Clément concludes, hysterics, charlatans, crazies, and the like succeed only in reinforcing social structures—or, as she puts it, in "mak[ing] them comfortable."

Ultimately, I would argue, it is an ambiguity inherent in the modern intellectual's own role as a mouthpiece for recuperated critique that has both fueled the contestatory/conservative debate and rendered the particular figure of the (recuperated) hysteric endlessly fascinating. Despite its frequent implication in a process of symptomatic working through, however, the contestatory/conservative debate is (on one level at least) ineluctable. Reading over Cixous's dialogue with Clément, most readers will be struck by the subtlety and suppleness of the latter's analytic mind, which seems constantly to get the better of its more intuitive and poetic—not to say "naive"—counterpart.

As I have worked with Cixous's manifesto writings, however, I have come to see how her apparent naiveté might be closer to the mark than Clément's neo-Marxist rigor. In order to make her recuperative analysis stick, Clément must suppress an effect of hysterical "contagion" that she had earlier evoked in these unequivocal terms: "The hysteric produces these stunning effects: remember Mr. K.'s accident. The electricity is the identification which, circulating from hand to hand, cannot be imputed to any one female subject but to everyone: 'sexual community' " (35; *69–70*). Seeing what might be particularly timely about such an electrical play of identifications will require us to look back to an effect of "moral contagion" once seen to underlie those two (now seemingly untimely) phenomena, anarchism and hysteria.

In 1833 the young Prosper Lucas submitted a *thèse de médecine* that recast in the terminology of the fledgling psychiatric movement the body of current medical wisdom on the subject of "moral contagion." Echoing the findings of a 1784 royal commission charged with investigating convulsive behavior among devotees of Mesmer's tubs, Lucas attributed nervous contagion to the "communication" of an "example"—"a pattern of heightened nervous vibration in one individual [that] would set up a corresponding pattern in other individuals in the vicinity" (Goldstein, "Contagion," 204). Like the royal commissioners before him, moreover, he advocated "suppression of the example" as the means of counteracting its noxious effect. In a remarkable article, historian Jan Goldstein has argued that this tactic took two principal forms. Afflicted individuals could be isolated and accounts of contagious events banned. Or "shows of authority," like the whipping once administered to a group of meowing nuns, could be mobilized to shock unruly imaginations into reasonable submission ("Contagion," 191, 205).

Theories of moral contagion were never more prevalent, however, than in the period between the Paris Commune and the First World War. In 1884, for instance, Gabriel Tarde looked to "imitative contagion" as the very basis of social cohesion; in the following decade Gustave Le Bon would examine "the establishment of psychological homogeneity through 'contagion' " and Durkheim the effect of moral contagion on the suicide rate (Goldstein, "Contagion," 182).

It is no accident, of course, that this period has also come to be known as hysteria's Golden Age. Throughout the early decades of the Third Republic, supporters and critics alike equated hysteria and moral contagion to specifically political ends. For the good republicans of Charcot's Salpêtrière, the systematic characterization of convents and clerical asylums as hotbeds of hysterical contagion served to buttress contemporary campaigns to laicize French schools and hospitals (Goldstein, "Diagnosis," 231). In their retrospective diagnosis of past phenomena as hysterical, Goldstein notes, the Salpêtrière school invariably chose "those phenomena originally construed as religious in nature: on the one hand, demonic possession, where the individual became the vessel of the malign forces of evil; on the other, privileged intercessions of the forces of the divine, and most notably, mystical ecstasies" ("Diagnosis," 235).

But for others, such as Le Bon or Maxime Du Camp, contagion theory served primarily to articulate the sense of a profound instability seen to be inherent in the Third Republic's nascent democratic order. Episodes like the Commune (one of Du Camp's *Convulsions de Paris*) and the populist Boulanger Affair were read as evidence of "a generic likeness, almost a continuity, between the pathological phenomenon of convulsive contagion and the political one of revolt" (Glazer, 64; Goldstein, "Contagion," 193–94).

Hysterics, the very models of convulsive mimicry, played a central role in these analyses as well. In a 1905 study of *La Contagion mentale*, for instance, the Drs. Vigouroux and Juquelier included the hysteric (together with the alcoholic and the degenerate) under the rubric of "les «contagionnables»"—dangerous elements "who in popular demonstrations are quickly perverted, becoming agents of contagion, and even setting a match to the powder-keg" (Glazer, 67).

In agreeing on the need to control moral contagion, the Republic's supporters and critics thus tended to echo one of French psychiatry's earliest and most fundamental mandates. From the time of Proudhon, however, anarchist theory had appropriated that effect of contagion for its own. "The Revolution," Proudhon was fond of asserting, "would be vain if it were not contagious" (Schatz, 116). This anarchist "inversion" would become all the more insistent by century's end, especially among apologists for anarchist bomb-throwing. Distrustful of all revolutionary organizations, and blocked by a doctrine of abstention from actively participating in political life, anarchist theorists sought to conjure the specter of individual and collective impotence by authoring a series of cataclysmic events said to exercise "the contagious and irresistible force of the example" (Emile Armand, cited by Maitron, *2: 178*). In his suggestively titled "Le rire de Ravachol" (Ravachol's laughter) (1892), a certain Victor Barrucand speaks of Ravachol's exercising "through the example of his life and death a salutary contagion, a sort of new morality, without obligation or punitive sanction, that would annul the old Law" (*280*).

From one point of view, that of dialectical materialism, the anarchist's contagion rhetoric was nothing more than an impossible attempt to square the revolutionary circle—to be revolutionary but not political, to bridge the gap between the individual incendiary act and real, social effects in the absence of any dialectical analysis of history. Relying on the age-old millenarist belief that a new and more just social order would arise phoenix-like out of the ashes of an old, corrupt society, the "theory" of anarchist bomb-throwing was (to this point of view) but an act of wishful thinking and the anarchist's bomb but a metaphor for the "ideal and dreamed of totality" that was the revolutionary *grand soir* (great red night).[8]

What such analysis misses, however, is the relationship of mutual self-interest that linked anarchism to the popular press. Just as the anarchist bomb-thrower needed the journalist to communicate his profound dissatisfaction, and thus to guarantee the exemplarity of his deed, so the journalist needed the anarchist's bomb to create the sort of "collective psychosis" that could radically increase his circulation (Maitron, *1: 258*). No account of the efficacy of anarchist bomb-throwing, I would argue, can fail to account for its place in the early history of our society of spectacle.

The introduction of Emile de Girardin's *La Presse* and Armand Dutacq's *Le Siècle* in 1836 marked more than just an important first stage in the development in France of the modern mass-market daily newspaper; it also marked a transformation in the very structures of political and cultural address. In a brilliant chapter of his *Discourse/Counter-Discourse*, Richard Terdiman has shown how the pressure (for Girardin and his successors) to make up in circulation what they had lost through cuts in subscription prices led increasingly to an "ideology of inclusiveness and 'objectivity,'" and hence to the practice of juxtaposing competing opinions on the page in a manner that effectively neutralized social contradictions (131). Whereas the *journaux d'opinion* that had so colored political life under the Restoration had addressed themselves to delimitable ideological constituencies, the dailies of the *fin de siècle* would attempt to address everyone and no one. They aimed to establish what one editorialist called "the sublime communion of souls across distances," and in the process to maximize revenues by agreeing as it were to address no one reader in particular (cited by Terdiman, 131).

Seen from the point of view of contagion theory, however, this "sublime communion of souls" was somewhat more than a simple ideological alibi. Writing three years before Girardin and Dutacq's journalistic "revolution," Prosper Lucas prophetically bemoaned the press's capacity radically to extend the otherwise limited range of a contagious spectacle's "sympathetic force" (Goldstein, "Contagion," 208–9). Worse yet, the daily papers were seen to intensify that force by recreating in the minds of otherwise upstanding citizens "the same order of ideas and sensations which, in monomaniacs and felons brought about the [fatal and newsworthy] act" (Lucas, cited in "Contagion," 209). Such sensationalist appeals to the readerly imagination—to a faculty whose potential for unruliness Lucas's contemporaries commonly ascribed to its "intimate connection with [the] visceral passions"—would, over time, prove extraordinarily profitable ("Contagion," 192). Thus, if commercial pressures had served to disrupt the organic linkage between the citizen and the *journal d'opinion*, they would set in its place a new relation of journal to reader based on the contagiousness of nondirected (or, if you will, disseminative) speech. It is on precisely this contagiousness that the anarchist deed would be ultimately predicated.

Relatively empty of any meaning uncoverable by a hermeneutic—indeed often unreadable to fellow anarchists—the anarchist's bomb was the product of a recognizably commercial logic of publicity or death.[9] In the late 1870s an article in the radical journal *Avant-Garde* praised the new doctrine of "propaganda by the deed" in these now familiar terms: "A deed on the other hand shakes things up. For or against, everyone becomes agitated . . ." (cited by Dubois, *153*). Viewed as a speech act, moreover, the anarchist's bomb possessed none of the organic necessity of a union organizer's address to his membership or the striking worker's message to management. Like the popular press on which it depended for its effect, it was so all-encompassing in its address as to be effectively nondirected: "the explosion of my bomb is not only the cry of the rebel Vaillant; it is the cry of an entire class demanding its rights" ("Déclaration de Vaillant").[10] An act of disseminative speech—in this sense not unlike the advertisements it accompanied on the journalistic page—it was meant to trigger a process of revolutionary self-selection among those who unknowingly possessed the anarchistic "temperament."[11]

Despite its apparent irrationality and the indeterminacy of its address, in other words, anarchist bomb-throwing was seen as an exemplary action, capable of giving rise—spontaneously, even magically—to communities of shared emotion: "Thus, consciously or not—but what does it matter?—whoever communicates the secret splendor of his dream to his brothers in suffering acts on the society around him in the manner of a solvent, making outlaws and rebels (often without their knowledge) of all those who understand him" (Quillard, *150–51*).

Since French anarchists exploded their first bomb at a luxurious Lyon nightclub with the provocatively ironic name of "L'Assommoir" (1882), the relationship between anarchist violence and avant-garde literary production has proven astonishingly symbiotic. Nowhere has this symbiosis been more acute than in the avant-garde manifesto, where bomb throwing, revolver shots, explosive contagions, and the like have typically figured ambivalences inherent in the very project of literary modernism.[12] For some, such as Tzara, they served both as the marker of a certain aggressivity and as a means of appealing to unwittingly kindred temperaments; abusing an audience thus became, in Tzara's words, a means of "hunting out men and nothing more" (cited by Breton, *132*). Others, such as Artaud, sought to compensate for modernist art's constitutive puzzlement about the identity and receptivity of its addressee by dreaming of a space of contagious hypercommunication, opened up by a primitivist refusal of rationality and utilitarian instrumentality. In *The Theater and Its Double*, Artaud dreams of theatrical events that would restore to the word its "old magic efficacy" by "go[ing] off" in the sensibilities of the spectator "with the force of an epidemic": "And, in an instant, the magic identification is complete: WE KNOW THAT WE OURSELVES WERE SPEAKING" (*4: 25, 4: 64*).

In many respects, Cixous's manifesto writings take their place within the long lineage of avant-garde manifestoes specifically beholden to the anarchist model. Yet they consistently inflect the rhetoric of explosion in ways that bring them back to hysteria and classic anarchism. Their explosions, like those of the hysteric, are patently explosions of the self; they show neither the bravado of Tzara's explosive pages nor that hostility to a public that led Artaud to imagine throwing bombs at his audience "in a gesture marked by aggression" (cited by Kristeva, *Polylogue, 92*; see note 12 above). At the same time, their implicit faith in the capacity of explosive speech acts to touch their readers is unbounded and unambiguous.

Like the anarchist bomb, in other words, Cixous's manifesto writings tend radically to deny the very indeterminacy of address that constitutes them as speech acts—an indeterminacy opened up, I have suggested, through the development of mass culture and reflected in the very ambivalence of the high modernist speech act. The final sentence of "The Laugh of the Medusa"—"Jamais nous ne nous manquerons"—means not only "In one another we will never be lacking" (the standard English translation), but also "We will never fail to reach one another (in communication)" (264; *54*). As it takes exception with the Lacanian economies of lack, in other words, this sentence also rejects Derrida's position on the impossibility of fully circumscribing the communicational act ("Signature"). The following passage, which conjoins the rhetoric of the exploding self with the assumption that women's signs and writings invariably reach their destination, perfectly illustrates the conception of exemplary action subtending Cixous's manifesto writings:

> I wished that that woman would write and proclaim this unique empire so that other women, other unacknowledged sovereigns, might exclaim: I, too, overflow [*moi aussi je déborde*]; my desires have invented new desires, my

> body knows unheard-of songs. Time and again I, too, have felt so full of luminous torrents that I could explode—explode with forms much more beautiful than those which are put up in frames and sold for a stinking fortune. ("Laugh," 246; *39–40*)

To the extent that Cixous's feminine manifestoes inflect the rhetoric of explosion back to specifically nineteenth-century models, they are emblematic of what is (at the very least) a curious historical discrepancy. In the cultural life of post-May France, both anarchism and hysteria enjoyed an unprecedented prestige, despite the fact that both had been in a state of near permanent decline (the former as a political movement, the latter as a somatic condition) since at least the onset of the First World War.[13] But as "anarchism" and "hysteria" seemed increasingly to refer to a constellation of eminently "reproducible" subversive gestures, the very possibility of a revolutionary moment ironically became ever more dependent on a contagion analogous to that which they were once thought to exercise.[14]

In his original contribution to *Mai 68: La Brèche*, Claude Lefort speaks of the centrality in the May events of what he calls "direct, exemplary action—action that strikes the collective imagination, inciting in all a desire to imitate and to go still further" (*50*). Rather than rely on the specific strategizing of enlightened, well-disciplined revolutionary vanguards (unions, parties, or *groupuscules*), the militants of May, he suggests, disseminated their message through relatively spontaneous acts of illegality in public squares. Drawing on the immense reserves of anxiety and alienation proper to a modern, melancholic world of pacified well-being, such acts served to stimulate the violence latent in our contemporary institutions of social control (specifically here, the C.R.S.). Like the anarchist deed and (more implicitly) the hysterical attack, they invited imaginative solidarity not only with the grounds of an initial dissatisfaction, but also with the fate of those who, in giving voice to that dissatisfaction, had become subject to repression. And, like the anarchist deed, they issued that invitation through the modern mass media.

Detailing those factors that had given "an epic, victorious, contagious dimension" to what might otherwise have remained a "hyper-rowdy eruption of the Latin Quarter," Edgar Morin underscores the importance for the events of live, on-the-scene reports by radio-telephone. Among other things, he suggests, such reports gave the otherwise unorganized rebels an "immediate knowledge of the global situation"; allowed them to launch their appeals "on a very large scale"; and, perhaps most important, served to attract "a generalized sympathy" for their fight against that brutally repressive "Goliath" that was the C.R.S. (*Brèche, 72–73*).

Reviewing the literature on May '68, one can easily come away with the impression that the objectives of the events were as multiple and as contradictory as the specific agendas of the individuals who participated in them. A call for popular revolution and a fight for direct democracy in the workplace; an act of generational revolt and a libertarian critique of social authority; a reformist struggle for jobs and a movement for the modernization of the university system—May was, in Morin's early assessment, a "revolution without a face because a revolution with a thousand faces" (*Brèche, 83*).

Of course, as Morin himself predicted, historical perspective has helped bring into focus some of the more characteristic features of May's physiognomy (see Chapter 2). And yet it would not be wrong to suggest that, on some fundamental level, the events of May *were* faceless and must be analyzed as such. For their "contagious dimension" depended on a certain vacancy at the heart of the "ideal and dreamed of totality" they embodied. In her *Psychoanalytic Politics*, Sherry Turkle speaks of the partisans of May adopting Lacan's concept of "intransitive demand" to justify "actions in political and social life that were, in their way, without concrete object"; only the pure, intransitive demand, as in the demand for analysis, will serve to "release the powerful force of past demands that have never been met" (85).

If Cixous is oddly right in ascribing efficacy to the hysteric's cry, "I want it all"; if there is something more than residual avant-gardism to her adaptation of anarchist rhetoric, this is because, in our age of advertising and mass media, demand is all the more contagious to the extent that it is absolute and intransitive—or, more precisely, to the extent that it is so radically burdened with objects as to be effectively without object. If there is magical thinking in Cixous's manifesto writings, it is a form of magical thinking whose efficacy advertising executives and media analysts have long known.

In Lieu of an Epilogue

Much has happened since the late 1970s that bears directly on issues central to this book. The world communist movement has imploded, bringing down with it most of our models of popular revolution. The democratic ideal has spread to nations where it would scarcely have been imaginable two decades ago, while the historical democracies have come to an ever more acute awareness of democracy's limitations. Racists and nationalists, not unreconstructed revolutionists, have become our principal examples of what is troubling about imaginary identification.

In France the intellectual has been declared dead—the victim of an all-too-friendly Socialist regime—and then reborn. Lacanian psychoanalysis is testing new highs, French feminism new lows. Continued interrogation of a collaborationist past has given a complex new resonance to the term "complicity." The politics of writing position has begun to look quaint. On the left the theme of community has arisen in response to a "crisis of 'class' politics" and a "growing awareness of the need for a new form of identification around which to organize the forces struggling for the radicalization of democracy" (Mouffe, 60).

To the extent that it attempts to remain faithful to the open-ended structure of history, a book such as this can only end in a more or less arbitrary manner. Among the possible endings suggested by developments of the intervening years, I have chosen two that are doubtless as arbitrary as the next, despite what may have seemed at the time a certain inner necessity, and included them as "afterthoughts."

In the first of these afterthoughts I jump from French theoretical work of the late 1960s and early 1970s to the Los Angeles riots of 1992. In so radically breaking the frame of this study, I want to ask whether the project behind the post-May generation's turn from paranoia to hysteria is in fact still adequate today—to a social conjuncture in which the proliferation of paranoid scenarios (racist fantasies, resurgent nationalisms, conspiracy theories on the right and left) is matched only by our ever-greater susceptibility to media hysteria. Specifically, I want to argue that the modern-day exemplarity of the hysterical subject, and indeed the possibility of a community that is "communal but singular, addressed to all yet carried out by each" (Kristeva), depends on forms of disseminative speech that, as products of our media age, effectively undermine the very distinction between paranoia and hysteria that has so often served to justify that exemplarity. In so doing, I shall briefly reflect on an ambivalence I take to be crucial to (indeed the very ethical dimension of) the conception of "hysterical community."

In my second afterthought I use readings of the Jacobinical Terror by François Furet (1978) and Slavoj Žižek (1991) to return to the question of a "terrorism" ostensibly built into Lacanian theory. How, I ask, can the paradox of counter-authoritarian enunciation that Žižek shows to be endemic to Jacobin politics help sharpen our understanding of what I have heretofore analyzed as a divorce between the intents and the effects of Lacanian theory? How might one begin to see Lacanian theory as a "vanishing mediator," an impossible moment of violence, the very foreclosure of which has given rise to new theorizations on the question of democracy? And what might these reflections, taken as a whole, have to tell us about that vicious circle of terrorism and counter-terrorism that is the contemporary Franco-American dialogue on the matter of "theory"?

PART IV

Afterthoughts

CHAPTER 9

Hysterical Communities

We are all hysterics.

— American feminist slogan, circa 1970

April 29, 1992: Twelve jurors in Simi Valley, California, vote for a near-total acquittal of the four Los Angeles Police Department officers charged in the beating of motorist Rodney King.[1] Rioting erupts in Los Angeles.[2]

April 30 to May 4: Chanting "No justice, no peace," protesters take to the streets in New York, Washington, Atlanta, and elsewhere. In Toronto white counter-demonstrators carry a sign reading, "L.A. burns, Toronto next?"[3]

May 3: Robert Conot, former member of the Kerner Commission and author of a book on the Watts riots, argues in the *Los Angeles Times* that what sets the 1992 riots apart from the events of 1965 is television's ability to create "not only a regional but national network of 'happenings,' of 'you too can be there,' and, if so inclined, participation [*sic*]." "Stimulated by TV," he concludes, "hysteria overtakes the population."[4]

May 4: In Simi Valley Mikhail Gorbachev accepts the first annual Ronald Reagan Presidential Library award at a $5,000-a-plate luncheon billed as a tribute to the two men "who ended the Cold War." He endorses the American ideals of "freedom, peace, democracy, human rights and justice."[5]

May 6: Gorbachev delivers a speech at Westminster College in Fulton, Missouri, site of the 1946 address in which Winston Churchill had warned of an "iron curtain" descending across the European continent.

Also May 6: The *Los Angeles Times* reports that the County Department of Health Services has joined forces with the Atlanta-based Centers for Disease Control (CDC) "in an unprecedented effort to find ways to 'vaccinate' communities against . . . the infectious violence that overtook Los Angeles, killing 58 people and causing property damage approaching $1 billion."[6]

May 18: After noting that the former leader of the Soviet Union had been jetting around the United States in a plane called the Capitalist Tool, *Newsweek* pronounces his speech at Westminster "rhetorically flat" (Watson).

This brief chronology, with the play of its multiple ironies, speaks eloquently of a shift in containment strategies proper to American society in our *fin de siècle*. What is uncovered by the eclipse of a contagion without—the plague of world communism—is a potential for internal contagion fostered by more than a decade of social neglect, a potential that it was arguably the very function of Reaganite Cold-warriorism effectively to mask.

I would approach the question of hysterical community by asking in what sense, and with what degree of terminological slippage, we might speak of the Los Angeles riots as a hysterical episode. In harping on the theme of "self-inflicted wounds," media pundits and community leaders alike have tended to portray the events as a classic instance of hysterical conversion—an expression of Oedipal rage acted out, spectacularly, on one's own body. It is clear that, on some level, those who beat passing motorists to cries of "That's how Rodney King felt, white boy" were engaged in an act of hysterical repetition driven by an identification with the very principle of power they appeared to combat. What is less clear is that the wounds to businesses and communities were in fact self-inflicted. For despite the looting and torching of numerous African-American and Latino businesses—including the Aquarian Bookshop, the oldest black-owned bookstore in the nation—there was a strong sense in which the riots' message was, as one commentator would put it: "These things weren't ours. We need redevelopment in our own image."[7]

Closer to the mark, I would suggest, is the argument that the riots made manifest a split between demand and desire which, although endemic to the human condition, is exemplified in hysteria (Žižek, *Sublime Object*, 111). Not knowing what he "really wants," the hysteric addresses the question of his desire to an Other presumed to know: "Why am I what you are saying that I am?" or "Why do I occupy this place in the Symbolic and not another?" (113). Conot's story of rioters who lit fires so they could go home and watch them live on television may well be apocryphal. Yet it underscores the extent to which television in general, and the voyeuristic minicam in particular, has come to figure the very gaze of the Other, that which emanates from that (ultimately empty) point where our meaning is presumed to resonate. As political subjects in our highly technologized, capitalist societies, we are all more or less hysterics, obsessively posing the question of our desire to the technological eye and its surrogate subjects presumed to know (a role that, as I write, is being brilliantly played by Ross Perot).

The L.A. riots unfolded according to the logic of hysterical desire in a second sense as well. Knowing that every object proposed to his desire is not "it," the hysterical subject will hasten after the next, which of course will not be "it" either (Žižek, *Sublime Object*, 192). In that Supermarket Sweep into which the events in L.A. ultimately degenerated, it often appeared as if the only ideal totality in play were the impossible totality of the commodity utopia. Yet, in their pursuit of that totality, the looters effectively acted out the very vacuity that assures the contagiousness of desire throughout consumer society: witness the story of the man who "ran from a pizza parlor with an insulated bag for transporting take-out pizzas" or of the childless nonsmoker who "brought home 35 cartons of cigarettes . . . and six boxes of disposable diapers."[8] To the extent that we are economic subjects of modern consumer society, we are all more or less hysterics, condemned to an endlessly renewed flight after the next object in sight despite our certainty that it too "procures *too little* enjoyment" (Žižek, *Sublime Object*, 192).

It is of course not surprising that television, as a primary instigator of that hysterical process of commodity appropriation on which the health of our social unit is commonly said to depend, should be seen to have unleashed a massive acting-out of that process in the L.A. riots. But television also serves as the principal agent of a certain paranoia—a suspiciousness on the part of the ostensibly whole and autonomous ego (together with its external analogues: home, family, and neighborhood) of a world that has become saturated with threatening significance. Av Weston has suggested that the primary function of television news, and particularly its local varieties, is to provide a changing array of answers to the viewer's (the ego's) eternal question: "Is my world safe?" (cited by Morse, 73). The endless succession of helicopter shots that dominated local coverage of the riots obsessively posed and reposed that question as they reenacted (and appeared to justify) a social distanciation chosen by those who had abandoned the city for the ostensibly secure, monied enclaves of the Valleys and Westside. Likewise, reporters "on the scene" functioned as walking metaphors for the anxieties of the affluent, for their fear that (as one writer put it) "the social problems we strive to distance ourselves from can get into their own cars and follow us."[9] In that urban agglomeration that is greater Los Angeles, where "community" has long tended to mean "homogeneity of race, class and, especially, home values," such fears took on well-nigh epic proportions (Davis, 153).

We need resist, however, any simple juxtaposition of hysterical looters and paranoid suburbanites. With the decline of hysteria as a condition of somatic conversion (already underway at the time of the Dora case), hysteria has increasingly come to be seen as a character disorder—specifically, as a "mode of defence against psychotic anxiety, coupled with exaggeration and dramatization" (Eric Brenman, summarized in Laplanche, "Hysteria," 463). It is in this sense that one might characterize as "hysterical" the behavior of the local television anchor who bemoaned the violence "encroaching" on the Westside or of shoppers in a gourmet market in West Hollywood turning to their neighbors to ask whether Beverly Hills had "fallen."[10]

Even more obviously hysterical would be that gesture whereby hordes of affluent Angelenos expressed their fear of a contagious alterity, a gesture that novelist Carolyn See has aptly dubbed "looting with a checkbook."[11] Brought face to face with a world of ominous hypersignificance uncannily like that which is lived every day in our inner cities (and especially by young men of color), the shoppers who descended on their upscale supermarkets in Encino, San Marino, and Pacific Palisades sought to assuage their anxiety by stocking up on goods they most often did not need. In so doing, they participated in a wave of contagious, hysterical mimicry, the very model for which was precisely those "others" whom the checkbook looters so patently feared.

The recent announcement that the County Department of Health Services and the CDC would join forces to find a "vaccine" against social mayhem suggests that we have by no means seen the last of that positivist dream of containing "moral contagion" on which supporters and critics of the Third Republic, I have argued, had tended to agree. But neither have we abandoned the task—variously essayed by the anarchists, Bataille, and Cixous—of turning such contagion to a specifically positive effect.

Jean-Luc Nancy's *The Inoperative Community* represents a radical attempt—in the wake of Bataille, Heidegger, and Derrida—to theorize a contagious state of community traceable to the very finitude of Being itself. The "mutual interpellation of singularities" that is constitutive of "community" in Nancy's sense arises with the suspension of a movement toward communion with an immanent meaning inherent in the project of community as traditionally conceived (28–29; *71–73*). What Nancy calls the sharing (*partage*) of community implies neither nostalgia for a lost communion (Christianity, fascism), nor the immanence of a communal subject (totalitarianism), nor even that "consensus of a single program that we call democracy" (25, *64*; xxxviii). Rather, it names a structure of reciprocal "resemblance" without origin or positive identity, that "remainder" of community that we are in common in the wake of the unraveling of a common, mythic meaning (220–21).

As a relationship of reciprocal "compearance" (*comparition*) whereby every "I" (*je*) is always already "another" (*autrui*), the sharing of community depends on an articulation of same and other nearly identical to that which Cixous puts into play under the rubric of "MetaFor" (*Portrait du Soleil*, 15; *42*): "What is exposed in compearance is the following, and we must learn to read it in all its possible combinations: 'you (are/and/is) (entirely other than) I' ('*toi [e(s)t] [tout autre que] moi*'). Or again, more simply: *you shares me* ('*toi partage moi*')" (29; *74*). Without such an articulation of compearing subjects, without such metaphoricity, the contagion of community is unthinkable. The passion for community, Nancy writes, is "not an absence, but . . . the communication of community itself that propagates itself or communicates its contagion *by its very interruption*" (60; *151*).

The events of late April and early May did nothing if not disrupt the myth of Los Angeles as a model of multicultural harmony for the twenty-first century—a myth largely fostered by Mayor Tom Bradley and investment interests on both sides of the Pacific Rim. In so doing, they served to expose something very much like that logic of "sharing" captured in the formula, *toi (e[s]t) (tout autre que) moi*. As the region's massive productive machine entered into an uncharacteristic state of inoperativeness (here too mimicking a certain reality of inner city life), individuals discovered themselves to be singular beings whose most insignificant gestures served to "indicate" and "inscribe" that limit between "you" and "I" without abolishing that limit "in the fiction of a common body" (67; *167*). They came to approximate, in short, what Nancy sees as the condition of "literature."

There have certainly been moments in the wake of the riots in which the experience of inoperative community has seemed little more than the pretext to a massive return to the politics of paranoid identity. As white candidates from across the political spectrum trip over one another in a rush to strike the "Law and Order" chord; as a small but vocal portion of the African-American community reaffirms its belief in "The Plan," a conspiracy "to wipe out black men with drugs and AIDS" (Mabry and Thomas); as television news pursues its traditional double injunction, recreating the myth of community (the so-called Southland) while playing to the paranoid fears of His Majesty the Domestic Monad, it might well appear as if the ultimate destiny of what Nancy would call an articulation of "you" and "I," or Cixous a "brief identificatory embrace," has been to reinforce a paranoid suppression of alterity in the ever-renewable quest for coherent (i.e., mythic) meaning. Or, more simply, it is as though "you and I" were only an alibi for "you are entirely other than I."

But to draw such a conclusion would be to reinforce a distinction between paranoid self-definition and the being in common of (hysterical) split subjects that my argument, and Nancy's, must ultimately call into question. An anecdote told recently by a friend and colleague will help make my point. As the streets of L.A. erupted in their apocalyptic revision of President Bush's "thousand points of light," a black woman and a white man carpooling back to a distant suburb chose to travel by what we slaves of the freeway refer to as "surface streets." As they passed through African-American communities, the black woman saw the white man shrink in his seat; he watched her do the same in Anglo neighborhoods; both found themselves uneasy in the predominantly Latino and Asian neighborhoods of East L.A.

Here it is precisely paranoid self-definition ("you are entirely other than I"), and the equally inevitable failure of the same, that serves to articulate two singular subjects in a relation of brief reciprocal identification that, following Cixous, one might well call hysterical. In this instance, hysterical community is not a means of escaping the paranoid drive toward communion so much as a way of turning paranoid self-definition against itself, of finding an articulation of "you and I" in the very gesture whereby "you are entirely other than I." It is founded on a common experience of the very abyss that separates us, and thus on the acknowledgment that alterity is a constitutive feature of community as such. Or, to borrow a Derridian turn from Verena Conley's text on Cixous: in community "separation is no longer identical to itself, reversible into its opposite; it is traversed by its own difference" (33).[12]

In this brief chapter the phrase "hysterical community" has been meant to function as both a warning and a challenge, as an ethical injunction to continue rethinking community in light of a necessary—and necessarily dangerous—complicity. The increasing importance of media spectacle in modern political life has fostered a contagious fascination for what Nancy calls "founding, original figures, places or powers of remainderless identification" (79; *194*). From Hitler to Reagan and Perot, there has been a disturbing linkage between technological advance and a reduction of the citizen to the role of hysteric demanding knowledge from the political subject presumed to know. The example of the L.A. riots, moreover, reminds us how quickly political statement in the society of spectacle can devolve into hysterical attention-getting, or political action degenerate into an equally hysterical process of commodity appropriation. But to theorize forms of community rigorously shorn of all spectacle, such as the community of lovers in Nancy and the later Bataille, is to risk articulating a purely virtual politic.[13] Likewise, to dismantle the *moi* on the grounds that it can be implicated in nearly all of our modern political pathologies is also to deny the *moi*'s empowering function; there are clearly situations that demand "redevelopment in [one's] own image." It is to parry these risks that I would propose understanding the phrase "hysterical community" to name a double injunction, a split project that expressly straddles the question of the appeal through public spectacle to an identificatory *moi*. At its most radical, the phrase enjoins us to explore forms of being in common realized by "*I*'s that are not *egos* [*des* je *qui ne sont pas des* moi]"; the function of lovers and literature in Nancy, or of the lovers in Cixous's literature, is plainly to anticipate a community of split subjects that, from a recognizably political point of view, is currently at the very limit of conceivability. But it also invites a rethinking of the ways in which mimic contagion between egos—between those newly born women who proclaim that "I, too, overflow" or even, indeed, among checkbook looters—might be seen to foster a reciprocal recognition that serves to found community on the experience of alterity itself. Pointing to our greatest danger and to a double project, "hysterical community" thus names the ambivalence of our ethico-political project on the far side of the specular impasse.

CHAPTER 10

The Terrors of Theory

It is the abyss opened up at the thought that a thought should make itself heard in the abyss that provoked resistance to psychoanalysis from the outset. And not, as is commonly said, the emphasis on man's sexuality. . . .

The intolerable scandal in the time before Freudian sexuality was sanctified was that it was so "intellectual." It was precisely in that that it showed itself to be a worthy ally of all those terrorists whose plottings were going to ruin society.

— Jacques Lacan, "The Agency of the Letter"

To speak of the "terroristic" implications of any body of theoretical work, and especially that produced under the name of Jacques Lacan, is to run the risk of a certain conceptual instability.[1] Should "terrorism" be taken to refer primarily to practices of coercive intimidation analogous to those of the historical Reign of Terror? To acts of destabilizing violence such as advocated by nineteenth-century anarchists under the rubric "propaganda by the deed"? Or perhaps to the still more recent rigors of political and intellectual Stalinism? Are we thus to recognize theoretical "terrorism" by its concern for doctrinal purity (and the denunciations that follow therefrom)? By its faith in the power of language, and particularly its recourse to what Edgar Morin once called "mana words [and] taboo words" (*Brèche,* 29)? By its obsession with spectacular violence? Or by a tendency to posit the charismatic theorist as an embodiment of collective power?

My aim in this final chapter is to negotiate some of these, the risks of the "terrorist" moniker, through a necessarily brief reexamination of the aims and effects of Lacanian theory. If Lacan's work can be patently, indeed self-consciously, terroristic—I will be sketching out some of the parameters of that argument here—it has also been frequently used to theorize the way out of a certain vicious circle of terrorism and counter-terrorism. It is worth recalling in this context that the words *terrorisme* and *terroriste* became naturalized in France after 9 Thermidor, at the moment of the Thermidoreans' disengagement from a Terror in which they themselves had been largely implicated (*Le Petit Robert*). Talk of theoretical terrorism has likewise tended to flourish at moments of generalized disengagement (the years 1976 and 1977 come to mind), yet such talk has all too frequently devolved into simple counter-terrorism of the sort best exemplified by the more programmatic pronouncements of Bernard-Henri Lévy.

My principal example here of the paradoxical attempt to use terroristic theory to think one's way out of the vicious circle of terror and counterterror will be derived from the work of Slavoj Žižek, the Slovenian Lacanian best known in Anglo-American circles for his 1989 *The Sublime Object of Ideology* and a series of books on Lacan and Hitchcock, but whose 1991 collection, *For They Know Not What They Do* (entirely different, as it turns out, from 1990's *Ils ne savent pas ce qu'ils font*) contains two remarkable essays on the Jacobin Terror. I shall also be referring to two works that, like Žižek's, tend to read the Terror through a post-Stalinist lens: François Furet's *Interpreting the French Revolution*, (1978) and Claude Lefort's *L'invention démocratique* (1981). My assumption throughout will be that the terrors of "theory," and particularly its Lacanian variety, are best elucidated from within, by a discourse that passes (or has passed) through "theory" itself. The precise forms such a passage might take will be the subject of some concluding remarks on the still embattled question of the Franco-American "Dialogue and Misreadings" (to borrow the symptomatic subtitle of a recent special number of the *Stanford French Review* [15.1–2]).

In the extract from the 1956 "The Agency of the Letter" that served as my epigraph, Lacan speaks of the scandalously "intellectual" nature of "Freudian sexuality" as making it a worthy supernumerary to "all those terrorists whose plottings were going to ruin society" (*Écrits*, 171; 523). Such a conjunction of terms clearly alludes to a decade, the 1890s, that witnessed, first, an epidemic of anarchist bomb-throwing, culminating in the 1894 *Procès des Trente*; second, the emergence of the concept of "the intellectual," again largely in anarchist circles; and finally, a preliminary codification of Freudian thought.[2]

It is curious, therefore, that this passage finds its place in an argument that is ultimately terroristic in the original, post-Revolutionary sense of that term. Lacan continues:

> At a time when psychoanalysts are busy remodelling psychoanalysis into a right-thinking movement whose crowning expression is the sociological poem of the *autonomous ego*, I would like to say, to all those who are listening to me, how they can recognize bad psychoanalysts; this is by the word they use to deprecate all technical or theoretical research that carries forward the Freudian experience along its authentic lines. That word is *intellectualization*. (*Écrits*, 171; 523)

In its insistence on differentiating an "authentic" Freudian experience from the right-thinking doctrines of those "bad psychoanalysts" whose shibboleth is "intellectualization," this passage calls for doctrinal purification—

the so-called return to Freud—with a well-nigh Robespierrean vehemence. Žižek's repeated references to Robespierre's "tragic greatness" (in the essay "Much Ado about a Thing") only serve to make explicit a constant linkage, in the later Lacan, between terror in both its political and physiological senses and an ethic of tragic purification aimed in large part at combatting the ideological miscognitions of American ego psychology (*For They Know*, 268). For just as the aim of the revolutionary Terror was, in Žižek's terms, to extract "the sublime pure object"—the People (capital P) as Freudian "Thing" (capital T)—from the "corrupted Body" of the people (small p), so did Lacan work tirelessly to extract the sublime kernel of Freudian thought from the corrupt, "pathological" mass of contemporary Freudianisms (268).[3]

The paradox here, of course, is that it is Lacanian theory that provides what are arguably the most powerful tools for theorizing its own terroristic effects. I have referred on several occasions to Lacan's reading of the Stalinist purges as an instance of that paranoid self-aggression characteristic of the beautiful soul. It was Lacan's great originality, moreover, to have seen such narcissistic aggressivity as but the extreme case of a more generalized miscognition whereby the *moi* of modern man ruthlessly denies its fundamental lack of self-identity. And yet all that separated Lacan's own quest for psychoanalytic purity from that of the beautiful soul, Stalinist or otherwise, was a certain self-ironic undertow. At the end of his diatribe against "bad psychoanalysts" or, more specifically, against those analytic Churches that had turned psychoanalysis into "the cradle and trysting-place of oblativity and attraction" Lacan evokes (with a subtle self-irony) a supposedly authentic form of Freudian oblation: "That word is *intellectualization*—execrable to all those who, living in fear of being tried and found wanting by the wine of truth, spit on the bread of men, although their slaver can no longer have any effect other than that of leavening" (*Écrits*, 171; *522–23*).

I would bring the specifically terroristic quality of Lacan's gesture here into focus by turning to a book that was very much a product of the watershed years of the late 1970s, François Furet's *Interpreting the French Revolution*. In this work, in which Furet rethinks the Revolution through the Terror and the Terror (explicitly, if not always consistently) through the Gulag, he pays particular attention to the role of the aristocratic plot (*complot aristocratique*) as Revolutionary antiprinciple. The idea of aristocratic plotting, he writes, constituted "the lever of an egalitarian ideology that was both exclusionary and highly integrative," an ideology that provided legitimacy to the integral body of the people precisely through the exclusion of traitors to the nation (55; *93*). In so doing, the "aristocratic plot" called forth a practice of "popular vigilance," which, by affirming a reciprocal transparency of action, power, and values, effectively gave birth to our modern conception of politics (52, 29; *89–90, 55*).

That the rhetorical couple *complot aristocratique / vigilance populaire* might be analyzable in terms of Lacan's theory of aggressivity is a point I need not belabor. For, like the Lacanian *moi*, the pure, undivided body of the people—or what Claude Lefort has called the *peuple-Un*—plainly depended on a constitutive miscognition, the belief that "all violence, corruption and egotism invaded the people from outside" (Blum, 217).[4] If democracy implies, as Lefort suggests, a necessary tension between two poles—between representations of popular unity on the one hand and a recognition on the other of "the dispersion of individuals, the fragmentation of activities, the antagonism of particular interests, the partition of classes"—then the Terror, like its Stalinist replay, sought to resolve that fundamental division by positing a strictly external division between the One People and its enemies (*Invention, 127*). There is thus something of the Terror in all nationalisms—a point to which I shall return in a moment.

The democratic idea, it has often been claimed, presupposes that the space of social power remains structurally empty, fillable through the mechanism of democratic suffrage, but never fully coextensive with the particular sway of any one leader, party, or governing body (see Lefort, *Invention, 126*). Terror begins when the regulated representation of social power, which necessarily implies revokability, gives way to an embodiment of that power, again in the form of a leader, party, or governing body.

The notion of "Stalinism" has served to designate a particularly willful, cynical attempt to resolve the tension constitutive of democracy by affirming, in Lefort's words, "the power and . . . will of the leader, which is supposed to coincide with the full affirmation of the people's power and will" (*126*). Such cynicism was of course not wholly foreign to the Jacobin Terror; one need only recall Saint Just's proposal that Robespierre assume dictatorial status, provided one also recall Robespierre's refusal. Indeed, for Žižek, the Jacobins were tragically great—and fundamentally different from their Stalinist progeny—to the extent that they refused to sanction the "re-emergence of the sublime political body in the shape of the Leader and/or the Party" (*For They Know*, 256). But a more subtle model is needed to account for the rise of the Terror, and especially, I would argue, for so-called theoretical terrorism.

According to the well-known thesis of François Furet, the revolutionaries of 1789 attempted to exorcise the traditional embodiment of power in the person of the King by turning to language—or, more precisely, to public speech—as "the sole guarantee that power would belong only to the people, that is, to nobody" (48; *83*). The possibility of Terror then arises from a paradox—Furet calls it an "ambiguity"—inherent in the revolutionary speech act itself: "It strove for power yet denounced the corruption power inevitably entailed" (49; *85*). Žižek reformulates this paradox in terms of a distinction between the *sujet d'énoncé* (subject of the utterance, the enunciated) and the *sujet d'énonciation* (subject of enunciation):

> On the level of the enunciated, the Jacobin safeguards the emptiness of the locus of Power; he prevents anybody from occupying this place—but does he not thus reserve for himself a privileged place, does he not function as a kind of King-in-reverse—that is to say, is not the very position of enunciation from which he acts and speaks the position of absolute Power? Is not safeguarding the empty locus of Power the most cunning and at the same time the most brutal, unconditional way of occupying it? (*For They Know*, 268–69)

Referring to the Jacobins' self-perception as protectors of this empty (i.e., purely symbolic) locus of Power, Žižek will read the Jacobinical Terror not as "a simple aberration or betrayal of the democratic project," but as a phenomenon of "strictly democratic nature" (268). And yet that quintessentially democratic act of protecting power's empty locus led the Jacobins into an impasse, a "vicious circle of Terror," whereby successful subjects of the enunciation were doomed to lose their heads. The way out of this vicious circle, Žižek suggests, is to materialize social power in the person of an empty and purely formal agent, such as Hegel's monarch, who will function as "nothing but a positivization, a materialization of the *distance* separating the locus of Power from those who exert it" (*For They Know*, 269). Only the "sublime, evasive body" of a King who knows he is not the Thing (for he is nothing apart from his subjects' recognition); only that "thing" of "pure semblance without substance" that is the *objet a* can provide what Žižek calls a "speculative solution" to the Jacobinical impasse (255, 269).

It is here that one rejoins the question of theoretical terrorism in its specific Lacanian manifestation. I have spoken on several occasions of an oft-remarked divorce between the intents and the effects of Lacanian theory.[5] Even if we grant, as I think we should, that Lacan sincerely sought to demonstrate that the position of the *sujet supposé savoir* (like the position of power in democracy) can be occupied only by usurpation, it is nonetheless the case that, in the act of demonstrating as much, he occupied that position all the more forcefully. (Let me note in passing that this paradox of counter-authoritarian enunciation was also very much at work in nineteenth-century anarchism, and thus serves as an important point of commonality between the various forms of "terrorism"—Jacobin, anarchist, and theoretical—I refer to in this chapter.)

Lacan's "solution" to this paradox, such as it was, was to found a psychoanalytic school, the École freudienne de Paris (EFP), within which an unprecedented statutory democratism—including equal voting rights for all members and elections of an administrative council by universal suffrage—coexisted with a no less evident monarchism (Roudinesco, 429; 436). For Lacan's role at the EFP was, as Elisabeth Roudinesco has argued, that of the thoroughly modern, "enlightened" monarch, one who knew (like de Gaulle) that he was nothing without the people he governed—that he was not "the Thing"—and who, at the same time, sought to restore "the risks of a Freudian republic" (432, 418; *439, 425*). Thus, within limits to which I shall return in a moment, Žižek's recourse to Hegel's monarch as "speculative solution" to the Jacobinical impasse should be seen as resonating with Lacan's own institutional profile within the EFP.[6]

But reading Žižek's neo-Lacanian analyses for resonances of Lacan's "solution" to the impasse of counter-authoritarian enunciation is ultimately less fruitful than reading Žižek (or reading Žižek reading Lacan) with an ear for the terrors of Lacanian theory. The reason for this is simple: for Žižek, as for Lacan, certain forms of terror are essentially ineluctable. According to standard democratic theory, it is the rule of law articulated in a constitution, together with specific procedures for the expression of public opinion, that serves to guarantee that the locus of social power will remain structurally empty. What Žižek calls the "vicious circle of terror" is considered fundamentally aberrational, since it arises only with the breakdown or supersession of those rules.

Against this position, Žižek would make two points. First, it is nonsensical to ask democratic law to save us from the vicious circularity of counter-authoritarian enunciation, since the authority of all law presupposes an analogous circularity. "It follows, from [the] constitutively senseless character of the Law," he has written, glossing Pascal, "that we must obey it not because it is just, good or even beneficial, but simply *because it is the law*—this tautology articulates the vicious circle of its authority, the fact that the last foundation of the Law's authority lies in its process of enunciation" (*Sublime Object*, 37).

Behind this analogy, moreover, lies a necessary historical linkage. Arguing against the overly simple equation of Stalinism and the Jacobin Terror, Žižek sees the latter not as a "proto-totalitarian aberration," but as a "vanishing mediator," an "impossible" moment of openness and violence that becomes invisible (or, in Lacanian parlance, "foreclosed") in the process of giving birth to that "new positivity" that is "'normal' pluralistic democracy" (*For They Know*, 215, 184, 188).[7] Every reign of law, including that of pluralistic democracy, has its "hidden roots" in a scandalous act of criminal transgression, which succeeds only to the extent that it manages to efface—or, more precisely, disavow—its scandalous character (208, 192–93). Such an "absolute, self-referential crime," Žižek continues, thinking of Kant's analysis of the trial and sentencing of Louis XVI, "cannot be properly 'forgotten' (undone, expiated and forgiven); it must persist as a repressed traumatic kernel, since it contains the founding gesture of the legal order—its eradication from the 'unconscious memory' would entail the disintegration of the very reign of law; this reign would be deprived of its (repressed) founding force" (*For They Know*, 208).

What holds the place of this repressed traumatic kernel, thereby assuring the normal functioning of the reign of law, is a paradoxical object Žižek variously calls the "sublime body" or (echoing Lacan) the "little piece of the real":

> The emergence of this sublime body is clearly linked to the illegal violence that founds the reign of law: once the reign of law is established, it rotates in its vicious circle, "posits its presuppositions," by means of foreclosing its origins; yet for the synchronous order of law to function, *it must be supported by some "little piece of the real" which, within the space of law, holds the place of its founding-foreclosed violence*—the sublime body is precisely this "little piece of the real" which "stops us" and thus conceals the void of the law's vicious circle. (*For They Know*, 260)

Žižek's principal example of such a sublime body is Lenin's in its mausoleum. In light of my analysis in Chapter 3, however, I would argue that this model applies to nothing so much as to the sublime body of the Lacanian theorist, the primary function of which has been to conceal a vicious circularity endemic to the Lacanian system, and thus proper to the Lacanian law.

Some day we will need to write the recent history of the notion of "theory" *tout court*: as a counterpart to "practice"; as an effect of expansions of the French university system; as the byproduct of structuralist ideology, including structuralist interdisciplinarity; as an American marketing ploy; and so on. When that history is written, it will, I suspect, reserve a significant place for the bracketing of the question of reference in Saussurean semiology. "Theory" would thus tend to designate modes of thought functioning in accordance with a "vicious circle of differentiality" (Žižek) proper to the order of the signifier as such (*Looking Awry*, 39). To this view, on whose hypothetical quality I should like to insist, Lacanian "thought" would have become Lacanian "theory" with the claim, first articulated in the 1953 Rome Discourse, that the unconscious is structured like a language—an act of founding violence to which Lacan hinted he had set himself "a bit late."[8]

In a preface to Marx's *Capital*, Althusser once suggested that, just as children learn to walk only by walking, so too does one "learn to walk in theory" only through an indispensable "apprenticeship in theory" (*Lenin*, 78). This seemingly unproblematic claim becomes circular to the extent that it is allied, as I have shown it to be for both Lacan and Althusser, with an extreme, rigorist version of the otherwise dialectical position that the objects of theory are determined by the very theoretical problematics commonly presumed to account *for* those objects (see Chapters 3 and 4). In the case of Lacan, the founding violence of the Rome Discourse produced a profound conceptual circularity which, when coupled with assimilationist/exclusionary rigor, resulted in a style of (neo-"terrorist") theorization that could only be "taken or left." And the only way to take such theory, if I may quote Žižek out of context, would be to "act *as if* you already believe, and the belief will come by itself"—a Pascalian procedure that, as Žižek notes, was once "very popular among French Communists" (*Sublime Object*, 39).

What Žižek is loath to acknowledge, however, is the extent to which this radically "vicious circle" of transferential belief is the product of specifically circular forms of theoretical practice. I would grant Žižek the point that all laws, once established, tend to rotate in a vicious circle, positing their presuppositions while foreclosing their origins; such is indeed the mechanism uncovered by Marx's analysis of "primitive accumulation" as the idyllic origin-narrative of modern capitalism. But it is not the case that all laws are equally vicious in their circularity. And the more viciously circular the law, the more it will tend to secrete a sublime body to conceal the void of that circularity, a sublime body always at risk of being taken for the Thing itself.

This argument brings me, in conclusion, to the divorce between current French and American attitudes on the question of "theory." At the risk of a certain caricature, let me couch the misunderstanding in the terms with which Žižek reads Revolutionary politics. Viewed from the American perspective, certain members of the French *haute intelligentsia* (most notably, the New Philosophers) appear to have subjected "theory," particularly that of late 1960s or early 1970s vintage, to what Žižek calls an "anamorphotic reversal." For just as the Jacobins transformed the King as the "charismatic embodiment" of his people into "a cancerous proturbance contaminating the body of the People," so did a cadre of terroristic antiterrorists work to change the "sublime body" of theory into (and here I quote Žižek quoting Lacan) a "gift of shit" (*For They Know*, 254). At the same time, more subtle thinkers have sought, like the Thermidoreans, to exorcise theoretical terrorism by dissociating their own power as critics and philosophers from an episode they saw to be, in the words of Babeuf, "an unfortunate deviation" (cited by Furet, 71; *117*). (Curiously, for Žižek it is the former—the terroristic antiterrorists—who are more tragically great.)

Seen from the French perspective, on the other hand, we in the United States look like nothing so much as monarchists, provincial dolts too libidinally tied to the sublime body of theory to have quite gotten around to cutting off the King's head. One reason for this apparent languor is surely the greater decentralization of American academic and intellectual culture, which is slow to accept new ideas, but "reluctant to relinquish those [it has] endorsed" (Pavel, 17). Another is the effect of economics—indeed, of commodity terrorism—on the American critical scene. It is not just that, for the American academic, the entree into theory can appear to be an indispensable prerequisite to entrance into the world of scholarly publishing, itself reflective of a culture industry for which, as Horkheimer and Adorno remarked many years ago, "the only choice is either to join in or be left behind" (148). Capitalism itself secretes an endless succession of sublime bodies, including of course theoretical ones.

As consumers of popular culture, we well "know" that such sublime bodies are radically contingent, always incipient "gifts of shit." Indeed, the speed and persistence with which our society of spectacle transforms erstwhile sublimity into abjection effectively guarantees the contemporary capitalistic and democratic order by materializing, far more profoundly than Hegel's monarch ever could, a distance separating power from those who exercise it. But, as critics and theoreticians, many of us have clung to our sublime bodies all the more tenaciously. One of the interests of Žižek's (itself highly commodified) body of work is the way it oscillates with such provocative ease from the sublime, all-knowing delirium of late Lacanian theory to the unabashed abjection of slasher films and drugstore fiction.

There are, of course, many alternative positions, on both sides of the Atlantic, to such an overly simple choice between terroristic antiterrorism and a monarchism driven by the terror of the commodity. Žižek, whose position with regard to this debate is itself consistently eccentric, articulates what I take to be the most powerful of these positions when he writes, in discussing Marx on "primitive accumulation," "The role of historical description is to 'go through' the fantasy which masks this vicious circle: to denounce the mythical narration by means of which the synchronous system retroactively organizes its own past, its own origins, and to render visible the contingent reality full of blood and brute force" (*For They Know*, 212).

Žižek himself will never apply historical description in an effort to go through the fantasy veiling the specific vicious circle that is Lacanian theory, to theorize (in other words) that absolute crime that gave birth to Lacan *qua* Lacan.[9] That critical task has fallen to such studies as François Roustang's *The Lacanian Delusion* and Mikkel Borch-Jacobsen's *Lacan: The Absolute Master*, to cite just two works central to my argument in this book. But in one significant respect Žižek's account of the Jacobinical Terror strikes me as particularly suggestive for future "historical description" of the phenomenon that was French "theory."

On the far side of the polemic over the "sublime body" of theory, the question I would ask is this: to what extent might theoretical "terrorism" itself have served as "vanishing mediator" for the emergence, in France and elsewhere, of new reflections on the question of democracy? To what extent, in other words, does "theory" name a "forgotten excess of negativity" that drops out once one looks at intellectual evolution "'backwards,' from its Result" (*For They Know*, 195)? What has disappeared, if not "theory" in its mediating role, in the general rush to rediscover or rehabilitate such liberal-democratic forebears as Alexis de Tocqueville, Raymond Aron, and Hannah Arendt? "Democracy after Lacan": such is the subtitle I should have liked to attach to this chapter, but which it must be the task of another paper—or another book—fully to earn.

Appendix

APPENDIX

Marx/Bakunin

As a concise statement of the grounds for dispute in the Marxist/anarchist polemic that rocked the First International, Marx's "Notes on Bakunin's *Statehood and Anarchy*" are quite useless. Their interest, which is exceptional, lies in the way they testify to an ongoing process of theoretical elaboration, a highly passionate process in which rival positions oscillate between indistinction and polarization, where one is just as adamant about translating the other's language back into one's own terms as about branding the other with the very flaws that he would project onto you. The complexities of this dynamic are particularly evident in the following passage near the end of the "Notes" (for the sake of clarity, I have put Marx's comments in boldface):

> By *our polemics* against them **[which appeared, of course, before my book against Proudhon and the *Communist Manifesto*, and even before Saint-Simon (a beautiful hysteron proteron)]** *we* have forced them to *admit* that freedom or anarchy **[Mr. Bakunin has only translated Proudhon's and Stirner's anarchy into the barbaric idiom of the Tartars]**, i.e., the free organization of the working masses from below **[nonsense!]**, is the ultimate goal of social development and that every 'state,' the people's state included, is a yoke which engenders despotism, on the one hand, and slavery, on the other. (521)

Marx's objections here are a textbook example of what in the wake of Freud has come to be known as kettle logic.[1] Into an argument whose dominant motive is one of devalorization and disseverance (you got all this "nonsense" from Proudhon and Stirner and only rendered it the more barbaric), Marx imports a contradictory gesture of valorization and reappropriation (you can't have brought me to this admission, because I was there *before you*). What Marx thinks Bakunin has backwards in his "beautiful *hysteron proteron*" is not priority in conceiving "the ultimate goal of social development," though in the "Notes" the impulse to distinguish between essentially similar visions is never more acute than on the matter of the future, classless society.[2] Rather he would seem to mean the priority of having first engaged the polemic (it was *I* who first took on the anarchists).

However trivial it may at first appear, this question of priority is highly significant in view of the paranoid structure of the exchange as a whole. For in situations where symmetrically determined antagonists plainly distinguish in the other's practice the very qualities they fail to recognize in their own, the honor of having originated the debate tends to confer a certain authenticity on the "originator"'s miscognition.[3] The question of who first initiated the polemical exchange asserts itself with especial vengeance here because what is at stake in this passage is Bakunin's claim that "every 'state,' the people's state included, is a yoke which engenders despotism, on the one hand, and slavery, on the other." In other words, the fact of having struck the first blow is perceived to be coextensive with the conclusion that it is the *other*—in this case Bakunin—who is responsible for the fall back into authoritarianism.

The most fundamental element of the Marxists' "persecution" (their word) of the Bakuninite Alliance circa 1872 was the charge that the doctrine of antiauthoritarianism served to conceal an inveterate taste for authority. In a June 1872 letter to C. Cafiero, Engels demanded to know whether previous letters to that correspondent "have been passed to my enemies [the *Bulletin Jurassien*] with or without [Cafiero's] consent":

> If with your consent, then I can only draw one conclusion: that you have let yourself be persuaded into joining the *Bakuninist secret society, the Alliance*, which, preaching the disorganisation of the International to the uninitiated, under the mask of autonomy, anarchy, and antiauthoritarianism, practices absolute authoritarianism with the initiated, with the aim of taking over leadership of the Association, treating the working masses as a flock of sheep blindly following a few initiated leaders, and imitating in the International the role of the Jesuits in the Catholic Church. (Marx, Engels, and Lenin, 78–79)

This oft-repeated accusation that the Alliance would remodel the International Working Men's Association along the lines of a Jesuit order plainly represented a way of throwing back in the anarchists' faces the charge that the Marxist state will be nothing more than "the highly despotic rule of the masses by a new and highly restricted aristocracy of real or pretended scholars" (Schatz, 163; also cited in Marx, "Notes," 520). In other words, the Marxists sought to operate a preemptive strike by tainting the anarchists with the same logic of repetition that anarchists since Proudhon had used to good effect against them.

There is textual evidence to substantiate the Marxist claim, most tellingly a letter of June 2, 1870, in which Bakunin speaks of the "collective dictatorship" of a small, unofficial band of anarchists dedicated to directing the spontaneous popular revolution "in accordance with a preexisting and well-defined common plan" (*Archives Bakounine*, 1: 237–38, cited by Maitron, 2: 205–6). To note that this letter was written prior to the split in the First International, and thus reflects an openness to the concept of revolutionary dictatorship absent in the later Bakunin, is not to deny that there might be within anarchism itself an ambivalence about power more deep-rooted than would suggest Bakuninite anarchism's official position—the apparently naive, absolute condemnation of power in all its forms.

Anarchist doctrine has long served to express the will to power of small elites who feel themselves endowed to a rare degree with the spirit of revolt. Repeated claims for the natural (and hence apolitical or antiauthoritarian) character of this supposed superiority have not effectively countered the objection, formulated here by Rémy de Gourmont, that "in the absence of all laws, the ascendancy of superior men would be the sole law and their just despotism uncontested" (*147*). Indeed the appeal of anarchism to intellectuals of the symbolist generation and beyond would seem to lie precisely in its conjunction of two contrary gestures: (1) an unconditional rejection of power, consistent with the intellectual's role as "specialist of the negative," and (2) a no less insistent appropriation of power on the basis of a "natural" superiority (Kristeva, *Revolution*, 97; 92).

However well-founded Engels's assertion that anarchist antiauthoritarianism served as the alibi for an absolute love of authority, the Jesuitic analogy through which both he and Marx make that accusation suggests that something more is at stake here than meets the eye. In the document by which they justify the expulsion of Bakunin and James Guillaume from the International, Marx and Engels "reveal the secret of all the Alliance's double and triple-bottomed boxes" by citing the Alliance's program, beginning with this passage: "It is necessary that in the midst of popular anarchy, which will make up the very life and all the energy of the revolution, *the unity of revolutionary thought and action should be embodied in a certain organ*. That organ must be the *secret and world-wide association of the international brothers*" (cited in Marx, Engels, and Lenin, 111).

Here is Marx and Engels's gloss of that passage: "Unity of thought and action means nothing but orthodoxy and blind obedience. *Perinde ac cadaver* [Loyola: Be like unto a corpse]. We are indeed confronted with a veritable Society of Jesus" (Marx, Engels, and Lenin, 112).

I argued in Chapter 1 that the logic of recuperation might be read as the sign of a narcissistic wound that Marx and Engels would inflict on an "emasculated" adversary, specifically to foreclose a castration endemic to the revolutionary project itself. Heightening the tone of this phallic drama is the characteristic anarchist insistence that revolutions "come about, as it were, of their own accord, produced by the force of circumstances. . . . They slowly mature in the depths of the instinctive conscience of the popular masses, then they explode" (cited in Marx, Engels, and Lenin, 111). The ejaculatory quality to this conception of revolution is fully consistent with Bakunin's tendency to conceive of historical development organically, through images of germination, eruption, and vitalistic overflow. But in maintaining that "the unity of revolutionary thought and action should be embodied in [the] certain organ" that is an association of "international brothers," Bakunin nonetheless feminizes the role of this "organ," perceiving it not as procreator but as midwife: "the only thing a well-organised secret society can do is first to assist the birth of revolution" (Marx, Engels, and Lenin, 111).

What then is at the bottom of the Alliance's "double and triple-bottomed boxes"? To Marx and Engels it is an "organ": monastic, dysfunctional, corpselike; there can be no doubt that Marx would hijack Loyola's *Perinde ac cadaver*, addressing it himself to the anarchist upstarts. If Bakunin's text tends to foreground interesting issues of homosexuality (the association of brothers) and anarchist cross-dressing (the brother as midwife), Marx's response is to emit the Loyolan injunction apotropaically, reducing the problem of revolutionary efficacy to a simple question of who "has it" (the Marxists) and who does not (the Bakuninite monks).

But it is precisely Marx's repudiation of the homosexual order that underscores the extent to which homosexual desires are at work in the Marx/Bakunin polemic. In his account of the Schreber case, Freud argued that the four principle forms of paranoia—delusions of persecution, delusions of grandeur, delusional jealousy, and erotomania—could "all be represented as contradictions of the single proposition: '*I* (a man) *love him* (a man),' and indeed . . . they exhaust all the possible ways in which such contradictions could be formulated" ("Psycho-Analytic Notes," 62).[4] Of interest to me here is not any speculative applicability of Freud's (necessarily ahistorical) claim that paranoia functions as a defense against the instinctual threat that is the homosexual wish. It would be by and large superfluous to claim, as a strict Freudian might, that the Marxian mimicry of Loyola's "Be like unto a corpse" represents the paranoid projection of a repressed "desire to be unmanned"; such a desire could only have been a luxury to the nineteenth-century revolutionary who "knew" himself to be always already "unmanned" by an irreducible indeterminacy at the heart of the historical process. Of interest to me rather is the way in which the logics of repetition and recuperation have historically found their places within relations of specular rivalry, marked by narcissistic aggressivity, paranoid projection, *and* a certain repressed homosexuality.

One last word on paranoia. Against what this analysis has shown to be the Marxist's paranoid repression of a homosexuality traversing the nineteenth-century revolutionary project, recent critical theory has tended to operate a "hysterical" blurring of gender-difference not unlike that associated with Bakunin above. By problematizing the internal/external opposition so crucial to the mechanism of paranoid projection, many of the theoretical projects of *l'après-Mai* have effectively called into question the polarization of power and impotence that underwrites the narcissistic phallodrama of the Marx/Bakunin polemic. In *A Thousand Plateaus*, for example, Deleuze and Guattari suggest that centers of power define themselves not so much by their zones of effective power as by their zones of impotence. Thus, in translating "as best they can flow quanta into line segments," these centers of power encounter "both the principle of their power and the basis of their impotence. Far from being opposites, power and impotence complement and reinforce each other in a kind of fascinating satisfaction" (225; 275)

I have suggested that the uncanny persistence of the argumentative structure of the Marx/Bakunin debate must be read as the repetition of an institutionalized tendency to paranoia, based on the projection onto an (internal) rival of a recuperative threat that plays throughout all revolutionary practice (including one's own) against an adversary whose powers of reappropriation are as highly developed as capitalism's. If Deleuze and Guattari have thus effaced the evident persecutorial ethos characteristic of revolutionary rivalries on the Marx/Bakunin model, and this through the problematization of those dichotomies on which paranoia in the Freudian sense depends (inside/outside, potency/impotence, same/other, etc.), this is not to say that paranoia has no place in their world.

Quite the contrary. Deleuze and Guattari clearly suffer no illusions as to capitalism's power of reappropriation, its uncanny capacity to regenerate itself through the reincorporation of hostile energies: "But it is precisely the most deterritorialized flow under the first aspect that always brings about the accumulation or conjunction of the processes, determines the overcoding, and serves as the basis for reterritorialization under the second aspect" (220–21; 269).

The interest of their work lies in its systematic refusal of that mechanism whereby forms of paranoia inherent in systems such as capitalism are projected onto relations between simple individuals, however world-historical they might be. Like much of the later work of Jean Baudrillard, *A Thousand Plateaus* might be read as an appeal for salutarily generalized forms of paranoia. Whereas the logics of repetition and recuperation operative in the Marx/Bakunin polemic attempt to explain away and externalize a certain impotence of revolutionary action, the "paranoid" systems of Deleuze/Guattari and Baudrillard share in the project of demonstrating the *internal necessity* of a certain impotence to any system—economic, hermeneutic, or otherwise.

Reference Matter

Notes

INTRODUCTION

1. "And now he approaches the Restoration, . . . at which not daring openly to repine, he vents all his Spleen on the happy Instrument [Monk] of that glorious Revolution" (B. Higgons, cited in "Revolution," *Oxford English Dictionary*, 1971 ed.).

2. As this list of authors tends to suggest, the principal theoretical domain to be explored in the readings that follow is that where Lacanian psychoanalysis meets post-structuralist textual theory. Doubtless there are other theorists, writing in the same domain or in related ones, whose work of the late 1960s and early 1970s could likewise be productively studied through the lens of the logics of failed revolt. But in aiming to write a book that is more suggestive than it is exhaustive, I have allowed myself the luxury of making only passing reference to a number of authors whose work might well have been included in a study of this kind (including Michel Foucault, Gilles Deleuze and Félix Guattari, Jean-François Lyotard, Luce Irigaray, Jean Baudrillard, Christian Metz, Bernard-Henri Lévy, André Glucksmann, François Furet, and many others besides).

3. I have of course borrowed this notion of the revolutionary "fused group" (*groupe en fusion*) from Sartre's analysis of the taking of the Bastille in his 1960 *Critique of Dialectical Reason*. Although familiar to the *enragés* (rabid ones) of Nanterre prior to the events of May, Sartre's *Critique* attained cult status only in their aftermath, in large part because it accounted so seamlessly for the birth of the student movement (Aron, *Revolution*, 125; *136*). For, like their revolutionary forebears of the Faubourg Saint-Antoine, those who stood on the barricades of May overcame their "seriality," their quotidian status as disjunctive

and self-alienated monads, as a result of the exterior negation of that seriality that was police action. The effect of a united front against the student unrest was to make each student conceive of him- or herself as a "singular incarnation of the common person" (357; *461*). From this conception there followed a recognition of the fellow militant as embodying one's own project, allowing both for the rebirth of a freedom based upon the reciprocal recognition of one another's liberty and for the constitution of an organically unified fused group.

4. In a 1975 seminar, for instance, Luce Irigaray would seek to justify the necessary marginality of woman's liberation movements, "[which] keep themselves deliberately apart from institutions and from the play of forces in power," on the grounds that "strictly speaking, political practice, at least currently, is masculine through and through" (*This Sex*, 127; *125–26*). And yet feminism, like writing in Sollers's recasting of Clausewitz, was clearly conceived to be a "continuation of politics by other means" (*Théorie d'ensemble*, 78).

5. This book began as a study of the afterlife of anarchist rhetoric in French theory after May '68. Although my focus has shifted markedly, traces of this original project remain throughout, especially in the chapters of Part III.

CHAPTER I

1. I return to this fascination on several occasions throughout this study, most notably at the end of Chapter 2, in the section of Chapter 7 entitled "The New Paranoid Systems," and in the Appendix.

2. See, for instance, this passage from Lacan's *Séminaire XX: Encore*: "All dimensions of being are produced in the ebb and flow of the master's discourse, the discourse of him who, in uttering the signifier, counts on one of its binding effects that is not to be neglected, an effect that follows from the fact that the signifier commands. The signifier is first and foremost imperative. . . . There is no prediscursive reality. All realities are founded on and defined by a discourse" (33).

3. I advance a second, complementary account of this recuperative effect in the section of Chapter 3 entitled "The Perils of Liberation."

4. "From whatever angle you take things, and however you may turn them, the property of each of these little four-legged diagrams is to allow each its cleft [*béance*]. At the level of the discourse of the master, it's precisely that of the recuperation of surplus value" ("Impromptu," 123–24; *23*). Lacan introduced his "four-legged" schemata for the analysis of the "four discourses" of the master, the university, the hysteric, and the analyst in the opening weeks of his *Séminaire XVII: L'envers de la psychanalyse*. See also *Séminaire XX: Encore*, 20–21.

5. Christian Jambet and Guy Lardreau make a similar point in *L'Ange*: "Because these terms—'desire' and 'discourse'—do not possess the same logical force, we can escape from the impasse we have seen. All desire belongs to the Master, but not all discourse" (34–35).

6. I discuss Barthes's use of paradox and Cixous's punning in Chapters 6 and 8, respectively. The most obvious of Derrida's verbal slights of hand was his practice of putting metaphysical concepts "under erasure" (as, for example, in *Of Grammatology*, 19; *31*).

7. Nineteenth-century anarchist theory serves as a major point of comparison throughout the present study, in large measure on account of its predilection for the "all-or-nothing" logic. As Peter Alexeivitch Kropotkin once remarked, anarchist "logics" commonly found their place within the quest for an absolute nonalienation modeled after the unity that Hegel proposed within Absolute Spirit ("Anarchism"). Yet such logics were invariably framed in profoundly antidialectical terms. Proudhon, for example, outlined his vision of the autonomous commune in these words: "There is no halfway house. The commune will be sovereign or subject, *all or nothing*. . . . As soon as there is a conflict *the logic of power* insures victory for the central authority, and this without discussion, negotiation, or trial, debate between authority and subordinate being impermissible, scandalous, and absurd" (cited by Guérin, 58; emphasis added).

The anarchist's refusal to admit the possibility of a dialectical reversal of established forms of power is particularly evident in those passages from Bakunin's *Statehood and Anarchy* that would later bear the brunt of Marx's satire. Here is but one example: "Where there is a state, there is inevitably domination and consequently there is also 'slavery'; domination without slavery, open or masked, is unthinkable—that is why we are enemies of the 'state' " (cited by Marx, "Notes," 518). Behind these, as behind so many arguments in anarchist literature, one can almost hear Bakunin repeat what he had said of an argument for the necessary abolition of God: "The severe logic that dictates these words is far too evident to require a development of this argument" (Schatz, 139).

As passages such as these tend to suggest, the anarchist's conjunction of logical rationality with political extremism was very much a phenomenon of the late nineteenth century, of a historical moment (chronicled in texts such as Villiers de l'Isle-Adam's *L'Eve future*) in which the cult of reason was shown to reveal an irrationality at its very core. The arguments of nineteenth-century anarchists frequently rested on that cusp where an excess of logic, of "straightforward judgment" (see below), slips over into a senselessness that both frustrates any distinction between appearance and reality and disallows all pragmatic calculation. Consider this curious passage from Paul Adam's well-known "Eloge de Ravachol," in which the author rejoices in the failure of the anarchist bomb-thrower François-Claudius Ravachol's act of grave robbing to feed "a family of poor souls": "By the very fact that his attempt was fruitless, and that the corpse was found to be unadorned, his act becomes all the more significant. It is stripped of all real profit-motive, and takes on the abstract demeanor of a logical and deductive idea" (28).

Rarely, however, was the anarchist's reliance on logic theorized in a more stunningly delirious fashion than in an 1895 text entitled *Physiologie de l'anarchiste-socialiste* by Dr. Auguste Hamon, himself an important figure in anarchist circles: "All beings who are more than normally moved by this sense [of justice] must also necessarily possess the sense of logic—that is to say, the faculty that allows one to follow a line of reasoning step by step, to be consistent and single-minded. We make *no hypothesis on the correctness or inaccuracy of the point of departure of that line of reasoning*. Indeed, the *natural disposition* to link ideas and reasons points, among those who possess it, to a conception of justice; they possess *clear, straight-forward judgment* (*le sens droit*), developed in proportion to their sense of justice. Hence it follows that the anarchists, manifesting the 'sense of justice' trait in their cerebral activity, must also manifest, in a more or less developed state, the 'sense of logic' trait" (cited by Dubois, 239; emphasis added).

Since the anarchist's sense of logic and justice is thus seen to be wholly independent of his initial assumptions, we should not be surprised to find the anarchist man of science slipping into an absolute circularity of reasoning where a delirious whirl of rational deduction and positivist "physiology" defies any attempt to assign priority to the rational or the experiential: "Hence logically, one is a rebel by the very fact of being an anarchist . . . that is to say, one is shot through with the spirit of revolt. . . . The positive method confirms the a priori reasoning advanced by the rationalist method" (Dubois, 223).

There then follows a series of first-hand accounts gathered by Hamon from his experience in anarchist circles. In response to the question of why he became an anarchist, the writer "O." (perhaps Octave Mirbeau) admits, "I am very tight in my logic; I follow a line of reasoning as far as it goes, without pausing or changing course in the process, no matter how fatally bold or impudent my conclusions. Most of my critics have acknowledged this 'excess of logic.'" A "Dr. H." (no doubt Hamon himself) writes, "I became an anarchist through reasoning, through logic." A certain "Ph.D." claims, "My mind has never been able to accommodate itself to moderate solutions, and thus it is always with a certain 'exaggeration' that I follow my ideas to the bitter end, to their last logical consequence" (cited by Dubois, 239).

In recent French theory, use of the word "logic" has typically implied an "all-or-nothing" standard analogous, but not identical, to that behind the nineteenth-century anarchist's claim to understand the "logic of power." Derrida, for instance, plainly acknowledges that "every [philosophical] concept that lays claim to any rigor whatsoever implies . . . [an] oppositional logic, which is necessarily, legitimately, a logic of 'all or nothing.' . . . It is impossible or illegitimate to form a philosophical *concept* outside this logic of all or nothing" (*Limited Inc.*, 116–17). Yet he ultimately deploys such a logic tactically and duplicitously so as to promote a practice of writing or of the trace that would perturb "every logic of opposition, every dialectic" (137). Far from being the object of a cult, in other words, logical rigor here serves as the pretext to a displacement outside logical closure. It might be argued, however, that certain "logics" of post-May theory rejoin their anarchist forebears to the extent that they are mere *semblances* of the logical, eternally subordinated to the project of guaranteeing an essential mobility of the spirit. In a comment to which Barthes, Kristeva, Cixous, or Lyotard might have had no trouble subscribing, the anarchist Jean Grave once wrote that "a unity of opinions is unachievable, and then again it would be deadly, because it would be immobility itself" (cited by Maitron, 1: 21).

8. On moral and political antinomies as constitutive of the intellectual's intervention in political and social debates, see Ory and Sirinelli, especially pp. 5–12.

9. The logics of specular doubling and recuperation were not "*absolutely* false"; received ideas seldom are (*pace* Jean Paulhan, 103). Still, the question Paulhan would pose of the commonplace is precisely right in this context: "It is useful, but how?"

10. As Arden Reed astutely remarked on reading a draft of this chapter, the act of conjuring the impasse that is revolutionary politics in the Stalinist mode is thus also a conjuration in the root sense of that word (from the Latin *con* + *jurare*, to swear together).

CHAPTER 2

1. On Lacan's use of the concept of *Verneinung*, see the French volume of the *Écrits*, 178–79 and 879–87.

2. "If socialism is the outpouring of the autonomous activity of the masses and if the objectives of this activity and its forms can spring only from the experience the workers themselves have of exploitation and oppression, it cannot be a question either of inculcating them with a 'socialist consciousness' produced by a theory or of acting as their substitute in directing the revolution or in constructing socialism" (Castoriadis, *Writings*, 1: 10).

The structural repetition inherent in the very conception of the Leninist vanguard could in turn be said to work to recuperative effect, not through any lack of strategic complicity, any essential impertinence (as many would find in May '68), but rather through a near-total complicity with a capitalist system of which it was but a simple or mechanical inversion. There is clearly no inherent incompatibility between analyses of specular or structural repetition and claims of recuperation (and all the less so the more one historicizes these claims). But the easier the slippage from specular doubling to structural repetition and ultimately to recuperation, the more inclined one should be to consider these logics as (strictly ahistorical) justifications for a change of political scene. See, in this respect, my analysis of Barthes's "Recuperation" fragment in Chapter 6.

3. It was, in turn, a short step from this disenchantment with the institutions of Marxist revolutionism to a disgruntlement with the proletariat itself (cf. Marcuse, *One-Dimensional Man*). Castoriadis and others would conclude from the relative failure of the CGT rank and file to question the counter-revolutionary decisions of its leadership that the industrial proletariat had come to abandon its traditional role as revolutionary avant-garde for that of a passive and mystified rear guard, concerned only with improving its lot within consumer society (*Brèche*, 116).

4. This alternative highlights an essential ambivalence within the so-called logic of recuperation. In its stronger form, "recuperation" implies an essential, if unwitting, complicity with the forces of counter-revolution—inscription, in other words, within a process of active co-optation. In its weaker guise, "recuperation" suggests a simple impertinence, the inherent inefficacy of all overly marginalized revolutionary action. In the interest of narrative economy, I have avoided making a formal distinction between these types—between logics, say, of "recuperation through active complicity" and "recuperation through impertinence"—although such a distinction is clearly justifiable.

5. "J'insiste beaucoup et sans cesse sur la nécessité de cette phase de renversement qu'on a peut-être trop vite cherché à discréditer" (*Positions*, 56). On the commonplace status of this "phase of overturning," consider the following "pragmatist answer" articulated by Althusser in his opening essay to the collective volume *Reading Capital* (1968): "In major historical situations it has hap-

pened and may happen again that one is obliged or forced to fight on the terrain of the ideological opponent, when it has proved impossible to draw him onto one's own terrain. But this practice, and the mode of employment of ideological arguments adapted to this struggle, must be the object of a *theory* so that ideological struggle in the domain of ideology does not become a struggle governed by the laws and wishes of the opponent, so that it does not transform us purely into subjects of the ideology it is our aim to combat" (56–57; *1: 68*). What Althusser, like Derrida, calls the "pragmatist" answer recognizes both the necessity of ideological battle on the opponent's terrain and the threat of repetition that shadows such a tactic. But, unlike Derrida's "double gesture," it is in no way a response to what I have called the revolutionary double bind. On Althusser's grounds for being left "hungry" by this "pragmatist answer," see my discussion of the "closed circle" of idealism and pragmatism in Chapter 4.

6. Significantly, Derrida rejoins the neither/nor in such a way that it also means "*at once* or else *or else*"; the logic of *différance* ultimately allows us to read the *pharmakon* as neither remedy nor poison, as both remedy and poison, and/or as remedy or poison (*Positions*, 43; 59).

7. Writing in 1969, Eric Hobsbawm noted the zeal with which the French publishing industry rushed to sate an "apparently unlimited demand" for commentaries on May '68: "By the end of 1968 at least fifty-two books about the May events had appeared, and the flow continues" (*Revolutionaries*, 234). In accordance with a deliriously commemorative logic peculiar to the world of Gallic publishing, anniversaries in 1978 and 1988 have since flooded the market with further memoirs, polemical essays, collections of documents, and scholarly studies. A useful annotated bibliography of this work can be found in Joffrin, pp. 344–59.

8. No one has taken the argument for a gap between revolutionary intentions and actual effects quite so far as Jean Baudrillard, for whom May has become "the first implosive episode" in reaction to the increasing supersaturation and overregulation of modern social life (*Simulacres*, 111). In accordance with his generalized principle that "an order of simulacra is only upheld through the alibi of the previous order," Baudrillard tracks a fundamental discordance between a "revolutionary" language that would be adequate to the postmodern, cybernetic order of simulation and a "revolutionary prosopopoeia" still very much in evidence in the commentaries on May, a discourse Baudrillard would relegate—together with its attendant values of expansion, liberation, and explosive violence—to a bygone era of production (96, 111).

9. On the intellectual as rebel brigand, see Camille Mauclair: "Intellectuals, we inherit with this title the most gloriously lamentable of fates: we are unacceptable in all gatherings of civilized beings."

CHAPTER 3

1. Lacan devoted one week of the seminar entitled "Encore" (1972–73) to arguing the proposition that "the written text, it is not to be understood [*l'écrit, ça n'est pas à comprendre*]"; another to glossing an improvised graph "[which] doesn't strike me as exemplary unless it be, as usual, for producing misunderstandings" (35, 73; Mitchell and Rose, 149). Likewise, in the seminar on "The

Ethics of Psychoanalysis" (1959–60), he insisted that his teaching had value precisely to the extent that it left his listeners "perplexed," unable to endow any one of his terms (the "symbolic," the "signifier," "desire") with the fetishistic power of an "intellectual amulet" (*S* VII, 252; *294*).

2. Roudinesco, 449–50; *456*. Lacan conceived the "pass" in 1967 as an alternative to the more bureaucratized mechanisms of promotion common to the member groups of the International Psychoanalytic Association—mechanisms, he argued, that failed to account for that critical "knot" that is the analysand's *désir de l'analyse*. The pass began with the candidate's recounting her training analysis—and most especially the moment in which the desire *for* her analyst passed over into her desire *to be* an analyst—before two colleagues of roughly similar training, known as "passers." The passers then presented the candidate's case before a jury composed of the director (Lacan), three "School Analysts" (*Analystes de l'École*), and three simple members (all but the director chosen at random). Successful candidates were accorded the title of School Analyst, in recognition not of their aptitude to perform clinical work—which was recognized by the subordinate title "Analyst Member of the School" (*Analyste membre de l'École*)—but rather of their capacity to derive specifically theoretical insight from their training analysis. On Lacan's conception of the *passe*, and on the firestorm it unleashed within the EFP, see Roudinesco, 443–61; *450–67*; Marini, 133–35, *138–40*; and Turkle, 123–38.

3. Turkle, 86. For a detailed discussion of the effects of Lacanian theory on the work of the young theorists who fought on the barricades of May, see Roudinesco, 478–546; *483–550*.

4. The essential characteristics that Ferry and Renaut attribute to "May thought" (*la pensée 68*) are marginally less banal than Castoriadis's list of topoi might be read to suggest. They include: (1) the "end of philosophy" theme (Althusser, Derrida); (2) recourse to genealogical paradigms (Foucault et al.); (3) a disintegration of the idea of truth; and (4) a "historicizing of categories and the end to any reference to the universal" (*French Philosophy*, 4–12; *40–51*).

5. On the *Quatrième groupe*, see Roudinesco, 470–77, *476–82*; Marini, 134–35, *138–39*; and Turkle, 260–61.

6. In a similar vein, Lacoue-Labarthe and Nancy discuss the "perverse effects" of Lacanian theory in their *Title of the Letter*, p. xxix. In this regard, see also Goux, "Lacan décentré," *44*; Cixous and Clément in *The Newly Born Woman*, 140–41, *259*; Kristeva, *Revolution*, 97; *92*.

7. *S* VII 243; *285*. Unless otherwise noted, all parenthetical notations in the present section refer to this text.

8. In the final week of the Ethics seminar, Lacan advances the following four propositions "in an experimental form": "First, the only thing one can be guilty of is giving ground relative to one's desire. / Second, the definition of a hero: someone who may be betrayed with impunity. / Third, this is something that not everyone can achieve. . . . For the ordinary man the betrayal that almost always occurs sends him back to the service of goods. / Fourth proposition: There is no other good than that which may serve to pay the price for access to desire—given that desire is understood here, as we have defined it elsewhere, as the metonymy of our being" (319, 321; *368, 370–71*).

9. Of Lacan's Other Malcolm Bowie writes: "More consistently than any

other of Lacan's terms 'the Other' refuses to yield a single sense; in each of its incarnations it is that which introduces 'lack' and 'gap' into the operations of the subject and which, in doing so, incapacitates the subject for selfhood, or inwardness, or apperception, or plenitude; it guarantees the indestructibility of desire by keeping the goals of desire in perpetual flight" ("Jacques Lacan," 134). However, when Bowie comes to list the Other's various "incarnations"—"as a father, a place, a point, any dialectical partner, a horizon within the subject, a horizon beyond the subject, the unconscious, language, the signifier"—the mother is conspicuously absent (136).

In putting together this account of the genesis of the Thing, I have benefited from a reading of Dor, 188–89.

10. Implicit in this analysis is a concept, the so-called *désir de la mère,* whose essential duplicity can be illustrated with reference to Freud's spool game. The spool that the child sends away (*Fort*) serves as a symbol (1) for the mother as object of the child's desire and (2) for the child himself as sole object of the mother's desire—i.e., as the phallus. With this rejection of the spool (this "murder of the thing"), the child rehearses that (Oedipal) repression of the phallic signifier, or signifier of the *désir de la mère,* that will both suspend him on the Symbolic and consolidate the Thing (and ultimately, the Real) as an impossible space of irretrievable loss.

11. Lacan's name for the signifier that functions as both the cause and the aim of desire is the *objet (petit) a*. Stand-in for the phallus and (often fetishized) guarantor of male fantasy and polymorphic perversion, the *objet a* is typically put into circulation by the woman in her dual role as object of desire and guardian of the phallus (*S* XX, *67–68*; Mitchell and Rose, 143). Lacan speaks of it as a piece of "exquisite trash"—a glance, tear, word, body part, or bodily excretion—that seems to fall (or have been expelled) from the Other (*Television*, 23; *40*). In the moment of acceding to the familial *Atè*, Antigone will fairly glow with the luminosity of the *objet a*. Thus Lacan tells of the Chorus losing its head over "this visible desire that emanates from the eyelids of the admirable girl" (281; *327*). It is in fact the desire of the mother, as it speaks in Antigone's gaze, that renders her so eternally fascinating.

Lacan would elaborate upon this conception of woman as the phantasmatic barrier through which the Other is glimpsed in the *Encore* seminar, particularly pp. 61–82 and 86–88. Among the many fine critiques of this conception, see Luce Irigaray's "Cosi Fan Tutte" (in *This Sex*, 86–105; *79–101*) and the Lacan chapter in Alice Jardine's *Gynesis* (159–72).

12. I address the question of this oscillation in the final section of the present chapter, and again in Chapter 5.

13. On the translation of this sentence, see Gallop, *Reading Lacan*, 145.

14. The importance of "rigor" in the Althusser/Lacan nexus is the subject of Chapter 4.

15. Marcelle Marini has suggested reading the evolution of Lacanian thought in terms of Lacan's own triad of the Imaginary, the Symbolic, and the Real. To this view, the early work on the psychoses, aggressivity, and the specularity of the mirror stage bespeaks a special focus on the imaginary dimension of human experience. This would give way in the early fifties, with Lacan's discovery of the structural anthropology of Claude Lévi-Strauss, to an insistence on the primacy of the Symbolic, most strikingly formulated in the conception of the unconscious as structured "like a language." Finally, it is in the 1959–60 seminar

on Ethics that Marini detects the first signs of an ascendancy of the Real that would come to fruition in the 1974–75 seminar entitled *R.S.I.* (Real, Symbolic, Imaginary) (43–44; *50–51*).

16. To this argument, the Real would not be a byproduct of the primary repression (as was the case with the Thing), but rather the effect of its failure.

17. This emphasis on abolition would in turn ground Lacan's argument for distinguishing foreclosure, as characteristic of psychosis, from the mechanism of repression common to the neuroses. If (as Serge Leclaire has argued) the repression of symbolic material leaves open the possibility that such material might eventually be "unveiled and reintegrated into the dialectical current of experience," foreclosure precludes such a dialectic by withholding even the judgment that its object might exist (cited by Lemaire, 231). The notion of "foreclosure" (*Verwerfung*), Lacan writes, "is articulated in this register as the absence of that *Bejahung*, or judgement of attribution, that Freud poses as a necessary precedent for any possible application of *Verneinung* (negation), which he opposes to it as a judgement of existence: whereas the whole article from which he detaches this *Verneinung* as an element of analytic experience demonstrates in it the avowal of the signifier itself that it annuls" (*Écrits*, 200–201; *558*).

18. Nearing the end of his argument, Roustang reads this passage as yet another instance of Lacan's hopeless ambition to found psychoanalysis as a "scientific delirium" (*Delusion*, 109; *107*). The puzzling "triumphalist" conjunction of psychotic delirium and logical rigor would represent one more Lacanian attempt to derive theoretical profit from the aggravation of a conceptual impasse—here specifically an inability to reconcile the conception of the real as unrepresentable (derived from the experience of psychosis) and a notion of the real as a suprasensible domain structured by physical and mathematical laws. Roustang makes plain his conviction that Lacan's later work does little more than gesture toward the real in this second sense, the real as object of mathematical interpretation, and never more so than when he concludes that, "like the psychotic, the Lacanian system is cut off from life, from affects, from subjectivity, and from all appropriation" (118; *115*).

19. Psychosis is a "trial (or attempt) in rigor" because the psychotic always aims for an impossibly coherent phantasmatic construction. In seeking to differentiate the neuroses from the psychoses in his 1924 paper on "The Loss of Reality in Neurosis and Psychosis," Freud would argue that, whereas the neurotic protects himself against one part of reality by endowing another part with a special, symbolical significance, the psychotic gives birth to an entirely "new phantastic outer world . . . [that] *attempts to set itself in the place of external reality*" (206; emphasis added).

20. *Reading Capital*, 53; *1: 63*. I explore Althusser's arguments to this effect, and their debt to Lacan, in Chapter 4.

21. On tragedy's compatibility with the logic of transgression, see Bataille, *Literature and Evil*, 23; *20*. I return to Bataille's concept of transgression in Chapters 6 and 7.

22. That Lacan would have sought to place the student militants in the role of "sexo-leftists" is not the least of the many misunderstandings that permeate the "Impromptu." On the institutional and political forces that helped shape this event, see Turkle, 174–82, and Roudinesco, 552–59, *557–63*.

23. As this passage might be read to suggest, Lacan was given to attacking

the notion that psychoanalysis might be "progressive" in any sense. In the "Impromptu," however, he would admit the term "in so far as it completes the circle that might perhaps allow you to situate what precisely is at stake, what it is that you are rebelling against" (128; *25*). Delimiting the circle against which one revolts would represent an advance in political rigor if it allowed one to avoid the structural circularity of a liberationist transgression that, in mistaking the origin of its imperative to *jouissance*, effectively veils "what precisely is at stake."

24. On Lacan's dialogue with the Hegel of Alexandre Kojève, see the opening chapters of Mikkel Borch-Jacobsen's superb *Lacan: The Absolute Master*.

25. In the 1948 essay on aggressivity, Lacan spoke of the "especial delusion of the misanthropic '*belle âme*' " as "throwing back on to the world the disorder of which his being is composed" (*Écrits*, 20; *114*). The evolution from this mechanistic language to a full reliance on miscognition in 1953 ("does not recognize the very reason") is symptomatic of the emergence, in the mid-1950s, of Lacan's concept of foreclosure to designate the specific mechanism of psychosis. In thus replacing the paradigm of psychotic projection with one centered around a primal deficiency and subsequent miscognition of fundamental signifers, Lacan might be said to use Hegel against himself, deploying Hegelian miscognition against the expulsion thematic in Hegel's own analysis of the heart as "expelling from itself the perversion [*Verkehrtheit*] which it is itself" (*Phenomenology*, 226).

26. "Such is the general formula for madness as one finds it in Hegel, for do not think I am breaking new ground, despite the fact I have thought it necessary carefully to present this formula to you in the form of an example" (*Écrits, 172*).

27. On the historical function of neither/nor rhetoric in the predominantly socialist "third way" tradition, as well as in the quest for a consensual centrism, see Chapter 6.

28. I return to Barthes's notion of "perversity" in Chapter 6.

29. Reflecting on his "excommunication" from the International Psychoanalytic Association in a seminar from January 1964, Lacan remarked: "I am not saying—but it is not out of the question—that the psychoanalytic community is a Church. But without doubt, the question arises if we are dealing with the echo of a religious practice" (cited by Turkle, 117). On Freud's "Copernican Revolution," see *S* II, 3; *11*.

30. I have borrowed this phrase from Lacan's critique of ontology in the *Encore* seminar: "Everything that has been articulated on the subject of being presupposes that one can shut one's eyes to the predicate and say for example 'man is,' without saying what he is. The very status of being is intimately linked to this cutting off [*section*] of the predicate. Henceforth, nothing can be said of it except in the form of impasse-bound detourings [*des détours en impasse*], demonstrations of logical impossibility, in and through which no predicate is allowed to suffice. That which is of being, of a being that would present itself as absolute, is only the fracturing, the breakage, the interruption of the phrase, 'sexed being' [*être sexué*], insofar as the sexed being has an interest in *jouissance*" (*S* XX, *16*). The force of this passage, read as a whole, is to take issue with ontology's dream of a return to a prediscursive (and hence precultural) reality by appealing to fundamental "*jouissance* of being" (of God, of The Woman, etc.) (*S* XX, *66*; Mitchell and Rose, 142). Whether the phrase "impasse-bound

detourings" actually applies to Lacan's own ethical project is a decision the reader will have to make after reading the present chapter. My decision to appropriate it may, however, prove less paradoxical than it first appears. For not only does Lacan speak of that "*jouissance* of being" he would seemingly throw in the face of ontology as itself "already intimated in the philosophy of being" (in Aristotle in particular), he goes on to say that, much like that specifically tragic experience on which I have focused throughout this chapter, it is approachable only "along the path of logic" (*S* XX 66, 69; Mitchell and Rose, 142, 146).

31. Asked at Yale in 1975 about the political implications of his psychoanalytic work, Lacan responded, "In any event, there is no progress. What we gain on one side we lose on the other. We think we have gained, only because we don't know what we have lost" ("Conférences," 37).

32. For a detailed discussion of these attempts, see Ragland-Sullivan 119–29, especially pp. 124–25.

33. Here is Ovid's version of the Diana and Actaeon story in a recent translation by Charles Boer:

> Bath Time As Usual for Diana: & here comes
> Cadmus's grandson! tired, straying, unsteady,
> woods unknown; but he finds the grove! fate brings him;
> enters cave: splashing fountains, naked nymphs!
> they beat their breasts: "Man!" loud outcry
> fills entire woods: they surround Diana, covering
> her body with theirs
> but the tall goddess towers over others
> by a neck! seen undressed, Diana's face
> goes scarlet dawn, sky color when
> clouds deflect sun; her troops crowd round:
> she, sideways, looks back, wishing
> she had arrows ready: instead throws water,
> soaks virile face, wets his hair, adds
> to water-vengeance words promising disaster:
> "Now say you saw me undressed!
> if you can!"
> no more threats: she sprouts old stag
> antlers on his wet head, expands neck, points
> his ears, lengthens arms & legs, spots on body;
> & adds fear: hero flees at his own speed
>
> . . .
>
> the whole pack is prey-happy: no path
> impassible: rocks, boulders, closed cliffs: pursuit!
> he moves through old hunting grounds: oh!
> flees even his own men; aches to cry,
> "It's Actaeon! can't you recognize your leader?"
> words fail: the air barks.
>
> . . .
>
> snouts all over tear master apart
> a false stag; & only when dead from wounds
> is angry Diana satisfied (53–54)

34. I suspect it is the "pass" that Alan Sheridan has in mind when, in his English translation of the *Séminaire XI*, he renders Lacan's "je me changerai sans doute en cerf" as "I will no doubt be changed into a stag" (188).

CHAPTER 4

1. Indispensable to such a task would be Pierre Bourdieu's *Homo Academicus*, Jean-François Sirinelli's *Génération intellectuelle* (despite its focus on the École Normale of the interwar years), and Althusser's posthumous autobiographies, recently published as *L'Avenir dure longtemps, suivi de Les faits*.

2. These shifts have been explored in some detail by Elisabeth Roudinesco; see especially pp. 373–85, 398–407; *381–93, 405–14*.

3. Lacan, of course, makes a similar argument in basing his "return to Freud" on linguistic models of which Freud himself knew nothing (*Écrits*, 162; *513*).

4. Althusser discussed Marx's "inversion" problematic on numerous occasions, most notably in *For Marx*, 72–73, 89–94; *69–70, 87–92* and *Reading*, 28–34, 46–48, 152–57; *1: 28–37, 1: 53–57, 2: 15–22*.

5. Althusser returned to specular recognition's role in the mechanism of ideology in his influential "Ideology and Ideological State Apparatuses" (1972); see especially pp. 177–83, *129–34*.

6. "The nothing of their philosophy is only the nothing of this inversion of the terms in an immutable categorical opposition (Matter/Mind) which represents in philosophical theory the play of the two antagonistic tendencies in confrontation in this opposition. The history of philosophy is thus nothing but the nothing of this repeated inversion" (*Lenin*, 55; *43*). Philosophy, in Althusser's reading of Lenin, enjoys no history of its own, no dialectical development. It only accedes to history vicariously, through the new scientific practices it helps to install (66; *55*).

7. Althusser's work is never more pathetic (in the root sense of that word) than when he speaks of the "prodigious efforts" with which Marx attempted to fight his way through the "crushing layer" of ideology "beneath which he was born"; of the "heroic struggles" of a "theoretical drama . . . lived, in absolute solitude, long ago" (*For Marx*, 74, 84; *71, 81* and *Reading*, 193; *2: 71*). In itself, such bathos clearly echoes the more patent transgressions of socialist realist style. But Althusser's readers have long sensed that this tone, like the motif of being father to oneself (so striking in "Freud and Lacan" and the Preface to *For Marx*), might prove more deeply symptomatic. The recent publication of Althusser's remarkable memoir, *L'Avenir dure longtemps*, has brought this symptomatic quality into the sharpest focus. "Yes, I had not had a father," Althusser writes in just one of many pertinent passages, "and had endlessly played at the game of 'the father's father' so as to delude myself that I had one. In fact, this meant giving myself the role of father to myself, since all the fathers I imagined or actually met [*pères possibles ou rencontrés*] were incapable of fulfilling the role. I belittled these potential fathers contemptuously by placing them beneath myself, in a position of manifest dependency" (163).

8. "Certainly," Lacan writes in the Four Fundamental Concepts seminar, "the unconscious has always been present, it existed and acted before Freud, but it is important to stress that all the acceptations given, before Freud, to this

function of the unconscious have *absolutely nothing to do* with the Freudian unconscious" (*S* XI, 126, *115*; emphasis added).

In one of his many attempts to rectify the "theoreticist deviation" of his work prior to 1967–68, and specifically its tendency to conceive philosophy on the model of science, Althusser suggests in *Réponse à John Lewis* that science differs from philosophy insofar as it has "(1) an *object*; (2) a *beginning* (the 'epistemological break' . . .); and (3) a *history*" (55). But to the extent that a science's theoretical object is defined restrictively, as absolutely incommensurable with that of its prescientific, ideological antecedents, these criteria are themselves circular (a science has a history *because* it has an object, an object because it has a beginning, a beginning because it has a history, and so on).

9. Be it out of embarrassment (at the call for incessant purification) or befuddlement (at the phrase "libre dans la nécessité de son histoire"), the English translator of *For Marx* gives us only this: "we know that a 'pure' science only exists on condition that it continually frees itself from the ideology which occupies it, haunts it, or lies in wait for it."

CHAPTER 5

1. Raymond Aron has explored this tension in *Revolution*, 131–33; *145–47*.

2. *L'Ange*, 83. Unless otherwise noted, all parenthetical references in this chapter are to this text.

3. Restating their commitment elsewhere to the model of revolution as harbinger of the absolutely new, Jambet and Lardreau trace the (ostensibly abject) idea that the new is "always contained within the old" from the Enlightenment through Marx and on to the "desiring ones" (Lyotard, Deleuze/Guattari). "The most insignificant apocalyptic monk of the Middle Ages, the most insignificant Joachimite," they argue, "conceived of the new in a far more radical manner" ("L'ange, entre Mao et Jésus," *55*).

4. On the points of possible compatibility between the Lacanian and Leninist notions of "rigor," see Chapter 4.

5. Lacan is referring here to his patient Lucien Sebag, a brilliant young ethnologist and ally of various "Third World" movements who in January of 1965 committed suicide by shooting two bullets into his face. "Overwhelmed by the violence of an act he was unable to prevent," Elisabeth Roudinesco writes, "Jacques Lacan confided his distress to his intimates. To some, he asked that they not tell anything, and to others he explained that he had done all he could to avoid what had happened. 'With him gone,' Claude Lévi-Strauss wrote of [Sebag], 'ethnology will never be the same.' And not only ethnology. If Lucien Sebag had lived, Lacanianism would undoubtedly have known a different fate" (384–85; *392–93*). For a more deeply critical evaluation of Lacan's comportment in the Sebag affair, see Althusser, *Avenir*, 180–81.

6. "It remains the case today that the Angel can have no more dogged, no more wicked an adversary than the *semblant*. . . . And it is Lacan, and Lacan alone, who at this time gives us the rules for the hunt after semblances" (37).

7. I read this desire not to let themselves be "Schreberized" as a refusal of Schreber's feminization, his role as "God's woman" (*S* III, 90). In *L'Ange* as, for instance, in Artaud's *Héliogable*, castration is ultimately a way of having done with the contradiction of a certain bisexuality, *while still remaining a man.*

8. In practice, it should be noted, Jambet and Lardreau's concept of Cultural Revolution is surprisingly restrictive. Thus Lardreau speaks of extending the Maoist notion of Cultural Revolution to encompass but two historical moments marked by the appearance of ascetic mass movements: first, the emergence and dissemination of heretic strains of Christianity throughout the Hellenic world, and second, the development after May 1968 of a Maoist-inspired conception of Cultural Revolution within "the capitals of imperialism" (84).

9. Maoists and anarchists tend to agree on the importance of fostering a revolutionary mind-set. Thus both commonly extol the virtues of simplicity, straightforwardness, and a will to absolute purity against the vacillations, mitigations, and amalgamations that characterize what Jambet and Lardreau call ideological revolution (110–11). But this parallel breaks down at the critical point where Maoism meets Christian asceticism, and ultimately Lacanian "rigor." For where the nineteenth-century anarchist placed his faith in an end to oppression brought on as if by the magic of political violence (see Chapter 8), the Lacanian Maoist *qua* Christian ascetic sees the process of Cultural Revolution as never ending, since the desire to refuse mastery as such is properly unsatisfiable.

On the family resemblance between the work of the New Philosophers and nineteenth-century anarchist theory, see Spivak and Ryan, especially pp. 68–69, and the book by Aubral and Delcourt.

10. To illustrate this process of codification, Ory and Sirinelli cite the work of two young authors whose subsequent political destinies took them far from the anarchist circles in which they cut their political teeth: an 1892 piece by Léon Blum in the *Revue Blanche* and an article by Maurice Barrès (written "in the wake of the anarchists' trial, the so-called *Procès des Trente*, at which the term ["intellectual"] was used on several occasions") entitled "La Question des intellectuels" (7). For a still earlier instance of the anarchist's espousal of the term "the intellectual," see note 9 to Chapter 2.

11. Foucault, "Truth and Power," in *Power/Knowledge*, 109–33. As I shall show in Chapter 7, Julia Kristeva has traced the pertinence of a new, specifically *transgressive* conception of revolution to the scientific and technological advances proper to late nineteenth-century capitalism. If Kristeva's analysis is correct, then nineteenth-century anarchism might itself be read as a last-ditch effort to maintain the desire for revolution as the creation of the absolutely new in the face of a recuperative potential, inherent to advanced capitalism, that guarantees the impossibility of such a revolution. But if anarchist rhetoric is thus essentially nostalgic, it also (as I shall go on to argue in Chapter 8) possesses an efficacy that is very much of our age, an efficacy attuned to what Guy Debord has called the "society of spectacle."

12. On the "question of the intellectuals," see Mao's "On the Correct Handling of Contradictions Among the People," in *Selected Readings*, 457–59.

13. Rémi Hess's claim to have found Maoism at the origin of the movements for women's and gay liberation would doubtless be grist for this argumentative mill (167).

14. This double concern haunts Lardreau's meditations on Christian monasticism. Having reduced the forms of Cultural Revolution to two general categories—a radical rejection of Labor and hatred of the body, the latter most strikingly manifested by a "refusal of sexual difference," understood as "an abolition

of the sex itself"—Lardreau argues that the historical function of Christian monasticism was to domesticate the heretic's "dualistic" cultural revolution (100). Monasticism, the argument goes, served to repeat *and* defuse the heretic's revolt against the body, his refusal of marriage and procreation, while at the same time reviving the obligation to labor (99, 115). By severing the linkage between the hatred of thought and the hatred of the Master that characterizes true Cultural Revolution, Christian monasticism, like Maoism in its time, transmuted the revolutionary injunction to spiritual simplicity into a simple submission to the very principle of authority.

15. "It lives in dread of besmirching the splendour of its inner being by action and an existence; and, in order to preserve the purity of its heart, it flees from contact with the actual world, and persists in its self-willed impotence to renounce its self which is reduced to the extreme of ultimate abstraction" (Hegel, *Phenomenology*, 400). The following section pursues an analysis begun in the section of Chapter 3 entitled "Toward the Beautiful Soul."

16. This resemblance is deceptive, because Jambet and Lardreau's libidinal investment in a fundamentally dualistic and paranoid world-view precludes precisely the sort of incessant and complicitous undermining of the field of mastery that the double gesture was meant to effect (see Chapter 2 above).

17. Fragment 484 (Brunschvicg) of the *Pensées*, in *Œuvres complètes*, p. 1134. Lacan was fond of citing this text when reflecting upon the necessarily psychotic effect of modern culture, where the subject is spoken by the accumulated mass of lifeless cultural stereotypes (*Écrits*, 71; *283*).

18. Of the analyst Lacan writes, "There is no better way of placing him objectively than in relation to what was in the past called: being a saint. . . . A saint's business, to put it clearly, is not *caritas*. Rather, he acts as trash [*déchet*]; his business being *trashitas* [*il décharite*]. So as to embody what the structure entails, namely allowing the subject, the subject of the unconscious, to take him as the cause of the subject's own desire" (*Television*, 15–16; *28*).

At its best, the analyst's role as "the *objet (a)* incarnate" serves to block the imaginary and narcissistic demand for love, raising the subject to the level of that exquisite love for the Symbolic father in which Lacan would locate analytic truth (*Television*, 15; *28*). The analyst, he remarks in the *Encore* seminar, "is he who, by putting the *objet a* in place of the *semblant*, is in the most suitable position to do what is right—namely, to ask (as one would ask of knowledge) what is up with truth" (*S* XX, 88). But the institutional history of psychoanalysis, and of its Lacanian variety above all, clearly justifies a fear that the analytic transference will not be overcome, that the analysand will fail to effect a desupposition of the analyst's knowledge. On this matter, see François Roustang's *Dire Mastery*.

19. As such, the Maoist intellectual's will to humility plainly inscribes itself within that logic of mastery that Pierre Legendre has derived from Lacan: "The true word of the Master is: 'under the threats I flourish at you, give way on your desire, and there will come to you from me, freely, this grace, this sprinkling of dew that is my love' " (*L'Ange*, 26).

20. Sartre wrote, "In our society . . . the intellectual has no meaning unless he be in perpetual self-contradiction, unless he suppress himself as an intellectual by doing exactly the opposite of what he wishes to do" (cited by Ory and Sirinelli, 217).

21. In the *Encore* seminar, Lacan would go further, speaking of the master-signifier as "the One incarnate" in that elemental language, shot through with puns and neologisms, he called *lalangue* (131). On *lalangue*, see Ragland-Sullivan, 206.

22. The phallus is imaginary, for example, in its status as object presumed to satisfy the mother's desire and yet symbolic as the signifier of desire's eternal flight.

23. "The Idea of cultural revolution is an ahistorical, but not eternalist, reassessment of the evidence for the Rebel. History exists [history defined, again tautologically, as epic struggle] to the extent that this Idea rises up in the face of a reassessment of the evidence for the Master, understood as the very eternity that will be taken advantage of by each successive ideological revolution" (92).

24. Jambet, *Apologie de Platon*, cited by Aubral and Delcourt, 91. In *L'Ange* Lardreau speaks of countering what he calls "Bouvard and Pécuchet thought"—the doctrine that human nature is changeable and diverse—with a trenchant, decisive form of thought (*une pensée qui tranche*) (139). Yet it is precisely the drive to take sides and conclude upon the nearly infinite range of questions thrown up by the world that constitutes the cycle of illusion and disillusionment into which Flaubert's two clerks clearly fall. Calling Jambet and Lardreau "our contemporary Bouvard and Pécuchet," Aubral and Delcourt rightly remark, "Illusions, disillusions; one believes, sends one's beliefs up in flames, and believes again. It's an infernal cycle. If there is nothing left but belief, is thinking still allowed?" (199, 50) In fact, Lardreau tacitly justifies the comparison when he implies that it is the urgent force of passion, not analytic acumen or political efficacy, that constitutes the true locus of their book's value: "We would like our readers to feel here the haste, the urgency, that moves us" (13). On Flaubert's grounds for likewise valorizing the urgent process of desire itself, see my "The Style of (Post-) Liberal Desire: *Bouvard et Pécuchet*."

25. Like the hysteric, Lacan remarks in the *Envers de la psychanalyse* seminar, the analysand fabricates a "man [his word] animated by the desire to know," a man to whom the analysand will address the question of his desire (*S* XVII, *36*). Later in this same seminar, Lacan effectively anticipates the drama of *L'Ange* when he speaks of the hysteric's assiduity in an attempt to "unmask" the workings of the master "by emphasizing the master's share in the One, from which she [again, his word] subtracts herself in her capacity as object of his desire" (107).

26. A full evaluation of this problematic would need to address at least four principal points: (1) how the precondition of writing (as Lacan understands it in *Encore*) is a certain *béance* opened up by the impossibility of sexual relations; (2) how "writing" thus derives from an ambiguity in Lacan's 1969 characterization of analysis as a therapeutic "hystericization of discourse" (*S* XVII, *35-36*); (3) how analytic discourse, and love for the analyst as subject-presumed-to-know, emerge from the rotation (the true "revolution"-ism) of Lacan's "four discourses" schema; and (4) how it is precisely writing's supplementarity to the *béance* of sexual relations that allows it, like feminine *jouissance*, to break out of the totality of the phallic function.

On the tone of the *Encore* seminar, see Irigaray, *Ce sexe*, 100–101, and Bowie, *Lacan*, 150–51.

27. I say "ostensible" because, as Elie Ragland-Sullivan perceptively remarks, Lacan pronounces this phrase as an ironic "joke-cum-challenge" to the MLF (269).

CHAPTER 6

1. This paragraph draws heavily on Ory and Sirinelli, 205–13. In *Teachers, Writers, Celebrities* (*Le pouvoir intellectuel en France*) (41–95; *51–113*), Régis Debray divides the history of the intellectual in France into three "cycles," each delimited by historical shifts in cultural hegemony—from the university (what Debray calls the "University Cycle" ran from 1880 to 1920) to the literary review and publishing house ("Publishing Cycle," 1920–60) and finally to the mass media ("Media Cycle," 1968–).

2. In his excellent *Michel Foucault: The Freedom of Philosophy*, John Rajchman suggests that "one need only glance at [Foucault's] writings until the *Archaeology of Knowledge* in 1969 and his assumption of his chair at the Collège de France (and it was his most prolific period) to see that no one pursued the question of writing more relentlessly than he" (11).

3. "At this point, different things ceaselessly and rapidly pass into each other, and the *critical* experience of *difference resembles* the naïve and *metaphysical* implications *within difference*, such that to an inexpert scrutiny, we could appear to be criticizing Artaud's metaphysics from the standpoint of metaphysics itself, when we are actually delimiting a fatal complicity. Through this complicity is articulated a necessary dependency of all destructive discourses: they must inhabit the structures they demolish, and within them they must shelter an indestructible desire for full presence, for nondifference: simultaneously life and death" (Derrida, *Writing and Difference*, 194; *291–92*).

4. At the time of the Dreyfus Affair, and thus at a crucial moment in the development of "the antinomic nature of the modern political image-repertory" (Castoriadis), the editors of *Le Temps* called for a union of those like-minded citizens "[who] wish to be neither revolutionaries nor internationalists along with certain defenders of Dreyfus, nor antisemitic or nationalist with certain adversaries of Dreyfus" (cited by Bredin, 283; *358*). But in the highly charged atmosphere of the affair, Jean-Denis Bredin noted, this effort toward a moderate consensus would "have no future."

5. On the vicissitudes of this aspiration to a "third way," see Ory and Sirinelli, especially chapters 5 and 8.

6. In his conclusion to the earlier *Writing Degree Zero*, Barthes had reflected on the writer's situation and vocation in a manner very much within the framework established by *What Is Literature?*: "Writing is therefore a blind alley [*impasse*], and it is because society itself is a blind alley. The writers of today feel this; for them, the search for a nonstyle or an oral style, for a zero level or a spoken level of writing is, all things considered, the anticipation of a homogeneous social state; most of them understand that there can be no universal language outside a concrete, and no longer mystical or merely nominal, universality of society. / There is therefore in every present mode of writing a double postulation: there is the impetus of a break and the impetus of a coming to

power [*avènement*]." On the one hand, literary writing is the consciousness of a "division of languages which is inseparable from the division of classes"; in its capacity as Freedom, literary writing is also consciousness of "the very effort which seeks to surmount [such division]." On the other hand, "it is none the less an imagination eagerly desiring a felicity of words, it hastens towards a dreamed of language whose freshness, by a kind of ideal anticipation, might portray the perfection of some new Adamic world where language would no longer be alienated" (*Writing Degree Zero*, 87–88; *64–65*).

7. The quotations throughout this paragraph have been modified so as to maintain Barthes's clear construction of an impasse. As for the English version's reference to "the left-wing writers and intellectuals who have been absorbed for the last *ten* years by the anti-Stalinist struggle," it is simply wrong—both with respect to history and to Barthes's published text (70; emphasis added).

8. It is tempting to conclude that this refusal of a direct revolutionary heritage places Barthes's Sollers in the lineage of those revolutionaries of 1789 who sought to foreclose the Oedipal struggle with the monarchical father by giving birth to themselves as virtuous republicans, by becoming (to paraphrase Althusser) "fathers to themselves." It is indeed true that Sollers's dictum "writing is a continuation of politics by other means" restates a notion of cultural politics that served the French Revolution as a means of attaining a specifically *comic* resolution to an apparent historical (Oedipal) bind. But Barthes and Sollers would claim to know, as the revolutionaries of 1789 and their utopian progeny did not, that such a resolution was not to be obtained by a quest for the radically new: "You have to recognize that with language, nothing really *new* is possible. There is no spontaneous generation—alas, language too is always filial. Consequently, the *radically new* (the new language) can never be anything but the old language pluralized. No force is superior to the *plural*" (*Writer Sollers*, 82; *65–66*).

9. As I showed in Chapter 4, there is at least one "father" to Barthes's theoretical generation, namely Althusser, for whom the enunciation of a repetitive doubling (that of "theory" and "practice") becomes the pretext to a plural solution—specifically, to the conception of the social formation as a complex articulation of diverse practices. But of course Althusser's work also gravitates incessantly back toward that very "definition," that "separation of Good and Evil," that Barthes found to be characteristic of the "Stalinist world."

10. Barthes was well aware that any escape from "the West's narcissistic game" might involve a narcissistic miscognition in its turn. The account of Japan he published as *The Empire of Signs* (1970) begins with the admonition that the "reality" of the Orient is "to me . . . a matter of indifference" (3; *10*). "Nothing is less certain than our having been in China in its space and time," Kristeva likewise remarked of the three-week trip to China by the *Tel Quel* group (Sollers, Kristeva, Barthes, Pleynet, Wahl) in the spring of 1974 (*Polylogue*, 520). To go to China was to satisfy a specifically Western fascination, "a fascination ultimately devoted to our own strange, foreign, feminine and psychotic side" ("Mémoire," 52). In his opening to the Japan book, Barthes speaks of the need someday to "write the history of our own obscurity—manifest the density of our narcissism, tally down through the centuries the several appeals to difference we may occasionally have heard, the ideological recuperations

which have infallibly followed and which consist in always acclimating our incognizance of Asia by means of known languages" (*Empire*, 4; *10*). But this analysis will be conspicuously deferred.

11. The etymological play by which Barthes would distance himself from anarchism proper ("for someone who, etymologically speaking, is an-archist") is thus at least triply ironic. Not only does Barthes have recourse here to a repetitive logic echoing that which embodied anarchism's central critique of its Marxist rival; not only does his (neo-Derridean) etymologism return him to an orthography (*an-archiste*) much in vogue among the libertarian communists of the First International; but, most important, his vision (here and elsewhere) of a specifically textual utopia grounded in the infinite, harmonious circulation of equal yet contradictory elements bears an appreciable resemblance to that which led Proudhon to characterize "the positive state of anarchy" as "the victory of Economics over Politics" (cited by Arvon, 43). On the orthography *anarchiste*, see Maitron, *Mouvement* 1: 15.

12. On Barthes's deep affective predilection for forms of circulation without mastery, consider the following short passage from *Roland Barthes by Roland Barthes*: "When I used to play prisoner's base [*quand je jouais aux barres*] in the Luxembourg, what I liked best . . . was to free the prisoners—the effect of which was to put both teams back into circulation: the game started over again at zero" (50; *54*).

13. Far from implying a relativist "in-difference," a "magnanimous" acknowledgment that all meanings possess their "share of truth," the liberal value of tolerance means according a right to exist to that which one firmly believes to be false (6; *12*).

14. "He could not get away from that grim notion that true violence is that of the *self-evident*: what is evident is violent, even if this evidence is gently, liberally, democratically represented" (*Roland Barthes*, 85; *88*).

15. I discuss this notion of a post-liberal textuality in my essay "The Style of (Post-)Liberal Desire."

16. *Polylogue*, 131, and *Revolution in Poetic Language*, 200; *178*. Keith Reader makes the "two Maos" argument by juxtaposing Mao the "arch 'anti-revisionist' " with "the 'other Mao'—the poster guru of May '68" (9). Of the latter he writes, "The idea that the cultural and intellectual spheres could become major areas of political struggle had an obvious appeal for the intellectuals of the Left, and the view of Chinese society as a hive of cultural democracy, buzzing with wall-newspapers and street theatre, was given credence by Mao's own activity as a poet and carefully cultivated image as the Third World's first Renaissance Man" (10).

17. On May 28, 1952, a violent demonstration led by the Communist Mouvement de la paix took place in Paris to protest the visit of General Matthew Ridgway, accused of being responsible for the deployment of bacteriological weapons in Korea (*Idées*, 106).

18. I shall have more to say on this specific language in the following chapter.

19. To appreciate the extent to which Sollers's evocation of the "Jacobin model" takes aim at the PCF, it is worth recalling that the mythology and historiography of the French Revolution had long remained the particular provinces of party ideologues and historians, respectively. On the Jacobin Terror as the

very model of that paranoid aggressivity typically decried by post-May theory, see Chapter 10.

20. The charge of "plastering over" fundamental psychic problems was one that Lacan had long leveled at ego psychologists and psychoanalytic pill-pushers alike. This rejection of a *replâtrage* complicitous with the bourgeois-capitalist order proved in turn one of the most powerful points of affinity between Lacanian doctrine and the various revolutionary ideologies that sprang up in France after 1965.

21. In 1977, for example, Sollers writes, "The truth is that many felt guilty, and still feel guilty, about going the 'American' way" ("Why the United States?" 284; *12*).

22. *S/Z*, 120; *126*. Marcel Gauchet writes of the period in question: "And yet this time, to cries of amazement and pain, resignation and rejection, the cocoon will be broken, the obscure sensation of the world economy's more ample pulse will sweep it entirely away. The international dimension takes hold. . . . [The year] 1977 could well have been a great secret milestone of our recent history: the year of alignment. A powerful process is set into motion . . . the beginning of the end of *l'exceptionnalité française*" (*Idées,* 339).

23. Thus she looks to America for one solution, not necessarily the most viable, to the "fundamental problem" ("Why?" 276; *5*) of learning to confront and parry the psychosis proper to Western capitalism: "The explosion of pornography, the various forms of mysticism, the proliferation of trans-psychotic aesthetic experiments, etc., which, while extremely troubling and perhaps so many dead ends, may also be ways of dealing with sublimation in a manner different from that of psychoanalysis, which, as we've all too frequently seen, produces its own particular churches and dead ends" ("Why?" 279; *8*).

24. On the institution of the inaugural lesson, see Ungar, 127–28.

25. "From this point of view, an institution differs from a conversation in that it always requires supplementary constraints for statements to be declared admissible within its bounds. The constraints function to filter discursive potentials, interrupting possible connections in the communication networks: there are things that should not be said" (*Condition,* 17; *34*). On the institution as space of discursive conflict, see Ansart, 43.

26. The French *leurre* habitually translates as "decoy," "bait," "allurement," or "imposture." What Barthes means by it here, I shall argue, is akin to what he elsewhere means by "fiction" and the "novelistic" (*romanesque*).

27. "One emerges from it [Antithesis]: either by the neutral [*le neutre*], or by the glimpse of reality (the Racinian confident seeks to abolish the tragic antithesis, as remarked in *On Racine*), or by supplemental material (Balzac supplements the Sarrasinian Antithesis, as remarked in *S/Z*), or by the invention of a (translational) third term [*par l'invention d'un troisième terme (de déport)*]" (*Roland Barthes,* 138; *142*).

28. In his reading of Balzac's "Sarrasine," Barthes will likewise speak of laughter as that which "breaches the wall of the Antithesis" (*S/Z,* 49; *35*).

Pascal Ory has noted a parallel development in a study of French culture between May '68 and May '81. In the "stupid-and-nasty humor" of magazines such as *Hari-Kari* and *Charlie hebdo,* as well as in the political cartoons of Reiser, Wolinski, and Cabu, Ory finds signs of a post-'68 revival of "that somewhat forgotten idea . . . that one can shake up the establishment just as easily, if not more so, with the coarseness of laughter than with formal sophistication" (*Entre-deux-mais*, 176).

29. "Nihilism: 'superior goals depreciate.' This is an unstable, jeopardized moment, for other superior values tend, immediately and before the former are destroyed, to prevail; dialectics only links successive positivities; whence the suffocation at the very heart of anarchism. How to *install* the deficiency of any superior value? Irony? It always proceeds from a *sure* site. Violence? Violence too is a superior value, and among the best coded. Bliss? Yes, if it is not spoken, doctrinal. The most consistent nihilism is perhaps *masked*: in some way *interior* to institutions, to conformist discourse, to apparent finalities" (*Pleasure*, 44; *71*).

30. I hear traces of Barthes's resistance in the opening qualification of a sentence such as this, from his discussion of the two "edges" of the Sadean text: "As textual theory would have it: the language is redistributed" (*Pleasure*, 6; *14*).

31. "Everything seems to suggest," he writes in *Roland Barthes*, "that his discourse proceeds according to a two-term dialectic: popular opinion and its contrary, *Doxa* and its paradox, the stereotype and the novation, fatigue and freshness, relish and disgust: *I like / I don't like*. This binary dialectic is the dialectic of meaning itself (*marked / not marked*) and of the Freudian game the child plays (*Fort/Da*): the dialectic of value" (68; *73*). See also *Pleasure*, 41; *67*.

32. Bliss for Barthes is precisely not a function of castration, as this language might be read to suggest. If in the Freudian scenario the phallus is the marked term and its absence the unmarked, castration becomes the mark of the unmarked. Bliss, on the other hand, serves to suspend the play of marked and unmarked terms constitutive of meaning itself (see preceding note).

33. *Pleasure*, 18; *32*. As early as *Writing Degree Zero*, Barthes had spoken of the impossibility of developing one's writing "within duration without gradually becoming a prisoner of someone else's words and even of my own"; indeed no literary style proves more susceptible to becoming habitual or mechanical than that "zero degree" of style he called "colorless writing" (17, 78; *16, 57*). In later years Barthes dwelt with evident horror on the prospect of an institutional recuperation of his work that would, as Lawrence Kritzman puts it, "preempt the possibility of futurity and thus threaten the writer's ongoing libidinal energy" ("Barthesian Free-Play," 189). Witness his reproduction in *Roland Barthes by Roland Barthes*, under the laconically eloquent rubric "Recuperation," of an exercise in *commentaire composé* based on a passage from *Writing Degree Zero* (155; *158*).

34. In his provocative new book *Bringing Out Roland Barthes*, D. A. Miller reads Barthes's *neutre* as a "pseudo-linguistic" transcription of the gay male's "double double bind"—the fact that "he must be, can't be, a man; he must be, can't be, a woman" (14, 11). I find Miller's reading both subtle and persuasive (especially the pages on *S/Z*), yet would resist reducing Barthes's discomfort with "the binary prison"—the weight of whose political history I have outlined in this chapter—to a simple matter of "protective coloring" (16).

35. In his discussions of the "double gesture" of disseminatory writing, Derrida suggests that no one text, no one name can inhabit and close down the "interval" between the "overturning" of previous conceptual hierarchies and

the irruptive emergence of new quasi-concepts (*supplément, pharmakon,* etc.); this interval can be marked only by what he calls a "*grouped* textual field" (an intertextual network), not by the punctuality of personal or textual positions. As a result, "responsibility and individuality are values that *can no longer predominate* here: that is the first effect of dissemination" (emphasis added; *Positions*, 42, *58*; *Dissemination*, 6; *12*).

36. As an example of the neutral as utopian disarming of value, consider Barthes's discussion of the "virile/non-virile" paradigm immediately following his fragment on "the neutral": "*Virile/non-virile*: this famous pair, which rules over the entire *Doxa*, sums up all the ploys of alternation: the paradigmatic play of meaning and the sexual game of ostentation. . . . Nonetheless, once the alternative is rejected (once the paradigm is blurred) utopia begins: meaning and sex become the object of a free play, at the heart of which the (polysemant) forms and the (sensual) practices, liberated from the binary prison, will achieve a state of infinite expansion" (*Roland Barthes*, 133; *137*).

37. On this dialectic, see note 31 above.

CHAPTER 7

1. Philip Lewis, "Revolutionary Semiotics," 28. Lewis proves especially astute on the matter of that curious movement proper to Kristevan semiology: "As an autocritical critique constructing the theory of its own criticology, Kristevan semiology is a perpetually self-revising, reflexive, open-ended, self-validating process, pursuing the formulation of a knowledge which is always immediately relativized, confronted with alien concepts, subjected to theoretical analysis. At the open end of a semiological investigation, there is nothing to be found other than the basic ideological gesture of its own movement, which it recapitulates and denies prior to reenacting the same critical trajectory, but with a modified object" (29).

Other worthwhile appreciations of Kristeva's work in the *Revolution in Poetic Language* phase include the Kristeva chapters of Toril Moi's *Sexual/Textual Politics* and Rosalind Coward and John Ellis's *Language and Materialism*; John Lechte's useful (if spotty) *Julia Kristeva*; Leslie Hill's essay in *Abjection, Melancholia and Love* (ed. John Fletcher and Andrew Benjamin); and Leon Roudiez's Introductions to *Desire in Language* and *Revolution in Poetic Language.*

In Britain and the United States, the theoretical apparatus of *Revolution* has received its most sustained attention in an ongoing dialogue around those questions of femininity and motherhood that Kristeva would explicitly address in subsequent writings. See in this respect Domna Stanton, "Language and Revolution" and "Difference on Trial"; Gayatri Spivak, "French Feminism in an International Frame"; Susan Rubin Suleiman, "Writing and Motherhood"; Alice Jardine, "Opaque Texts and Transparent Contexts"; and the Kristeva chapter of Elisabeth Grosz's *Sexual Subversions*. Kelly Oliver's recent *Reading Kristeva* is particularly good on the debates that Kristeva's work has elicited within Anglo-American feminist circles.

2. Throughout this chapter, parenthetical references to Part I of Kristeva's *Revolution* refer first to Margaret Waller's excellent translation for Columbia

University Press and second to the original French text. All translations from Parts II and III of the French text, absent from the Columbia edition, are my own.

3. It has become common practice to translate *sujet unaire* as "unitary subject"—perfect English, but apt to elide the always split nature of the *sujet unaire*. For this reason, I have come to prefer the more barbaric "unary subject" (first employed by Alice Jardine and Tom Gora in the translations for *Desire in Language*).

4. "With Kristeva," Kelly Oliver rightly notes, "it is always impossible to pinpoint an origin. . . . In some places Kristeva says that the semiotic is both logically and chronologically prior to the symbolic, while in other places she maintains that the symbolic is both logically and chronologically prior to the semiotic" (105). I shall explore the grounds for this second claim in a moment.

5. "From this ['analytic position'], modern philosophy only retains either the notion of a *position*, in order to offer a specialist or totalizing point of view (as in Marxism, Freudianism, Phenomenology and various forms of empiricism); or else it retains only the notion of analysis as *dissolution*, and writes in a style similar to that of an outmoded avant-garde such as symbolism. Torn between being the guardian of the law and that instance which disavows the law, hasn't philosophy turned away from thought?" ("Dissident," 8; *Kristeva Reader*, 300).

In lieu of a full account of Kristeva's complex appreciation of Derridean grammatology, consider this brief passage from *Revolution*: "Grammatology . . . is, in our view, the most radical of all the various procedures that have tried, after Hegel, to push dialectical negativity further and elsewhere. . . . But in its desire to bar the thetic and put (logically or chronologically) previous energy transfers in its place, the grammatological deluge of meaning gives up on the subject and must remain ignorant not only of his functioning as social practice, but also of his chances for experiencing *jouissance* or being put to death" (*Revolution*, 140–42; *128–30*). There can be no doubt that Derrida "gives up on" the subject as Kristeva understands it. She has a point, moreover, when she writes in *Revolution* that, in the texts of Derrida (inter alios), the "'theoretical' subject sets himself up with even more power . . . inasmuch as he will mime the dissolution of all positions" (*Revolution*, 97; *93*). But it is patently false, as my reading of the "double gesture" in Chapter 2 begins to show, that Derrida would "bar the thetic" in such a way that might ally him with those who would nihilistically negate the Law.

6. "Is it 'useless to insist'?" Derrida asks. "Can one, as Bataille says, understand the movement of transgression under the Hegelian concept of *Aufhebung*, which, we have seen often enough, represents the victory of the slave and the constitution of meaning? Here we must interpret Bataille against Bataille, or rather, must interpret one stratum of his work from another stratum" (*Writing and Difference*, 275; *404–5*).

In a note to this final sentence, Derrida specifies, "The greatest force is the force of writing which, in the most audacious transgression, continues to maintain and to acknowledge the necessity of the system of prohibitions (knowledge, science, philosophy, work, history, etc.). *Writing is always traced between these two sides of the limit*" (338, *405*; emphasis added).

7. Laplanche and Pontalis, *Language*, 364. In the entry of *The Language of*

Psychoanalysis on the "Psychical Representative," Laplanche and Pontalis present the ambivalence in Freud's notion of the drive as follows: "Sometimes the instinct [*pulsion, Trieb*: i.e., the drive] itself is presented as 'the psychical representative of the stimuli originating from within the organism and reaching the mind.' At other times the instinct becomes part of the process of somatic excitation, in which case it is represented in the psyche by 'instinctual representatives' which comprise two elements—the ideational representative and the quota of affect" (364).

A good example of Kristeva's tendency to dialectize that "frontier between the mental and the physical" on which Freud had situated the drives occurs in a passage to which I shall return in more detail below, in which she speaks of the *sujet en procès* as "a passage-way, a non-place [*non-lieu*], where there is a struggle between conflicting tendencies, *drives* whose stases and thetic moments . . . are as much rooted in affective relations (parental and love relations) as they are in class conflict" (Freud, *Three Essays*, in *Standard Edition*, 7: 168; *Revolution*, 203; *179–180*).

8. "Thus, even while maintaining Kantian oppositions [negation/affirmation, quality/quantity, singular/universal, etc.], the Hegelian dialectic moves toward a fundamental reorganization [*refonte*] of these oppositions—one that will establish an *affirmative negativity*, a *productive dissolution* in place of 'Being' and 'Nothing' " (*Revolution*, 113; *105*). Kristeva commonly uses the concept of *la refonte* ("recasting," "reorganization") to designate the sort of open-ended, productive/destructive dialectic that is our subject here. See, for example, "A New Type of Intellectual: The Dissident," where she opposes "recast[ing]" to the "dialectical trap" (293; *3*).

9. In his "Réponse au commentaire de Jean Hyppolite sur la 'Verneinung' de Freud" (Response to Jean Hyppolite's remarks on Freud's *Verneinung*), Lacan speaks of expulsion (*Ausstossung aus dem Ich*) as "[that] which constitutes the real insofar as it is the domain of that which subsists outside symbolization" (*Écrits*, 388). As will become apparent, Kristeva would retain expulsion's function as constitutive of "the real," while wresting the latter from that "rigorously" psychotic logic in which Lacan bemires it (see Chapter 3).

10. Clearly informing this argument is Lacan's second thesis in "Aggressivity in psychoanalysis": "Aggressivity in experience is given to us as intended aggression and as an image of corporal dislocation, and it is in such forms that it shows itself to be efficient" (*Écrits*, 10; *103*).

11. Unlike those forms of separation proper to the thetic moment—the separation from the mother that founds signification and desire or that which constitutes the self as fiction in the mirror stage—the separation of anal rejection "is not a lack, but a discharge, and which, although privative, arouses pleasure" (*Revolution*, 151; *137*).

12. Jean Laplanche, for example, has discussed this "confusion" (his word) on at least two occasions: in chapter 6 of *Life and Death in Psychoanalysis* and in *The Language of Psychoanalysis* (with J.-B. Pontalis), pp. 102 and 346.

13. On the place of this dialectic in nineteenth-century vitalist biology, see François Jacob, *La Logique du vivant*, 102–3, as well as my own "Science and Confusion," 207–8.

14. Like Althusser, in other words, Kristeva uses the specular impasse as im-

petus to the recovery of a certain dialectic. Yet her theoretical project is marked by a radical open-endedness that stands in sharp contrast to the aggressive circularity that follows from Althusser's demand to maintain the purity of Marxist science's theoretical object (see Chapter 4).

15. "This heterogeneous process [*signifiance*], neither anarchic, fragmented foundation nor schizophrenic blockage, is a structuring and de-structuring *practice*, a passage to the outer *boundaries* of the subject and society [*passage à la* limite *subjective et social*]. *Then—and only then—can it be jouissance and revolution*" (*Revolution*, 17; *15*; emphasis added).

16. "Revolutionary Semiotics," 29. On the tendency of metalanguage to reduce heterogeneity to positivity and on its relation to specifically paranoid forms of the social bond, see *Revolution*, 93–95; *89–91*.

17. On this point, see note 15 above.

18. Bataille takes a more sanguine approach to this inherent promise in the following passage from "The Notion of Expenditure": "In the agitation that is history, only the word Revolution dominates the customary confusion and carries with it the promise that answers to the unlimited demands of the masses. As for the masters and the exploiters, whose function is to create the contemptuous forms that exclude human nature . . . a simple law of reciprocity demands that we hope for the time when they will be condemned to fear, for the great night (*grand soir*) on which their beautiful phrases will be drowned out by the death screams of the riots" (127–28; *42*).

19. The Mallarmean epigraph with which Sollers introduces *Théorie d'ensemble* is also to the point here: "Nothing easier than to anticipate, by abstraction, and purely, verdicts included in the future, which is nothing more than the conceptual lethargy of the masses" (cited on p. 7).

20. In *Revolution in Poetic Language*, Kristeva reads Mallarmé's phrase from "Un coup de dés," "Nothing will have taken place but the place [*Rien n'aura eu lieu que le lieu*]" as emblematic of a "*second overturning*" of that "history of a subject always present to himself" that is the Hegelian dialectic (215; *188*). Through this "second overturning," said to be "as fundamentally radical" as Marx's recentering of history around the means of production, history comes to be driven by the sumptuary practice of a *sujet en procès*, always already absent from herself within the position of practical activity, and anticipating herself "in an always anterior future [*dans un futur toujours antérieur*]" (*Revolution*, 215; *188*). And yet nothing will have taken place but the place, for the negativity unleashed by this activity will only have been readable as a transformation of those "place(s)" that "support" it (*lieu-support*): namely, language, the means of production, relations of production and reproduction, and the like (*Révolution*, *365*).

21. See, for example, Sollers, *Logiques*, 13; Derrida, *Positions*, 57; *78*; Kristeva, *Polylogue*, 61.

CHAPTER 8

1. Born of a women's study group at the Université de Paris-Vincennes, where Cixous had taught since 1968, Psych et po took a militantly psychotextual approach to the question of woman's liberation. Unlike those groups

such as Questions feministes that argued that the apparent self-evidence of sexual difference was but an alibi for continued male domination, Psych et po sought to uncover a specifically feminine libidinal economy repressed under patriarchy, and so to operate (with and against Lacan) a "revolution of the Symbolic." For a useful articulation of the aims and vicissitudes of Psych et po, see Duchen, 32–39.

2. Throughout this chapter, "hijacking" should be read as a (necessarily imperfect) translation of the concept of *détournement* theorized and practiced by Guy Debord and the members of the Internationale Situationniste. On this concept, see Knabb, 8–14.

3. Jan Goldstein gives this useful summary of Charcot's model: "In the hysterical attack, he taught, four periods follow one another with the regularity of a mechanism." These were (1) tonic rigidity; (2) clonic spasm or *grands mouvements*, also called, with a whimsical pun, *clownisme* because of the circus-like acrobatics produced; (3) *attitudes passionnelles*, or vivid physical representations of one or more emotional states, such as terror, hatred, love; the patient, who was endowed with an acrobat's agility in the second period, was now said to display the talents of a mime or dramatic actress; and (4) a final delirium marked by sobs, tears, and laughter and heralding a return to the real world" ("Diagnosis," 214).

4. I have derived the phrase "metaphoric condensation" from Leslie Rabine's excellent study "*Ecriture féminine* as metaphor." "When it erupts as a symptom of the unconscious," Rabine notes, metaphoric condensation "disrupts the unity of that symbolic order and the Oneness of the subject based on it. It frees the difference repressed by metaphor as substitution [between proper and figural, for example], since in condensation the two forms of metaphor alternate with each other in the same signifier" (36).

5. Jane Gallop has written that the exchange between Clément and Cixous that closes *The Newly Born Woman* "seems to be a struggle to keep the hysteric an 'obsolete' figure, to keep the hysterical identification in the past" ("Keys," 203). But this struggle plays itself out quite clearly within Cixous's own discourse, as the sort of historical distanciation that is evident here collapses under the pressure of her capacity for "brief, identificatory embraces": "The hysterics are my sisters . . . "

6. In the margins of Cixous's comments on the "sphere of hysteria" in the English edition of *La jeune née*, the typography of a passage from the earlier *Portrait du soleil* has been reworked to show how the play of subjects and objects caught up in the hysteric's "hideous merry-go-round" can give rise to the spacing of those subjects and objects on the typographically "exploded" page. Here is a brief excerpt (*Newly Born Woman*, 147, 274; cf. *Portrait*, 120):

not Mummy— put me to sleep—some gold for Dora
DADDY— MUMMY— DORA—

Mr. K. only for Mrs. K.—only for Daddy—not Mrs. K.—
MONSIEUR K.— MADAME K.— DADDY MADAME K.—

only for Dora—will have Daddy
adore some gold for Daddy—
golden case— won't get— not my lady—
DORA— DADDY— MADAME K.—

7. The following, from *Portrait du soleil*, is one (untranslatable) instance of such a divine frenzy: "A savoir Dieubis Jeor Mr ou Mme K Freud être Efeu Efypte Vienne Z et Je: restent non négligeables mais où d'où vers où le faux Dieubis le faux Jeor le faux Mr ou Mme K le faux Freud être le faux Afeu le faux Egypte et Vienne lc faux Z et Je. Reste, qui que je sois où que je sois, ma lettre de souffrance portant le cachet d'Egypte adressée à qui je sais on ne sait jamais qui à côté de qui on ne sait jamais à côté de qui par quelqu'un qui a été en Egypte ou en Autriche" (155–56).

8. In his marginalia to Bakunin's "Statism and Anarchy," Marx writes: "He [Herr Bakunin] understands absolutely nothing about social revolution; all he knows are its political phrases. . . . *Will power* and not economic conditions is the basis of his social revolution" ("Notes," 517).

9. The unreadability of the anarchist bomb was of course never more evident than during the period of blind violence. After Emile Henry launched his bomb at the Café Terminus on February 12, 1894, Octave Mirbeau remarked: "A mortal enemy of anarchy could not have acted more effectively than did Emile Henry when he threw his inexplicable bomb into a group of peaceful, anonymous folk who had simply gone to a café to have a glass of beer before returning home to bed. The ineptitude of this act was such that many with novelistic imaginations [including Jean Grave] initially took Henry for an agent of the police" (cited by Dubois, 179).

10. Cixous echoes a long lineage of explosive anarchist "cries" when she speaks of the woman's "Voice-cry" as "the spoken word exploded, blown to bits by suffering and anger, demolishing discourse" or characterizes the woman's "Prise de la Parole"—her seizing the occasion to speak—as a "shattering entry *into History*, which has always been based *on her repression*" (*Newly Born Woman*, 94, *174*; "Rire," 250, *43*).

11. "The individualist-anarchist engages in 'propaganda' so as to select out those who unwittingly possess the individualist-anarchist temperament, or at the very least to give rise to an intellectual climate favoring their development" (Armand, 8).

12. The full-scale adoption of this metaphor in literary circles is traceable to the so-called *ère des attentats* (era of attempted attacks), a spectacular wave of anarchist violence that began with Ravachol's dynamiting of the residence of President Benoît on March 11, 1892, and ended with Santo Jeronimo Caserio's assassination of Sadi Carnot and the subsequent *Procès des Trente* (August 1894). Lecturing on free verse at Oxford and Cambridge in March 1894, for instance, Mallarmé spoke of the poct in these terms: "to him it is, all the same, that one attributes the presentation, insofar as it's explosive, of an overly virginal concept, to Society" (651). Some two decades later, Tzara's "Manifeste Dada 1918" would speak of the typographically explosive page as marking a typically anarchist *entre-deux* (interval) between the decline of a "tottering" old order and the advent of "new men": "Every page should explode, either because of its profound gravity, or its vortex, vertigo, newness, eternity, or because of its staggering absurdity, the enthusiasm of its principles, or its typography. On the one hand there is a world tottering in its flight, linked to the resounding tinkle of the infernal gamut; on the other hand, there are: the new men" (7; *362*). Likewise, Artaud strikes the anarchist chord with extraordinary insistence in the early "Théâtre Alfred Jarry," where he speaks of "bombs to be placed . . . at

the feet of most of the habits of contemporary thought" or proclaims of Roger Vitrac's *Victor ou les Enfants au pouvoir*: "I am as sure of it as of a mechanism set to unleash its explosive charge at a given hour" (*Œuvres complètes*, 2: 33, 2: 43).

The historical basis for this introduction of anarchist images and problematics into the language of the literary avant-garde has been richly documented. See Pierre Aubéry's useful overview in "L'anarchisme des littérateurs au temps du symbolisme." Also Maitron, *Mouvement*, 1: 137–38, 1: 480–81; Kristeva, *Révolution*, 421–40.

13. By all standards of measure, the grand period of the anarchist movement was relatively short. Born as a revolutionary force with the split of Bakunin and the Jura Federation from the First International (1872), political anarchism passed through an era of political violence (the "black terror" of the 1880s and 1890s), gave birth to syndicalism in the first decade of this century, then entered, with the advent of the October Revolution in 1917, into what Jean Maitron has aptly called a state of "permanent regression" (2: 134).

In a paper for a panel on "Hysteria Today," Alfredo Namnum likewise argues that cases of *grande hystérie* had all but disappeared in Freud's time. As early as the Dora case, symptomatic conversion had begun to give way "to renewed emphasis on the idea that the primary object of hysteria is the management and avoidance of anxiety" (reported by Laplanche, 462).

14. I have taken this notion of the reproducible gesture from the early Baudrillard: "At the extreme, the subversive act is no longer produced *except as a function of its reproducibility*. It is no longer created, it is produced directly as a *model*, like a gesture" (*Critique*, 174; *215*). I would argue that, rather than attempt to critique (as here) or to celebrate such reproducibility (as Baudrillard tends to do in his later work), we need to explore its ineluctability for any contemporary understanding of effective political action.

CHAPTER 9

1. A first version of this chapter was written in late May of 1992. In revising that version for incorporation into this book, I have suppressed some obvious redundancies with Chapter 8, while nonetheless preserving its sense of topicality. Hence certain effects of tense structure, the references to Bush and Perot, and (perhaps too) several symptomatic touches.

2. In the months immediately following the events of late April to early May 1992, there arose a consensus among politically sensitive commentators that what had taken place was a "civil disturbance," an episode of civil "unrest." What these formulas clearly miss, I would argue, is that sense of contagious transgressive festivity implied by the word "riot" (and so central to my argument here). "Rebellion" is clearly better, but it strikes me as far too wishful on the whole. (The violent demonstrations at the Parker Center on the night of the verdicts were acts of rebellion; much of the looting was not.)

3. "Anger Resonates Over Continent," *Los Angeles Times* (May 5, 1992), A8.

4. Robert Conot, "When Watts' Lessons Are Forgotten," *Los Angeles Times* (May 3, 1992), M1.

5. Jenifer Warren, "Old Cold War Foes Rekindle a Firm Friendship," *Los Angeles Times* (May 5, 1992), A28.

6. Irene Wielawski, "Experts Hope Riots Will Yield 'Vaccine' Against Violence," *Los Angeles Times* (May 6, 1992), A1.

7. Jonathan Peterson and Hector Tobar, "South L.A. Burns and Grieves," *Los Angeles Times* (May 1, 1992), A5. David Dante Troutt, "Fires Cleared South L.A.—Now Residents Can Redefine It," *Los Angeles Times* (May 15, 1992), T3.

8. Ashley Dunn, "Years of '2-Cent' Insults Added Up to Rampage," *Los Angeles Times* (May 7, 1992), A1.

9. William Fulton, "All of Us in Southern California, Like It or Not, Are Angelenos," *Los Angeles Times* (May 10, 1992), M6.

10. Steve Weinstein, "News Directors: We Made the Right Call," *Los Angeles Times* (May 6, 1992), E1.

11. Carolyn See, "Los Angeles Is Still Being Born," *Los Angeles Times* (May 14, 1992), T8.

12. To measure how my analysis of the Los Angeles riots ultimately differs from that of a Lacanian, consider what would emerge if one read those events through the following passage from Slavoj Žižek's *Looking Awry*: "There is, perhaps, an experience in the field of politics that entails a kind of 'identification with the symptom': the well-known pathetic experience 'We are all that!,' the experience of identification when we are confronted with a phenomenon that functions as the intrusion of unbearable truth, as an index of the fact that the social mechanism 'doesn't work.' Let us take, for example, Jew-baiting riots. A whole network of strategies . . . allow us to evade the fact that the persecution of Jews pertains to a certain repressed truth of our civilization. We attain an authentic attitude only when we arrive at the experience that—in a sense that is far from being simply metaphorical—'we are all Jews.' And it is the same for all traumatic moments of the intrusion into the social field of some 'impossible' kernel that resists integration: 'We all live in Chernobyl!,' 'We are all boat people!,' and so on. Apropos of these cases, it should also be clear how 'identification with the symptom' is correlated with 'going through the fantasy': by means of such an identification with the (social) symptom, we traverse and subvert the fantasy frame that determines the field of social meaning, the ideological self-understanding of a given society, i.e., the frame within which, precisely, the 'symptom' appears as some alien, disturbing intrusion, and not as the point of eruption of some otherwise hidden truth of the existing social order" (140).

13. In this regard, see Christopher Fynsk's highly nuanced exploration of the "gap *and the bridge* between [Nancy's] thought of community and any existent political philosophy or program" in his forward to *The Inoperative Community*, pp. ix–xi.

CHAPTER 10

1. A preliminary version of this chapter was delivered at a colloquium on "Terror and Literature" at the Maison Française of Columbia University, April 2–3, 1993. My thanks to the colloquium organizers, particularly Antoine Compagnon, for the invitation that led to this work.

2. Despite such occasional borrowings of anarchist rhetoric, Lacan was careful to distinguish his project from anarchism proper, which promised a liberation from the Law that "authentic" psychoanalysis, he argued, must see as

purely illusory. See, for example, Lacan's response to Marie-Claire Boons in the *Envers* seminar (*S* XVII), 137–51.

3. In this regard, see the section of Chapter 3 entitled "A Trial in Rigor."

4. Lefort defines the *peuple-Un* as follows: "A Great Living Being, society understood as a collective individual that acts, creates itself, and takes possession of all its faculties so as to bring itself to fruition while ridding itself of all that is foreign to it—in short, society conceived as a *body* capable of controlling the movements of each of its organs and each of its members" (*Invention*, 127).

5. See the opening pages of Chapter 3, especially note 6.

6. Need I add that I am reading Žižek here very much "against the grain"?

7. Thus the Jacobins universalized the democratic-egalitarian project while helping to institute precisely that "'dirty' acquisitive activity" they regarded—wrongly—as a betrayal of their egalitarian ideals. "The illusion proper to the 'vanishing mediators,'" Žižek writes, "is precisely that of the Hegelian 'Beautiful Soul': they refuse to acknowledge, in the corrupted reality over which they lament, the ultimate consequence of their own act—as Lacan would put it, their own message in its true, inverted form" (*For They Know*, 185).

Žižek will likewise apply the logic of the "vanishing mediator" to the question of what he calls "the Nation-Thing." In the face of the recent resurgence of nationalisms and ethnic hatred throughout both the democratic and the post-communist worlds, he argues that nationalism, as "the privileged domain of the eruption of enjoyment into the social field," must be seen not simply as democracy's greatest risk, but also as a foreclosed, "pathological stain" that has served, and continues to serve, as "a positive condition of the 'democratic break'" (*Looking Awry*, 164–65).

8. At the end of the French text of "The 'Agency' of the Letter" there appears the enigmatic notion, "T.t.y.m.u.p.t.," which Jacques-Alain Miller has suggested be read, "Tu t'y es mis un peu tard" (You set yourself to it a bit late) (*Écrits*, 528).

9. By using Žižek's work to theorize the terrors of Lacanian theory, I have sought to exploit a deep, but necessary, ambivalence within that work. Although largely faithful to the later Lacan, Žižek's texts strike me as marked by the very same fetishistic split he sees as "the very source of the strength of democracy": "*I know very well* (that the democratic form [read: Lacanian theory] is just a form spoiled by stains of 'pathological' imbalance [in the case of democracy, the nationalist Thing]), *but just the same* (I act as if democracy [or: a Lacanian ethic] were possible). Far from indicating its fatal flaw, this split is the very source of the strength of democracy" (*Looking Awry*, 168).

APPENDIX

1. After that story of the copper kettle that Freud so often told to illustrate the proposition that the "mutual cancelling-out by several thoughts, each of which is in itself valid, is precisely what does not occur in the unconscious": "It will be recalled that the borrower, when he was questioned, replied firstly that he had not borrowed the kettle at all, secondly that it had had a hole in it already when he borrowed it, and thirdly that he had given it back undamaged and without a hole" (*Jokes*, 205). My treatment of kettle logic in the paragraph that follows has been informed by Derrida's note on Lacan in *Positions* (107–11; *112–19*).

2. Asking what the Marxists intend by the notion of a proletariat organized as a ruling class, Bakunin writes: "The entire people will rule, and no one will be ruled." Marx responds with all the rigor of a knuckle-slapping *Privatdozent*: "When a person rules himself, he does not do so according to this principle; for he is only himself and not another." Yet this "objection" precisely borrows from Bakunin's aversion of government in principle in order to foreclose Bakunin's own conclusion: "Then there will be no government, no state" ("Notes," 519). The effect of Marx's gloss is thus two-fold: (1) to register an objection that is not one, and (2) to forestall Bakunin's argument that "if there is a state, there will be both rulers and slaves" by staging an implication of priority through a purely "typographical" ruse.

3. The Marxian heist: This quest for the authenticity of an originary utterance reemerges in one of the most curious of Marx's argumentative tics—his habit of translating Bakuninist perversions *back into* authentic Marxian terms with the magisterial flourish of a *das heißt* (*d.h. nur, d.h. bloß*, etc.). Marx will respond, for example, to Bakunin's question as to why a "people's state" should abolish itself by saying, "Apart from his harping on Liebknecht's *people's state*, which is nonsense directed against the *Communist Manifesto*, etc., *this only means* [emphasis added] that, as the proletariat in the period of struggle leading to the overthrow of the old society still acts on the basis of the old society and hence still moves within political forms which more or less correspond to it, it has at that stage not yet arrived at its final organisation, and hence to achieve its liberation has recourse to methods which will be discarded once that liberation has been attained" ("Notes," 521).

4. At work in the Marx/Bakunin exchange is a combination of two of Freud's four permutations on this proposition, those corresponding to the delusions of grandeur ("I do not love at all—I do not love anyone [I love only myself]") and persecution ("I do not *love* him—I *hate* him [because he persecutes me]"). On paranoia and homosexuality in Freud, see Wilden, *System*, 289–301.

Bibliography

Adam, Paul. "Eloge de Ravachol." *Entretiens politiques et littéraires* 28 (July 1892): 28–30.

Althusser, Louis. *L'avenir dure longtemps, suivi de Les faits.* Ed. Olivier Corpet and Yann Moulier Boutang. Paris: Stock, 1992.

———. *For Marx.* Trans. Ben Brewster. London: Verso, 1979. A translation of *Pour Marx.*

———. "Freud and Lacan." In Althusser, *Lenin and Philosophy,* pp. 195–219.

———. "Freud et Lacan." In Althusser, *Positions,* pp. 17–39.

———. "Idéologie et appareils idéologiques d'État (Notes pour une recherche)." In Althusser, *Positions,* pp. 81–137.

———. "Ideology and Ideological State Apparatuses (Notes towards an Investigation)." In Althusser, *Lenin and Philosophy,* pp. 127–86.

———. *Lenin and Philosophy and Other Essays.* Trans. Ben Brewster. New York: Monthly Review Press, 1971.

———. *Lénine et la philosophie.* Paris: Maspero, 1969.

———. *Positions.* Paris: Editions sociales, 1976.

———. *Pour Marx.* Paris: Maspero, 1965.

———. *Réponse à John Lewis.* Paris: Maspero, 1973.

Althusser, Louis, and Etienne Balibar. *Lire le Capital,* 2nd ed. 4 vols. Paris: Maspero, 1975 [1968].

———. *Reading Capital.* Trans. Ben Brewster. London: Verso, 1979 [1970].

Anderson, Perry. *Considerations on Western Marxism.* 4th ed. London: Verso, 1984.

———. *In the Tracks of Historical Materialism.* Chicago: University of Chicago Press, 1984.

Ansart, Pierre. *Les idéologies politiques.* Paris: PUF, 1974.

Armand, E[mile]. *Petit manuel anarchiste-individualiste.* Paris: L'en-dehors, 1934.

Aron, Raymond. *The Elusive Revolution: Anatomy of a Student Revolt.* Trans. Gordon Clough. New York: Praeger, 1969. A translation of *La révolution introuvable.*

———. *L'opium des intellectuels.* Paris: Calmann-Lévy, 1955.

———. *La révolution introuvable: Réflexions sur les événements de Mai.* Paris: Fayard, 1968.

Artaud, Antonin. *Œuvres complètes,* 19 vols. Paris: Gallimard, 1971–.

Aubéry, Pierre. "L'anarchisme des littérateurs au temps du symbolisme." *Le Mouvement social* 69 (Oct.–Dec. 1969): 21–34.

Aubral, François, and Xavier Delcourt. *Contre le nouvelle philosophie.* Paris: Gallimard, 1977.

Bakunin, Michael. *Bakunin on Anarchism.* Ed. and trans. Sam Dolgoff. Montreal: Black Rose, 1980.

Barrucand. "Le rire de Ravachol." *La Révolte, Supplément littéraire* 5, no. 45 (Aug. 6–12, 1982): 279–80.

Barthes, Roland. *The Barthes Reader.* Ed. Susan Sontag. New York: Hill and Wang, 1982.

———. *Le degré zéro de l'écriture, suivi de Nouveaux essais critiques.* Paris: Seuil, 1972 [1953].

———. *L'empire des signes.* Geneva: Skira, 1970.

———. *Empire of Signs.* Trans. Richard Howard. New York: Farrar, Straus and Giroux, 1982.

———. *Essais critiques IV: Le bruissement de la langue.* Paris: Seuil, 1984.

———. *Fragments d'un discours amoureux.* Paris: Seuil, 1977.

———. "Inaugural Lecture, Collège de France." In Barthes, *The Barthes Reader,* 457–78. A translation of *Leçon.*

———. *Leçon.* Paris: Seuil, 1978.

———. *A Lover's Discourse: Fragments.* Trans. by Richard Howard. New York: Hill and Wang, 1978. A translation of *Fragments d'un discours amoureux.*

———. *Mythologies.* Paris: Seuil, 1957.

———. *Mythologies.* Trans. Annette Lavers. New York: Hill and Wang, 1972. A partial translation of *Mythologies.*

———. *Le plaisir du texte.* Paris: Seuil, 1973.

———. *The Pleasure of the Text.* Trans. Richard Miller. New York: Hill and Wang, 1975.

———. *Roland Barthes by Roland Barthes.* Trans. Richard Howard. New York: Hill and Wang, 1977.

———. *Roland Barthes par Roland Barthes.* Paris: Seuil, 1975.

———. *The Rustle of Language.* Trans. Richard Howard. New York: Hill and Wang, 1986. A translation of "*Essais critiques IV: Le bruissement de la langue.*

———. *S/Z.* Paris: Seuil, 1970.

———. *S/Z.* Trans. Richard Miller. New York: Hill and Wang, 1974.

———. *Sade, Fourier, Loyola.* Paris: Seuil, 1971.

———. *Sade, Fourier, Loyola.* Trans. Richard Miller. New York: Hill and Wang, 1976.

———. *Sollers écrivain*. Paris: Seuil, 1979.
———. *Writer Sollers*. Trans. Philip Thody. Minneapolis: University of Minnesota Press, 1987.
———. *Writing Degree Zero*. Trans. Annette Lavers and Colin Smith. New York: Hill and Wang, 1968. A translation of *Le degré zéro de l'écriture*.
Baruch. "Propagande par le fait." *L'Endehors* 82 (Nov. 27–Dec. 4, 1892): 1.
Bataille, Georges. *The Accursed Share: An Essay on General Economy*. Trans. Robert Hurley. New York: Zone, 1988. A translation of *La Port maudite*.
———. *Erotism: Death and Sensuality*. Trans. Mary Dalwood. San Francisco: City Lights, 1986.
———. *L'Erotisme*. Paris: Minuit, 1957.
———. *Literature and Evil*. Trans. Alastair Hamilton. New York: Marion Boyars, 1985.
———. *La littérature et le mal*. Paris: Gallimard, 1957.
———. "La notion de dépense." In Bataille, *La Part maudite, précédé de La notion de dépense*, pp. 25-45.
———. "The Notion of Expenditure." Trans. Allan Stoekl. In Bataille, *Visions of Excess*, pp. 116-29. A translation of "La notion de dépense."
———. *Œuvres complètes*. 10 vols. Paris: Gallimard, 1970–.
———. *La Part maudite, précédé de La notion de dépense*. Paris: Minuit, 1967.
———. *Visions of Excess: Selected Writings, 1927–1939*. Ed. Allan Stoekl. Trans. Allan Stoekl, Carl R. Lovitt, Donald M. Leslie, Jr. Minneapolis: University of Minnesota Press, 1985.
Baudelaire, Charles. *Œuvres complètes*. Ed. Claude Pichois. 2 vols. Paris: Gallimard, 1975.
Baudrillard, Jean. *For a Critique of the Political Economy of the Sign*. Trans. Charles Levin. St. Louis: Telos, 1981.
———. *Le miroir de la production*. Paris, 1973.
———. *The Mirror of Production*. Trans. Mark Poster. St. Louis: Telos, 1975.
———. *Pour une critique de l'économie politique du signe*. Paris: Gallimard, 1972.
———. *Selected Writings*. Ed. Mark Poster. Stanford, Calif.: Stanford University Press, 1988.
———. *Simulacres et simulation*. Paris: Galilée, 1981.
———. *Simulations*. Trans. Paul Foss, Paul Patton, and Philip Beitchman. New York: Semiotext(e), 1983. A partial translation of *Simulacres et simulation*.
Benjamin, Walter. "Theses on the Philosophy of History." In Hannah Arendt, ed., *Illuminations*, pp. 253–64. Trans. Harry Zohn. New York: Schocken, 1969.
Bensaïd, Daniel, Alain Krivine, and Henri Weber. *Mai 68: Une répétition générale*. Paris: Maspero, 1968.
Bernheimer, Charles, and Claire Kahane, eds. *In Dora's Case: Freud, Hysteria, Feminism*. New York: Columbia University Press, 1985.
Blum, Carol. *Rousseau and the Republic of Virtue: The Language of Politics in the French Revolution*. Ithaca, N.Y.: Cornell University Press, 1986.
Borch-Jacobsen, Mikkel. *The Freudian Subject*. Trans. Catherine Porter. Stanford, Calif.: Stanford University Press, 1988.
———. *Lacan: The Absolute Master*. Trans. Douglas Brick. Stanford, Calif.: Stanford University Press, 1991.

Bourdieu, Pierre. *Homo Academicus.* Paris: Minuit, 1984.

Bouscasse, Sylvie, and Denis Bourgeois. *Faut-il brûler les nouveaux philosophes? Le dossier du 'procès'.* Paris: Nouvelles éditions Oswald, 1978.

Boussinot, Roger. *Les mots de l'anarchie: Dictionnaire des idées, des faits, des actes, de l'histoire et des hommes anarchistes.* Paris: Delalain, 1982.

Bowie, Malcolm. "Jacques Lacan." In J. Sturrock, ed., *Structuralism and Since,* pp. 116–63. Oxford: Oxford University Press, 1979.

———. *Lacan.* Cambridge, Mass.: Harvard University Press, 1991.

Bredin, Jean-Denis. *The Affair: The Case of Alfred Dreyfus.* Trans. Jeffrey Mehlman. New York: George Braziller, 1986.

———. *L'Affaire.* Paris: Juilliard, 1983.

Breton, André. *Manifestes du surréalisme.* Paris: Gallimard (Idées), 1972.

Breton, André, Diego Rivera, and Leon Trotsky. "Manifesto: Towards a Free Revolutionary Art." In Paul N. Siegel, ed., *Leon Trotsky on Literature and Art,* pp. 115-24. New York: Pathfinder, 1970.

Callinicos, Alex. *Althusser's Marxism.* London: Pluto Press, 1976.

Castoriadis, Cornelius. "Les mouvements des années soixante." Rpt. in Edgar Morin, Claude Lefort, and Cornelius Castoriadis, *Mai 1968: La Brèche, suivi de Vingt ans après.*

———. *Political and Social Writings.* Trans. and ed. David Ames Curtis. 2 vols. Minneapolis: University of Minnesota Press, 1988.

———. "La suspension de la publication de *Socialisme ou Barbarie.*" In Castoriadis, *L'expérience du mouvement ouvrier.* Vol. 2, pp. 417–25. Paris: U.G.E. (10/18), 1974.

Caws, Mary Ann. "Tel Quel: Text & Revolution." *Diacritics* 3, no. 1 (Spring 1973): 2–8.

Chambers, Ross. *Room for Maneuver: Reading (the) Oppositional (in) Narrative.* Chicago: University of Chicago Press, 1991.

Cixous, Hélène. *"Coming to Writing" and Other Essays.* Trans. Deborah Jenson et al. Cambridge, Mass.: Harvard University Press, 1991. A partial translation of *Entre l'écriture.*

———. *Entre l'écriture.* Paris: Des femmes, 1986.

———. "The Laugh of the Medusa." In Elaine Marks and Isabelle de Courtivron, eds., *New French Feminisms: An Anthology,* pp. 245–64. New York: Schocken, 1981. A translation of "Le rire de la méduse."

———. *Neutre.* Paris: Grasset, 1972.

———. *Portrait de Dora.* Paris: Des femmes, 1976.

———. *Portrait du soleil.* Paris: Denoël, 1973.

———. *Portrait of Dora.* Trans. Sarah Burd. *Diacritics* 13, no. 1 (Spring 1983): 2–36.

———. "Le rire de la méduse." *L'Arc* 61 (n.d.): 39–54.

———. "La Venue à l'écriture." In *Entre l'écriture,* 9–69.

Cixous, Hélène, and Cathérine Clément. *La jeune née.* Paris: U.G.E., 1975.

———. *The Newly Born Woman.* Trans. Betsy Wing. Minneapolis: University of Minnesota Press, 1986.

Clément, Catherine. "Lettre à Lacan, ou l'oiseau pris." *Le Magazine littéraire* 121 (Feb. 1977): 18–20.

———. *The Lives and Legends of Jacques Lacan.* Trans. Arthur Goldhammer. New York: Columbia University Press, 1973.

———. *Vies et légendes de Jacques Lacan.* Paris: Grasset, 1981.

Cohn-Bendit, Daniel, and Gabriel Cohn-Bendit. *Obsolete Communism: The Left-Wing Alternative.* Trans. Arnold Pomerans. New York: McGraw-Hill, 1968.

Condé, Michel. "*Tel Quel* et la littérature." *Littérature* 44 (Dec. 1981): 21–32.

Conley, Verena Andermatt. *Hélène Cixous: Writing the Feminine.* Lincoln: University of Nebraska Press, 1984.

———. "Missexual Misstery." *Diacritics* 7, no. 2 (Summer 1977): 70–82.

Coward, Rosalind, and John Ellis. *Language and Materialism: Developments in Semiology and the Theory of the Subject.* London: Routledge & Kegan Paul, 1977.

Crownfield, David, ed. *Body/Text in Julia Kristeva: Religion, Women, and Psychoanalysis.* Albany: State University of New York Press, 1992.

Culler, Jonathan. *On Deconstruction: Theory and Criticism after Structuralism.* Ithaca, N.Y.: Cornell University Press, 1982.

———. *Roland Barthes.* New York: Oxford University Press, 1983.

David-Ménard, Monique. *L'hystérique entre Freud et Lacan: Corps et langage en psychanalyse.* Paris: Editions universitaires, 1983.

Davis, Mike. *City of Quartz.* New York: Vintage, 1992.

Debord, Guy. *La société du spectacle.* Paris: Gérard Lebovici, 1987 [1967].

Debray, Régis. *Modeste Contribution aux cérémonies officielles du dixième anniversaire.* Paris: Maspero, 1978.

———. *Le pouvoir intellectuel en France.* Paris: Ramsay, 1979.

———. *Teachers, Writers, Celebrities: The Intellectuals of Modern France.* Trans. David Macey. London: NLB, 1981. A translation of *Le pouvoir intellectuel en France.*

"Déclaration sur l'hégémonie idéologique bourgeoisie/révisionnisme." *Tel Quel* 47 (Fall 1971): 133–41.

de Gourmont, Rémy. "L'Idéalisme." *Entretiens politiques et littéraires* 25 (April 1892): 145–48.

Deleuze, Gilles, and Félix Guattari. *L'Anti-Oedipe.* Paris: Minuit, 1972.

———. *Anti-Oedipus.* Trans. Robert Hurley, Mark Seem, and Helen R. Lane. New York: Viking, 1977.

———. *Mille plateaux.* Paris: Minuit, 1980.

———. *A Thousand Plateaus: Capitalism and Schizophrenia.* Trans. Brian Massumi. Minneapolis: University of Minnesota Press, 1987.

Derrida, Jacques. "Afterword: Toward an Ethic of Discussion." *Limited Inc.* Trans. Samuel Weber. Evanston: Northwestern University Press, 1988.

———. *De la grammatologie.* Paris: Minuit, 1967.

———. *La dissémination.* Paris: Seuil, 1972.

———. *Dissemination.* Trans. Barbara Johnson. Chicago: University of Chicago Press, 1981.

———. *L'écriture et la différence.* Paris: Seuil, 1967.

———. *Marges de la philosophie.* Paris: Minuit, 1972.

———. *Margins of Philosophy.* Trans. Alan Bass. Chicago: University of Chicago Press, 1982.

———. *Of Grammatology.* Trans. Gayatri Chakrovorty Spivak. Baltimore: Johns Hopkins University Press, 1976.

———. *Positions.* Trans. Alan Bass. Chicago: University of Chicago Press, 1981.

———. *Positions: Entretiens avec Henri Ronse, Julia Kristeva, Jean-Louis Houdebine, Guy Scarpetta.* Paris: Minuit, 1972.

———. *Writing and Difference.* Trans. Alan Bass. Chicago: University of Chicago Press, 1978. A translation of *L'écriture et la différence.*

Descombes, Vincent. *Le même et l'autre: Quarante-cinq ans de philosophie française (1933–1978).* Paris: Minuit, 1979.

———. *Modern French Philosophy.* London: Cambridge University Press, 1980. A translation of *Le même et l'autre.*

Dor, Joël. *Introduction à la lecture de Lacan, 1. L'inconscient structuré comme un langage.* Paris: Denoël, 1985.

Dubois, Félix. *Le Péril anarchiste.* Paris: Flammarion, 1894.

Duchen, Claire. *Feminism in France: From May '68 to Mitterand.* London: Routledge & Kegan Paul, 1986.

Duchet, Claude, ed. *Manuel d'histoire littérature de la France.* 6 vols. Paris: Editions sociales, 1975–.

Ducrot, Oswald, and Tzvetan Todorov. *Dictionnaire encyclopédique des sciences du langage.* Paris: Seuil, 1972.

———. *Encyclopedic Dictionary of the Sciences of Language.* Trans. Catherine Porter. Baltimore: Johns Hopkins University Press, 1979.

Eisenstein, Hester, and Alice Jardine, eds. *The Future of Difference.* Boston: G. K. Hall, 1980.

Ferry, Luc, and Alain Renaut. *French Philosophy of the Sixties: An Essay on Antihumanism.* Trans. Mary H. S. Cattani. Amherst: University of Massachusetts Press, 1990. A translation of *La pensée 68.*

———. *La pensée 68: Essai sur l'anti-humanisme contemporain.* Paris: Gallimard, 1985.

———. *68–86: Itinéraires de l'individu.* Paris: Gallimard, 1987.

Flaubert, Gustave. *Bouvard et Pécuchet.* Ed. Claudine Gothot-Mersch. Paris: Gallimard, 1979.

Fletcher, John, and Andrew Benjamin, eds. *Abjection, Melancholia and Love: The Work of Julia Kristeva.* London: Routledge, 1990.

Foucault, Michel. *The History of Sexuality: Volume 1, An Introduction.* Trans. Robert Hurley. New York: Random House, 1978. A translation of *La volonté du savoir.*

———. *Les mots et les choses.* Paris: Gallimard, 1966.

———. *The Order of Things: An Archaeology of the Human Sciences.* New York: Random House, 1973. A translation of *Les mots et les choses.*

———. *Power/Knowledge: Selected Interviews and Other Writings, 1972–1977.* Ed. Colin Gordon. New York: Pantheon, 1980.

———. "Preface to Transgression." In Donald F. Bouchard, ed., *Language, Counter-Memory, Practice: Selected Essays and Interviews,* pp. 29–52. Trans. Donald F. Bouchard and Sherry Simon. Ithaca, N.Y.: Cornell University Press, 1977.

———. *La volonté du savoir.* Paris: Gallimard, 1976.

Foucault, Michel, and Gilles Deleuze. "Les Intellectuels et le pouvoir." *L'arc* 49 (n.d.): 3–10.

Freud, Sigmund. "The Aetiology of Hysteria." In *Standard Edition,* vol. 3, pp. 191–221.

———. *Beyond the Pleasure Principle.* Ed. and trans. James Strachey. New York: Norton, 1961.

———. "A Child Is Being Beaten: A Contribution to the Study of the Origin of Sexual Perversions." In *Standard Edition*, vol. 17, pp. 179–204.
———. *Dora: An Analysis of a Case of Hysteria*. Ed. Philip Rieff. New York: Collier, 1963.
———. "Fetishism." In Philip Rieff, ed., *Sexuality and the Psychology of Love*, pp. 214–19. New York: Collier, 1963.
———. "Hysterical Phantasies and their Relation to Bisexuality." In Philip Rieff, ed., *Dora: An Analysis of a Case of Hysteria*, pp. 145–52. New York: Collier, 1963.
———. *Jokes and Their Relation to the Unconscious*. Trans. James Strachey. New York: Norton, 1963.
———. "The Loss of Reality in Neurosis and Psychosis." In Philip Rieff, ed., *General Psychological Theory: Papers on Metapsychology*, pp. 202–6. New York: Collier, 1963.
———. "Negation." In Philip Rieff, ed., *General Psychological Theory: Papers on Metapsychology*, pp. 213–17. New York: Collier, 1963.
———. *The Origins of Psychoanalysis: Letters to Wilhelm Fliess*. Trans. Eric Mosbacher and James Strachey. New York: Basic Books, 1954.
———. "Psycho-Analytic Notes on an Autobiographical Account of a Case of Paranoia (Dementia Paranoides)." In *Standard Edition*, vol. 12, pp. 3–82.
———. *The Standard Edition of the Complete Psychological Works of Sigmund Freud*. Trans. James Strachey. 25 vols. London: Hogarth, 1975.
———. "The Unconscious." In Philip Rieff, ed., *General Psychological Theory: Papers on Metapsychology*, pp. 116–50. New York: Collier, 1963.
Frye, Northrop. *The Anatomy of Criticism: Four Essays*. Princeton, N.J.: Princeton University Press, 1957.
Furet, François. *Interpreting the French Revolution*. Trans. Elborg Forster. Cambridge, Eng.: Cambridge University Press, 1981. A translation of *Penser la Révolution française*.
———. *Penser la Révolution française*. Paris: Gallimard, 1978.
Fynsk, Christopher. "Forward." In Jean-Luc Nancy, *The Inoperative Community*, vii–xli.
Gallop, Jane. *The Daughter's Seduction: Feminism and Psychoanalysis*. Ithaca, N.Y.: Cornell University Press, 1982.
———. "Keys to Dora." In Charles Bernheimer and Claire Kahane, eds., *In Dora's Case: Freud, Hysteria, Feminism*, pp. 200–220.
———. *Reading Lacan*. Ithaca, N.Y.: Cornell University Press, 1985.
Glazer, Catherine. "De la Commune comme maladie mentale." In Ruth Amossy and Elisheva Rosen, eds., *Les discours du cliché*, pp. 63–70. Paris: C.D.U.-S.E.D.E.S., 1982.
Glucksmann, André. *Les Maîtres penseurs*. Paris: Grasset, 1977.
Goldstein, Jan. "The Hysteria Diagnosis and the Politics of Anticlericalism in Late Nineteenth-Century France." *Journal of Modern History* 54 (June 1982): 209–39.
———. "'Moral Contagion': A Professional Ideology of Medicine and Psychiatry in Eighteenth- and Nineteenth-Century France." In Gerald L. Geison, ed., *Professions and the French State: 1700–1900*, pp. 181–222. Philadelphia: University of Pennsylvania Press, 1984.
Goux, Jean-Joseph. *Economie et symbolique: Freud, Marx*. Paris: Seuil, 1973.
———. "Lacan décentré." *Stanford French Studies* 15, nos. 1–2 (1991): 37–46.

Greimas, A. J., and J. Courtés. *Sémiotique: Dictionnaire raisonné de la théorie du langage.* Paris: Hachette, 1979.

Grisoni, Dominique. "Politique de Lacan." *Le Magazine littéraire* 121 (Feb. 1977): 25–27.

Grosz, Elizabeth. *Jacques Lacan: A Feminist Introduction.* London: Routledge, 1990.

———. *Sexual Subversions: Three French Feminists.* Sydney: Allen and Unwin, 1989.

Guérin, Daniel. *Anarchism: From Theory to Practice.* Trans. Mary Klopper. New York: Monthly Review Press, 1970.

Hamon, H., and Rotman, P. *Les Intellocrates: Expédition en haute intelligentsia.* Paris: Editions Ramsay, 1981.

Harari, Josué, ed. *Textual Strategies: Perspectives in Post-Structuralist Criticism.* Ithaca, N.Y.: Cornell University Press, 1979.

Hegel, Georg Wilhelm Friedrich. *Logic.* Trans. William Wallace. Oxford: Oxford University Press, 1975.

———. *Phänomenologie des Geistes.* Ed. Hans-Friedrich Wessels and Heinrich Clairmont. Hamburg: Felix Meiner, 1988.

———. *Phenomenology of Spirit.* Trans. A. V. Miller. Ed. J. N. Findlay. Oxford: Oxford University Press, 1977.

Hertz, Neil. "Dora's Secrets, Freud's Techniques." *Diacritics* 13, no. 1 (Spring 1983): 65–76.

———. "Medusa's Head: Male Hysteria under Political Pressure." In Hertz, *The End of the Line: Essays in Psychoanalysis and the Sublime,* pp. 161–93. New York: Columbia University Press, 1985.

Hess, Rémi. *Les maoïstes français: Une dérive institutionnelle.* Paris: Anthropos, 1974.

Hirsh, Arthur. *The French New Left: An Intellectual History from Sartre to Gorz.* Boston: South End Press, 1981.

Hobsbawm, E. J. *Revolutionaries: Contemporary Essays.* New York: Pantheon, 1973.

Holley, David. "Anger Lingers on Beijing Campuses; Intellectual's Role Now in Question." *Los Angeles Times,* Sept. 6, 1989: A5.

Hollier, Denis. "Le dispositif Hegel/Nietzsche dans la bibliothèque de Bataille." *L'Arc* 38 (n.d.): 35–45.

———, ed. *A New History of French Literature.* Cambridge, Mass.: Harvard University Press, 1989.

Horkheimer, Max, and Theodor W. Adorno. *Dialectic of Enlightenment.* Trans. John Cumming. New York: Continuum, 1972.

Hunt, Lynn Avery. *Politics, Culture, and Class in the French Revolution.* Berkeley: University of California Press, 1984.

Les idées en France: 1945–1988, Une chronologie. Paris: Gallimard, 1989.

Irigaray, Luce. *Ce sexe qui n'en est pas un.* Paris: Minuit, 1977.

———. *Ethique de la différence sexuelle.* Paris: Minuit, 1984.

———. *Speculum de l'autre femme.* Paris: Minuit, 1974.

———. *Speculum of the Other Woman.* Trans. Gillian C. Gill. Ithaca, N.Y.: Cornell University Press, 1985.

———. *This Sex Which Is Not One.* Trans. Catherine Porter and Carolyn Burke. Ithaca, N.Y.: Cornell University Press, 1985.

Jacob, François. *La Logique du vivant: Une histoire de l'hérédité*. Paris: Gallimard, 1970.

Jambet, Christian, and Guy Lardreau. "L'ange, entre Mao et Jésus." *Magazine littéraire* 112–13 (May 1976): 54–57.

———. *L'Ange: Pour une cynégétique du semblant*. Paris: Grasset, 1976.

Jameson, Fredric. *The Ideologies of Theory: Essays, 1971–1986*. 2 vols. Minneapolis: University of Minnesota Press, 1988.

———. *Marxism and Form: Twentieth-Century Dialectical Theories of Literature*. Princeton, N.J.: Princeton University Press, 1971.

———. *The Political Unconscious: Narrative as a Socially Symbolic Act*. Ithaca, N.Y.: Cornell University Press, 1981.

Jardine, Alice A. *Gynesis: Configurations of Woman and Modernity*. Ithaca, N.Y.: Cornell University Press, 1985.

———. "Opaque Texts and Transparent Contexts: The Political Difference of Julia Kristeva." In Nancy K. Miller, ed., *The Poetics of Gender*, pp. 96–116. New York: Columbia University Press, 1986.

Joffrin, Laurent. *Mai 68: Histoire des Evénements*. Paris: Seuil, 1988.

Johnson, Barbara. *The Critical Difference: Essays in the Contemporary Rhetoric of Reading*. Baltimore: Johns Hopkins University Press, 1980.

Judt, Tony. *Marxism and the French Left*. New York: Oxford University Press, 1986.

———. *Past Imperfect: French Intellectuals, 1944–1956*. Berkeley: University of California Press, 1992.

Kamuf, Peggy. "Ashes to Ashes (On Faithful Translation)." Unpublished essay.

———. "Replacing Feminist Criticism." *Diacritics* 12 (1982): 42–47.

Knabb, Ken, ed. and trans. *Situationist International Anthology*. Berkeley, Calif.: Bureau of Public Secrets,1981.

Kojève, Alexandre. *Introduction à la lecture de Hegel*. Ed. Raymond Queneau. Paris: Gallimard, 1947.

Kristeva, Julia. *About Chinese Women*. Trans. Anita Barrows. New York: Urizen, 1977.

———. *Des Chinoises*. Paris: Editions des Femmes, 1974.

———. *Desire in Language: A Semiotic Approach to Literature and Art*. Ed. Leon S. Roudiez. Trans. Thomas Gora, Alice Jardine, and Leon S. Roudiez. New York: Columbia University Press, 1980.

———. "La littérature dissidente comme réfutation du discours de gauche." *Tel Quel* 76 (Summer 1978): 40–44.

———. "Mémoire." *Infini* 1 (Winter 1983): 39–54.

———. "A New Type of Intellectual: The Dissident." In Toril Moi, ed., *The Kristeva Reader*, pp. 292–300. New York: Columbia University Press, 1986.

———. "Un nouveau type d'intellectuel: Le dissident." *Tel Quel* 74 (1977): 3–8.

———. *Polylogue*. Paris: Seuil, 1977.

———. "Psychoanalysis and the Polis." Trans. Margaret Waller. In Toril Moi, ed., *The Kristeva Reader*, pp. 301–20. New York: Columbia University Press, 1986.

———. *La révolution du langage poétique*. Paris: Seuil, 1974.

———. *Revolution in Poetic Language*. Trans. Margaret Waller. New York: Columbia University Press, 1984. A partial translation of *La révolution du langage poétique*.

———. *Les Samouraïs*. Paris: Fayard, 1990.

———. *Semeiotikè: Recherches pour une sémanalyse*. Paris: Seuil, 1969.

Kristeva, Julia, Marcelin Pleynet, and Philippe Sollers. "Pourquoi les Etats-Unis?" *Tel Quel* 71/3 (Fall 1977): 3–19.

———. "Why the United States?" In Toril Moi, ed., *The Kristeva Reader*, pp. 272–91. New York: Columbia University Press, 1986.

Kritzman, Lawrence D. "Barthesian Free Play." *Yale French Studies* 66 (1984): 189–210.

———. "The Changing Political Ideology of Tel Quel." *Contemporary French Civilization* 2 (1978): 405–21.

———. "The Discourse of Desire and the Question of Gender." In Steven Ungar and Betty R. McGraw, eds., *Signs in Culture: Roland Barthes Today*, pp. 99–118.

Kropotkin, Peter Alexeivitch. "Anarchism." *Encyclopaedia Brittanica*. 11th ed. 1910–11.

Lacan, Jacques. "Conférences et entretiens dans les universités nord-américaines." *Scilicet* 6–7 (1975): 7–63.

———. *Écrits*. Paris: Seuil, 1966.

———. *Écrits: A Selection*. Trans. Alan Sheridan. New York: Norton, 1977. A partial translation of *Écrits*.

———. *The Four Fundamental Concepts of Psychoanalysis*. Trans. Alan Sheridan. Ed. Jacques Alain Miller. New York: Norton, 1978. A translation of *Le Séminaire, Livre XI*.

———. "Impromptu at Vincennes." In Lacan, *Television*, pp. 117–28. New York: Norton, 1978.

———. "L'impromptu de Vincennes." *Le Magazine littéraire* 121 (Feb. 1977): 21–25.

———. "Letter of Dissolution." In Lacan, *Television*, pp. 129–31.

———. *Le Séminaire, Livre II: Le moi dans la théorie de Freud et dans la technique de la psychanalyse*. Paris: Seuil, 1978.

———. *Le Séminaire, Livre III: Les psychoses*. Paris: Seuil, 1981.

———. *Le Séminaire, Livre VII: L'éthique de la psychanalyse*. Paris: Seuil, 1986.

———. *Le Séminaire, Livre XI: Les quatre concepts fondamentaux de la psychanalyse*. Paris: Seuil, 1973.

———. *Le Séminaire, Livre XVII: L'envers de la psychanalyse*. Paris: Seuil, 1991.

———. *Le Séminaire, Livre XX: Encore*. Paris: Seuil, 1975.

———. *The Seminar of Jacques Lacan, Book II: The Ego in Freud's Theory and in the Technique of Psychoanalysis, 1954–1955*. Trans. Sylvana Tomaselli. Ed. Jacques Alain Miller. New York: Norton, 1991.

———. *The Seminar of Jacques Lacan, Book III: The Psychoses, 1955–1956*. Trans. Russell Grigg. Ed. Jacques Alain Miller. New York: Norton, 1991.

———. *The Seminar of Jacques Lacan, Book VII: The Ethics of Psychoanalysis, 1959–1960*. Trans. Dennis Porter. Ed. Jacques Alain Miller. New York: Norton, 1991.

———. *Télévision*. Paris: Seuil, 1974.

———. *Television*. Trans. Denis Hollier, Rosalind Kraus, and Annette Michelson. Ed. Joan Copjec. New York: Norton, 1990.

Laplanche, Jean. *Life and Death in Psychoanalysis.* Trans. Jeffrey Mehlman. Baltimore: Johns Hopkins University Press, 1976.

———. "Panel on 'Hysteria Today.'" *International Journal of Psychoanalysis* 55 (1974): 459–69.

———. *Vie et mort en psychanalyse.* Paris: Flammarion, 1970.

Laplanche, Jean, and J.-B. Pontalis. *The Language of Psycho-Analysis.* Trans. Donald Nicholson-Smith. New York: Norton, 1973.

———. *Vocabulaire de la psychanalyse.* Paris: PUF, 1971.

Lautréamont, Comte de (Isidore Ducasse). *Les Chants de Maldoror.* In Lautréamont and Germain Nouveau, *Œuvres complètes*, pp. 46-256.

———. *Poésies.* In Lautréamont and Germain Nouveau, *Œuvres complètes*, pp. 257-92.

Lautréamont, Comte de, and Germain Nouveau. *Œuvres complètes.* Ed. Pierre-Olivier Walzer. Paris: Gallimard, 1970.

Lechte, John. *Julia Kristeva.* London: Routledge, 1990.

Lefort, Claude. *L'Invention démocratique: Les limites de la domination totalitaire.* Paris: Fayard, 1981.

Lemaire, Anika. *Jacques Lacan.* Trans. David Macey. London: Routledge & Kegan Paul, 1977.

Lenin, V[ladimir] I[lyich]. *Materialism and Empirio-Criticism.* Peking: Foreign Languages Press, 1972.

———. "What Is to Be Done?" In Robert Tucker, ed., *The Lenin Anthology*, pp. 12–114.

Lévy, Bernard-Henri. *Éloge des intellectuels.* Paris: Grasset, 1987.

———. "Les Nouveaux Philosophes." *Les Nouvelles littéraires* 2536 (June 10, 1976).

Lewis, Philip E. "Revolutionary Semiotics." *Diacritics* 4, no. 3 (Fall 1964): 28–32.

Link, Perry. "The Chinese Intellectuals and the Revolt." *New York Review of Books*, June 29, 1989: 38–41.

Lipovetsky, Gilles. *L'ère du vide: Essais sur l'individualisme contemporain.* Paris: Gallimard, 1983.

Lombardo, Patrizia. *The Three Paradoxes of Roland Barthes.* Athens: University of Georgia Press, 1989.

Lyotard, Jean-François. *La Condition postmoderne: Rapport sur le savoir.* Paris: Minuit, 1979.

———. *Economie libidinale.* Paris: Minuit, 1974.

———. *Libidinal Economy.* Trans. Iain Hamilton Grant. Bloomington: Indiana University Press, 1993.

———. *The Postmodern Condition: A Report on Knowledge.* Trans. G. Bennington and B. Massumi. Minneapolis: University of Minnesota Press, 1984.

———. *Tombeau de l'intellectuel et autres papiers.* Paris: Galilée, 1984.

Mabry, Marcus, and Evan Thomas. "Crime: A Conspiracy of Silence." *Newsweek*, May 18, 1992, 37.

Macalpine, Ida, and Richard A. Hunter, eds. *Memoirs of My Nervous Illness* by Daniel Paul Schreber. Cambridge, Mass.: Harvard University Press, 1988.

MacCannell, Juliet Flower. *Figuring Lacan: Criticism and the Cultural Unconscious.* Lincoln: University of Nebraska Press, 1986.

Maitron, Jean. *Le mouvement anarchiste en France.* 2 vols. Paris: Maspero, 1983 [1975].

Major, René. "The Revolution of Hysteria." *International Journal of Psychoanalysis* 55 (1974): 386–92.

Mallarmé, Stéphane. *Œuvres complètes.* Ed. Henri Mondor and G. Jean-Aubry. Paris: Gallimard, 1945.

Mao Tsetung. *Selected Readings from the Works of Mao Tsetung.* Peking: Foreign Languages Press, 1971.

Marcuse, Herbert. *One-Dimensional Man: Studies in the Ideology of Advanced Industrial Society.* Boston: Beacon, 1964.

Marini, Marcelle. *Jacques Lacan: The French Context.* Trans. Anne Tomiche. New Brunswick, N.J.: Rutgers University Press, 1992. A translation of *Lacan.*

———. *Lacan.* Paris: Belfond, 1986.

Marks, Elaine, and Isabelle de Courtivron, eds. *New French Feminisms.* Amherst: University of Massachusetts Press, 1980.

Marx, Karl. *Class Struggles in France: 1848–1850.* New York: International Publishers, 1964.

———. "The Eighteenth Brumaire of Louis Bonaparte." In Karl Marx and Friedrich Engels, *Collected Works,* vol. 11, pp. 99–197.

———. "Notes on Bakunin's Book *Statehood and Anarchy.*" In Karl Marx and Friedrich Engels, *Collected Works,* vol. 24, pp. 485–526.

Marx, Karl, and Frederick Engels. *Collected Works.* 45 vols. New York: International Publishers, 1975.

Marx, Karl, Friedrich Engels, and Vladimir Lenin. *Anarchism and Anarcho-Syndicalism.* New York: International Publishers, 1972.

Marx-Scouras, Danielle. "The Dissident Politics of *Tel Quel.*" *L'Esprit Créateur* 27, no. 2 (Summer 1987): 101–8.

Mauclair, Camille. "Petits théorèmes d'art social." *L'Endehors* 46 (March 20, 1892): 2.

Mehlman, Jeffrey. *Revolution and Repetition: Marx/Hugo/Balzac.* Berkeley: University of California Press, 1977.

Méric, Victor. *A travers la jungle politique et littéraire.* 2 vols. Paris: Valois, 1930–31.

Miller, D. A. *Bringing Out Roland Barthes.* Berkeley: University of California Press, 1992.

Mirbeau, Octave. "Ravachol." *L'Endehors* 52 (May 1, 1892): 1.

Mitchell, Juliet, and Jacqueline Rose, eds. *Feminine Sexuality: Jacques Lacan and the école freudienne.* Trans. Jacqueline Rose. New York: Norton, 1983.

Moi, Toril. *Sexual/Textual Politics: Feminist Literary Theory.* London: Methuen, 1985.

———, ed. *The Kristeva Reader.* New York: Columbia University Press, 1986.

Morin, Edgar. *Journal de Californie.* Paris: Seuil, 1970.

Morin, Edgar, Claude Lefort, and Cornelius Castoriadis. *Mai 1968: La Brèche, suivi de vingt ans après.* Paris: Editions complexe, 1988 [1968].

Morse, Margaret. "The Television News Personality and Credibility." In Tania Modleski, ed., *Studies in Entertainment: Critical Approaches to Mass Culture,* pp. 55–79. Bloomington: Indiana University Press, 1986.

Mortimer, Armine Kotin. "Roland Barthes: Writing by Subtraction." Twentieth-Century French Studies Colloquium. Iowa City, April 21, 1990.

Mouffe, Chantal. *The Return of the Political.* London: Verso, 1993.

Nancy, Jean-Luc. *La Communauté désœuvrée.* Paris: Bourgois, 1986.

———. *The Inoperative Community.* Trans. Peter Conner et al. Minneapolis: University of Minnesota Press, 1991.

Nancy, Jean-Luc, and Philippe Lacoue-Labarthe. *The Title of the Letter: A Reading of Lacan.* Trans. François Raffoul and David Pettigrew. Albany: State University of New York Press, 1992.

———. *Le titre de la lettre.* Paris: Galilée, 1973.

Nietzsche, Friedrich. "On the Uses and Disadvantages of History for Life." In Nietzsche, *Untimely Meditations,* pp. 57–124. Trans. R. J. Hollingdale. Cambridge, Eng.: Cambridge University Press, 1983.

Oliver, Kelly. *Reading Kristeva: Unraveling the Double-bind.* Bloomington: Indiana University Press, 1993.

Ory, Pascal. *L'aventure culturelle française: 1945–1989.* Paris: Flammarion, 1989.

———. *L'entre-deux Mai: Histoire culturelle de la France, Mai 1968–Mai 1981.* Paris: Seuil, 1983.

Ory, Pascal, and Jean-François Sirinelli. *Les Intellectuels en France, de l'Affaire Dreyfus à nos jours.* Paris: Armand Colin, 1986.

Ovid. *Ovid's Metamorphoses.* Trans. Charles Boer. Dallas: Spring Publications, 1989.

Pascal, Blaise. *Œuvres complètes.* Ed. Jacques Chevalier. Paris: Gallimard, 1954.

Paulhan, Jean. *Les fleurs de Tarbes, ou La Terreur dans les Lettres.* Paris: Gallimard, 1941.

Pavel, Thomas G. "The Present Debate: News from France." *Diacritics* 19, no. 1 (Spring 1989): 17–32.

Perloff, Marjorie. *The Futurist Moment: Avant-Garde, Avant Guerre, and the Language of Rupture.* Chicago: University of Chicago Press, 1986.

Pessin, Alain. *La Rêverie anarchiste.* Paris: Méridiens, 1982.

Pleynet, Marcelin. "Les problèmes de l'avant-garde." *Tel Quel* 25 (Spring 1966): 77–86.

Poggioli, Renato. *The Theory of the Avant-Garde.* Trans. Gerald Fitzgerald. Cambridge, Mass.: Harvard University Press, 1968.

Poster, Mark. *Critical Theory and Poststructuralism: In Search of a Context.* Ithaca, N.Y.: Cornell University Press, 1989.

———. *Existential Marxism in Postwar France: From Sartre to Althusser.* Princeton, N.J.: Princeton University Press, 1975.

Proudhon, Pierre-Joseph. *Proudhon: Textes et débats.* Ed. Pierre Ansart. Paris: Livre de poche, 1984.

Quadruppani, Serge. *Catalogue du prêt-à-penser français depuis 1968.* Paris: Balland, 1983.

Quillard, Pierre. "L'Anarchie par la littérature." *Entretiens politiques et littéraires* 25 (April 1892): 149–51.

Rabine, Leslie. "*Ecriture féminine* as metaphor." *Cultural Critique* 8 (Winter 1987–88): 19–44.

Ragland-Sullivan, Ellie. *Jacques Lacan and the Philosophy of Psychoanalysis.* Urbana: University of Illinois Press, 1987.

Rajchman, John. "Lacan and the Ethics of Modernity." *Representations* 15 (Summer 1986): 42–56.

———. *Michel Foucault: The Freedom of Philosophy.* New York: Columbia University Press, 1985.

Reader, Keith A. *Intellectuals and the Left in France since 1968.* New York: St. Martins, 1987.

Reszler, André. *L'esthétique anarchiste.* Paris: P.U.F., 1973.

Richman, Michelle. *Reading Georges Bataille: Beyond the Gift.* Baltimore: Johns Hopkins University Press, 1982.

Roger, Philippe. *Roland Barthes, roman.* Paris: Grasset, 1986.

Rose, Jacqueline. "Introduction-II." In Juliet Mitchell and Jacqueline Rose, eds., *Feminine Sexuality*, pp. 27-57.

Roudiez, Leon S. "Twelve Points from *Tel Quel.*" *L'Esprit Créateur* 14 (Winter 1974): 291–303.

Roudinesco, Elisabeth. *La bataille de cent ans: Histoire de la psychanalyse en France, 2.* Paris: Seuil, 1986.

———. *Jacques Lacan & Co.: A History of Psychoanalysis in France, 1925-1985.* Trans. Jeffrey Mehlman. Chicago: University of Chicago Press, 1990. A translation of *La bataille de cent ans.*

Roustang, François. *Un destin si funeste.* Paris: Minuit, 1976.

———. *Dire Mastery.* Trans. Ned Lukacher. Baltimore: Johns Hopkins University Press, 1982. A translation of *Un destin si funeste.*

———. *Lacan: De l'équivoque à l'impasse.* Paris: Minuit, 1986.

———. *The Lacanian Delusion.* Trans. Greg Sims. New York: Oxford University Press, 1990. A translation of *Lacan: De l'équivoque à l'impasse.*

Ryan, Michael. *Marxism and Deconstruction: A Critical Articulation.* Baltimore, Johns Hopkins University Press, 1982.

Sartre, Jean-Paul. "L'ami du peuple." In Sartre, *Situations VIII, Autour de 68,* pp. 456–76. Paris: Gallimard, 1972.

———. *Critique de la raison dialectique, précédé de Questions de méthode.* 2nd ed. Vol. 1. Paris: Gallimard, 1985.

———. *Critique of Dialectical Reason.* Trans. Alan Sheridan-Smith. Vol. 1. London: NLB, 1976.

———. "Plaidoyer pour les intellectuels." In Sartre, *Situations VIII, Autour de 68,* pp. 375–455. Paris: Gallimard, 1972.

———. *Qu'est-ce que la littérature?* Paris: Gallimard, 1948.

———. *Situations X.* Paris: Gallimard, 1976.

———. *What Is Literature? and Other Essays.* Cambridge, Mass.: Harvard University Press, 1988.

Sauvageot, J., A. Geismar, D. Cohn-Bendit, J.-P. Duteuil, *La Révolte Étudiante, Les animateurs parlent.* Ed. Hervé Bourges. Paris: Seuil, 1968.

Schatz, Marshall S., ed. *The Essential Works of Anarchism.* New York: Quadrangle, 1972.

Sirinelli, Jean-François. *Génération intellectuelle: Khâgneux et Normaliens dans l'entre-deux-geurres.* Paris: Fayard, 1988.

Smith, Steven B. *Reading Althusser: An Essay on Structural Marxism.* Ithaca, N.Y.: Cornell University Press, 1984.

Sollers, Philippe. "Division de l'ensemble." In *Tel Quel: Théorie d'ensemble,* pp. 7–10.

———. "Écriture et révolution: Entretien de Jacques Henric avec Philippe Sollers." In *Tel Quel: Théorie d'ensemble,* pp. 67–79.

———. "L'Ecriture fonction de transformation sociale." In *Tel Quel: Théorie d'ensemble*, pp. 399–405.

———. *Logiques*. Paris: Seuil, 1968.

Sonn, Richard D. *Anarchism and Cultural Politics in Fin de siècle France*. Lincoln: University of Nebraska Press, 1989.

Spivak, Gayatri Chakravorty. "French Feminism in an International Frame." *Yale French Studies* 62 (1981): 154–84.

Spivak, Gayatri Chakravorty, and Michael Ryan. "Anarchism Revisited: A New Philosophy." *Diacritics* 8, no. 2 (Summer 1978): 66–79.

Stanton, Domna C. "Difference on Trial: A Critique of the Maternal Metaphor in Cixous, Irigaray, and Kristeva." In Nancy Miller, ed., *The Poetics of Gender*, pp. 157–82. New York: Columbia University Press, 1986.

———. "Language and Revolution: The Franco-American Dis-Connection." In Hester Eisenstein and Alice Jardine, eds., *The Future of Difference*, pp. 73–87.

———. "The Matter of the Text: Barthesian Displacement and Its Limits." *L'Esprit Créateur* 25, no. 2 (Summer 1985): 57–72.

Starr, Peter. "Science and Confusion: On Flaubert's *Temptation*." In Harold Bloom, ed., *Gustave Flaubert: Modern Critical Views*, pp. 199–218. New York: Chelsea House, 1989.

———. "The Style of (Post-)Liberal Desire: *Bouvard et Pécuchet*." *Nineteenth-Century French Studies* 18, nos. 1–2 (1989/90): 74–91.

Stoekl, Alan. *Politics, Writing, Mutilation: The Cases of Bataille, Blanchot, Roussel, Leiris, and Ponge*. Minneapolis: University of Minnesota Press, 1985.

Suleiman, Susan Rubin. "1960: As Is." In Denis Hollier, ed., *A New History of French Literature*, pp. 1011–18.

———. "Writing and Motherhood." In Shirley Nelson Garner, Claire Kahane, Madelon Sprengnether, eds., *The (M)other Tongue: Essays in Feminist Psychoanalytic Interpretation*, pp. 352–77. Ithaca, N.Y.: Cornell University Press, 1985.

Swain, Gladys. "L'âme, la femme, le sexe et le corps: Les métamorphoses de l'hystérie à la fin du XIXe siècle." *Le Débat* 24 (1983): 107–27.

Tel Quel: Théorie d'ensemble. Paris: Seuil, 1968.

Terdiman, Richard. *Discourse/Counter-Discourse: The Theory and Practice of Symbolic Resistance in Nineteenth-Century France*. Ithaca, N.Y.: Cornell University Press, 1985.

Touraine, Alain. *L'après-socialisme*. Paris: Grasset, 1980.

———. *Le communisme utopique: Le mouvement de Mai 68*. Paris: Seuil, 1972 [1968].

———. *The May Movement: Revolt and Reform*. Trans. Leonard F. X. Mayhew. New York: Random House, 1971. A translation of *Le communisme utopique*.

Trotsky, Leon. *The Struggle Against Fascism in Germany*. New York: Pathfinder, 1971.

Tucker, Robert C., ed. *The Lenin Anthology*. New York: Norton, 1975.

———. *The Marx/Engels Reader*. 2nd ed. New York: Norton, 1978 [1972].

Turkle, Sherry. *Psychoanalytic Politics: Freud's French Revolution*. New York: Basic Books, 1978.

Tzara, Tristan. "Sept Manifestes Dada." In Henri Béhar, ed., *Œuvres complètes*, vol. 1, pp. 355–90. Paris: Flammarion, 1975.

———. *Seven Dada Manifestos and Lampisteries.* Trans. Barbara Wright. London: Calder, 1992.

Ungar, Steven. *Roland Barthes: The Professor of Desire.* Lincoln: University of Nebraska Press, 1983.

Ungar, Steven, and Betty R. McGraw, eds. *Signs in Culture: Roland Barthes Today.* Iowa City: University of Iowa Press, 1989.

Vaillant, Auguste. "Déclaration de Vaillant." *La Révolte* 7, no. 19 (Jan. 20–27, 1894): 1–2.

Veith, Ilza. *Hysteria: The History of a Disease.* Chicago, University of Chicago Press, 1965.

Villiers de l'Isle-Adam. *L'Eve future.* Paris: Corti, 1977.

Watson, Russell. "Gorbachev: Capitalist Tool." *Newsweek,* May 18, 1992, 50.

Weber, Samuel M. *The Legend of Freud.* Minneapolis: University of Minnesota Press, 1982.

White, Hayden. *Metahistory: The Historical Imagination in Nineteenth-Century Europe.* Baltimore: Johns Hopkins University Press, 1973.

Wilden, Anthony. *The Language of the Self.* Baltimore: Johns Hopkins University Press, 1968.

———. *System and Structure: Essays in Communication and Exchange.* 2nd ed. London: Tavistock, 1980 [1972].

Zegel, S. *Les Idées de Mai.* Paris: Gallimard, 1968.

Žižek, Slavoj. *Enjoy Your Symptom! Jacques Lacan in Hollywood and Out.* New York: Routledge, 1992.

———. *For They Know Not What They Do: Enjoyment as a Political Factor.* London: Verso, 1991.

———. *Ils ne savent pas ce qu'ils font: Le sinthome idéologique.* Paris: Point Hors Ligne, 1990.

———. *Looking Awry: An Introduction to Jacques Lacan through Popular Culture.* Cambridge, Mass.: MIT Press, 1991.

———. *The Sublime Object of Ideology.* London: Verso, 1989.

Index

In this index "f" after a number indicates a separate reference on the next page, and "ff" indicates separate references on the next two pages. A continuous discussion over two or more pages is indicated by a span of numbers. *Passim* is used for a cluster of references in close but not consecutive sequence.

Library of Congress
Cataloging-in-Publication Data

Starr, Peter.
Logics of failed revolt : French theory after May '68 /
Peter Starr.
p. cm.
Includes bibliographical references and index.
ISBN 0-8047-2445-8 (alk. paper)—ISBN
0-8047-2446-6 (pbk. : alk. paper)
1. Critical theory. 2. Philosophy, French—20th century.
3. France—Politics and government—1958– I. Title.
B809.3.S72 1995 94-46160 CIP

∞ This book is printed on acid-free
recycled paper.